HANDBOOK OF CONVEYANCING PRACTICE IN SCOTLAND

For Sandra

HANDBOOK OF CONVEYANCING PRACTICE IN SCOTLAND

John Henderson Sinclair BA (QUB), LLB (Glas)

Solicitor in Scotland
Emeritus Professor of Conveyancing Practice
and Director of Legal Practice in the
University of Strathclyde and Glasgow Graduate School of Law
Visiting Professor, Glasgow Caledonian University
Formerly Clerk Treasurer and Fiscal, now an Honorary Member of the
Royal Faculty of Procurators in Glasgow

4th Edition

Butterworths
LexisNexis™
Law Society of Scotland

Members of the LexisNexis Group worldwide

United Kingdom	LexisNexis Butterworths Tolley, a Division of Reed Elsevier (UK) Ltd, 4 Hill Street, EDINBURGH EH2 3JZ and Halsbury House, 35 Chancery Lane, LONDON WC2A 1EL
Argentina	LexisNexis Argentina, BUENOS AIRES
Australia	LexisNexis Butterworths, CHATSWOOD, New South Wales
Austria	LexisNexis Verlag ARD Orac GmbH & Co KG, VIENNA
Canada	LexisNexis Butterworths, MARKHAM, Ontario
Chile	LexisNexis Chile Ltda, SANTIAGO DE CHILE
Czech Republic	Nakladatelství Orac sro, PRAGUE
France	Editions du Juris-Classeur SA, PARIS
Hong Kong	LexisNexis Butterworths, HONG KONG
Hungary	HVG-Orac, BUDAPEST
India	LexisNexis Butterworths, NEW DELHI
Ireland	Butterworths (Ireland) Ltd, DUBLIN
Italy	Giuffrè Editore, MILAN
Malaysia	Malayan Law Journal Sdn Bhd, KUALA LUMPUR
New Zealand	LexisNexis Butterworths, WELLINGTON
Poland	Wydawnictwo Prawnicze LexisNexis, WARSAW
Singapore	LexisNexis Butterworths, SINGAPORE
South Africa	Butterworths SA, DURBAN
Switzerland	Stämpfli Verlag AG, BERNE
USA	LexisNexis, DAYTON, Ohio

Law Society of Scotland
26 Drumsheugh Gardens, Edinburgh EH3 7YR

A CIP Catalogue record for this book is available from the British Library.

3rd edition reprinted and revised in 2000

ISBN 0 406 95705 3

Typeset by Phoenix Photosetting, Chatham, Kent
Printed and bound in Great Britain by Thomson Litho Ltd, East Kilbride, Scotland

Visit Butterworths LexisNexis *direct* at : www.butterworthsscotland.com

PREFACE

This is the fourth edition of this book, which was and is written principally for the benefit of Diploma students, Professional Competence Course students and young trainees, whom I hope will continue to find it useful.

Land registration has now almost completely taken over in Scotland, and the book is written with this in mind, and the Sasine element of previous editions has largely disappeared. However, as a recent Keeper's Report reminds us, Sasine registrations are still quite buoyant, thanks to the amount of remortgages of unregistered properties, and a look is therefore taken at the Sasine Registers, where this is still relevant. One further point to note is that with the imminent passing of the Title Conditions (Scotland) Bill, land obligations will come to be known as title conditions. I have retained the current terminology in this edition.

Thanks are again due to the Keeper of the Registers of Scotland and his staff, to the Secretariat and to Ian Stubbs, convenor of the Insurance Committee of the Law Society of Scotland, and to Millar & Bryce for information provided gladly over the years. I would also like to thank the Library staff of the Strathclyde Law School and Royal Faculty of Procurators in Glasgow for all the help they have kindly provided.

Thanks are also given to Brian Rigby, a tutor in Finance and Investment, for providing financial information, and to Scott Wortley and Euan Sinclair, for keeping me up to date, as best they can, with recent developments in the legislature and the courts, and the future of electronic conveyancing.

Vitally, I would like to thank my neighbour, Eric Dewhurst for all his help with my computer, which I was about to throw out of the window, until he came along and rescued me, and the machine.

Lastly, I would like to thank all of my students over the years. Every year I have thought to be the best, only to revise my opinion the following year. I am pleased to say that many are fulfilling the potential observed at University, and I hope that many more will do so in years to come. I am not, as you will understand, one of the moaners at today's students, but then I have had the cream of the crop!

John H Sinclair
Crail
August 2002

CONTENTS

Chapter eight
NOTES ON TITLE, SEARCHES, REPORTS,
OBLIGATIONS AND DRAFTS

Chapter nine
THE DRAFT DISPOSITION

Chapter ten
THE FINAL STEPS BEFORE SETTLEMENT

Chapter eleven
THE SETTLEMENT, FEEING-UP AND TIDYING-UP

Chapter twelve
BORROWING ON HERITABLE PROPERTY

Chapter thirteen
FIRST REGISTRATION

Chapter fourteen
THE DEALING

TABLE OF STATUTES

TABLE OF ORDERS, RULES AND REGULATIONS

TABLE OF EUROPEAN LEGISLATION

TABLE OF CASES

PROCEDURAL TABLES

Procedural Table I

CHRONOLOGICAL STEPS IN A TRANSACTION INVOLVING REGISTRATION OF DOMESTIC PROPERTY IN THE GENERAL REGISTER OF SASINES

Note: This example includes repayment of the sellers' loan and the constitution of the purchasers' loan.

SELLERS	PURCHASERS
1 Ideally the sellers inform their solicitor of intention to sell. Solicitor then:— (a) informs lenders of clients' intention and asks for the title deeds; (b) obtains the writs referred to for burdens (or quick copies) if these are likely to be required and are not with the title deeds, and requests Local Authority Certificate *re* roads and planning, required permissions for any work done on the building and any guarantees for work done.	
2 The solicitor may or may not act in the marketing of the property. If so instructed, advertisements are placed, the property is registered with the property centre, a schedule is drawn up, enquiries answered and arrangements made to show potential buyers around the property. If solicitors do not act at this stage, they may not be instructed until the purchaser has been found, in which case steps 1(a) and 1(b) are taken at the earliest opportunity.	
	3 Purchasers inspect property and consult their solicitors, who intimate purchasers' interest to selling agents. Further details of the property are obtained at this stage, and preferably a copy of the particulars of the property for particular reference to moveables included. Purchasers' solicitors enquire if there is a closing date for offers.

SELLERS	PURCHASERS
	4 Purchasers are advised to contact lenders *re* loan. If lenders are satisfied as to purchasers' income and credit rating, they will arrange to have the property valued. If the valuation covers the amount of the loan, the lenders will indicate what offer of loan they will make.
	5 Once the purchasers' finances are seen to be in order, solicitors submit offer on behalf of the purchasers.
6 (a) Offers are considered and sellers' instructions taken. Best offer is accepted conditionally or unconditionally, and others are informed. Advertisements are cancelled and boards removed. Property is deregistered with property centre. Fire insurance is maintained, unless in special circumstances. (b) Lenders are informed of sale and date of entry, and are asked to state how much is to be repaid at the date of entry. (c) Diary entries as to various steps in transaction are made.	
	7 Purchasers' solicitors accept sellers' qualifications and generally ensure that parties are completely in consensus and there are no loose ends in Agreement. Due consideration should be given to any time limits in the acceptance, within which the purchasers' solicitors must satisfy themselves as to conditions of title and also that loan application has been enclosed and can be processed and funds available in time for settlement. Temporary insurance cover is arranged, unless sellers accept responsibility in terms of missives which is the usual case. Diary entries are made.

GOLDEN RULE:– Fire insurance is cheap, and double insurance is always better than no insurance!

8 Sellers' solicitors send purchasers' solicitors (a) title deeds; (b) draft discharge of security; (c) draft letter of obligation; (d) search; (e) draft memorandum for continuation of search and in the computerised presentment book; (f) draft state for settlement and all other relative receipts; (g) all certificates of permission and guarantee available; (h) property enquiry certificates and (i) any other information that may be useful.

SELLERS	PURCHASERS

PURCHASERS

9 Purchasers' solicitors:– (a) examine title, approve sellers' drafts and draft disposition in favour of purchasers;

(b) carefully peruse lenders' loan instructions, and accordingly draft standard security and assignation of any policy;

(c) If loan is taken in one name only, or in the names of two persons who are engaged, or who have the potential of being married, the appropriate affidavit(s) under MH(FP)(S)A 1981 is prepared to protect lenders' interest; separate advice should be made available to consenting spouse.

(d) If the loan is an `endowment loan', assignation of policy is prepared;

(e) The draft disposition with the title deeds and all other papers are now returned to sellers' solicitors, and

(f) purchasers' solicitors also make observation on title at this stage.

10 Purchasers' solicitors make any enquiries that the sellers' solicitors have not undertaken in missives (eg Roads certificates et cetera).

11 Solicitors report to clients on any important feuing conditions or other important matters of title.

12 Sellers' solicitors serve notice of redemption of feuduty if this has not already been attended to, and inform council tax office of the local authority to intimate change of ownership; also remind the sellers to contact gas, electric and telephone companies to arrange final meter readings.

13 (a) Sellers' solicitors revise disposition and return this to purchasers' solicitors, answering observations on title at the same time.

(b) Discharge of loan is typed and sent to lenders asking them to execute this and return it on understanding by sellers' solicitors to hold it as undelivered pending repayment of loan.

(c) Interim report on search is obtained and sent to purchasers' solicitors.

SELLERS	PURCHASERS
	14 (a) Disposition is engrossed, compared with draft and returned to sellers' solicitors for signature, with the draft for comparison. (b) Standard security, assignation of policy, and appropriate affidavit are signed in good time for settlement. (c) Report on title and request of cheque is sent to lenders, allowing at least five days for return. Purchasers are requested to provide balance of price in order to have cleared funds ready at settlement. (Another GOLDEN RULE: see Chapters 10–11.)
15 Sellers' solicitors either get keys or arrange for their transfer on date of entry. The engrossed disposition is compared with draft, and signed by sellers together with any affidavit. Draft disposition is returned to purchasers' agents. Solicitors ensure discharge of security and retrocession of any policy are available and put in testing clauses. Letter of obligation is typed.	
16 Once everything is ready, sellers' solicitors arrange settlement. Have letter of obligation signed.	**16** Purchasers' solicitors having ensured there are sufficient funds in clients' account to settle, and that no points are outstanding, arrange settlement.
17 *Settlement*	*Settlement*
Sellers' solicitors hand over: 1. keys (or have arranged for their collection by purchasers); 2. signed disposition and draft (if not already returned); 3. deliverable title deeds and writs referred to for burdens; 4. letter of obligation and draft. 5. Feu duty redemption receipt. 6. Receipted sale for settlement and draft. 7. Any matrimonial affidavit and draft. 8. Discharge of standard security and draft. 9. Signed letter to keeper requesting registration of discharge and cheque for dues. 10. Permissions and guarantees.	Purchasers' solicitors hand over cheque. Check all items handed over, with drafts where appropriate, and return drafts to sellers' solicitors.

SELLERS	PURCHASERS
	18 (a) Testing clause is added to disposition, and disposition is stamped (if appropriate) and sent to register of sasines with a cheque for recording dues and standard security and discharge with Keeper's letter signed by sellers' solicitors. All deeds are checked before dispatch to ensure that they are sufficiently stamped, testing clauses are correct, all signatures of granters and witnesses are furnished, and that the warrant of registration is signed. (b) Purchasers' solicitors ensure that fire insurance arrangements have been made. (c) If appropriate, notice of assignation of life policy in duplicate is sent to life assurance company who are requested to receipt and return the duplicate. (d) Notify lenders of completion of transaction and encashment of cheque.
19 (a) Loan is repaid. (b) Having deducted the loan, all fees and outlays, sellers' solicitors send cheque for proceeds to sellers with statement of accounts. Alternatively payment may be made to sellers' bank (designating sellers' account on the cheque) or as otherwise instructed, or proceeds applied to purchase of new house. (c) Fire insurance is cancelled and all standing orders for premiums, rates et cetera.	**19** Purchasers' solicitors should send statement of account showing receipts and payments, fees and outlays to clients with explanatory letter.

20 BOTH PARTIES SHOULD NOW CHECK FILE AGAIN FOR ANY LOOSE ENDS.

SELLERS	PURCHASERS
	21 The recorded disposition and standard security are received. After a reasonable interval, sellers' solicitors are asked for search.
22 When completed search is received, this is sent to purchasers' solicitors.	
	23 On receipt of search, the letter of obligation is returned to sellers' agents marked as 'implemented'.
	24 Disposition, standard security, title deeds and other certificates (eg NHBC, roads and planning, woodworm treatment et cetera) are sent to lenders with life policy, assignation and receipted intimation of assignation.

SELLERS	PURCHASERS

25   BOTH FILES ARE CLOSED AND PUT AWAY.

Notes: The Land Registers (Scotland) Act 1995 provides that registration fees will are payable at the time of presentation of the deeds to the Register.

Procedural Table II

CHRONOLOGICAL STEPS IN A TRANSACTION INVOLVING THE FIRST REGISTRATION OF DOMESTIC PROPERTY IN THE LAND REGISTER

Note: This example includes repayment of the sellers' loan and the constitution of the purchasers' loan.

SELLERS	PURCHASERS
R1 Ideally the sellers inform their solicitors of intention to sell. Solicitors then: (a) inform lenders of clients' intention and asks for the title deeds; and (b) obtain the writs referred to for burdens (or quick copies) if these are likely to be required and are not with the title deeds, and request Local Authority Certificates *re* roads and planning; (c) send Form 10 in DUPLICATE and Form P16 to Keeper of Land Register or searchers requesting reports. (**Note**: P16 Report is not necessary for flats.)	
R2 The solicitors may or may not act in the marketing of the property. If instructed to act, advertisements are placed, property is registered with the property centre, enquiries answered, and arrangements made to show potential buyers round the property. If the solicitors do not act at this stage, they may not be instructed until the purchaser has been found, in which case steps R1(a), R1(b) and R1(c) are taken now or at the earliest opportunity.	

SELLERS	PURCHASERS
	R3 Purchasers inspect property and consult their solicitors, who intimate purchasers' interest to selling agents. Purchasers' solicitors enquire if there is a closing date for offers. Further details of the property are obtained at this stage, and preferably a copy of the particulars of the property, for particular reference to moveables included in the sale. Solicitors enquire if property is already registered – if in doubt an enquiry to the Keeper can be made on a Form 10 or 14.
	R4 Purchasers are advised to contact lenders *re* loan. If lenders are satisfied as to purchasers' income and credit rating, they will arrange to have property valued. If the valuation covers the amount of the loan, the lenders will make an offer of loan.
	R5 Once the purchasers' finances are seen to be in order, solicitors submit offer on behalf of purchasers.
R6 (a) Offers are considered and sellers' instructions taken. Best offer is accepted conditionally or unconditionally, and others are informed. Advertisements are cancelled, property centre informed and boards removed. Fire insurance is maintained, unless in special circumstances. (b) Lenders are informed of sale and date of entry, and are asked to state how much is to be repaid at the date of entry. (c) Diary entries as to various steps in transaction are made.	
	R7 Purchasers' solicitors accept sellers' qualifications and generally ensure that parties are completely in consensus and there are no loose ends in agreement. Due consideration should be given to any time limits in the acceptance, within which the purchasers' solicitors must satisfy themselves as to conditions of title. Temporary insurance cover is arranged, unless sellers accept responsibility in terms of missives. Diary entries are made.

SELLERS	PURCHASERS

GOLDEN RULE: Fire insurance is cheap, and double insurance is always better than no insurance!

R8 Sellers' solicitors send purchasers' solicitors (a) title deeds; (b) Form 10A and P16 Reports; (c) draft Form 11; (d) draft discharge of security; (e) draft letter of obligation; (f) the search but without a draft memorandum for its continuation; (g) draft state for settlement and all relative receipts; (h) permissions and guarantees; (i) property enquiry certificates and (j) any other information that may be useful.

R9 (a) Purchasers' solicitors examine title, approve sellers' drafts, and draft disposition in favour of purchasers and Forms 1 and 4.

(b) Carefully peruse lenders' loan instructions, and accordingly draft standard security and Form 2 (Blue) in respect of the standard security which is treated as being the first dealing in registered land. (**Note**: Where the same solicitors act for purchasers and lenders, it is only necessary to prepare one Form 4 – to include the standard security – in duplicate.) If loan is taken in one name only, or in the names of two persons who are engaged, or who have the potential of being married, the appropriate affidavit(s) under MH(FP)(S)A 1981, is prepared to protect lenders' interest.

(c) If the loan is an 'endowment loan', assignation of policy is prepared.

(d) The draft disposition and draft Forms 1 and 4, the title deeds, and all other papers are returned to the sellers' solicitors.

Purchasers' solicitors also make observations on title at this stage.

R10 Purchasers' solicitors make any enquiries that the sellers' solicitors have not undertaken in missives (eg roads certificates et cetera).

R11 Solicitors report to clients on any important title conditions or other important matters of title.

SELLERS	PURCHASERS

R12 Sellers' solicitors serve notice of redemption of feuduty if this has not already been attended to and contact council tax office of the local authority to intimate change of ownership; also remind the sellers to contact gas, electricity and telephone companies to arrange final readings.

R13 (a) Sellers' solicitors revise disposition and Forms 1 and 4 and send these to purchasers' solicitors, answering observations on title at the same time.
(b) Discharge of loan is typed and sent to lenders with letter asking them to execute this and return it on the undertaking by sellers' solicitors to hold it as undelivered pending repayment of loan.

R14 (a) Disposition is engrossed, compared with draft and returned to sellers' solicitors for signature, with the draft for comparison.
(b) Forms 1 and 4 are typed, the latter in DUPLICATE.
(c) Standard security, assignation of policy and appropriate affidavit are signed in good time for settlement.
(d) Report on title and request of cheque is sent to lenders, allowing at least five days for return. Purchasers are requested to provide balance of price in order to have cleared funds ready at settlement. (Another GOLDEN RULE: see Chapters 10–11.)

R15 Sellers' solicitors either get keys or arrange for their transfer on date of entry. The engrossed disposition is compared with draft, and signed by sellers together with any affidavit. Draft disposition is returned to purchasers' agents. Solicitors ensure discharge of security is available, put in a testing clause and prepare Form 2 for discharge. Letter of obligation is typed.

SELLERS	PURCHASERS

R16 Once everything is ready, sellers' solicitors arrange settlement. Have letter of obligation signed (see Appendix 11.18(b)).

The sellers should also arrange for a Form 11A Report to be sent by the Keeper just prior to settlement (allow five working days). If short of time, a faxed report may be obtained, at an additional fee.

R16 Purchasers' solicitors having ensured there are sufficient funds in clients' account to settle, and that no points are outstanding, requisition cheque, have this signed and arrange settlement.

R17 *Settlement*
Sellers' solicitors hand over:
1. Keys (or have arranged for their collection by purchasers);
2. signed disposition and draft and particulars of signing (if not already returned);
3. deliverable title deeds and writs referred to for burdens;
4. letter of obligation and draft;
5. feu duty redemption receipt;
6. receipted state for settlement and draft;
7. any matrimonial affidavit and draft;
8. discharge of standard security and draft and Form 2 for discharge (signed by sellers' solicitor);
9. Form 11A Report;
(**Note**: The discharge is registered in the Land Register and no warrant or registration is put on discharge.)

R17 *Settlement*
Purchasers' solicitors hand over cheque. Check all items handed over, with drafts where appropriate, and return drafts to sellers' solicitors.

R18 (a) Testing clause is added to disposition, and disposition is stamped (if appropriate).
(b) Form 1 is *signed* and *dated* and sent to Land Register with Form 4 (IN DUPLICATE) cheque for registration dues and all documents mentioned in Form 4 (which includes discharge of sellers' loan and relative Form 2). Check all deeds and forms to ensure that they are sufficiently stamped, testing clauses are correct, all signatures of granters and witnesses are furnished, and that the Form 1 is signed.

SELLERS	PURCHASERS
	R18 (continued) (c) Form 2 is sent to Land Register with standard security and the appropriate fee. Sellers' solicitors' Form 2 is sent to Register with discharge and the appropriate fee. (d) Purchasers' solicitors ensure that fire insurance arrangements have been made. (e) If appropriate, notice of assignation of life policy in duplicate is sent to life assurance company who are requested to receipt and return the duplicate. (f) Notify lenders of completion of transaction and encashment of cheque.
R19 (a) Loan is repaid. (b) Having deducted the loan, all fees and outlays, sellers' solicitors send cheque for proceeds to sellers with statement of account. Alternatively payment may be made to sellers' bank or as otherwise instructed (ensuring that cheque is designated with sellers' names), or proceeds applied to purchase of a new house. (c) Fire insurance is cancelled and all standing orders for premiums and rates et cetera.	**R19** Purchasers' solicitors should send statement of account showing receipts and payments, fees and outlays to client with explanatory letter. Fee note should include land registration dues for disposition and standard security.

R20 BOTH PARTIES SHOULD NOW CHECK FILE AGAIN FOR ANY LOOSE ENDS.

SELLERS	PURCHASERS
	R21 Purchasers' solicitors await any observations from Land Register. If any are received these are dealt with if possible or referred to sellers' solicitors for clarification under terms of letter of obligation.
	R22 Eventually the land certificate and charge certificate are received together with documents submitted to Land Register. Both are checked for any exclusion of indemnity or other irregularity. Upon satisfaction, the letter of obligation is returned to sellers' solicitors. Land certificate and charge certificate and any other certificates (eg NHBC, roads, planning, woodworm treatment et cetera) are sent to lenders with life policy, assignation and receipted intimation of assignation. Any writs referred to for

SELLERS	PURCHASERS
	R22 (continued) burdens which were borrowed from a third party are returned to the sellers' solicitors.

R23 BOTH FILES ARE CLOSED AND PUT AWAY.

Note: The Land Registers (Scotland) Act 1995 provides that registration fees will be payable at the time of presentation of the deeds to the Register.

Procedural Table III

CHRONOLOGICAL STEPS IN A TRANSACTION INVOLVING A SECOND OR SUBSEQUENT REGISTRATION OF DOMESTIC PROPERTY

Note: This transaction closely resembles the First Registration in Procedural Table II, and many steps are given only by reference to Procedural Table II to avoid repetition.

SELLERS	PURCHASERS
SR1 Ideally the sellers inform their solicitors of intention to sell. Solicitors then: (a) inform lenders of clients' intentions and ask for the Land Certificate and Charge Certificate, and any other papers that were sent (see **R22**); (b) obtain local authority planning certificate to date, and (c) send Form 12 in duplicate requesting report. (**Note:** Form 12 replaces Form 10 and a Form P16 is not now sent as the boundaries are plotted on the ordnance survey map in the land certificate.)	
SR2 as in **R2**	
	SR3 as in **R3**.
	SR4 as in **R4**.
	SR5 as in **R5**.
SR6 as in **R6**.	
	SR7 as in **R7**.
SR8 Sellers' solicitors send purchasers' solicitors (a) land certificate and charge certificate; (b) Form 12A report; (c) draft Form 13; (d) draft discharge of security;	

SELLERS	PURCHASERS

SR8   (continued)
(e) draft letter of obligation; (f) draft state for settlement and all relative receipts; (g) permission and guarantees and (h) any other information that may be useful.

SR9   (a) Purchasers' solicitors examine the land certificate and charge certificate and draft disposition and Form 2 (Blue) if the whole of the registered holding is being transferred or Form 3 (Green) if only part of a registered holding (eg a new house on a building estate) and Form 4.
(b) Carefully peruse lenders' loan instructions and accordingly draft standard security, Form 2 (blue) in respect of the standard security. (**Note:** Where same solicitors act for purchasers and lenders it is only necessary to prepare one Form 4, incorporating the standard security, in duplicate. If purchase is taken in one name only, the appropriate affidavit(s) under MH(FP)(S) Act is prepared to protect lenders' interest.)
(c) If the loan is an 'endowment loan' assignation of policy is prepared.
(d) The draft disposition and draft Form 2 or 3 and Form 4, the land and charge certificates and all other papers are returned to the sellers' solicitors. Purchasers' solicitors also make observations on title at this stage.

SR10 as in **R10.**

SR11 as in **R11.**

SR12   R12 (redemption of feu duty) is no longer appropriate as this will have been done, unless the feu duty is unallocated in which case it will remain in force until voluntarily redeemed. Sellers' solicitors contact council tax office of the local authority to intimate change of ownership.

SELLERS	PURCHASERS
SR13 (a) Sellers' solicitors revise disposition and Form 2/3 and 4 and send these to purchasers' solicitors, answering obligations on title at the same time; (b) as in **R13**(b).	
	SR14 (a) Disposition is engrossed, compared with draft and returned to sellers' solicitors for signature, with the draft for comparison. (b) Forms 2/3 and 4 are typed, the latter IN DUPLICATE. (c) and (d) as in **R14**(c) and (d).
SR15 as in **R15**.	
SR16 as in **R16** (except read Form 13A Report for Form 11A, which is only competent on first registration).	**SR16** as in **R16**.
SR17 Sellers' solicitors hand over: 1. keys (or have arranged for their collection); 2. signed disposition and draft (if not already returned); 3. land certificate and change certificate; 4. letter of obligation and draft; 5. receipted state of settlement and draft; 6. any matrimonial affidavit and draft; 7. discharge of standard security and draft and Form 2 for discharge; 8. Form 13;	
	SR18 (a) Testing clause is added to disposition and disposition is stamped (if appropriate). (b) Form 2/3 is signed and dated and sent to the Land Register with Form 4 IN DUPLICATE and all documents mentioned in Form 4 (which includes discharge of sellers' loan). (c) Form 2 for standard security and Form 4 (latter in duplicate) are sent to Land Register with standard security and the appropriate dues. All deeds are checked before dispatch to ensure that they are sufficiently stamped, testing clauses are correct, all signatures of granters and witnesses are furnished, and that the form 2/3 is signed.

SELLERS	PURCHASERS
	SR18 (continued) (d) Purchasers' solicitors ensure that fire insurance arrangements have been made. (e) If appropriate notice of assignation of life policy in duplicate is sent to life assurance company who are requested to receipt and return the duplicate. (f) Notify lenders of completion of transaction and encashment of cheque.
SR19 as in **R19.**	**SR19** as in **R19.**

SR20 BOTH PARTIES SHOULD NOW CHECK FILE AGAIN FOR ANY LOOSE ENDS.

SR21 as in **R21.**

SR22 as in **R22.**

SR23 BOTH FILES ARE CLOSED AND PUT AWAY.

Notes: See Notes under First Registration above.

Part one

GENERAL CONSIDERATIONS

Chapter 1

WELCOME TO THE PROFESSION (?)

'Having seen the cost to his father of having no qualification to fall back on, Sir Denys determined to finish his law training at Aberdeen University and at a lawyer's office, despite finding it "singularly dull".'

(*Daily Mail*, on Sir Denys Henderson, formerly Chairman of ICI and Zeneca PLC)

'Never ask an instructing solicitor if his leg is better. This is as fatal as asking a client if he happens to be guilty, you run a terrible danger of being told.'

(John Mortimer QC *Rumpole A la Carte*)

'I believe that, for our firm at least, the independence issue related to providing both auditing and consulting services is one of perception only. However, in the current environment, we cannot expose our clients to possible criticism because of the perception problem surrounding the scope of services audit firms may provide to clients.'

(James Copeland, Chief Executive Officer of Deloitte Touche Tohmatsu, in a press release announcing that it was spinning off its consulting arm (Deloitte Consulting) in the 'post-Enron era').

'Whenever I see someone in power, I ask myself five questions. Who gave you this power? What did you do to get this power? What are you going to do with this power? To whom are you giving power? And how can we get rid of you? In a true democracy, everyone should be made to answer these questions.'

(Tony Benn)

1.1   A conveyancer is, at present, a solicitor who deals in practice mainly with the purchase and sale of heritable property. A solicitor in Scotland is a person who is qualified to practise as such by having obtained a law degree from one of the five Scottish universities at present offering this degree (or passing equivalent examinations assessed by the Law Society of Scotland), Diploma in Legal Practice, and then having served a two-year traineeship in a solicitors' office, attending a Professional Competence course, and completing a Test of Professional Competence to prove that the lessons have been learnt. This rigorous basic training occupies at the very least six years, which is the equivalent of the basic medical training. The aspiring Scottish solicitor must also be shown to be a fit and proper person to be a solicitor.

Admission to the profession is regulated by the Law Society of Scotland, in terms of the Admission as Solicitor (Scotland) Regulations 1991 and 2001, also the EC Qualifying Lawyers Transfer (Scotland) Regulations 1994.

The solicitor is governed by the Solicitors (Scotland) Acts 1980 and 1988, which supersede the Solicitors (Scotland) Act 1949, the foundation Act which set up the Law Society of Scotland as the governing body for the profession. Section 5 of the 1980 Act empowers the Council of the Law Society to make regulations, with the concurrence of the Lord President of the Court of Session. Many of these regulations will be referred to throughout this chapter, and are printed in full in *Parliament House Book* (W Green, looseleaf), or in the off-print known as *Solicitors' Compendium* (W Green).

A practising solicitor must be a member of the Law Society of Scotland under the Solicitors (Scotland) Act 1980, s 4, (unlike English solicitors who need not belong to their Law Society) and must hold a practising certificate in terms of the Solicitors (Scotland) Practising Certificate Rules 1988.

1.2   The reasons for entering the profession are perceived to be: (a) it should ensure a comfortable lifestyle, and a safe job for life, although it is doubtful if any such thing now exists; (b) despite the comments of the media, it is still a profession that inspires a certain amount of respect in the general public, especially in smaller communities; (c) there is a genuine sense of satisfaction in helping out people in the worst times of crisis in their lives, although it should be noted that even the nicest clients can turn into monsters in a crisis, and a good job well done does not necessarily imply that your fee will be unquestioningly paid; (d) law can become a totally absorbing discipline, and a great deal of intellectual stimulation can be obtained from solving its complexities; and (e) if it all gets too much, the lawyer is fairly qualified to turn to another career in, for example, commerce, industry or politics (see Sir Denys Henderson quoted above). Well, er, that's it, as *Private Eye* would say. What of the disadvantages?

You have probably chosen the most tightly regulated of occupations. The main problem is that while the legal profession handles huge amounts of clients' money—even a small practice can have an annual turnover of several million pounds in its clients' account—many solicitors take a perverse pride in being innumerate. This breeds problems, which in turn breed regulations.

Where there is money, there is temptation for the dishonest, the weak, and the badly organised. The *Journal of the Law Society of Scotland* (JLSS) regularly carries a dismal little column detailing the offences of solicitors who have come to grief through misuse of their clients' account, as does the *Annual Report* of the Disciplinary Tribunal. While some offences are hair-raising in their dishonesty, the remainder are committed by people who have simply got out of their depth.

What is even more alarming is where solicitors have entrusted the running of the cashroom to a cashier, who has then done the embezzling. Not only do the solicitors have to refund the money from their own pockets (failing which the profession does through the Guarantee Fund), but the solicitors are guilty of an offence under the Accounts Rules of the Law Society, as the liability is strict. The firm must designate a cashroom partner, who is responsible for the actings of the staff. In one such case in 1993, the tribunal ruled that 'even although an established shortfall may be attributable to dishonesty among members of a solicitor's staff, such circumstances do not necessarily provide an answer to a charge of professional misconduct on the basis that it always remains the solicitor's duty to take all reasonable steps to ensure that clients' funds are safeguarded'.

Even the most trusted members of staff, if left entirely to their own devices, may turn dishonest. It usually starts in a small way, by the taking of a small sum. If this is not detected, the tempation the next week is to take a slightly larger sum, and so it goes on. In no time at all a great sum has been taken, especially if gambling is involved. At some stage it is all going to come into the open, usually with disastrous consequences to employer and employee alike.

There are many instances where a trusted cashier has yielded to the temptation of too much freedom, and it is essential that a close check be kept on all cash handling staff to make sure that a minor defalcation is not allowed to grow into something more serious. This is the only fair procedure from the point of view of both employer and employee.

1.3   The Law Society of Scotland (hereinafter referred to—following the practice of good conveyancers—as 'the Law Society' or as 'the Society' although this name, without territorial designation, officially belongs to the English counterpart) governs the actions of Scottish solicitors from its offices at 26 Drumsheugh Gardens, Edinburgh EH3 7YR (Telephone: 0131 226 7411; Fax: 0131 225 2934). The Society also has a Brussels office (Telephone: 00 832 502 2020; Fax: 00 322 502 2292).

In terms of the Solicitors (Scotland) Act 1980, s 1(2) the objects of the Law Society shall include the promotion of (a) the interests of the solicitors' profession in Scotland and (b) the interests of the public in relation to that profession. It might be said that these two objects are contradictory, but this proposition demands rather closer examination.

The Law Society has to walk a very thin line between representing the interests of its members, and representing the interests of members of the public who think, rightly or wrongly, that they may have been ill-treated by their solicitor. Thus, while many lay persons might think of the Law Society as being 'a lawyers' trade union', many solicitors would equally think of the Society as a body which exists to wrap the solicitor in a web of petty regulations, and to punish the solicitor for any minor transgression of these. The Society was called by one member, somewhat unfairly, 'a rotweiler society', because rotweilers are the only breed of dog known to bite their owners. I shall attempt to explain in this book why that perception is false.

There is, however, an apparent conflict of interest between these two duties, which may some day blow out of control.

1.4   The Law Society, as part of the first object of the Solicitors (Scotland) Act 1980, is responsible, among other things, for the training and admission of solicitors, compulsory continuing professional development, legal education, practice development, maintaining links with other societies, publications, giving advice on numerous professional topics through a network of specialist committees and the secretariat, scrutinising proposed legislation and making representations as necessary, ensuring that accounting rules and the regulations under the Financial Services Act 1986 are observed, liaising with the Scottish Executive and the Scottish Law Commission, corporate public relations and advertising, arranging mediation proceedings through an organisation called 'Accord' and negotiating professional indemnity insurance.

1.5   The Law Society, as part of the second object of the Solicitors (Scotland) Act 1980, maintains a Client Care Committee and secretariat, which has five Clients Relations Committees considering complaints received from members of the public against solicitors. According to the Annual Report of the Society for 2001, 1,262 complaints were lodged in that year by members of the public, compared to 1,094 in 2000.

Where the Society concludes that there has been Inadequate Professional Service (IPS), which means very much what it says, it may modify a solicitor's fee, order a solicitor to correct the fault, or to pay for having the fault corrected. In 2001, IPS sanctions were imposed as follows: number of formal sanctions (27); refund or abatement of fees (19); compensation only (69); fees and compensation (36); order to solicitors to carry out work in the interest of the client (5).

The Law Reform (Miscellaneous Provisions) (Scotland) Act 1990 places a statutory duty on the Society to investigate complaints, which means that all mail received has to be analysed and categorised. The complaints are duly categorised in the Society's 2001 Report: conduct unbecoming a solicitor (19); failure to communicate (279); failure to follow instructions (122); breach of Practice Rules (40); failure to advise adequately (175); delay (339); dishonesty (8); failure to prepare adequately (53); and breach of code of conduct (227). Total, 1,262.

Many complaints (852 in 2001) can be dealt with administratively. If, however, a complaint cannot be resolved in this way, it is then referred to one of five complaints committees, made up mainly of lawyers, but with lay members on each committee. The Solicitors (Scotland) Act 1988 widened the powers of the Society in this respect—formerly the Society might deal only with complaints about the professional conduct of solicitors; now it may act where the solicitor has provided an inadequate professional service. In these circumstances, the solicitor concerned may be required to reduce or waive the fee charged, rectify the defect, or pay for someone else to rectify it.

Of course not all complaints are justified, and 256 were abandoned without reference to a complaints committee, 281 had no action taken, 156 were referred to dispute resolution, and 159 were referred to conciliation. Of complaints that went to a committee, 137 were dismissed.

1.6   In serious cases of professional misconduct arising from complaints received, or from the investigations of the Society, principally under the Solicitors (Scotland) Accounts, Accounts Certificate, Professional Practice and Guarantee Funds Rules 2001, the Society may make a complaint to the Discipline Tribunal. This body operates under the Scottish Solicitors Discipline Tribunal Procedures Rules 1989, and its members are appointed by the Lord President of the Court of Session. The members of this tribunal are predominantly, but not exclusively, lawyers, but it must be stressed that the tribunal operates wholly independently of the Society. The Society is not, as some may suspect, therefore judge and prosecutor.

The tribunal has power to order a solicitor's name to be struck from the roll of practising solicitors or to suspend or restrict their practising certificates. An appeal against the tribunal's decision lies to the Court of Session.

1.7   Disgruntled members of the public who cannot be appeased by any of these means, may additionally make a complaint to the Scottish Legal Services Ombudsman. The Ombudsman replaced the Lay Observer as a result of the Law Reform (Miscellaneous Provisions) (Scotland) Act 1990, s 34 (1), which gave the Ombudsman wider powers than the former Lay Observer had, including a power to raise a matter in the Disciplinary Tribunal, and a jurisdiction over advocates.

In the year to July 2002 the Ombudsman received 153 complaints and enquiries, of which she investigated 74. In only 35% of cases did she consider that the Law Society 'acted fairly, thoroughly and reasonably'. The Ombudsman said in her report, dated July 2002, that she was having 'a bit of a battle with the Law Society', and certainly her report is overall critical of the Society, and, indeed, of the Faculty of Advocates.

There has been a move to impose independent regulation on the profession. Nigel Griffiths MP has been quoted (*Sunday Times*, 28 August 1994) as saying:

> 'There is need for a truly independent body to regulate this industry (*sic*) in Scotland. The time has come to set up such a body and I would expect the legal profession to fund it.'

The latest report from the Ombudsman can scarcely have defused this argument.

1.8   While there is no room for complacency, it will be seen that a remarkably small proportion of the many transactions that must be carried out by solicitors every year in Scotland, actually come to grief. It should be a matter of pride that this is so, and the standard should be maintained and improved in the interest of the profession. It will also be seen that the Society is fairly vigilant in rooting out its bad apples. While this does necessitate a high degree of regulation of its members, it should be appreciated that the disciplinary functions of the Society are a vital part of the Society's broad duty to represent the interests of the profession, by maintaining public confidence. The two objects of the Solicitors (Scotland) Act 1980 (para **1.3**) are not, therefore, self-contradictory after all.

1.9   Despite this many solicitors, especially those in smaller firms, still feel that, in the event of their getting into trouble with the Society or otherwise, they are left with no professional body to assist them. For this reason, there was established the Legal Defence Union (LDU), which is analogous to the well-established Medical and Dental Defence Union (MDDU). In the medical world, the disciplinary function is dealt with by the General Medical Council (GMC), the doctor's trade union is the British Medical Association (BMA) and the members' interests under the disciplinary function are dealt with by the MDDU. There is a clear separation between the three functions. For lawyers in Scotland, the Law Society deals with the first two functions.

Membership of the LDU (274 Sauchiehall Street, Glasgow G2 3EH (Telephone: 0141 307 5000; Fax: 0141 307 5005), which is purely voluntary, offers members insurance cover for legal expenses incurred in respect of complaints and disciplinary proceedings, criminal and certain civil proceedings, and employment disputes for employed solicitors, and industrial tribunal proceedings for partnerships. In addition a solicitor with a professional problem should be able to obtain advice through the local Faculty of Solicitors.

1.10   The solicitors' profession was the last of the non-specialising professions, and a solicitor is qualified to advise on a great number of matters, although inevitably specialisation is becoming increasingly prevalent. The solicitor, like other agents, is bound by duties of agent to client imposed by the law of agency which may be summarised as follows:

(a) The agent must carry out the principal's instructions.
(b) The agent is in a personal relationship with the principal, and may not therefore, in general, delegate, without the principal's instructions.
(c) The agent must keep the money and property of the principal separate from the agent's own money and property, and keep accounts of dealings with it.
(d) The agent must give the principal the full benefit of contracts made with third parties. Any secret commission must not be gained without the principal's consent.

In return, the agent is entitled to receive a reasonable remuneration, reimbursement of expenses, to be relieved of all liabilities incurred in the performance of the agency, and to the agent's lien over the property of the principal in the agent's hands in the course of the agency, until remuneration has been received.

1.11   To the law of agency there must now be added statutory controls, most importantly under the Financial Services Act 1986 as amended by the Financial Services and Markets Act 2000. This Act was introduced with the stated intention of offering an investor protection from incompetent and unscrupulous advisers and dealers, of whom there was apparently no shortage.

While the Act is framed on the basis that investors must accept personal responsibility for the risk involved in every investment to be made, and are thus not protected from the consequence of their own folly, they are nevertheless entitled to sound and impartial advice from a well qualified professional adviser. This advice is known technically as 'best advice' and is similar in concept to the obligations laid down in the law of agency.

Best advice is therefore precisely what every competent solicitor, registered as a financial adviser under the Act, would, or should, have offered anyway. The Act is aimed at rather more colourful figures on the financial spectrum. Nevertheless solicitors who give financial advice, as do most, are inevitably brought into the regulatory net. Again this involves the Law Society.

1.12   Solicitors who give any form of financial advice must now be registered under the Financial Services Act 1986. The giving of financial advice, without registration, is a criminal offence, punishable by up to two years in prison. The communication of a stockbroker's report, for example, on investments to a client, without comment, is not however covered by the Act. Sales of heritable property are not covered by the Act, but often the solicitor will be asked to give financial advice to clients as part of sale or purchase.

Investor protection is under the overall control of the Department of Trade and Industry (DTI). The DTI delegates regulatory powers to the Financial Securities Authority (FSA). FSA, in turn, has recognised a number of self-regulating organisations (SROs) and recognised professional bodies (RPBs) which, subject to the supervision of the SIB, are empowered to monitor the conduct of investment business by their members.

The Law Society of Scotland is an RPB, and thus is the regulatory body under the Financial Services Acts of the solicitors' profession in Scotland. The Society has enacted the Solicitors (Scotland) (Conduct of Investment Business) Practice Rules 1994 and the Solicitors (Scotland) (Incidental Investment Business) Practice Rules 2001. Thus the solicitor who wishes to give investment advice is at the end of this chain of acronyms, and must comply with the Practice Rules, and submit to regular inspection to ensure that this is so.

While the whole question of Financial Services Acts and the Law Society Rules requires a separate and detailed study, the main requirements of the Act and Rules, so far as concerning solicitors, may be summarised thus:

(a) There is a polarisation choice open to financial advisers (see below) but this is not open to solicitors in private practice. The polarisation choices require agents who sell financial services to decide whether they are either 'independent intermediaries' or 'authorised representatives'. The former approximates to the older concept of an 'insurance broker', who had access to the products of a number of companies—the larger the brokerage, the more products available—and advised which product was currently the best available in the circumstances. The latter approximates to the older concept of the 'insurance agent' (e g 'the man from the Pru'), who sold the products of only one company, and did not make any pretence to the contrary.

Unfortunately the two concepts had become hopelessly mixed, and agents might have represented themselves as 'brokers' but in reality were selling the products of one company, and stating that the product was the best available in the market. The truth was usually that it was not, only that it paid the best commission to the agent. That is the reason why the agent must decide which status to adopt (the polarisation option), and must advertise this clearly, and maintain that status.

No one person can be both independent intermediary and authorised representative, although large bodies like banks and building societies may be authorised representatives at branch level and independent intermediaries at head office level. Of the top ten lenders only one is an independent intermediary, while the others are tied to a particular life office. This does not seem to be entirely within the spirit of the Act, which was intended to make good and impartial financial advice available to everybody, at local level, and not just in gilded banking halls.

(b) The solicitor in private practice is not allowed to be an authorised representative (rule 3.5) nor have an exclusive arrangement with another intermediary. This does not, however, apply to solicitors employed in public service or commerce, whose employers may maintain an exclusive arrangement with an insurance or other financial company.

(c) A solicitor may not give or receive any gifts, services or inducements which might be regarded as likely to influence, improperly, a recommendation for a particular service (rule 3.7). There have been instances where inducements have been given, to get around the requirement on an agent to give the benefit of financial commission to the client (see the law of agency).

(d) A solicitor is required to know the client's personal and financial circumstances, and the investments available on the market. The solicitor must have an adequate and reasonable basis for any recommendation of an investment, and where the investment is a life policy or unit trust the solicitor must be sure that there are no other investments which would be more advantageous to the client. Further the solicitor must be satisfied that the investment is suitable for the client's purposes (best advice rule—rule 4.1). The solicitor must also take reasonable steps to ensure that the investment is effected on the best terms available at the time (best execution rule—rule 4.2).

(e) The solicitor must maintain records to demonstrate compliance with the best advice and best execution rules. The required records are fully detailed in the Conduct of Investment Business Rules 1994 and obviously must be complied with. The Law Society makes frequent periodical inspections of solicitors' books to ensure compliance with the Practice Rules.

(f) The solicitor must now disclose the commission to be received in respect of a packaged product, which includes commission. If the solicitor is to be paid a commission by a third party to whom business is passed, the amount of the commission must be disclosed to the client, and not be hidden as a fee paid to the solicitor.

The Practice Rules do not, however, particularly affect conveyancing as such, as purchase and sale of heritable property are not counted as a financial service. When, however, the conveyancing solicitor offers advice as to financial services in connection with the purchase of heritage, that is financial advice and is dealt with in greater detail in chapter 12.

Financial regulation is much more strictly applied than previously, and these rules are ignored at your own peril, as several 'household name' insurance companies have found out to their cost.

1.13   Other duties incumbent on the solicitor are:

(a) To effect through the Law Society's Master Policy, professional indemnity insurance, covering the solicitor's clients against any loss through the solicitor's negligence (Solicitors (Scotland) Professional Indemnity Insurance Rules 1995); as a guideline only, the maximum payment under the Master Policy is £1.25 million, unless an additional premium is paid. The total premium required from the profession in 2001 was £7,780,000. There were 8,768 people with practising certificates. The Law Society's Insurance Committee should be congratulated on the reduction of the premium by 9.5% in 2001, at a time when professional indemnity insurance is generally becoming more expensive.

(b) To subscribe to the solicitors' Guarantee Fund, which reimburses persons who have been defrauded by their solicitor (Solicitors (Scotland) Accounts, Account Certificates, Professional Practice and Guarantee Fund Rules 2001); again as a guideline the amount payable in 2000/01 was approximately £195, and the compensation paid was £249,000.

(c) To observe the Solicitors' (Scotland) (Advertising and Promotion) Practice Rules 1995. These Rules have been substantially liberalised, but solicitors must follow rule 8 which does not allow solicitors to claim superiority over other solicitors, nor make any reference in advertisements to volume of business or fee income, the identity of their clients or item of business without the prior written consent of the client, any item of business entrusted to them, or the outcome of any such business. Solicitors may not compare their fees with those of any other solicitor, make any inaccurate or misleading statements, nor bring the profession into disrepute. These Rules differ quite markedly from those of other professions, particularly accountants. In summary therefore, the solicitor is still restricted very much to advertising a corporate image.

(d) To observe the Accounts etc Rules mentioned above. In as much as these concern conveyancing in particular, they are discussed at paragraph **10.16**. The general reminder is merely given that 'each partner of a firm of solicitors shall be responsible for securing compliance by the firm with the provisions of these Rules'. The operation of this rule is slightly mitigated for junior partners who were given no responsiblity in accounting matters (*Sharp v The Council of the Law Society of Scotland* 1984 SLT 313 at 316), but basically lawyers cannot stand by and ignore accountancy matters, muttering how they are 'men of letters' and therefore, apparently, quite innumerate.

The Accounts Rules are a separate and very important study. The Disciplinary Tribunal Report for 1993 devotes a whole chapter to cases concerning a failure to comply with the Rules. Reliance on staff, reliance on computer programmes, without understanding them, and the 'particularly distressing' case of a solicitor who committed his client account to a withdrawal of almost three million US dollars, without ensuring that there were cleared funds to meet the transaction.

Some larger practices now employ chartered accountants as their partnership accountants or secretaries, and they may also employ other professional people, such as chartered surveyors and social workers, for specialist functions within the firm. The names of such persons may be printed on the firm's letterhead, provided that the public are in no way misled as to the status of the individual within the firm (Solicitors (Scotland) (Associates, Consultants and Employees) Practice Rules 2001). A smaller practice could not probably justify having a chartered accountant in the practice, but there should certainly be access to the services of a competent bookkeeper, who is preferably trained in the excellent courses run by the Society of Law Accountants (SOLAS).

(e) To accept unlimited liability for the debts of the partnership, and even, in extreme cases, of the other partners. The financial obligations of this requirement are, however, to some extent mitigated by compulsory professional indemnity insurance (see App VI).

In a case of major embezzlement in a firm, the Law Society will appoint a trustee to run the business, and will settle immediate claims from the Guarantee Fund. The Society will look first to the firm itself and then to the partners of the firm for recompense, to the limit of their assets. The indemnity policy will cover the partners for the first £1.25 million, but that may not be enough to protect their assets being sold. Any balance, in the last resort, will then be met by the Guarantee Fund.

(f) Not to act in the same matter for two parties who might have a conflicting interest (Solicitors (Scotland) Practice Rules 1986). It must be said that formerly a solicitor might have acted, and often did, for both seller and purchaser. In most cases, where there was no substantial conflict of interest, the result was usually satisfactory to all. It should be stressed, however, that where one person is selling, and another buying, however amicably, there is always a latent conflict of interest, and it was the cases where a dispute arose in the course of the transaction that gave tremendous difficulty. A solicitor cannot obviously act for both parties in a court case. By logical extension, the same applies in house purchase.

Having said that, there is considerable difficulty in country areas, where there are few solicitors, and certain exemptions are therefore made, to cover transactions between parties who are related, where both parties are established clients of the solicitor, or where there is no other solicitor in the area whom the client could reasonably be expected to consult.

Probably the most major exemption is that a solicitor may act for an institution, such as a building society or bank, which is lending money to the client in connection with a purchase, provided that the terms of the loan have been agreed before the solicitor is instructed to act. This last exemption is dealt with at rule 5(f) of the 1986 Rules. However, this is moderated by a change in banking practice set out in the terms of a circular from the Law Society in March 1994, which states that the banks now intend to instruct separate solicitors to represent their interest in commercial transactions. A further discussion of this topic follows in chapter 12.

Further, the building societies are known to be unhappy with the conveyancing services they are getting in English cases where the solicitors are acting for both borrower and the Society, and there has been a run of cases in the English courts dealing with instances where a solicitor acted for both borrower and lender. These cases usually produce an adverse result for the solicitor, and a claim on their indemnity insurance.

(g) To observe the code of conduct contained in Schedule 1 to the Code of Conduct (Scotland) Rules 1992, Admission as a Solicitor with Extended Rights (Scotland) Rules 1992 and Solicitors (Scotland) Order of Precedence, Instructions and Representations Rules 1992, which relate to general conduct, and particularly in court by solicitors and solicitor-advocates.

(h) To observe the Money Laundering Regulations 1993. Briefly these Regulations are intended to cover the placing of 'dirty' money (e g profits from drug-dealing or terrorism) into a 'clean' investment, such as a house or bonds. The investment can be subsequently sold, and the resulting proceeds are 'clean'. A person may commit five money laundering offences: assistance, concealment, acquisition, failure to disclose or tipping off. Basically, if you are approached by a client whom you have not known for at least two years, with a lot of unexplained cash, you are expected to 'verify' that the money has been legally obtained. If you are still not certain you would be well-advised to discuss the matter, on a confidential basis, with the National Crime Intelligence Service (Telephone: 0171 238 8271). It is appreciated that this is against the whole concept of client confidentiality, but this is an occasion where the solicitor has no right to silence. Desperate problems require desperate measures. It should be noted that an English solicitor was jailed in 2002 for six months. The offence related to receiving a sum of money from a client to account of expenses, and then refunding it in a laundered condition.

(i) To maintain complete confidentiality and silence as to a client's affairs. This confidentiality is even stricter than the confidentiality of the confessional, and the only exception to it is the duty to reveal details of possible money laundering (see (h) above). Solicitors should not even reveal their clients' names, in case someone puts two and two together, and perhaps even reaches four. In particular a major difficulty can arise where solicitors are asked to act against a former client, and the rule is that the knowledge they have gained of the former client's affairs should not be used against the interest of that former client, to the benefit of the new client. This is dealt with by a system of 'Chinese walls' which means that a solicitor who was involved with the former client, should not assist in any way with preparing the case for the new client. The landmark case in this respect is *Prince Jefri Bolkiah v KPMG* ([1999] 1 All ER 517). Also see *Koch Shipping Inc v Richards Butler* (2002) Times, 21 August.

(j) The solicitor will also, like other mortals, be subjected to visits from VAT and tax inspectors, none of which are, not even remotely, social in character.

1.14 Having outlined how difficult it is to become a solicitor, and how carefully regulated one's conduct is after that, and perhaps having indicated how expensive all of this is going to be for the solicitor, it is now appropriate to consider the benefits of being a solicitor, before too many people take fright and run. Quite apart from the intangible benefits of the profession, which are many and which depend in their intensity upon the individual, the most important privilege is the so-called 'solicitors' monopoly' of conveyancing matters. This is contained in the Solicitors (Scotland) Act 1980, s 32 which states:

> 'a person including body corporate, not being qualified as a solicitor or advocate who draws or prepares a writ relating to heritable or moveable estate shall be guilty of an offence.'

Section 32(3) then continues to exclude from the definition (a) a will or other testamentary writing; (b) a document *in re mercatoria*, missive or mandate; (c) a letter or power of attorney; and (d) a transfer of stock containing no trust or limitation thereof.

Thus, of the four major steps of a property transaction: marketing, completing missives, completing title and drafting the deed, and settling up, it is only the third that is protected by the conveyancing monopoly. A person who is not legally qualified may market heritable property, and even complete a missive on behalf of purchaser or seller. When, however, it comes to drawing up formal deeds (i e those deeds not excepted by s 32(3)) this work must then be done by the solicitor.

Nothing said above, however, limits the ability of non-qualified parties selling or buying houses, to act entirely or partially on their own behalf in the matter. As a rough analogy, if you have a sore tooth, you may pull it out yourself, but do not even ask an undentally qualified person to do the job for you, for that will be an offence. Thus, if the Smiths buy a house, there is no reason why they should not complete their own missives and disposition, and present the disposition for recording. A solicitor need not be employed, but a non-solicitor may not be employed, at a fee, to draw up a writ covered by the solicitors' monopoly. If that person will perform the service gratuitously, that is permitted. It might be mentioned that the lender will insist on a lawyer acting on their behalf, at the borrowers' expense, and the Smiths will therefore still have to pay for a lawyer.

Further it should be noted that advocates are covered by the conveyancing monopoly as well, but as a matter of tradition they do not handle conveyancing.

1.15 Monopolies are, however, currently not at all in favour, and are gradually being dismantled, the ultimate authority being the Treaty of Rome, arts 88 and 89, which set out prohibitions on restriction of trade. These articles are being enthusiastically implemented throughout the European Union, not least in the United Kingdom.

For example, opticians have lost their monopoly on providing spectacle frames, and newspapers now advertise that you can buy reading spectacles for a few pounds at a variety of places, which include service stations and tobacconists. The person who had predicted this a few years ago would have been labelled as unquestionably insane. I recall hearing a prosecution, a few years ago, of an optician who had dared to advertise his services in the telephone directory IN BLOCK CAPITALS, thus presumably unfairly attracting business! He was duly prosecuted for this heinous crime, but was admonished, the defence agent having poured scorn on the prosecution case, and having very logically suggested that those who needed the service most would perhaps have been more at ease with block capitals!

It tends to be the case that other peoples' monopolies are seen to be monopolistic and oligarchic, whereas one's own monopoly is 'in the public interest'. Bearing this in mind, one turns to the Law Reform (Miscellaneous Provisions) (Scotland) Act 1990, which unleashed two new legal animals: the licensed conveyancer or licensed executry practitioner, and the solicitor-advocate. A licensed conveyancer would be a person not qualified in law, but in the particular discipline of conveyancing or executry practice. Licensed conveyancers practise happily in England, although mainly as part of a solicitor's business, but not yet in Scotland. For a definition of the limit of services that should be offered by licensed conveyancers, see *Hall v Eade, The Times*, 18 January 1989.

The government set up a Licensed Conveyancer's Board to draw up rules, but the whole project was dismantled in 2002 when it became apparent that there was not enough work to go around, even to keep solicitors busy and there was little demand for this qualification. Had the project materialised, licensed conveyancers would have been under similar constraints as to financial probity and conduct as solicitors and in truth, without much extra effort, could have become solicitors.

1.16 Solicitors have traditionally been known as 'men of business' who were willing and able to advise on the whole spectrum of business affairs. Formerly solicitors performed a wide variety of tasks, including accountancy, being bank agents in smaller communities, and being part-time clerks to smaller local authorities, clerks of court in smaller jurisdictions, as well as running their own practices. In the present century, however, there has been a drive towards specialisation, and inevitably the man of business is yielding to the specialist—both inside the legal profession and outside it.

1.17 This removing of items of general practice into specialist niches can, and does, produce friction. By and large the legal profession enjoys fairly amicable links with other professional bodies.

Frankly, however, a fair amount of animosity exists between some solicitors and some estate agents, whom solicitors see as removing a very important part of their livelihood. It is not only the mere fact that estate agents will market their clients' houses that troubles solicitors; it is that estate agents, who are predominantly now owned by banks, building societies and life assurance companies, will sell them life policies of their own tied company, suggest that they surrender other policies, and direct the client to a 'tame' solicitor, who offers a low fee. It really all boils down to a single question: who has control of the transaction, the solicitor or the estate agent?

Of course, the only answer to competition is to go out there and compete; if you think that an estate agent is taking your business, there is nothing to stop the conveyancer practising as an estate agent.

Solicitors may, however, justly feel that they are entitled to compete on 'a level playing field', with a referee who is not wearing reading spectacles he bought at the filling station that morning. Solicitors with their complex training, and intricate web of self-regulation should not be asked to contend with someone who was selling groceries last week, and who has no real professional regulations as to conduct.

In particular solicitors may rightly feel aggrieved that they have to avoid conflicts of interest while some estate agents openly are happy to act for anyone they can find. The worst example of this case is where estate agents are instructed to act in a sale; a buyer expresses interest, and the estate agent immediately suggests that they see their financial adviser. Some estate agents even make this a condition of inspecting the house. Thus the sellers know exactly how much the buyers can afford and may favour buyers who are willing to instruct the agents in the sale of their own house. They are thus able to act for both seller and buyer, and arrange a loan for the latter, backed by a financial arrangement which brings in further commission. Contrast that with the solicitors' position under para **1.13(f)** above, and ask if a level playing field exists? Again, the defence is one of 'Chinese walls', but bear in mind walls in China are paper thin.

1.18   Estate agents were virtually unknown in Scotland until about 1960, except in the sale of specialised properties. Landed estates, very grand houses, farms and industrial properties might have been marketed by specialised agents, but solicitors handled the bulk of routine property sales as part of the whole selling process. Quite frankly, they had become extremely complacent about this, and the fact that nearly all property throughout the English-speaking world was marketed by estate agents, did not seem to ring any warning bells.

In 1963, however, the first commercial or 'high street' estate agency came to Scotland, in the shape of the Villa Estate Agency in Glasgow. The proprietor of this venture, one James Davidson, a chartered surveyor (it should perhaps be mentioned that two solicitors were also initially involved, but both the Royal Institution of Chartered Surveyors and the Law Society did not want their members practising as commercial estate agents, and they had to choose one or the other) attracted customers to the agency by his cheerful advertising. This was quite different from anything house buyers in Scotland had seen before, although the great Roy Brooks had been using this technique in England for many years. (See his two books of advertisements *A Brothel in Pimlico* and *Mud, Straw and Insults*, both available from Roy Brooks, 395 Kings Road, London.)

As an example of James Davidson's advertising:

'POLLOKSHIELDS (Ayton Road) Well—what a bargain for anyone who wants to make a home out of a decrepit mausoleum. The electricity bills in this 6/7 apartment SEMI greystone VILLA are nil, simply because there is no electricity. Yes, dignified Victorian gas lighting sets the Dickensian scene where the grotty dull ancient decoration somehow seems in place. Massive two tractor and car garage (there presently are two tractors and what once passed for a car in it now!). Regardless of your fears of "strange houses" surely £1,850 must tempt a lot of viewers.'

You will incidentally note the price, merely 40 or so years ago. Such a house would now attract an offer in excess of six figures , but that is another matter.

1.19   These advertisements were allied with considerable marketing flair, attractive shops, attentive receptionists, block advertising and informative details. Further, lists of potential sellers and buyers were maintained, and these were constantly updated and cross-referenced, so that a seller who went to an estate agent would be impressed when the agent could produce a list of potential buyers. The seller would be even more impressed if a sale resulted, without the property being advertised.

These techniques are standard nowadays, but were not then, and one winces at the thought of the amateurism of the legal profession at that time. House sales were usually deputed to the newest apprentice, who had probably never seen the house, did not even know where it was, and had no idea of the asking price. As a result, estate agents were able to secure a fairly firm beachhead on the market very quickly, and have since then made very substantial inroads into this business.

To the chagrin of the legal profession, many estate agents subsequently sold their businesses to banks, building societies and life assurance companies at very large sums. This has often resulted in tears, and large institutions have learnt the hard way that a small personal business like estate agency cannot be easily institutionalised, and that cobblers should stick to their lasts. In October 1994 the Nationwide Building Society was reported as selling its estate agency chain of 305 branches for the sum of £1. They had made a loss of £200m in seven years. In 1993 Abbey National sold its 347-branch chain for one-tenth of the price paid for each outlet. The Prudential lost £340m on its 500-branch chain. (Financial figures: *Daily Telegraph*, 12 October 1994.)

This whole process hopefully taught the legal profession a never-to-be-forgotten lesson in the joys of competition. What was perhaps even worse, in many cases the legal profession surrendered the opportunity of first contact with the client.

1.20   It should be pointed out that, nationally, solicitors still market around 70% of residential property. In most areas, solicitors fought the fire of competition with fire, and in most areas solicitors have been able to maintain a healthy share of a greatly increased market. In most cities and towns, solicitors' property centres exist where the individual solicitor can enjoy the benefits of a main street shop window, corporate advertising, solicitor referral schemes, property matching, financial advice, and a permanent staff to answer enquiries. These solicitors' property centres have proved highly successful throughout Scotland; until 1993 everywhere except Glasgow and its environs. Further details of the services available are given in chapter 2.

The property centre concept was not initially successful in Glasgow, and when the original centre collapsed it was replaced by the Solicitors Estate Agency Ltd (SEAL), a limited company owned by participating solicitors, but run by professional estate agents. In addition, several solicitors ran their own agencies, either under their own names or under an independent company. In 1993 the property centre idea was revived in Glasgow, and the Glasgow Solicitors Property Centre (GSPC) is the result. SEAL ceased to be owned by solicitors. The GSPC appears to be doing well: it is claimed that the centre accounts for around 40 per cent of residential sales in Glasgow and the West of Scotland, and that a sale is made every 22 minutes (*Scotland on Sunday*, 23 June 2002) The GSPC is centrally sited: 145/147 Queen Street, Glasgow G1 3BJ (Telephone: 08457 229922). For details of other centres, consult the Legal Directory, or the Law Society website (www.lawscot.org.uk).

1.21   Further, to add fat to the flames, a group of Aberdeen estate agents, complained that they were unable to advertise in the highly successful

Aberdeen Solicitors Property Centre weekly newsletter, which contained details of properties being sold by solicitors. They claimed that this position restrained competition, and the matter came to court (*Aberdeen SPC Ltd v Director General for Fair Trading* 1996 SLT 523). The court decided that ASPC were not in restraint of fair trade. The Office of Fair Trading then persuaded the Monopolies and Mergers Commission to make a formal hearing under the Fair Trading Act 1973. This again was not successful, and the MMC concluded that ASPC were not operating unfairly.

1.22 Formerly, solicitors might not refer to themselves as 'estate agents' but have been permitted to do so for some years now. Solicitors may also refer to themselves by some of the more traditional designations, such as Writers to the Signet, Writers, or Advocates (member of the Society of Advocates in Aberdeen as opposed to a member of the Faculty of Advocates). This often causes confusion, as where the first edition of Yellow Pages in Glasgow listed all firms describing themselves as 'writers' under the generic heading of 'authors'.

A further designation widely used by solicitors is that of 'notary public'. A notary public is a person who can administer solemn oaths to persons signing deeds, the most common being affidavits prepared in terms of the Matrimonial Homes (Family Protection) (Scotland) Act 1981, as amended (see App III). A notarial instrument had originally to be signed by a notary public, but the Conveyancing (Scotland) Act 1924 provided for a new notice of title, with the same feudalising function of the notarial instrument, which could be signed by any solicitor, whether a notary or not.

A notary public may also perform, in Scotland, the function of the roughly similar English functionary, known as the commissioner of oaths, and vice versa. When signing an English document, the Scottish notary signs as 'Notary Public, and as such a Commissioner of Oaths'. The office of the notary public is an ancient one, said to date from the Holy Roman Empire, and the admission and conduct of notaries is now regulated by the Solicitors (Scotland) Act 1980, Pt V, and administered by the Law Society.

1.23 Writing in 1990, I then quoted an article entitled 'Big Bang for the City's Law Firms' (*The Economist*, 9–15 September 1989) which prophesied:

'By the end of the next decade there will probably be ten giant commercial law firms in the City of London, some of which will be American. They will each have a gross fee income of around £500 million. Alongside them will be niche firms, specialising in insolvency, tax, intellectual property, and entertainment etc. Partnerships will be a thing of the past. Most firms will have incorporated and are likely to belong to multi-disciplinary practices (ie part of a holding company of accountants, architects and surveyors), with Chinese walls and all.'

'Chinese walls' are, incidentally, an informal arrangement devised under the restructuring of the City (which allowed stockbrokers to be owned by banks). The concept purports to prevent one part of these huge businesses (e g stockbrokers dealing in shares) from benefiting from confidential information imparted to another part of the business (e g merchant banks who are selling a company, whose shares are being traded by the stockbroking arm of the business). The efficacy of this arrangement remains questionable, and there are still many allegations of persons with inside knowledge trading in the stock market, although this is now a criminal offence.

This forecast has proved remarkably accurate. In London, there are many huge legal firms, with wide international links, whose turnover in fees every year is staggering. In Scotland this process is not so evident, but there are several mega-firms who are developing in the same way.

Basically the conveyancer has four main worries at this time:

(1) Are we making sufficient money to meet overheads and provide the partners with a decent living?

While property prices have risen relentlessly in recent years, conveyancing fees have fallen. The question of the fee to be charged should depend on the quality of the work done, and the time spent. The techniques of fee charging are dealt with in Chapter 11, but it is emphasised that a conveyancer's fee depends on how much the market will bear, and how much the competition are charging. There are firms that will quote a fee that can scarcely cover their overheads, hoping to attract volume business and make a good profit in that way. Such firms naturally attract business on price alone, although in some cases the quality of their service is suspect.

Any question of centrally regulating fees, as was the case a few years ago, would be viewed as anti-competitive, and not allowed. Each firm must therefore keep their efficiency under constant control, to provide a decent turnover and profit margin. This may involve heavy investment in training and computer equipment, and the delegation of routine tasks from conveyancers to trainees and para-legals. Many routine tasks in the conveyancing process should simply not be done by qualified lawyers, whose expensive time should be otherwise occupied. Remember that all lawyers have to sell is their time, and this has been an expensive commodity to purchase.

(2) Are the partners protected against professional liability claims?

Recent years have seen the development of a blame culture, in which if anything goes wrong, a claim for damages follows. Conveyancers have not escaped this, and this book will deal with techniques to ward off such claims, and to protect yourselves if one is made. It is a condition of practice, of course, that indemnity insurance is carried, and if a claim is made, the indemnity insurers will step in to defend it and to pay the award, if any. However, as with any insurance, the amount insured must be sufficient, and this can be expensive in premiums.

Then there arises, as mentioned above at paragraph **1.13(d)** and **(e)**, the dismal prospect of a partner in a firm fraudulently dealing with clients' funds, as unfortunately happens from time to time. The Law Society, which in the last resort pays the claims of defrauded clients, through the Guarantee Fund, makes and enforces rules that are designed to make such frauds unlikely, but there are a few cases each year despite this.

If a fraud does happen, a trustee for the firm is appointed. The indemnity insurers will pay a sum of £1.25 million under the Master Policy, but no more. This sum is not paid to single partner firms, or to firms where complicity in the offence is suspected. Then the Law Society looks to the firm, and each of the partners, for payment of the sum owing, and each of the partners may be declared bankrupt. Finally, when these sources are exhausted, the Guarantee Fund pays the balance, and all members of the Law Society are levied for a contribution to repay the Fund. This contribution varies from year to year, depending on the claims record.

It is obviously in the interests of the entire profession, and the individual partners of each firm, that such fraud be kept to a minimum, and while the Law Society auditors may seem formidable and unhelpful, it should be appreciated that they are providing a vital service to each and every partner and to the entire profession.

Each firm must therefore keep a careful eye on its accounts, and ensure that each partner is not enjoying a life style substantially in advance of the other partners, with no apparent reason, such as private means. This form of control becomes very difficult when the partnership is a large or international one. Partners in these should realise that they are effectively allowing anyone in the partnership to sign cheques on their personal bank account. When entering partnership, a solicitor should remember this, and that the actions of a maverick in Texas or elsewhere, may bring down the whole house of cards, with appalling consequences.

Probably advantage should be taken of the terms of the Limited Liability Partnership Act 2000 and the Limited Liability Partnerships Regulations 2001. Limited liability partnerships (LLPs) came into being on 6 April 2001, and already there have been registrations under the Act. The LLP is a corporate body, and is not subject to partnership law. It may grant floating charges (Limited Liability Partnerships (Scotland) Regulations 2001). The LLP has unlimited liability for claims against it, but the assets of individual partners are protected (or 'ring fenced') from liability. In return for these privileges, some concessions must be made: annual accounts must be made public, drawn under the requirements of UK GAAP, and the income of the highest paid member of the LLP must be disclosed. In summary, the LLP is like a cross between a limited company and a partnership, and legal firms might like to consider the advantages of converting to LLP.

(3) Is the practice organised to maximum effect?

Legal firms should give independent advice, and not be trammled by extraneous considerations. Thus, if a solicitor thinks that the client is going in a wrong direction, the solicitor should be able to say so, even if it means losing the business of the client. Good advice is not always popular.

For that reason solicitors are not, at present, allowed to enter into multi-discipline practices (MDPs). The concept of having a number of specialities under one roof is not an unattractive one, but it does present a danger to the concept of independent advice. Thus, if the lawyer in the practice gives certain advice, which the client does not like, the accountants or surveyors in the practice may lose a client. Accordingly the lawyer may be persuaded by the others to withhold the advice that should be given.

Multi-discipline practices have not been approved by the Law Society, which was consequently thought to be a bit stick in the mud. Then came the Enron affair, and critics have had to think again. Enron was a multi-national energy company with its head office in Texas, and had as its auditors the huge international accountancy firm of Arthur Andersen, who while being principally accountants, also offered consultancy services. These consultancy services included such matters as recruitment, advising on management services, and legal advice. Arthur Andersen had stated the intention to be the biggest law firm in the world, as well as the biggest accountancy firm, and were well on their way to achieving that intention, through the acquisition of big legal firms, including one in Scotland. Needless to say such legal advice given would not include advice to Mr and Mrs AB on their boundary dispute with their neighbour. The firm were only interested in big and expensive legal advice, and smaller business was quickly spun off to a 'private client' firm.

Enron got into major financial difficulties, and allegations were made that Arthur Andersen had been complicit in preparing accounts which did not reveal the true position of the firm, and had not only been Enron's internal auditors, but also its external auditors, and had supplied Enron with major consultancy services. Its audit fee from Enron was $25 million in the final year, and its fee for consultancy services in the same period was $27 million. The independence of its advice and of its audit was suspect. In the subsequent scandal, and the developing scandal of WorldCom, Arthur Andersen has ceased to be a firm, and the 'Big Five' accountants worldwide incredibly became the 'Big Four'.

It was thus perceived that it might not be such a good idea for lawyers to link up with a big international firm as had been thought, because accountants seem, in many cases, unable to accept that they are acting in a conflict situation (see quotation at the head of this chapter in which the CEO of Deloitte Touche grudgingly admits that there may be a conflict of interest in auditors offering consultancy services) by offering audit and consultancy services, and that this can affect the independence of a lawyer's advice when they are part of the accounting firm.

All that having been said, there is a trend to larger and larger firms, and international link-ups. Firms that wish to remain small really must offer specialist advice. There is no room for firms that deal with all aspects of legal business, but aren't very good at anything special.

(4) The future of conveyancing, if any?

Conveyancing for many years has been the mainstay of many legal practices. Suddenly it is not so. With the universal onset of land registration, the development of automated registration of titles to land (ARTL), the future abolition of the feudal system and the introduction of computerised conveyancing, allied with the refusal of the public to pay high conveyancing fees, the future of conveyancing practice suddenly looks bleak, and conveyancers, normally a jolly breed, are unhappy.

Progress cannnot, however, be denied, and conveyancers must adapt to the new conditions, and learn to charge realistically for their services. If the work is cut down, conveyancers cannot expect to be paid on the old labour–intensive basis. They must find other outlets for their talents. Since the original report on land registration was produced some 35 years ago, the legal profession has seen the introduction of divorce in the sheriff court, the right of audience in the higher courts, and many new areas of practice, such as intellectual property, employment law, social security law, immigration law, plus an enormous expansion in such fields as corporate law, civil court practice, and investment practice.

Thus the picture is not entirely bleak, it is simply a matter of finding a new direction. My own feeling, for what it is worth, is that conveyancing will continue to need attention, despite the best intentions of Parliament. The feudal system, in particular, will take some killing off.

I do not think, in summary, that you have made a bad decision to choose the law as a career. It is simply a matter of being fast on your feet, and adapting to new conditions as they come along. You are indeed welcome to the profession.

Part two

THE TRANSACTION

Chapter 2

MARKETING THE PROPERTY

'We were very concerned, bearing in mind the Property Misdescriptions Act, that we would be misleading by not telling about a ghost, but also misleading if we did come clean about it and then it didn't appear. We felt that if we knew of a ghost which eventually appeared it would only seem fair to tell the purchasers in case they freaked out later when they saw it.'

(Christopher Calcutt, estate agent in Kent, discussing the problems of haunted houses: *The Sunday Times*)

2.1 Most sale and purchase transactions start with houseowners deciding to move, and putting their property up for sale, although it is not unknown for the purchaser to initiate the process. It has been suggested that the entire contracting process could be speeded up if the seller issued an offer of sale, rather than the other way around. This idea has yet to be tested thoroughly.

As discussed (para **1.14**) the marketing process is not part of the solicitors' monopoly, and may be done by anyone. The choice between solicitor and estate agent is the houseowners', and to a large extent the answer to this question will depend on the services respectively offered, and the part of the country in which the house is situated.

2.2 For present purposes we shall assume that the houseowners choose to employ a solicitor to market the property, and that the solicitor is a member of a solicitors' property centre (SPC). It should be made quite clear, however, that property marketing has become a separate skill, and if a solicitor is to market property it must be done professionally and properly.

2.3 Some solicitors, particularly in Glasgow, may prefer to pass the marketing of houses to estate agents, and this is usually done on a reciprocal basis of instruction. In the case of a reciprocal arrangement being reached it should be remembered:

(a) That a solicitor may not share with any unqualified person any profits or fees derived from any business transacted by solicitors in Scotland in the course of or in connection with their practice.

(b) Formerly under Practice Rules, a solicitor might not share an office in conjunction with a person who was not legally qualified. This rule has now been relaxed, provided that there is no question of breach of confidentiality in the sharing of staff, and provided that the accommodation is self-contained, and provided there is no suggestion of business being channelled unfairly to the solicitor by the other party involved. If you contemplate such an arrangement, it would be best to obtain a waiver from the Law Society. Among waivers granted are for small offices in supermarkets, and a solicitor and accountant in a remote area using the same premises on alternate days.

(c) That the basic philosophy of the Law Society is that the only acceptable form of channelling clients to a solicitor is on the personal recommendation of a satisfied client, although the Society admits that it is not always possible to prevent 'less desirable' forms of enticement (Law Society Annual Report 1981, p 14).

(d) Any suggestion of unfair enticement of clients should be most scrupulously avoided.

In essence the question of whether or not to use an estate agent is one of circumstances, and the only important criterion is the interest of the clients, which in the long run is also the interest of the solicitor.

2.4   If your clients are going to employ an estate agent, it is as well that the wording of the contract is carefully considered. A contract is only likely to diminish the rights of the client. The estate agents will seek sole selling rights, that is they are entitled to commission if the property is sold during the agreed period, whoever finds the buyer—even if it is the clients themselves. Some agents will try to make the agreed period a long one—six weeks should be sufficient, and not any longer. As to commission, the law is quite clear on the subject: if the estate agent is instrumental in the sale of the house, the agent is entitled to claim commission at the standard rate (*Walker Fraser & Steele v Fraser's Trustees* 1910 SC 222). If the agent is unsuccessful, the agent is then entitled to a reasonable remuneration for work done (*quantum meruit*) and for refunding of outlays incurred.

In particular, the clients should not be panicked into employing two agencies. The dangers of this arrangement were highlighted in an unreported case in Paisley Sheriff Court.

Mr and Mrs A decided to sell their house, and asked estate agents F to handle the sale. F duly advertised the sale, and several parties, including a Mr Q, inspected the property. No sale resulted. Mr and Mrs A then saw a property advertised by estate agents Z, and while negotiating with Z, they decided to entrust the sale of their own house to Z. They signed Z's standard sale contract, which required a commission to be paid on sale, whether they were instrumental in effecting a sale or not.

In the meantime, Mr Q returned from abroad, looked again at Mr and Mrs A's house, and bought it. Agents F claimed a commission as they had introduced Mr Q to the sellers. Agents Z also claimed a commission in terms of their contract, which granted them a sole selling agency. It was held that Mr and Mrs A had to pay both agents. (See also *Lordsgate Properties v Balcombe* [1985] 1 EGLR 20, (1985) 274 EG 493, and an article 'Double Jeopardy' in the *Scottish Law Gazette* December 1985.)

2.5   At whatever stage the solicitor is instructed (and we are assuming here that it is at the outset, although sometimes it is not so simple—the first thing you know about your client's intention to sell is when an offer drops onto your desk) the first thing is to obtain the title deeds of the property. This is important in order that you can ascertain whether or not the title is a registered one, and if there are any unusual conditions of title, such as rights of pre-emption or unusual servitude rights.

If the titles are missing, extracts or quick copies may be obtained from the Register, or in the case of a registered title, a new land and charge certificate can be obtained from the Register. It is also helpful at this stage to obtain a planning certificate from the local council (para **3.21**), a roads certificate from the local council (para **3.24**), planning certificates, building warrants, completion certificates, a coal mining report, superior's consent certificate authorising any development of the property which requires these permissions, or some of them (para **3.25**), and guarantees of timber treatment, and double glazing (para **3.26**). In the case of a first registration, it is also important to receive a Form 10A report, which is equivalent to a Sasine Register search, and Form P16 Report (para **13.3**) lest there be any major discrepancy in the boundaries.

These papers should all be scrutinised carefully to ensure that there is nothing in them which would make a sale difficult, such as a clause of pre-emption (see para **7.29**) or in land registration cases, an exclusion of indemnity (see para **13.15(b)**) on the land certificate. Bearing in mind the complexity of offers, and the number of warranties that are now required (see ch 3) it is as well to know your title before entering into missives, and if there is a weakness in your title, to compromise it with the purchasers' agents before missives are concluded. Better that than to reveal the weakness after conclusion of missives, when the purchasers may be happy to accept a breach of warranty, given blindly, as an excuse to resile from the transaction.

2.6 Armed with as much knowledge as possible, the solicitors who are marketing the property through their own firm, can then prepare property details and instruct advertising.

It is, therefore, suggested that the solicitor who engages in selling houses should adopt a procedure broadly similar to that outlined here (although practice will obviously vary from office to office).

(a) **Visit the house in question, and take measurements and details.** Take a photograph for publicity purposes. Digital cameras will facilitate the production of attractive sales particulars but if a digital camera is not available commercial processors will be able to provide you with 'sticky-backed' prints for annexing to particulars. Arrange the viewing—the easiest arrangement is to have the owners show the property, at times that suit them. If the house is empty, you can arrange to show it, but you may wish to agree extra remuneration for this. It is advisable that, wherever possible, two people conduct the viewings, and a representative of your firm should not be alone in an empty house, especially at night. If the house is empty, make sure that you have the key, and at least one spare in the office. NEVER let the key out of your control.

(b) **If the clients ask you to advise them on how to make the property more attractive to buyers, there are a few basic rules:** make the house and garden appear attractive from the street; attend to essential repairs; don't spend money on expensive redecoration which may not be to potential buyers' tastes, and is thus a waste of money; keep the house clean and tidy and well lit; avoid cooking and other smells; make sure that there is a parking space for buyers' cars; be ready to show the house at short notice. While furnishing, decor and personal items are usually insignificant compared to structure and location, it is nevertheless important to make a good impression on potential buyers.

(c) **Form a reasoned evaluation and advise the client.** If in doubt, consult a chartered surveyor for a valuation. The question of the surveyor's fee should, however, be discussed with the client before the surveyor is instructed.

(d) **Prepare an attractive, concise and truthful advertisement, giving rough details and a telephone number for further details and viewing.** If the house is not constantly occupied, do not indicate this by saying, for example 'viewing after 6 p m'. You might as well put a notice in the *Crooks Gazette* intimating that the house will be unoccupied all day. Do not waste your clients' money on wasteful and over-elaborate advertisements. Eschew the temptation to advertise your firm more than the property. Outline your advertising proposals to your client, and provide a rough guide to the cost. When writing the advertisement, stick to the facts—try to avoid 'estate agentese'; some actual examples:

'Situated at a desirable crossroads';
'Designed by the celebrated Scottish architect, Ronnie Mackintosh';
'set in a child-safe cul-de-sac within this sought-after developing area';
'with a field for the possible horse';
'suitable for the disearning (*sic*) purchaser';
'with an Adam TV den';
'positively oozing with olde worlde charm';
'with a 9ft high widow, overlooking the garden';
'with a glazed door in vestibule leading to hell'
'property situated in a beautiful curved cresent'.

Such language is a casualty of the Property Misdescriptions Act 1991 (PMA 1991), which insists on property being accurately described. Prosecutions under this Act and its associated regulations are relatively rare in Scotland, as breaches of the law are usually dealt with by compensation. There are, however, recorded instances in England of prosecutions where a house was described as 'south facing' when in fact it faced north, and did not accordingly enjoy the same amount of sun. Another case was where a farm building was described as having a three-phase power supply, which was not the case.

   Travel agents have had this problem for years and have evolved a new form of language which describes the property in an attractive way but cannot be held as untruthful. Thus 'rapidly developing resort' means tower cranes and 'ideal for sun worshippers' means there's nothing else to do. Resorts described as 'lively' should generally be avoided by the elderly. Estate agents are following suit.

(e) **Similarly, prepare a schedule of particulars to be handed out to reasonably interested enquirers, giving truthful and accurate particulars of the house, preferably with a photograph and location plan (if available) attached.** Moveable items included in the sale should be clearly specified. Bear in mind PMA 1991 which makes it a criminal offence for an agent to misdescribe a property, or to 'touch up' a photograph to give a false impression. A semi-detached house can be photographed in such a way as to make it appear detached, but this is not allowed. The Property Misdescriptions (Specified Matters) Order 1992 gives a list of specified matters that must be correctly stated in particulars of the property.

   Oddly enough PMA 1991 ignores a misdescription by a person who sells the house personally.

(f) **Set a sensible asking price in consultation with the client.** If this is set too low, people will wonder what is wrong with the property. If it is set too high, they will be scared off. Estate agents have a practice of setting a low price, and expecting offers at least 15–20% above. The asking price is thus equivalent to the upset price in an auction, and potential purchasers are left in the dark as to what price is acceptable.

(g) **Register the house with the local solicitors' property centre,** if that is the chosen method of sale, which will help with the marketing by providing a 'high street' display facility for all properties, and will publish an advertisement in its weekly property list. The centres charge a one-off fee, and will hold the property until it is sold. If the sale is slow after a period of months the SPC may seek a re-insertion fee. The solicitor will supply the SPC with details of the property and a supply of Property Schedules. Bear in mind that the SPC will not arrange for sale boards. These are the responsibility of the solicitor. The SPC will put the details on the internet, display them in its centre, and publish them in its weekly newspaper. It will also make available to prospective purchasers copies of the Property Schedule.

(h) **Obtain as much information as you can, as soon as you can.**   The sellers' solicitor should at this stage obtain letters from the council (as to the roads and planning etc) and any necessary affidavits required in terms of the Matrimonial Homes (Family Protection) (Scotland) Act 1981 (see App III). The reason for this is to avoid unfortunate delays by others at a future date, when the pressure is on you.

(i) **Keep main details (e g price, entry, moveables included, rateable value etc) preferably on computer or a card index.**   Keep a list of all serious enquiries for future reference. Note in particular all formal notifications of interest, preferably on the back of the card.

(j) **Fix a closing date and advise all parties who have notified interest when it becomes clear that there is going to be competition (rough rule: when two surveyors have been to the property).**   Collect all offers, and arrange to discuss these with the sellers, giving them your advice. Accept the offer most attractive to your clients (see para **4.1**) and advise all unsuccessful offerors.

(k) **When missives are concluded, inform the property centre, cancel all advertisements and remove all boards etc.**   Nothing so much infuriates the general public as applying for details of an advertised house and being informed that 'it's sold'.

Chapter 3

THE PURCHASERS MAKE OVERTURES

'How can we have a standardised offer for property when offers differ not only from town to town, but from firm to firm, and in our case from husband to wife?'

(Letter from a married solicitor whose husband worked in a different firm)

'The enquiry reporter took the view that an estate agent's office, although classified as an office, was by nature a quasi-retail function involved in the buying and selling of property. The frequently changing window display was compulsive viewing for many people, necessary for others, and had a drawing power that could benefit other enterprises.'

(Scottish Planning Appeals, no 6, 117)

3.1 Really the first thing the purchasers should do is tell their solicitor that they are 'house-hunting'. This can hardly be done soon enough, as it gives the solicitors an opportunity to make available to the purchasers their expertise in the property market. The solicitors may even know of a suitable house on the market, and can give general advice on areas, neighbourhood schools and shops, price ranges and so on. The solicitors should at this stage also be able to give a good indication of the costs involved as these may make a substantial difference to the purchasers' target.

In particular, purchasers tend to forget that they may be liable to pay stamp duty on their purchase, and it really hurts them when they find that they have (say) an extra £700 to pay on a house costing £70,000. It hurts even more when the purchaser has to pay a minimum of £7,500 in stamp duty on a house costing over £250,000 (the cost of a good flat in Edinburgh); it is even worse when the purchaser has to pay a minimum of £20,000 on a house costing over £500,000 (the cost of a good flat in London).

The solicitors should warn the clients about this and other charges that may be overlooked. An estimate of fees and outlays should be given (see App I.2) and agreed. In terms of the Solicitors (Scotland) Act 1980, s 61A(a), where the solicitor and the client shall have reached a written agreement as to fees, it shall not be competent, in any litigation as to those fees, for the court to remit the solicitor's account for taxation. In terms of the Solicitors (Scotland) (Written Fee Charging Agreements) Practice Rules 1993 a written fee charging agreement shall not contain a consent to registration for preservation and execution, which would permit summary diligence to be done against the client.

Persons who buy a house at £200,000 may seem very rich to you but remember that they may be selling their old house at say £150,000 and finding the rest of the price by an increased loan. They are, therefore, paying by transfer of paper, and never really have this money: this is vulgarly referred to as 'buying with monopoly money'. If the purchasers do their sums wrongly, they have to make up the difference in 'real money', and usually at fairly short notice. It is only correct to advise them as to the costs involved, even if this has the effect of changing their mind about moving at all! Particular care should be taken to state whether or not a fee includes the VAT content—it can make a very significant difference (see para **11.12**).

3.2   At the first meeting with the intending purchasers, the solicitors should take down the purchasers' instructions clearly and in detail, so that they are in a position to make an offer. Obviously the price and date of entry are the most crucial matters, but instructions should also be taken on every point that may arise in the missives.

The solicitors will also want to satisfy themselves that the clients can afford the property that they are bidding for. While the solicitors are only agents, and not financially responsible, if the clients default, the solicitor is nevertheless left in a very embarrassing position. Anyone can make a mistake, but solicitors who get the reputation of acting for a series of defaulting clients can hardly expect their offers to be taken seriously in future. Like so many financial institutions the house market still depends on a measure of mutual trust, which should not be breached lightly.

Solicitors should have a good idea of the financial worthiness of their existing clients and of persons recommended by existing clients. When, however, they do not know the clients, solicitors now have extra responsibilities under the Money Laundering Regulations 1993 (see para **1.13(h)**) to verify the means of clients whom they have not known for two years. They are recommended, in these circumstances, to seek proof of identity by seeing full (not visitors') passports, full driving licences or signed company identity cards, with a photo forming an integral part of the card or a shotgun licence. Addresses can be verified by inclusion on the voters' roll, invoices for utilities payments, and a full driving licence. This may seem petty, but it is necessary. If you or I were to open a bank account, we would have to produce the same evidence of identity.

Many lenders will now issue mortgage certificates which state exactly how much they will lend on the borrowers' income. This involves verifying income details in advance of the purchasers choosing a house, and puts the clients on the starting blocks while the rest are still in their tracksuits. These are not, however, guarantees of loan, and are subject to satisfactory survey and credit rating.

3.3   The solicitors should then notify the selling agents of their clients' interest in the house concerned. To respectable agents, this means that a sale will not be concluded without notifying all those who have notified an interest (see para **2.6(i)**) and giving them a chance to offer, even on a short time limit. You should also note carefully the terms of the Law Society Guidelines on Closing Dates 1991, which, in summary, do not permit a solicitor, who has been instructed by a client to enter into negotiations with a party to complete a bargain, to accept subsequent instructions to enter into negotiations with, or accept an offer from, another party. This unattractive process is given an equally unattractive name—gazumping—where the first offer received is used as a lever to extract higher offers from others. Gazumping is a problem which occurs where there is a seller's market. The equally unattractive process of 'gazundering' occurs where there is a purchaser's market, and the purchaser uses the lack of demand to drive the price down.

At this stage the solicitors should also ask for full details of the property, if they have not already received these.

3.4   The next point to be considered is that of survey, probably the single most controversial topic in the whole process of house purchase. The difficulty is the apparently very high cost of surveys. Having said that, like any other good professional advice, a good survey can save thousands of pounds and much heartache. The difficulty arises when a survey is not properly done, and the purchasers find themselves without recourse against the surveyors who were negligent.

Surveys are broadly of four types:

(a) *The 'walkthrough' valuation.* This means exactly what it says; the surveyor walks through the property, and gives what all understand to be a rough valuation for whatever purpose it is required. This valuation confers no rights on the persons instructing it.

(b) *A mortgage valuation survey*, which is instructed usually by a lending institution, and is rather more thorough than (a), but less thorough than (c). The institution requires to know what value could be realised in the event of the property having to be sold on default by the borrowers before it lends money (see para **3.6**). No liability to the prospective purchaser is accepted by the surveyors, as to the condition or value of the property. (A rough indication of price is £130–£250, depending on value.)

(c) *A full structural or building survey*, which is a very thorough survey, with a full written report, and which gives the persons instructing the survey a right to reparation in the event of there being negligence on the part of the surveyor. This survey obviously is very much more expensive than the others, but should be seriously considered in every case, but especially where an older or unusual house is being bought. (A rough indication of price is £500 plus, again depending on value.)

(d) *Housebuyer's report and valuation*, which is a halfway house between (b) and (c). Building societies will arrange for the surveyor making a valuation (b) for them to prepare a short, written report for the purchaser. This will cost more than (b) and less than (c), and will give much less detail than (c). The surveyor will generally not move fitted carpets or heavy furniture, climb onto sloping roofs, or test drains, electrical, gas, heating and water services. This report, which is written on a standard RICS form, is also heavily hedged with recommendations that a specialist survey be obtained, if the surveyor has any suspicion that there might be something wrong with the house, such as dry rot, wet rot or woodworm. (The approximate cost of this survey is £250–£500.)

Formerly it was the practice of surveyors to issue reports which were full of disclaimers of liability, if anything proved to be wrong in the house surveyed. A classic example of the effects of such a disclaimer may be found in the case of *Robbie v Graham & Sibbald* (1989 SLT 870, 1989 SCLR 578).

The Law Reform (Miscellaneous Provisions) (Scotland) Act 1990 amended the law to apply Part I of the Unfair Contract Terms Act 1977 to Scotland, and thus to bring Scottish law in line with English law on the point of disclaimers, which do not therefore now protect the negligent surveyor. Surveyors, however, now combat the danger of litigation by suggesting that the report of a specialist contractor be taken if there is any sign of a defect in a house, such as dry rot, wet rot or woodworm.

3.5   When purchasers are buying solely from their own resources, and the house is old or unusual, the advice of the solicitors to their clients clearly must be to have a structural survey done. If, despite this advice, the purchasers say they do not want a survey, that is their privilege. The solicitors should, however (as a matter of self-preservation), obtain a letter from the purchasers stating that they were advised by the solicitors to have the property surveyed, but decided against this on their own volition, or at least the solicitors should write to the purchasers advising a survey, and keep a copy of the letter on file. The question of surveys turns up, time after time, to be the least satisfying part of the purchasing process, simply because if the purchasers are unlucky in a series of offers, they incur heavy fees to surveyors with no tangible result. Surveyors can hardly be blamed for this, but it is a constant aggravation to house buyers. The Scottish Executive established a task force to look into the purchasing process, and it in turn commissioned a report from DTZ Pieda Consulting Ltd, who reported on 9 May 2002. This report established that the Scottish system works well, with low costs by international standards. For details of this continuing debate, see an article *The House Buying process in Scotland:Does it need to be fixed?* by Ken Swinton in June 2002 the *Scottish Law Gazette* 69.

3.6   The real trouble arises, however, where a building society is involved. The building society will require (Building Societies Act 1986, s 13) its own valuation survey to be prepared. While the fee is payable to the surveyor by the society, and then refundable by the purchasers, but the purchasers have no rights under this contract, they are not parties to the contract and cannot therefore take advantage of it (Gloag, *Law of Contract* (2nd edn, 1929), ch XIII).

Complaints are, therefore, frequently made by purchasers: (a) that the house they have bought is in some way defective, and why did the surveyor instructed by the society not tell them? (b) what did they pay a surveyor for? (c) further, have they a claim for damages against the surveyor?

The answer to these questions is (a) the surveyor is not in contractual relationship with the purchasers, and need not tell them anything; (b) the surveyor is paid by the society technically; and (c) for the same reason, no! The surveyor may, however, be liable in delict (see para **3.4**). In any event the survey is a valuation survey, which costs less than a structural survey but is also much less rigorous than a structural survey, and it usually means that the surveyor has not checked under the floor, the roof space, or the plumbing and electrical systems, and followed the trail of any rot which shows on the surface of the building.

All the surveyor is doing is telling the building society that the property is sufficient security for the loan requested, although as a matter of practice, if the surveyor sees a defect he will point it out to the society, who will tell the borrowers.

3.7   While this is impeccable law, it is poor common sense, and purchasers having (in their minds) paid for a surveyor, will obviously be aggrieved to find that they have no recourse against that surveyor. Really the only safe course open to the purchasers is to instruct a structural survey for themselves (the halfway house: see para **3.4**) as well as paying for the society's valuation survey. These can be done simultaneously, with an appropriate reduction in fees. It is nevertheless an expensive business, but particularly to be recommended, even with new properties.

3.8   One might ask why, in a perfect world, the sellers should not instruct a survey, which would be available to all interested parties? There are, however, tremendous problems of privity of contract, and liability in negligence, to say nothing of fairly strenuous opposition from building societies and surveyors. This item surfaces from time to time but nothing much seems ever to be done about it. The possibility of the seller offering a 'seller's pack' giving a survey and other details of the house has been raised, particularly in England, but nothing so far has come of it.

3.9   Having looked at the property, obtained full details, satisfied themselves that the clients can afford the property and that the house has had some sort of survey, the purchasers' solicitors are now in a position to lodge their clients' offer.

3.10   The offer should be made by the purchasers' solicitors, on behalf of and to the instructions of their clients, to the sellers or the selling agents. Only in the most unusual circumstances should the principals' name not be disclosed, bearing in mind the liabilities upon agents for undisclosed principals.

If solicitors or estate agents are selling the house, do not send an offer directly to the clients and, conversely, if you have been dealing exclusively with the owners ask them to whom the offer should be sent. Do not in the latter case send an offer to someone who claims to be the selling agent. Not only is it discourteous to do so, but you may land the purchasers as witnesses in the middle of a squabble between the sellers and their agents.

Only in the most unusual circumstances should the principals' names not be disclosed, bearing in mind that solicitors who do not disclose the fact that the offer is on behalf of named clients may be personally liable to fulfil the contract, and definitely liable if the fact is not disclosed at all that the offer is made on behalf of clients.

3.11   The offer is made (generally) in the form of a letter on the solicitors' notepaper, and signed by a partner of the firm, and witnessed, indicating an intention to make the offer 'self-proving' and therefore binding upon their clients (Requirements of Writing (Scotland) Act 1995, s 11(3)(b)). It is not necessary to sign the letter on every page (Conveyancing and Feudal Reform (Scotland) Act 1970, s 44 (CFR(S)A 1970)) but a cautious practitioner will normally at least initial each page.

3.12   If the solicitors do not wish their name to be involved in the contract, for whatever reason, the offer may be drawn up in the offerors' name and be signed by the offerors themselves.

Every firm has its own style of missive, but a reasonably typical exchange of letters is printed in Appendix I and explanations are made in paragraph **3.13** of their different forms. Please do not forget that every house has its own different features, and each offer must be very carefully drawn up on its merits, and not merely copied uncritically from your last offer.

3.13   As mentioned, every firm has its own letter of offer, and there is no style that I can hold before you as 'totally typical'. The letter of offer should be simply a letter containing the full offer, but it is probably more common today for the letter to be quite short and to contain only essential details (address, price, date of entry, and specification of moveables contained in the sale) and for there to be a schedule annexed containing compendious and all-embracing clauses.

In England there is a National Conveyancing Protocol (Third Edition 1994) which very much standardises the documentation of conveyancing, but not so in Scotland. The Law Society introduced a standard offer for property, but this met with derision from the profession, for a variety of reasons, some bad, some good. Suffice it to say that the standardised offer has not caught on in Scotland. On reflection, this may not have been a good thing. In Inverness and Dundee the local faculties introduced a variant of the standard offer for use by their members, and these seem to have worked perfectly well.

While the production by firms of their own conditions of offer (as opposed to the proposed standard Law Society conditions) is attractive for the sake of speed and uniformity, it has these drawbacks:

(a) as every firm has its own, sometimes very lengthy, conditions, each of these long offers must be carefully evaluated against a variety of equally long offers from other firms. This can be a very complex business.

(b) From the point of view of the offeror, the temptation exists to use these schedules uncritically, thereby leaving in conditions that have become out of date or are inappropriate, and omitting new conditions framed to suit changed circumstances. Stories abound of solicitors receiving offers for a farm, and finding in it a clause relating to common parts of a tenement, or of solicitors selling a chip shop receiving an offer which demanded a matrimonial affidavit to be produced. The reply to the latter demand was that this particular shop was not a matrimonial chip shop. This, however, is careless conveyancing, and surely with the aid of modern technology, the profession can do better.

(c) A less scrupulous firm may be tempted to insert a 'poison pill'—that is a provision prejudicial to the seller hidden in a long formal clause that the eye is tempted to skip.

(d) While offers may be superficially the same, the order of the contents is quite different.

(e) Solicitors who use standard forms uncritically and repetitively may remember the arguments that it doesn't require a qualified lawyer to press the start button on a word processor or photocopier (compare para **1.18**).

3.14   Having said that, I have printed in Appendix I a long letter of offer which is really a set of standard conditions that are disguised to look like a letter. I would like to examine this letter in detail, and explain its purpose, because it does include a lot of points that should be remembered. I should point out that I do not claim that this is a perfect offer, just that it is a reasonably standard one. (The best offer is always the one used by the person or firm who employs you.)

The paragraphs that follow are referenced to the offer in Appendix I

The preamble

3.15   The client's name and address should be stated quite clearly so that the principal is fully 'disclosed' in the legal sense. A selling solicitor should think very carefully before accepting an offer that does not disclose the principal, lest the missives have to be enforced. The question then is 'against whom?' and why not the solicitor? The subjects are then clearly described, but a postal address, rather than a full conveyancing description will suffice. A postcode, wherever possible, should be used, to help avoid ambiguity. People tend to be vague about postcodes, but try and get this information. It can always be obtained from the postcode directory at the Post Office.

The price (clause 1)

3.16 The price should be fully and frankly detailed. A split may be made between heritable property and moveable property. You are reminded of the strictures contained in paragraph **3.18** as to the honest apportionment of the price.

The date of entry (clause 2)

3.17 This is the date when the price is paid and possession is given and titles handed over. The date is a matter for negotiation between the parties but it should allow time for both parties comfortably to meet their obligations. A small point to be considered by both parties is the availability of removal firms. For example, the last Friday of any month is a popular date for flitting and it may be very difficult to make suitable arrangements.

It was decided in *Gordon District Council v Wimpey Homes Holdings Ltd* (1988 SLT 481) that a stated date of entry is not essential to the validity and enforceability of missives, but if a date of entry is not specified there is no legal method of fixing one.

Specification of moveables (clause 3)

3.18 The more carefully these are specified the better, especially in cases where there may be genuine doubt as to whether an object is heritable or moveable. While it may appear to be a bit fussy to include bulbs and flexes, please bear in mind that these indispensable objects are fully moveable. They may be removed by the seller if not specified to be included in the sale—and often are! By and large the law of fixtures applies, except as modified by agreement, but nothing should be left to the mercy of this vague law. Consider, for instance, the telephone. Formerly this instrument was hired from British Telecom and was not removable except by one of their engineers, and for that reason it was heritable. Now you can buy a plug-in telephone, which is moveable, and remove it on leaving.

A price for moveables only may be stated in the offer, for only heritage bears stamp duty. Stamp duty currently starts at £60,001 and is at a rate of 1% of the total price. Thus, if you buy a house at £61,000, you will pay stamp duty of £610. But if the seller can fairly certify that the moveable property is valued at £1,000, then the value of the heritage is £60,000 and no stamp duty is payable. It must be stressed, however, that the valuation of moveables must justify the certificate given by the seller, who does not enjoy the benefit anyway. The Stamp Office have now issued a practice note which states that if they find the valuation to be dubious, they may call upon the parties to produce detailed inventory and valuation to justify the valuation. An incorrect statement is tax evasion, which is an offence.

Further, consideration should be given to the case of *Saunders v Edwards* ([1987] 1 WLR 116, CA) where it was stated that if the valuation of moveables is artificially inflated, the court may not enforce other parts of the contract, and that a solicitor indulging in this practice may be guilty of professional misconduct.

The seller should give a warranty that none of the moveable items purchased are the subject of financing agreements. The price should be reduced accordingly if it turns out that they are, or the financing agreements should be cleared by the seller, to the satisfaction of the buyer. Of course, if the seller is a rogue, this clause will be of little comfort but at least the conveyancer's back is covered.

Title conditions (clause 6(b))

3.19   This is a reasonable clause, but these are technically matters for the purchasers to satisfy themselves on, when examining titles. In particular, the term 'unusual' conditions is a vague one, and this term invites an answer from the sellers' solicitors, sending the title deeds and inviting the purchasers' solicitors to satisfy themselves on the point within so many days. The case of *Morris v Ritchie* (1992 GWD 33–1950) commented on in the *Scottish Law Gazette* in March 1993, makes it clear that all unusual conditions, including servitudes, should be disclosed before missives are concluded.

Maintenance of property (clause 7(b))

3.20   The common law rule, enshrined in this clause, is that the person who orders the repairs shall pay for them, unless the contract provides otherwise. The prudent purchasers' solicitors may want confirmation that no such repairs have been ordered and not yet done, or have been done but not yet paid for. This may be verified by a certificate from the appropriate district council.

Planning etc certificates and environmental matters (clause 9)

3.21   The entire question of local authority notices is dealt with at paragraph **17.7** in connection with flats. Such notices are more likely to be a problem in flatted property, but the notices can basically be served on any property. It is considered generally to be a primary responsibility of the sellers to obtain the certificate, in the view of the Law Society, and sellers' solicitors should not be allowed to contract out of this, unless in exceptional circumstances. It is obviously a matter of some importance to ensure, for example, that the district council is not about to acquire the house, or knock it down for any one of a multiplicity of purposes.

The existence of any such notices may be ascertained by writing to the planning department of the local council, who will issue a letter stating either that there are no such notices, or alternatively that there are. The correct addresses of various councils, and the fees currently charged, are detailed on the Law Society's website (www.lawscot.org.uk).

In purchases of development property particularly, it will now be important to obtain a clear environmental audit, for in many cases houses are built on land that has been used for contaminative uses. In its very useful booklet 'Buyer Beware', Friends of the Earth tells of land near Chatham on which it was intended to build 2,000 houses. Although the land was thought to be virgin agricultural land, it turned out to be heavily contaminated with heavy metals and blue asbestos, and had been part of the nearby naval dockyard during the war. The developers were forced to spend £30 million on cleaning up the site before building work commenced. There are many such examples in Scotland as well, and obviously a builder would not want to purchase such land, and such a liability.

Further, owning a building listed as of special architectural or historical interest, or a piece of land listed as a site of special scientific interest (SSSI—the rural equivalent of a listed building) may be very pleasant, but there are many restrictions on development, which a purchaser may not wish to undertake.

Sellers' obligations (clause 12)

3.22   This is an extremely long clause because it contains the sellers' obligations in (a) a register of sasines sale, (b) a first land registration sale and (c) a second or subsequent land registration sale.

The obligation in (a) is to produce a disposition, marketable title and a clear search. In the other two cases (b) and (c), the sellers have to produce a disposition but then the obligations vary widely. They are further discussed at paragraphs **7.4** and **13.2**. The most significant difference between the sasine obligation and the land register obligation is that in the former the sellers more or less disappear at settlement, it being a case of *caveat emptor*, while in land registration the sellers are kept 'on the hook' until a land certificate is issued, which is clear of any restrictions of indemnity.

A charges register report is only competent when a limited company is the seller of property or granting a security over the property.

Rates, council tax and feu duty (clause 4)

3.23   (See ch 11.) The absence of this clause would not prejudice the offer. A reasonable rateable value and feu duty are presumed by law and the redemption provisions for feu duties and other pecuniary burdens are statutory. A slight misstatement of either of these figures (or of the council tax rate band) would be ignored under the rule *de minimis non curat lex*, but a serious misstatement might lead to the purchaser resiling. Thus in *Bremner v Dick* (1911 SC 887) the contract stated that the feu duty was £2.25 but in fact this was an unallocated portion of a feu duty of £4.40. The purchaser was entitled to resile. While under the CFR(S)A 1970, ss 3 to 6, this could not happen today, for the feu duty could be allocated, the general principle probably still remains.

Settlements are dealt with in chapter 11. This clause sets out the division of rates between the parties at that time.

Rates do not now apply to domestic properties (see ch 10) and any reference to rates is only applicable to commercial properties.

The seller should be bound to report the sale to the council tax office, who will amend their records, and apportion the sum payable for the year between the seller and purchaser.

Roads, footpaths, and sewers (clause 7(d))

3.24   Generally the local council will maintain these artefacts, but if they do not, the purchasers will want to be assured that there is no liability for formation or maintenance. This is most crucial in the purchase of a newly-built house and in rural areas.

Most houses in cities, towns and even villages in Scotland have public roads, mains water and mains drainage. This may not be the case in the country. In which case please consider:

(a) has the house got sufficient access for the needs of the purchasers, and what are the rights of other parties over the road? Who pays for maintenance?
(b) is there a sufficient water supply (*tantum et tale*), as to amount and quality and adequate rights to pipe this water into the house (vice versa drainage)?

Extensions and alterations (clause 8)

3.25   If these are material the sellers should obtain planning consent, building warrant and if required, superior's consent. When the work is done a completion certificate from the building sub-committee should additionally be obtained, vouching that the work has been properly done. The purchasers should require to see all of these documents. In *Winston v Patrick* (1981 SLT 41: see para **3.29**) there was a building warrant but the work was not properly done, and a completion certificate obtained. All sorts of trouble was caused by this, because the house had been accepted without this point being verified.

Treatment certificates (clause 10)

3.26   These should be produced by the sellers as stated, and may be simply assigned to the purchasers if desired.

NHBC Buildmark certificates (inappropriate to offer)

3.27   These certificates guarantee the owner against loss through faulty workmanship not being corrected by the builder (see para **7.34**) in various degrees for a period of ten years. The buildmark certificate should be handed over on the first and every subsequent sale in the ten-year period. This request should not be made for an older house (as in this example) which is obviously more than ten years old. In the case of a small builder who is not a member of NHBC, the purchasers should see an architect's certificate of inspection, which certifies that, in the architect's opinion, work is complete (see para **7.34**). This clause does not appear in the offer as the property is over ten years old, and the cover has therefore expired.

Insurance risk (clause 11)

3.28   The rule is *res perit suo domino*: the thing perishes to (the risk of) its owner. In the case of *Sloans Dairies Ltd v Glasgow Corporation* (1979 SLT 17) it was clearly reaffirmed that once missives have been concluded the risk of damage or destruction of the subject passed to the purchasers (even where, as in this case, a date of entry had not yet been agreed). Technically the *emptio* becomes *perfecta* on completion of missives. (See the comments on this case by Professor Robert Black in 1982 JLSS 405.) It may not seem entirely logical that risk should pass without possession, which is the reason for inserting this clause which returns the risk to the sellers. The sellers, of course, sensibly maintain their fire insurance until the date of entry.

Where this clause is not inserted, risk passes to the purchasers, who must insure this interest forthwith by taking out fire cover. Their insurable interest is 'as purchaser, price unpaid', a clearly defined category of insurance.

It is, of course, up to the solicitors to make sure that this is done, because a layman could not be expected to understand this quirk of property law. If the solicitors are worried about forgetting this, they can buy a lot of contentment for a small price by having their own 'longstop' fire insurance policy—which gives block cover against damage over all houses the firm is handling in the event of their being uninsured elsewhere. The Scottish Law Commission has prepared a discussion paper on this topic entitled Passing of Risk in Contracts for the Sale of Land (1989 Scot Law Com Discussion Paper no 81), but no action has been taken on this point.

Survival of provisions in missives (not now appropriate)

3.29 This clause was formerly incorporated because of the decision in *Winston v Patrick* (1981 SLT 41). In *Winston*, the pursuers were the purchasers of a detached bungalow which had an extension at the rear, which extension had been constructed by the removal of part of the original wall. The defenders had obtained a building warrant for this extension and had undertaken to construct it in accordance with the approved plans.

Clause 9 of the missives provided:

'The seller warrants that all statutory and local authority requirements in connection with the erection of the subjects and any additions, extensions and alterations thereto have been fulfilled.'

The pursuers accordingly contended that the defenders were in breach of contract and thus liable in damage. The defenders argued successfully that the disposition had been delivered to the pursuers and accepted by them, and that the missives were accordingly superseded.

The basic rule of Scots law in the sale of heritage is that:

(a) formal missives supersede all prior communings (e g property circulars etc), unless there is a misrepresentation when reference may be made to these prior communings; and

(b) that the disposition on delivery supersedes missives unless:
  (i) the point at issue is not one that would normally arise in a contract for the sale of heritage, e g furniture included in the sale (see *Jamieson v Welsh* (1900) 3 F 176);
  (ii) where there is essential error in the description of the heritage in the disposition, but the description is correct in the missives, then the missives may be referred to (*Anderson v Lambie* 1954 SC (HL) 43);

(iii) where the disposition is ambiguous but the missives are not, the missives may be referred to (*Duke of Fife v Great North of Scotland Railway Co* (1901) 3 F (HL) 2);

(iv) where the disposition is delivered, but there turns out to be a conflicting interest under previous missives, the disposition will be reduced (*Rodger (Builders) Ltd v Fawdry* 1950 SC 483);

(v) where the parties agree to leave the missives or any part of them applicable.

Winston v Patrick did not displace this provision of law, rather it confirmed it. Where it did create difficulties was for the practical conveyancer who wished to keep a personal or collateral obligation in force despite the delivery of the disposition, owing to the confusing and contradictory litigation and comment that has followed *Winston* (for a full account of this see 6 *Stair Memorial Encyclopaedia* para 566 and its updating service).

Accordingly it was necessary: (i) to put a clause into missives, keeping the missives alive for a two-year period; (ii) to insert a non-supersession clause in the disposition which has the same effect; and (iii) to deliver a letter after delivery of the deed at settlement, stating more or less the same thing. This procedure was cumbersome and repetitive, but above all it was safe. To the great relief of conveyancers, section 2 (1) of the Contract (Scotland) Act 1997 provided that a deed should not be automatically superseded, and it is not now necessary to take these precautions outlined above. Section 2(2) however allows the parties to agree a supersession, and this clause is occasionally seen.

Matrimonial affidavits (clause 14)

3.30   This clause reflects the provisions of the Matrimonial Homes (Family Protection) (Scotland) Act 1981, as amended by the Law Reform (Miscellaneous Provisions) (Scotland) Act 1985. The 1981 Act was one of impeccable social purpose, but which neglected to allow for the problems it might create in numerous cases where there was no particular social purpose to fulfil. It is a matter of great pleasure to record that the 1985 Act considerably simplified the operation of the 1981 Act, without diminishing the social usefulness of that Act.

A matrimonial home is a house, caravan, houseboat etc, provided by one spouse for the use of his or her spouse and their family (MH(FP)(S)A 1981, s 22). The scope of the legislation also includes persons who co-habit without being married to the extent mentioned in the 1981 Act.

If the title stands in the name of one spouse only ('the entitled spouse') and a sale is to be made of the matrimonial home, or if the matrimonial home is to be burdened with a security in favour of a third party, it is required that the other spouse ('the non-entitled spouse') should either be a consenter to the sale document, or should sign a renunciation of his or her right to remain in occupation of the property, or (if not in occupation) his or her right to re-enter the home and reoccupy it.

Styles of the forms of consent and renunciation are given in Appendix II with detailed notes as to their preparation. The form of renunciation requires to be signed before a notary public or any other person outwith Scotland who is authorised by law to administer oaths or receive affirmations in the country of signature. In England, this would be a commissioner of oaths (see para **1.22**). As this all requires a great deal of additional work, it is usually simpler to include the consent in the deed, and to have the non-entitled spouse sign the deed as a consenter (App II).

If the title to a matrimonial home is in joint names of the two spouses, as is increasingly the case these days, both will sign the deed transferring or burdening the property, and nothing further is required under the legislation.

Where the property being sold is not a matrimonial home (e g an investment property, or a holiday house), or the proprietor is not married, the proprietor is required to sign an affidavit to the effect that the property is not a matrimonial home (App II).

The necessary consent, renunciation or affidavit formerly had to be delivered at or before delivery of the disposition or standard security in favour of the third party, but now may be retrospective (LR(MP)(S)A 1985, s 13(5)(b)(iii)). In registration of title cases the Keeper must be satisfied by a statement from the solicitor presenting the deed for registration that this is the case. (Forms 1, 2, and 3, and question 8 in Form 1, reproduced in App I).

Where the seller has signed a power of attorney authorising another person to conclude the documentation on his or her behalf, please note that an attorney cannot sign a matrimonial document, and that alternative measures should be taken in this respect.

Failure to observe these rules can have disastrous consequences. The worst things that could happen are as follows:

(1) You act for clients purchasing a house from a person who produces a title in his or her own name. You forget to ask for a consent, renunciation or affidavit from the non-entitled spouse. Your clients settle into their new home. The non-entitled spouse of the previous owner then asserts his or her right to reoccupy the house.
(2) Alternatively, although the occupancy right is not claimed, your clients try to sell the house within the five-year period, in which the non-entitled spouse could have asserted the right. Your clients will have considerable difficulties in selling, because the title is simply not marketable, owing to the risk of reoccupancy. In land registration cases, the Keeper will restrict indemnity in respect of the missing document.

The second possibility is stronger than the first, but neither is fanciful. The only way out of the dilemma is for an insurance indemnity to be obtained against the possibility of the non-entitled spouse re-appearing (see para **7.42(f)**). Clearly you, not having done your job properly, should pay the single premium involved. It is actually not very expensive, when compared to the possible embarrassment that might result otherwise.

Family Law (Scotland) Act 1985 (clause 15)

3.31   The Family Law (Scotland) Act 1985, s 8(1)(aa) enables either party in an action of divorce to apply to the court for an order transferring property to him or her by the other party to the marriage. Such a decree will of course be registered in the General Register or Land Register, but purchasing solicitors should be careful in case such an order has been granted, but not yet registered. The sellers' warranty that there are no such orders is an additional protection. This provision has given many difficulties, principally with valuation of the property, but difficulties can also arise where the divorcing couple owns the property on a survivorship destination (see John H Sinclair 'Conveyancing Aspects of Property Transfer Orders' 1993 Fam LB 1–3).

Time limit (clause 19)

3.32   A time limit may be put in the offer to put pressure on the sellers. If this device is used, it should be a realistic time limit and should allow time for the letter to arrive and for the sellers' agents to take instructions according to circumstances (i e a solicitor in Glasgow should not put a 24-hour time limit on an offer to a solicitor in, say, Inverness, unless special arrangements are made). If the sellers' solicitors do not wish to be put under pressure, or if they have another buyer 'up their sleeve', they should inform the purchasers' solicitors accordingly, and delete this clause if they do accept the offer ('condition 17 of your offer is deleted'). Please also note that the time limit contained in the offer in question states that the offer must be received 'here' by such and such a time, which cuts out ambiguity. The entire negotiation process can be telescoped by intelligent use of Fax (see para **4.7**).

A modern difficulty which frequently recurs is that the missives are not concluded within a reasonable time. In fact they are in some cases concluded shortly before settlement, which is a very dangerous practice. A time limit may be inserted to the effect that missives must be concluded by a certain date, which seems a good idea.

Minerals clause (clause 6(a))

3.33   'The minerals are included in the sale only in so far as belonging to the seller.' This clause is really a nonsense, but it has to go in, unless you are sure that you are in a position to sell the minerals, which is very seldom the case— certainly in urban areas.

The reason for this is a logical one—although the practical result is ridiculous. When you buy land, you buy the slice of earth's crust from the centre of the earth to the heaven (*a coelo usque ad centrum*). If someone else owns the minerals, you cannot give this layer, and the missives must therefore be qualified to that effect. The case of *Campbell v McCutcheon* (1963 SLT 290) quite clearly sets out this doctrine, and in this case missives not containing the clause were declared to be non-binding because the sellers could not give what they have contracted to sell. What is more, the sellers were not allowed time to acquire these mineral rights. The Halliday Committee (Cmnd 3118, 1966) suggested that the requirement for this clause be made unnecessary, but nothing was done about this apparently quite uncontroversial recommendation, presumably an oversight, which could easily be remedied. If the minerals do not belong to the sellers, the purchasers' solicitors may want to provide that the minerals cannot be exploited by a third party without adequate compensation being paid to the house owner.

Actio quanti minoris (not now appropriate)

3.34   This phrase can be very literally translated as 'the action of how much less'. (Literal translations of Roman maxims usually produce such clumsy results, which is why we tend to retain the original Latin.) It is an action of Roman law that was imported into Scots law for moveable property, but not for heritable property. (For a fuller discussion of the law on this topic, see 6 *Stair Memorial Encyclopaedia* para 566.)

This action allows the purchasers of property that is subject to a fault, which was not apparent at the time of purchase, to recover part of the purchase price, while retaining the property. Strangely enough this equitable solution was not available in Scots law for heritable property, unless it is specifically included in the contract (see *Fortune v Fraser* 1993 SLT (Sh Ct) 68, where the sheriff principal held that the contract contained no provision for the *actio*, and as it did not exist in Scots law, the pursuer had no remedy). If it is not included, the purchasers who discover a fault in the property have no remedy other than *restitutio in integrum* (total restitution of the property to the sellers and the price to the purchasers) which is usually impossible by the time the fault is discovered. It seems rather odd that Scots law, which so enthusiastically welcomed other Roman law equitable remedies, did not accept this one, and left people to include it by a term of contract.

In the case of *Campbell v McCutcheon* (1963 SLT 290) (see para **3.33**) if the *actio* had been available, a reduction in the purchase price might simply have been ordered, and the sale might have proceeded as agreed.

Section 3 of the very useful Contract (Scotland) Act 1997 effectively made this clause unneccessary.

3.35   These are the most standard of conditions contained in missives, but there may of course be many others. The only 'right' offer is the one your firm uses.

Acceptance of this offer constitutes a binding contract which the courts will enforce (see *Rodger (Builders) Ltd v Fawdry* 1950 SC 483; *Johnstone v Harris* 1978 SLT (Notes) 81 and many others). The sellers should not therefore accept any of the conditions of the purchasers' offer unless they are sure they can fulfil these.

It is, however, permissible in certain circumstances to insert a suspensive condition; eg you buy a house intending to turn it into a hotel; you offer £100,000 instead of the market value of £60,000 but only if you get planning permission for use of the house as a hotel. You therefore 'suspend' the deal until this permission is obtained; if it is not granted, the deal falls. A prudent seller will put a time limit on the suspension. In such circumstances see *Imry Property Holdings Ltd v Glasgow Young Men's Christian Association* (1979 SLT 261). On this topic see also the article by R B Wood 1980 JLSS 129.

If purchasers insert a suspensive clause which permits them to withdraw if planning permission is not 'to their satisfaction', the courts will construe this clause as excluding capriciousness and arbitrary actings, and will imply a condition of reasonableness (*Gordon District Council v Wimpey Homes Holdings Ltd* 1989 SLT 141). If the date of entry is left unascertainable, the courts will have little power to fix a date of entry which is indeterminate. Thus, while the C(S)A 1924, s 28, allows a date of entry to be fixed in conveyances, this does not include missives (see *Gordon District Council v Wimpey Homes Holdings Ltd*). Given that the date of entry is generally fixed in missives, this seems an omission of law, which might be easily corrected.

Such clauses are drawn up so as to permit the buyers, in their own discretion, to withdraw the suspensive clause, even though its terms have not yet been met. On this topic see the cases of *Ellis & Sons v Pringle* (1975

SLT 10), *Imry Property Holdings Ltd* and *Manheath v H & J Banks & Co Ltd* (1996 SC 42).

Suspensive conditions are not normally found in domestic missives, but a buyer might insert a suspensive condition to make the offer conditional on a satisfactory survey report, or environmental report, or even a feng shui report, as has been the case in England. In one instance a purchase in England was made subject to a satisfactory feng shui report. The report concluded that a front wall of the property was 'unpropitious' and the purchaser duly withdrew. Of course it should be noted that is much easier to do in England, where the purchasers are not bound until contracts are exchanged and may change their minds for any reason, or even no reason.

Chapter 4

THE SELLERS ACCEPT

'When acting for an elderly lady, I was instructed to accept a far lower offer for her house than had been made by someone else. In enquiring the reason for this, the lady explained that the higher offeror owned an Alsatian, and the cat next door would not like that.'

(Clydebank conveyancer, as told to the author)

4.1   The sellers' agents receive all offers and submit them to the sellers for instruction together with such advice as they may feel necessary.

Thus a slightly lower offer may actually be preferable to a higher offer, if there is a significant difference in the dates of entry and the lower offeror is prepared to name a date of entry suitable to the sellers, while the higher offeror is not. If the sellers want to sell in a month's time, a slightly lower offer with this date of entry may well be preferable to a higher offer with a date of entry in two months. You should consider the interest the sellers may lose by accepting the second offer.

That apart, the highest offer should in normal circumstances be preferred although in law the sellers are not bound to accept the highest offer, or indeed any offer. However, there have doubtless been many occasions on which a lower offer has been accepted for extraneous reasons, e g 'they were such a nice young couple' is a very common syndrome. Sellers can also take a violent dislike to viewers who criticise the house too volubly.

This pleasure of accepting a poorer offer from someone you like is not, however, open to persons acting in a fiduciary capacity, such as trustees, heritable creditors, etc. Please note also the possibly contrary effects of the Race Relations Act 1976, ss 21, 22, 43 and 57.

4.2   What is important is that there must be fair dealing by the sellers' agents, and that everyone should get a fair chance. Our selling system of closed bidding is a fertile breeding ground if not for malpractices, then for suspicion and accusation of malpractice, which are in many cases misplaced, but not all.

The rule is that the terms of no one's offer should ever, under any circumstances, be made known to another offeror. This is an ethical rule, not enforceable at law, but solicitors break it at the peril of their good reputation. You may, by bending the rule, have some cheap triumph at the start, but sooner or later your reputation will overtake you. If you are tempted, as with all ethical considerations, think 'Would I like someone to do that to me?'.

4.3   The following practices are extremely dubious.

(a) Dutch auction.   Anybody who has been at a flower auction in Holland will tell you that a 'Dutch auction' is simply a sale in which the auctioneer offers the goods at gradually decreasing prices, the first bidder to accept being the purchaser. This is just as legitimate as a system of starting with a low bid and moving progressively higher.

The words 'Dutch auction' have, however, acquired a slightly sinister meaning (compare the British habit of blaming the Dutch and the French for everything as in Dutch courage, Dutch treat, Dutch talent, Dutch uncle etc) of an underhand sale, where the sellers take advantage of our system of closed bidding by revealing genuine offers to other bidders in an attempt to force up the price. You should not get involved in this, especially as a seller, but also as a lawyer. If the purchasers are suspicious that a Dutch auction may develop, they should put an offer in with a very short time limit. Quite apart from moral considerations, if someone says to you 'We have an offer of £X, can you beat it?' you have not the slightest idea whether they are telling the truth or not, and if you accept their word then you may be the laughing stock.

(b) Referential bid.   Similarly any such arrangement as an offer of '£5 more than the highest offer received by you' should be avoided, because it makes reference to another offer and it is unfair to put the highest offeror to expense and trouble of survey and putting in an offer without giving this offer a fair chance. Further, if two or more such offers are received the whole thing is a nonsense. (On this topic generally see 1967 JLSS 2, and see the case of *Harvela Investments Ltd v Canada Royal Trust Co Ltd* [1985] 2 All ER 966, [1985] 1 All ER 261, where a referential bid was briefly approved by the court, but the decision was reversed by the House of Lords.)

(c) Progressive bid.   Here a bidder frames a number of offers that are identical except that the price in each is progressively higher than the last. They are then put in numbered envelopes, and the sellers are told to open them in sequence, until a satisfactory price is reached. The snag from the bidders' point of view is that the sellers must be tempted to open only the envelope last in the sequence!

4.4   Other perfectly legitimate ways around the problem have been tried, and may commend themselves:

(a) Raffle.   There seems to be nothing to prevent you from copying Mr Barney Curley of Dublin, who raffled his country house and made a profit of £1 million in the process, except that a public raffle on this scale in Scotland is probably illegal in terms of the Betting, Gaming and Lotteries Act 1963, s 45, in that 9,000 tickets were sold at £175 each, which exceeds the permitted ticket price and the value of the offerable prize. What you can do, however, is have a 'test of skill', requiring entrants to answer questions and complete a tie-breaker. This form of enterprise was last heard of in use in the sale of the Royal Hotel in Anstruther.

(b) 'Fixed price offer'.   This is basically an acceptable idea, in that the first offer of the price fixed by the seller is accepted. It is abused, however, when the price fixed is too high. Sellers who adopt this method really should inform their solicitors, otherwise embarrassing situations may arise. Two examples:

(i)   Prospective purchasers saw a house being sold on a fixed price basis, and informed their solicitors, who intimated the clients' interest and instructed a building society valuation. When the valuation was received, the solicitors were instructed to lodge an offer which was posted by first class mail. The following day, having received no reply, the solicitors telephoned the sellers' solicitors and were told that the house had been sold to an offer received earlier on the previous day. The solicitors concerned were, to say the least, extremely unhappy (see 1985 JLSS 346).

(ii) A house was advertised personally by the sellers at a fixed price of £X. Offerors had a valuation made and instructed their solicitors to offer for the property at the fixed price. The solicitors hand-delivered the offer because there was word of another party being interested. The sellers' solicitors informed the offerors' solicitors that although their offer was the first received, it would not be accepted and that a closing date had been fixed. The selling solicitors had not apparently been informed of the method of sale. In due course the offerors' solicitors received a letter stating that a higher offer had been accepted. Furious exchanges followed, but the offeror had no grounds for action. (**Reason**: see *Pharmaceutical Society of Great Britain Boots Cash Chemists (Southern) Ltd* [1983] 1 QB 401, CA, the advertisement is only an offer to treat, and the bargain must be concluded by written offer and acceptance, as is the rule with heritable property generally.)

(c) Auction. There is no reason why the property should not be sold by auction, or to use the old Scots word, 'roup'. This was the method by which many sales were formerly made, and sales under bonds had to be made in this manner. The modern law of securities now, however, allows sales under securities to be made by private bargain, provided that the best price is obtained. There is a fairly brisk market in auctions of unusual properties, such as railway and telecom property, and a legal firm in Edinburgh specialises in such auctions. Auction sales of heritable property generally are making a modest revival. There is a body of opinion that says that sale by auction, being open and fair, and producing a fair market price, should be used universally.

When there is a sellers' market, as there was—with occasional slips—from 1950 to 1990, the sellers of property can choose the method of sale, and will usually prefer a sale by closed offer. The reason for this is that this method will probably produce not so much a fair market price, as a much higher 'shutout' bid, that will easily top all the other offers. For that reason a return to full-scale sale by roup is not foreseeable.

The process of a sale by roup is (i) the sellers prepare articles of roup, which is effectively an open offer to sell; (ii) the auction takes place, and when the hammer falls, the highest bidder is preferred; (iii) the successful bidder and the auctioneer then sign a minute of enactment and preference, which has the effect of an acceptance of the offer, yielding a binding contract, similar in effect to missives.

Sales may also be made by auction on the internet. Details of the property are given on the sellers' website, and bids are requested. The size of bids are publicised on the website, and interested parties are given a certain time to raise the bid. If this is not done, the highest bid received is the succesful one. The difficulty here is that a signature to the documents must be given, which is not, at present, possible electronically. The necessary framework for electronic signatures is, however, contained in the Electronic Communications Act 2000 and the Electronic Signatures Regulations 2002. The Law Society has appointed consultants to advise it, and will, no doubt, issue regulations for the guidance of solicitors in this direction.

4.5   When one offer has been identified as being better than the rest, the offeror should be told, and the disappointed bidders should also be told. They will want to know how much they missed out by, and a vague indication may be given. Do not, under any circumstances, tell people that they missed by only a few pounds, for the immediate reaction will be to increase the bid, and under the Law Society Guidelines on Closing Dates 1993, you are not allowed to negotiate with anyone other than the chosen offeror.

There may be allegations of shady dealings made, and allegations of Dutch auctions. You only have your own clear conscience to defend you against these allegations. The practice followed in Aberdeen is worth noting: all parties who have bid are invited to the opening of the offers, and can thus see that there is no shady dealing. The prices are not, however, revealed.

4.6   When a successful purchaser has been selected by any method other than roup, the sellers' agents then send a formal acceptance, which again is in the form of a letter (see App II.15). Technically it should be sufficient to simply say 'On behalf of A, I hereby accept your offer of yesterday's date for the property at . . .'. Unfortunately, life is not so simple, and more complex offers produce more complex acceptances. An example of such, and more detailed remarks as to acceptance of offers are contained in Appendix I.

What must always be uppermost in your mind is that there must be a complete agreement as to details (*consensus in idem*) before a binding contract exists.

4.7   If a complex offer is followed by a complex acceptance, there is still no *consensus in idem*, and the purchasers' agents will have to write again formally, accepting the qualifications made by the seller before a binding contract can exist. Theoretically this process can go on indefinitely. It should not be allowed to do so. A 'three letter contract' is ample. The more letters that are exchanged, the more complex the contract becomes, and the longer the missives remain unconcluded, thereby yielding uncertainty and the possibility of the whole deal collapsing.

It is suggested that, rather than exchanging letters like tennis lobs, you have a meeting with the other solicitors, thrash out the differences, and then the purchasers should produce a new offer, reflecting the agreement, to be accepted *de plano* (i e unconditionally) by the sellers. The dire consequences of having too many letters can be seen in the case of *Rutterford Ltd v Allied Breweries Ltd* 1990 SLT 249 (OH).

If the other solicitors are far away, the same result can be achieved by the sensible use of fax, which can greatly speed up a transaction. Thus you can have points clarified by return, and have an offer in another solicitors' hands immediately, thus enabling them to take instructions right away. It should however be remembered that faxes are not self-proving or formally valid, as they are not signed, and it is, therefore, recommended that the original of the fax be sent to the addressee forthwith. Again you are reminded that an electronic signature cannot be added, and a faxed contract is not binding on the parties (see para **4.4**).

It should also be remembered that we have a very good document exchange post service (DX) guaranteeing next day delivery, unless the weather is very bad, and also an excellent postal service. Non-urgent mail should be sent by these methods, and not fax. Writing in the *Journal of the Law Society of Scotland* (1994 JLSS 197) Mr Graeme Pagan from Oban says: 'In an uncomplicated non-urgent conveyancing transaction, I received by fax, twenty minutes before the office closed, a seventeen page draft feu charter, the principal of which reached me at 7.45 am the following morning.' This is a wasteful practice which should be avoided. The recipients of such junk mail can feel aggrieved, because it is their paper that is used for printing the document, and their machine is tied up for a few minutes, when somebody might be trying to send an important document—known in the jargon as 'opportunity costs'.

4.8 A typical acceptance of offer is printed at Appendix I. The contents of the acceptance are, of course, dictated by the contents of the offer. Typically, however, the acceptance should contain the following matters:

(a) Interest clause. This clause rectifies by agreement (*ex pacto*) the complex situation outlined in paragraph **10.9**. It makes the date of entry and the price material conditions, and provides that interest shall be payable at overdraft rate (base rate plus 4 or 5%) if the price is not paid on the date of entry. It reserves the right to the sellers to resile if settlement is not made by a certain date; and to claim damages from the defaulting purchasers, which are assessed in terms stated in 6 *Stair Memorial Encyclopaedia* para 575.

This clause will normally be accepted substantially by the purchasers, but care should be taken, from the purchasers' point of view, that these fairly drastic remedies apply only if the purchasers are at fault. They will not apply if the delay is the sellers' fault, when the rule is that contained in *Bowie v Semple's Executors* (1978 SLT (Sh Ct) 9): the purchasers need not take entry, and if they do the agreement has to be re-made to this extent, usually to favour the purchasers.

It should also be noted that following the case of *Lloyd's Bank v Bamberger* (1994 SLT 424) it has been necessary to recast this clause completely to allow the sellers to claim interest on the price when the price is not paid through the sellers breaking the contract. The use of the word 'resile' in the context of such a clause is inappropriate, and the word 'rescind' should be used in preference. The remedies should also be specified. Two tentative clauses are given, one by Professor Robert Rennie and one by Professor Douglas Cusine, in (1993 JLSS 450 (Nov).

The clause printed in Appendix I contains such a clause. In summary it provides:

(i)   That the price and the date of entry be material or essential features of the contract, and that if the purchasers do not meet the agreed price and date, they are automatically in breach of contract (see *Wade v Walton* 1909 SC 571).

(ii) That in the event that settlement is late, the purchasers shall pay to the sellers a sum of interest at four or five % over bank minimum lending rate, to compensate for the interest the sellers will have to pay to the bank to borrow money, which they should have had from the sellers, if they only had kept to their bargain.

(iii) The interest runs from the original date of entry that was originally fixed until the date when the seller actually receives the money, either from the purchaser or from a new purchaser. This was the whole point of *Lloyd's Bank v Bamberger*.

(iv) If payment of the price is not made by the original purchaser within 14 days of the original date of entry, the sellers may end the contract, and proceed to resell the property, without any further consent from the original purchaser or from the court.

(v) When the second sale is concluded the sellers may seek damages for economic loss from the defaulting purchasers. 'Economic loss' includes interest on the price, any diminution of the price, expenses of resale, and any other losses arising directly from the default by the original purchaser. The sellers are under a duty to minimise the loss. No claim for solatium is competent, although the loss of a sale can be a very shattering blow to peoples' health.

(vi) If the delay in settlement is caused by the purchasers, or their agents, the above provisions shall not apply.

While this may seem a very draconian clause, it really only compensates the sellers for their losses due to the purchasers' carelessness in not meeting their agreed date of entry. For that reason, the purchasers' agent should never allow the purchasers to fix an entry date that may not be attainable.

(b) Detailed alterations to furnishings etc included.   If the purchasers have included an item or items of furniture in the offer, which the sellers would rather keep, now is the time to delete it, and to put the matter beyond doubt.

(c) Deletion of time limit offer.   It is as well to delete any time limit, to stop any future argument as to whether the time limit was in fact met. At the same time, the sellers may want to place a time limit for acceptance of the qualifications imposed by this letter, and for conclusion of the contract.

(d) Deletion of provision of certain certificates.   The purchasers may provide for roads and superior's certificates, which the sellers are disinclined to provide, because they feel that they are not really required. The provision can therefore be altered, to exclude the provision of these. If the purchasers really want these, they can apply themselves. The Law Society has ruled, however, that the provision of a planning certificate is a duty which the sellers should not attempt to avoid, as it is so fundamental to the nature of the transaction.

(e) Clearing away redundant clauses.   If for example the offer stipulates that the sellers should provide a charges register search, and the sellers are not a limited company, you can delete the clause. On the other hand you might equally take the attitude that it is clearly inapplicable, and just leave it. It is a matter of personal choice.

(f) Deletion of anything else that is clearly wrong.   This helps to achieve the great goal of *consensus in idem*.

Chapter 5

THE PURCHASERS CONCLUDE

'A verbal contract isn't worth the paper it's written on.'

(Samuel Goldwyn)

5.1 The bargaining process has already been discussed in chapter 4. As contract lawyers say 'these remarks are held to be herein repeated *brevitatis causa*' (for the sake of brevity).

5.2 Similarly, the topic of risk was covered at paragraph **3.27**. It is important, however, to underline that the risk passes to the purchasers on completion of the missives unless that risk is shifted back to the sellers in missives (see App II.11, cond 11). It is unusual for the sellers not to accept the insurance risk until entry. If the risk is not so shifted back, it should be insured again immediately on completing missives by instructing cover in the name of the purchasers 'as purchaser, price unpaid'.

At this stage, as always, the insurance cover should be for full reinstatement value, and not for market value. In a modern house there may not be much difference between the two values but in an older house, built of traditional materials, the cost of repairing the house to the same standard may well be considerably in excess of what the house cost to buy.

5.3 The solicitors then tell the purchasers of their good fortune and advise them to get their finances and the removal van ready.

5.4 The purchasers might also be reminded that they have entered into a formal binding contract, and the consequences of failing to meet the commitment are severe. They should have been kept informed at all stages of formation of the contract.

5.5 A regrettable feature of modern conveyancing is the long delay in conclusion of missives, sometimes until the date of settlement! This is very bad practice and it equates to the English system of the contract only being complete when contracts are exchanged. This allows the English features of gazumping, gazundering and contract chains to enter Scottish conveyancing. In Scotland, we have long prided ourselves on the superiority of our binding missives, and we should not let it be eroded. The principal culprits are the lending institutions, which are taking longer and longer to issue loan papers (see 'Lenders offer late service by Graeme Pagan of Oban in July 2002 JLSS 15. I suspect also that some solicitors, faced by increasingly complex contracts, are quite happy not to conclude them. The Law Society has issued a Practice Note urging conveyancers to conclude contracts at an early stage, and I can only agree with them. See Appendix I.

Chapter 6

INTRODUCTION TO LAND REGISTRATION

'Objectives: to extend, as required by statute, the operation of the Land Register throughout Scotland in order to bring the benefits of cheaper conveyancing to the Scottish public and to phase out the General Register of Sasines.'

(Keeper's Report, 1993–94)

The land registration scheme

6.1 The applicable law, and the prescribed forms, are contained in the Land Registration (Scotland) Act 1979 (LR(S)A 1979) and also in the Land Registration (Scotland) Rules 1980, SI 1980/1413, as amended by the Land Registration (Scotland) (Amendment) Rules, SI 1982/974, SI 1988/1143, SI 1995/248 and SI 1998/3100. Practitioners should also have available the *Registration of Title Practice Book* (2nd edn, 2000) and refer to the Registers of Scotland website: www.ros.gov.uk).

6.2 Registration in the Register of Sasines is a perfectly sound system, but it has some major defects:

(a) It is time-consuming.
(b) It is repetitive, and potentially involves several people doing exactly the same work in a short space of time. Thus for example, solicitors A may note title for their client X. When everything is complete X sells to Y, whose solicitors B then have to repeat the same process, and so on *ad infinitum*.
(c) Once the sellers' solicitors hand over the title deeds at settlement in a sasine transaction, the sellers' responsibility for the title ceases, unless a successful claim for warrandice is established. This is not the case with Land Register transactions where the sellers' responsibility for the title does not cease until the letter of obligation, which contains the obligation to obtain a land certificate without any exclusion of indemnity, is discharged (see para **6.9** and App I).
(d) If there are two solicitors involved in the same transaction, both have to do the same work, and the unfortunate clients have to pay for the repetition. Thus if A buys a public house, A's solicitors have to note the title; if simultaneously a loan is obtained from brewery B, their solicitors will also have to note title. In terms of the standard loan documents (CFR(S)A 1970, Sch 3, standard condition 12), A has the doubtful pleasure of paying both of them.
(e) Much of the work and the process involved in a sasine transaction is out of date and labour intensive and better suited to more spacious days,

when such work could be done cheaply. Because there is a lot of work involved, sasine registration is obviously expensive.

(f) The Sasine Register is a perfectly good register, but it was created in the seventeenth century. It has been substantially modernised by the introduction of microfilming of record volumes, and optical reading of presentment forms, leading to a computerised presentment book, thence to a computerised Sasine Register. The staff of Register House are highly efficient and can find any deed you want within minutes even though there are tens of thousands of deeds. It is, however, as a system, susceptible only to limited further modernisation.

(g) Further the Sasine Register is a register of deeds and not of land. The only information it can disclose is that disclosed by the deeds registered. If you do not know exactly what you are looking for, you may have great difficulty in finding what you want.

(h) Many plans presented to the Sasine Register are badly prepared and inaccurate. Further they follow no consistent pattern of scales, or even north points, and matching plans of adjoining lands is difficult.

In his fascinating book *Who Owns Scotland* (2nd edn, 1981) John McEwan tells of the difficulties he had drawing up a coherent picture of the ownership of vast acres of land in Scotland, which may only be described in the Sasine Register by a general description. An example of this is 'the Lands of Assynt in the County of Sutherland'. Nowhere is there, at present, an accurate delineation of the Lands of Assynt, which I believe extend to some 50,000 acres, and considerable knowledge of the area provides the only answer.

The principal difficulty was that under the sasine system huge areas of land, thousands of acres in the country areas, can be transferred by deeds containing only a vague general description, and with no map attached to illustrate the land transferred. Thus no coherent record of land ownership in Scotland exists.

6.3   The idea of registration of title, which seeks to correct these defects, is by no means new. A system of this kind was established in Prussia in 1700, and it was introduced in the whole of united Germany in 1872.

In the English-speaking world, a system of registration known as the 'Torrens System' was introduced into South Australia in 1858 and this system spread widely in the Dominions. It was principally a system for virgin land and was not thought to be a suitable system for introduction to Britain, where some land holdings go back to Domesday.

In Scotland, as far back as 1903, Professor Wood wrote in his lectures on conveyancing: 'I am unable to see any real difficulty in the way of introducing registration of title into Scotland'.

In 1959 the Secretary of State for Scotland set up a committee under Lord Reid to investigate the introduction of registration of title into Scotland. This committee reported favourably (Cmnd 2032) and recommended that another committee be set up to devise a scheme. This committee under Professor Henry reported in 1969 (Cmnd 4137) with a workable scheme, which after a trial in Register House, was introduced by LR(S)A 1979.

6.4   The scheme is based on the Ordnance Survey of Scotland using the scale 1:1250 for urban areas where modern house plots are small, 1:2,500 in villages and small towns where plots are rather larger, and 1:10,000 for farms and moorland areas. Ordnance Survey maps are extremely accurate, and are consistently updated. It should be noted, however, that they reflect boundaries as they actually exist on the ground, and not as they exist in title plans registered in the Sasine Register. This difficulty is met by asking the Keeper, in a Form P16 (see para **13.3**) to compare the title plan with the Ordnance Survey map.

It should be noted that the Land Register is based, like the General Register of Sasines, on the old Scottish county system, which was phased out for local government purposes in 1974. Thus regions and district, introduced by the Local Government (Scotland) Act 1973 have no significance in land registration, nor the unitary authorities, introduced by the Local Government etc (Scotland) Act 1994 that took over from them in 1996. The old county system was left untouched so far as the Land and Sasine Registers were concerned, as any change would have been too complicated and expensive. Comparative maps of these local government areas are given at Appendix V.

The original intention was to make all Scotland operational in nine years, starting year one on 6 April 1981 with the County of Renfrew; then in year two—The City of Glasgow; year three—Lanark; year four—Midlothian; year five—Rest of Central Belt; year six—Angus, Kincardine, Aberdeen; year seven—Ayr, Dumfries and Galloway; year eight—Southern Rural Areas; year nine—Northern Rural Areas.

6.5 This scheme (para **6.4**), however, proved wildly over-optimistic, and by 1990 only four counties were operational: Renfrew, Dumbarton, Lanark and Glasgow. It appeared at that time that the scheme was irretrievably stalled, for the Register was under-staffed, and could not keep pace with the applications pouring in, let alone the arrears that were building up. Long delays were commonplace, and the Keeper acknowledged this problem in his 1988 report, and explained that the backlogs on his shelves would generate a fee income of £9 million, if only he could process them.

The property boom of the late eighties coupled with the success of the 'right to buy' legislation led to a soaring demand for the services of the Registers of Scotland at a time when the department was subject to both staffing and accommodation constraints. The situation was steadily deteriorating and invidious comparisons were being drawn with the English system, which had only covered 50–52% of the country after 63 years. Fortunately the position in both countries has since been rectified.

The Department of the Registers of Scotland was created Scotland's first Executive Agency in 1990 and the consequent removal of constraints enabled the Agency to tackle its problems and meet targets set for it at its creation. These targets included:

(a) to reduce turnround times on registering dealings (i e sales of registered land) in the Land Register from 39 to 15 weeks;
(b) to present a phased programme for the extension of the Land Register throughout Scotland, to provide cheaper conveyancing, and to phase out the General Register of Sasines;
(c) to have in operation by April 1993 a branch office of the Land Register in Glasgow;
(d) to eliminate progressively the older casework by the end of 1996–97.

6.6 It is very pleasing to note that these targets have been met, or are well on the way to being met. In particular the land registration process has picked up momentum, as shown by the extension of land registration to the counties of Clackmannan (1 October 1992); Stirling (1 April 1993); West Lothian (1 October 1993); Fife (1 April 1995); Aberdeen and Kincardine (1 April 1996); Ayr and Dumfries, Kirkcudbright and Wigtown (1 April 1997); Angus, Perth and Kinross (1 April 1999); Berwick, East Lothian, Peebles, Roxburgh and Selkirk (1 October 1999); Argyll and Bute (1 April 2000); Inverness and Nairn (1 April 2002); and Banff, Caithness, Moray, Orkney and Zetland, Ross and Cromarty, and Sutherland (1 April 2003). As at June 2002 this timetable has been met, and only Banff, Caithness, Inverness, Moray, Nairn, Orkney and Zetland, Ross and Cromarty, and Sutherland remain outside the Land Register system. These are enormous geographical areas, but fairly lighly populated, and their assimilation into the Land Register system in April 2003 should be a mere formality. Then the whole of Scotland will be on the land registration system.

6.7   When an area becomes operational for land registration, all transfers for value must be registered (i e new securities on existing holdings and gratuitous transfers, as opposed to transfers for value, do not need to be registered). Transfers of long leases must be registered, whether gratuitous or not (LR(S)A 1979, s 3(3)).

Thus, if Mr and Mrs A had bought a house in the county of Renfrew in 1975, and if they had lived there continuously, the deed in their favour, and the standard security to their building society, would have been registered in the Sasine Register. The reason for this is that in 1975 the Land Register was not yet established.

If Mr and Mrs A then sold their house to B in 1994, the necessary documentation would then be registered in the Land Register.

If, however, Mr and Mrs A decided to transfer their house to their children as a gift (there are possible inheritance tax benefits in this action), the documentation would be recorded in the Sasine Register, as the transfer was not for valuable consideration. Rather oddly, if Mr and Mrs A gave the house to a child as a gift in contemplation of marriage (this has slightly greater possible inheritance tax benefits), that would then be treated as a transfer for valuable consideration, and the documentation would be registered in the Land Register.

If, however, Mr and Mrs A decided that they were staying put, but would get another loan, for their own purposes, the documentation would again be recorded in the Sasine Register, as a loan is not treated as being a valuable consideration.

Once, however, the title is registered in the Land Register, all relevant documents are registered in that register, irrespective of whether the consideration is valuable or not.

The Register of Sasines still operates in parallel with the Land Register (see App IV), and will continue to do so until it is finally phased out. Paradoxically, the Keeper of the Registers report for the financial year 2001–02 shows that the intake in the Sasine Register is 35% over that forecast. This is thought to be because of the upturn in remortgages caused by lower interest rates.

After all areas have become operational, it may be provided that all land shall be registered, whether transferred or not, to give a complete picture of land ownership in Scotland, kept on standard Ordnance Survey maps, and all stored on computer. That date is, however, still a rather long way off.

6.8   In 2001–02 the Keeper reported that there had been an intake of 77,200 titles for first registration, 22,200 for registration of part of a registered title (i e new houses built by builders on registered land), and 144,200 dealings (i e resales of registered land). There were 123,800 registrations in the Sasine Register, mainly explained at paragraph **6.7**.

6.9 It should, however, be made plain that there is nothing tricky about land registration. The first registration does, however, require extra work as the sellers' solicitors not only have to satisfy the purchasers' solicitors as to the sellers' title, but the purchasers' solicitors have immediately to satisfy the Keeper of the Land Register that a sufficient title is being registered, and that no restriction of indemnity is called for. If the Keeper is not happy he will notify the purchasers' solicitors who will in turn revert to the sellers' solicitors, demanding answers in terms of the obligation under missives (see App I).

Thus it may be said that while the sasine system is one of *caveat emptor* (buyer beware), the land registration system is one of *caveat vendor* (seller beware), as there is much more of an onus on the sellers' solicitors to prove a good title than there is on the purchasers' solicitors to be satisfied that the title is good.

When the Keeper is satisfied, a comprehensive land certificate is issued, which contains all necessary information on the title (but not the planning or building or other information) and it is conclusive evidence of ownership, the extent of the property, and the land obligations affecting the land.

6.10 In the case of *Short's Trustee v Keeper of the Registers of Scotland* (1996 SC (HL) 14) the House of Lords decided that the Keeper was not obliged to register a decree reducing a transfer of land, as the appropriate course for the holder of the decree is to apply for rectification of the register under LR(S)A 1979, s 9. This section allows the Keeper to rectify the title sheet where an error is brought to his notice, or if ordered to do so by the Lands Tribunal. This provision is, however, restricted by the terms of section 9(3), which does not allow rectification to the prejudice of the proprietor in possession, except in very limited circumstances:

(a) to note an overriding interest, which does not prejudice the proprietor because an overriding interest is overriding, whether noted or not;
(b) where all concerned consent;
(c) where the error is caused by the fraud or carelessness of the proprietor in possession;
(d) where rectification relates to something for which the Keeper has previously refused to indemnify the proprietor in possession. An example of this would be where the proprietor in possession has only an *a non domino* title, but this has now been perfected by positive prescription, and the proprietor wants the title to be rectified to the extent that the exclusion of indemnity is removed.

In the Inner House hearing of *Short's Trustee* (1993 SCLR 242) Lord President Hope said that if a decree of reduction was automatically registrable in the Land Register, that would subvert the whole system of land registration in that any person dealing with the registered proprietor would require to check the previous history of the title, which was what land registration was designed to avoid. However, this decision has now been undermined by the subsequent case of *Short's Trustee v Chung (No 2)* 1998 SC 105.

It should be noted that the Keeper asks (Annual Report 1992–93) to be cited in any action for rectification that is raised, although the action is not directed primarily against the Keeper. This is in order that he can enter an appearance if the integrity of the Register appears to be under threat in any way.

6.11   Furthermore if the registered title is successfully challenged in any respect, on the grounds of a matter on which indemnity has not been excluded, the loss is state guaranteed and falls on the Keeper. For that reason the Keeper inspects the title very carefully, and seeks certain information from the presenter of the title (see the questions in LR(S)A 1979, Forms 1, 2, and 3) before full indemnity is given.

Due to the care taken by the Keeper and his staff, the claims record for the first few years was modest, but ominously has taken an upturn recently. Such claims usually refer to inaccuracies in Agency reports (replies to LR(S)A 1979, Forms 10, 11, 12 and 13) but in recent years rather large sums have been paid (over £100,000 in 1993–94) in respect of lost leasehold casualty rights. These grotesque survivals are discussed at chapter 21.

6.12   The first registration involves a considerable amount of detailed work for it is effectively a sasine transaction, with the land registration work added. A positive weighting of fees may be justified. The case of any future transfer should be a comparatively simple matter, but there should be a negative weighting in fees for the reduction in work involved. Under the old Scale of Fees, the positive and negative weighting allowed was 25%, but the guidelines for fee charging in paragraph **11.11** should be followed in all cases. The government call for cheaper fees is thus met, by greater productivity, and fewer time-wasting procedures.

6.13   Thus the land registration system is a very good and modern one, with digitalised maps, optical reading, computerised land certificates either in operation or planned. It seems barely credible that all this sophisticated technology is imposed on a feudal system which derives from medieval times and still talks of superiors and vassals, and still accords the superior major powers over land that other people have bought, and would have bought outright in most other parts of the world. However, we eagerly await the implementation of the Abolition of Feudal Tenure etc (Scotland) Act 2000, which should allow the rest of the conveyancing system to catch up with the progress in registration.

Chapter 7

THE STUFF OF CONVEYANCING

'This registration of title is all very well, but it's not the stuff of conveyancing.'

(A Glasgow solicitor)

7.1 Missives having been concluded, it is now for the sellers' solicitors to show that the sellers have a valid marketable title, and for the purchasers' solicitors to be satisfied that this is so. This is truly the stuff of traditional conveyancing. In their book *Conveyancing* (2nd edn, 1999, p 91) Professors Reid and Gretton define a marketable title as one:

(a) which makes the buyer the owner of the property;
(b) contains no heritable securities adverse to the new owner's interest;
(c) contains no unusual conditions of title; and
(d) contains no leases adverse to the new owner's interest.

To this might be added that, in land registration areas, a marketable title is one that can be sent to the Keeper immediately after purchase, and on the basis of which the Keeper will, without making further enquiries or requisitions, issue a land certificate without restriction of indemnity.

7.2 Modern conveyancing practice has placed much more emphasis on the preparation of missives than previously, and many of the matters formerly dealt with at the examination of title stage are now dealt with before missives are completed.

Thus, for instance, it is a usual stipulation of missives that the title shall contain 'no unduly onerous conditions or restrictions' (see para **7.4**). It is very hard to know exactly what is meant by this statement, and its meaning depends very much on the circumstances of each case. This is not satisfactory at all, as the word 'unusual' is subjective. If the sellers give this warranty in missives, purchasers can claim at a later date that there is, in their opinion, an onerous condition or restriction in the title, and the matter will have to be argued and compromised, although, at worst, the purchasers may withdraw.

The question of what is an 'unusual condition' is considered in *Whyte v Lee* ((1879) 6 R 699 at 701), where Lord Young commented on the phrase as follows:

'If a man simply buys a house he must be taken to buy it as the seller has it, on a good title of course, but subject to such restrictions as may exist if of an ordinary character, and such as the buyer may reasonably be supposed to have contemplated as at least not improbable.'

The leading modern case is *Armia Ltd v Daejan Developments Ltd* (1979 SC (HL) 56), where a property in Kirkcaldy High Street, which had been bought for redevelopment, was found to be subject to a servitude right of access, which included a ten-foot frontage with the street. It was held that this was a sufficiently unusual condition to allow the purchaser to resile.

In the case of *Morris v Ritchie* (1992 GWD 33–1950) a piece of ground being sold turned out to be burdened by a servitude right of access, which would have reduced the number of car parking spaces by 7 out of 18, and would therefore have a bad effect on turnover and thus market value of the property. This only became known to the pursuer after missives had been concluded, and a deposit had been paid. The pursuer was allowed to withdraw from the purchase because of the diminution in value of the ground. On a practical note, sellers who know of restrictions of this nature should disclose them to the purchasers before missives are concluded.

The chief ambition of the conveyancer must be never to let any matter near the court, as, at best, a reference to court entails expense and delay, and, at worst, an adverse decision, whether right or (even worse still) wrong. For that reason it has been suggested (see para **6.1**) that the sellers' agents should obtain the titles, and as many other relevant certificates etc as possible, before exposing the property for sale. When an offer is received, containing the stipulation as to unusual or unduly onerous conditions, the sellers' agents should then send the title deeds, and other relevant papers, with the acceptance, and require the purchasers' agents to satisfy themselves prior to completion of the contract. This is good practice and will save arguments at a later date, probably arising shortly before the date for settlement (see App II.21(a) and following letter).

7.3   For the purposes of this chapter, we shall assume that such matters have not been dealt with before missives are completed, and that the full examination of title takes place after completion of missives. It is not always possible to assemble title deeds and other papers, and as indicated previously (see para **2.5**) the first intimation the solicitor may receive of a sale is when an offer drops through the letter box, requiring urgent attention. In that case, the missives must proceed on the basis of warranties given and proved to be correct when the title is available.

7.4   The obligations of the sellers for (a) a sasine transaction, (b) a first registration in the Land Register and (c) a subsequent dealing in registered land, are set out in clause 12 of the offer in Appendix I.11. In the disposition the sellers grant absolute warrandice, that is to say, they undertake to compensate the purchasers for any title defect. When a title is registered in the Land Register, the Keeper will issue a land certificate with a guarantee of indemnity.

Why then should the purchasers' agents have to examine the title in such detail? The reasons are (a) professional pride dictates that the purchasers shall get a title that can be passed on without question when the purchasers eventually sell, be that next month or next century; (b) the person who prepared the sellers' title may not have had the same standards, or perhaps there has been an innocent mistake perpetuating itself over the years; (c) warrandice is not in practice a particularly effective remedy, as it depends on 'eviction' having taken place, and the victim has to go through the process of losing his case before he can claim warrandice (see *Welsh v Russell* (1894) 21 R 769). It should be noted that 'eviction' in this case means any interference with the property right, rather than being put out of the property. Even if there is a valid remedy under warrandice, you may not be able to trace the granters of warrandice, or if appropriate, their predecessors in title; (d) lawyers are not paid to get their clients into dispute, quite the opposite; and (e) the *caveat emptor* rule applies, in sasine transactions at least, although less so in Land Register transactions.

7.5 If the house had been situated in a county where there is Land Registration (see para **6.6**) the procedures for registration of title would apply where a sale of the property is made. You would, therefore, require now to turn to chapters 13 to 16, and Appendix I and follow the procedure outlined there.

In a first registration, the procedure of examining title is very much the same as with a sasine title, but in a subsequent dealing, the title deeds are replaced by a land certificate. This contains all the essential parts of the title, and none of the non-essential, and should therefore be read very thoroughly. The fact that all inessential details are stripped out, and the remainder is clearly printed, should make this a very much easier business than reading through a lot of old titles written in spidery handwriting on disintegrating paper.

7.6 For ease of treatment, we are assuming that your clients are not obtaining a loan. The additional procedure to be adopted when they are getting a loan is contained in chapter 12.

7.7 In a first registration, or in a sasine transaction, the first thing that you must do is to check the title deeds against the inventory and (assuming they are in order) return the inventory marked 'borrowed the above title deeds; to be returned on demand' and signed. Then put all the title deeds into order and check them against the search, making sure that all the deeds mentioned in the Search or Form 10A have been sent to you. Form in your mind a rough history of the property, and in particular spot any split-offs or acquisitions and the writs referred to for burdens.

7.8 Next, put to one side the writs that do not concern you, bearing in mind the following provisions of statute that are designed to make life easier for you (see paras **7.9–7.13**).

Prescription and Limitation (Scotland) Act 1973, s 1

7.9 Section 1 provides (in paraphrase) that where a person has possessed land openly, peacefully and without interruption for ten years, on the basis of a sufficient title, then after ten years the title shall not be challengeable on the ground that it was not valid *ex facie* (on its face), the only exception being if it turns out to have been forged. This process is known as positive prescription.

It is not thought that many pieces of land are acquired in this way, yet this is, for another reason, a vital provision for the conveyancer. What it means, in effect, is that if you take the first transfer of the land that you are buying, which is more than ten years old, and find that it is free from an intrinsic objection (that is an objection showing on the face of the title, and not requiring proof from outside sources) then that is a valid foundation for a prescriptive title, and you need look back no further. Therefore you may set aside all older transfers of the land, unless these contain valid land obligations to which you must refer. You must, however, check this foundation writ for any intrinsic objection, and check everything after it to make sure that it correctly flows down to the present seller. An intrinsic objection is one which can be observed from the terms of the deed itself.

An example of what might have been called an intrinsic objection is given in *Cooper Scott v Gill Scott* (1925 SC 309), where a destination detailed in the narrative clause did not correspond with a further narration of the same destination in the dispositive clause. A majority of the seven judges, however, held that this deed was not intrinsically null and was therefore a good foundation for prescription (see also *Simpson v Marshall* (1900) 2 F 447).

An extrinsic objection, that is to say an objection which can only be proved from outside evidence, or an intrinsic objection that can be proved only by extrinsic evidence, does not affect the use of the disposition as a foundation of title.

7.10   As an example of the power of prescription, consider the disposition *a non domino* (a disposition granted by someone who is not the owner). If a piece of land lies vacant, and the owner cannot be traced, it is possible for someone who does not own that land to obtain a disposition, granted by anyone in favour of a grantee. Only simple warrandice is given, for the granter has no claim to the land at all. The disposition is then recorded to make it public and the disponee occupies the land 'openly and peaceably', as if it was owned, so that anyone who has a better title may see the occupation and object. If no objection is made by anyone having a better title, within ten years, the disponee then becomes the owner of the land.

If prescription can cure a disposition that is so obviously bad, it will be seen that it can also cure any minor defect in a deed.

Prescription and Limitation (Scotland) Act 1973, s 8

7.11   Section 8 provides (again in paraphrase) that where a right has not been enforced or exercised for a continuous period of 20 years, then that right shall be extinguished. This is known as negative prescription.

Again, this does not clearly state the benefit to the conveyancer, who only need look back for securities over a 20-year period. Thus (writing in August 2002), if a bond was recorded before August 1992, and no interest has been paid on it in that time, and it has not been enforced, it can be said to have prescribed. The snag is to know whether or not interest has been paid, and this will be dealt with under searches in chapter 8. All kinds of out-of-date obligations can be cleared in this way.

Succession (Scotland) Act 1964, s 17

7.12   Section 12 provides that where a person for good faith and for value (i e the average house purchaser) acquires title to land from an executor, or from somebody who has derived title directly from an executor, the title shall not be challengeable on the ground that the confirmation of the executor was reducible, or had in fact been reduced, or even that the title should not have been transferred by the executor to the person who is offering the title.

Thus, for example, you may be offered a title by X and Y, who produce (a) a confirmation in the estate of their uncle (V), whereby Z is appointed executor and (b) a docket in terms of the Succession (Scotland) Act 1964, s 15 transferring that property to X and Y, as, say, the persons entitled to take the property under V's will. Provided your client is buying in good faith and for value (i e the average house purchaser), it need not concern you (a) if someone produces a later dated will appointing A as executor and B the legatee, or (b) someone alleges that the will is a forgery. In summary, you need look no further than the confirmation itself.

An analogous provision is made in the Trusts (Scotland) Act 1961, s 2 which provides that titles acquired from trustees or executors are also protected from challenge on the ground that the transaction was at variance with the terms or purpose of the trust.

Conveyancing and Feudal Reform (Scotland) Act 1970, s 41

7.13 Section 41 provides that where a discharge of a security bears to be granted by a person entitled to do so (e g the creditor) subsequent acquirers of land bona fide and for value, shall not have their title to the land challenged after the expiration of a five-year period from the recording of the discharge, merely by reason of the discharge being reduced.

Thus, if a discharge is more than five years old, and appears to have been granted by the creditor of the security that is discharged, you need not examine the origins of that discharge any further.

7.14 The first step in examining title is to identify your foundation writ, and examine it for intrinsic defects. Then examine the writs that follow the foundation writ, ensuring that one follows on from another smoothly. If the grantee of one deed is not the grantee of the next deed, examine the deduction of title, and ensure that the link in title is in order. (*Example*: if a writ is in favour of Brown, and the next deed is granted by Black, check exactly why Black is selling a house that appears to be owned by Brown. Generally there will be a good reason, and if Brown has died and Black is his executor, or if Brown is bankrupt and Black is the trustee, ensure that title is properly deduced in the second writ using confirmation to vouch this.)

Recall two reminders contained in the Halliday Report (Cmnd 3118) (1966) (ch 4):

(a) that only certain deeds in terms of C(S)A 1924, s 3 (dispositions of land, or assignations, discharges or restrictions of heritable security) may be granted by uninfeft proprietors, and, for instance, feu grants and deeds of conditions may not. A surprising number of these deeds are granted by uninfeft proprietors, and are invalid until a recorded title is obtained, usually by means of a notice of title which is recorded, and which cures the defect by accretion. Formerly, heritable securities could not be granted by persons without a recorded title, but standard securities and their transmissions may now be granted by uninfeft proprietors in terms generally of CFR(S)A 1970, Pt II;

(b) that the style of deduction of title in C(S)A 1924, Sch A, Form 1, requires a designation of the person last infeft, and is ineffective otherwise. Thus, the designation of the granter, which appeared in the narrative clause, must be repeated. While this may seem harsh and inconsistent with the liberal terms of C(S)A 1924, Sch D, Note 1, that is nevertheless the law, and it must be followed.

7.15   Check carefully the first description of the land, either with your own observations or with a survey plan of the property and make sure that the first full description has been validly referred to throughout the progress in titles in conformity with the Conveyancing (Scotland) Acts 1874 and 1924. Note all additions to the land and disposals of any part of the land.

7.16   Examine the burdens contained in all writs referred to for burdens in the title, and assess their possible impact on your client. Properly created burdens do not, of course, ever prescribe, and thus you must still examine writs outwith the prescriptive periods that are referred to as burdens. Have all feuing conditions been implemented? If they have not (eg if walls and fences around the plot are not in conformity with the feuing conditions) the purchaser may be called upon to remedy the defect and this may prove expensive. If in doubt ask the sellers' agents to obtain a superior's certificate stating that feuing conditions have been implemented. If they will not obtain this (and they are probably under no compulsion to do so, unless the missives state that they shall or if the title is not marketable because of this) write to the superior's agent in terms similar to this:

Messrs Morrison & Goodfellow
Solicitors
23 Hamill Street
GLASGOW

Dear Sirs,

Mr James Meikle, Strathclyde Estates Limited,
3 Barrie Drive, Glasgow

Please confirm that all feuing conditions, other than those of a continuing nature, have been implemented to the satisfaction of the superiors, Strathclyde Estates Limited.

When sending this confirmation, please let us have a note of your fee in this matter.

Yours faithfully,

DAVIDSON & CARSWELL (signed)

7.17   Superiors roughly fall into three categories: (a) caring superiors, who genuinely care about the appearance of the estate, and who coincidentally own the superiorities (in the meantime) of some of the finest residential property in Scotland, such as the New Town in Edinburgh, the terraces in the West End of Glasgow, the fine shipbuilders' houses in Helensburgh and so on; (b) the commercial superiors, who are in it for the money (see ch 17) ((a) and (b) are not mutually incompatible categories); and (c) the uncaring superior, who has lost interest, or has disappeared. In many ways, the last is the most dangerous superior, because while no permissions are necessary from uncaring superiors, they may sell on to commercial superiors, who will start to delve into the estate and make life difficult.

   It should be noted that if an uncaring superior was a limited company which has probably been dissolved, the superiority, if not transferred will belong to the Crown, and a waiver may be received from the Queen's and Lord Treasurer's Remembrancer who is at the Crown Office (tel: 0131 226 2626).

A bit of common sense is required about this condition. If the house is over ten years old, say, to ask for this information is probably to waste everyone's time, and it may be expensive. If the superiors have not objected in this time, they are highly unlikely to do so now, and if they do, they will possibly have lost their right through acquiescence. It may be more useful in the case of a new house, where it is not immediately obvious that all feuing conditions have or have not been complied with. Do not ask for this information as a matter of course without considering what other ways you might obtain it.

7.18 Check that all parties granting deeds had the capacity to do so, that the form of all deeds is correct, that they are properly executed and that the testing clause is correctly completed, that all deletions, interlineations, additions and erasures have been properly stamped and recorded in the General Register of Sasines. This will require a knowledge of the law both before and after the Requirements of Writing (Scotland) Act 1995.

Planning permission and building warrants are obtained from separate committees of the council, and both must be obtained separately. The grant of one does not necessarily imply that the other will be given. Planning permission is given where (broadly) you are building the right kind of building for the zoning laid down. (Thus where an area is zoned for residential purposes, you should have little difficulty obtaining permission to build a house; if, however, you wish to build even a small factory or shop you will have difficulty.) Building warrant is given (again broadly) where a planned building complies with the building regulations, as to materials used, space available, hygiene arrangements, fire precautions, ventilation, etc. Failure to obtain or comply with either of these provisions may eventually lead to the owner having to reinstate the property to its original condition.

Incidentally, even councils are not exempt from this provision of law: Dundee District Council was ordered by the Scottish Development Department to reinstate Camperdown House (built in 1824) to its original state after modernisation was carried out without planning consent. Retrospective consent had also been refused by the department (*Sunday Standard*, 14 November 1982).

Similarly, all new buildings and extensions to buildings and proposals for such buildings should comply with the feuing conditions. If they do not, the owners will have to deal with the superior. Even worse, they may have to deal with a number of 'tertii' (that is persons who enjoy a *jus quaesitum tertio*)— groups of property owners are notoriously hard to deal with, as they seldom seem to agree. The superior and the *tertii*, or both, may interdict the owner, if the condition is breached. The only way around this problem is to negotiate a waiver of the feuing condition (presumably for a consideration) or, if that fails, to take the matter to the Lands Tribunal under the CFR(S)A 1970, s 1. (For a case dealing with the interests of both superiors and *tertii*, see *Main v Lord Doune* 1972 SLT (Lands Tr) 14).

7.19 Check that the house possesses suitable rights of access. This applies particularly to property in the country. Land is obviously useless unless it enjoys proper access, unless, of course, you own a helicopter. On 4 August 2002, it was reported in the press that a couple had bought a farmhouse (for £130,000) from a bank who had repossessed it. Unfortunately, however, the original owner still owned a small strip of land controlling access, and he wasn't selling it. This is the last thing you would want to happen.

The problem is not so acute in the city and towns where, generally, but not universally, the streets have been taken over and are maintained by the local authority. In that case anyone can use the road, but the downside is that the local authority can paint yellow lines on 'your' road and, even worse, charge you for parking outside your own house.

The local authority maintains the road, and is responsible for any accident that occurs through lack of maintenance. Where the road remains private, and this can be found even in towns and cities, the frontagers own the road to the centre point, along the length of their frontage. They are responsible for maintenance, and usually don't trouble to do any, because of the near impossibility of getting agreement from all the frontagers to pay for the work. If there is an accident through lack of maintenance, the appropriate frontagers are responsible, but should be covered by the public liability of their household insurance.

If a road is built to a certain standard, the builders can, and will, ask the local authority to take over the maintenance of the road. Owners of existing private roads seldom do this, again usually for lack of agreement to spending money on turning their quiet road into a public highway.

In the country, purchasing solicitors must ensure that purchasers enjoy an unrestricted right to all necessary rights of access, and are not expected to pay a disproportionate amount of maintenance. A servitude right of access is a licence to use someone else's ground for certain purposes, and if the owners of the dominant tenant exceed this use they can be interdicted. The division of large estates, and the sale of redundant estates and farm houses, has led to an increasing number of 'townspeople' now living in the country, often not happily with the country people. There have been an increasing number of cases that have illustrated the trend towards bad relations between the two (see an article on the subject by Douglas Patience (1993 *SLG* 127)).

In Caveat (a monthly article outlining the mistakes, hopefully, of others) (1993 JLSS 490), there is a cautionary tale of a couple who bought a house in the country, with an adjoining disused water mill. The access to the mill was over a farmer's land. There was nothing in the titles about this right, which had arisen from use, and positive prescription. The farmer objected to the proposed use of the road to the mill, which was intended for use as a holiday cottage. It was held by the court that the access had been created for use of the building as a mill, and not as a cottage. The solicitor who had acted for the pursuers was liable for the costs of forming an alternative access, and loss of income.

In addition, the owners of the dominant tenement cannot increase the burden on the servient tenement, and cannot therefore increase the usage. Professor Halliday (*Conveyancing Law and Practice in Scotland* (2nd edn, 1996) vol II, 20, 11), suggests that when a servitude of access is created, words such as the following should be used: 'The servitude has been granted with reference to the present state of the property and shall not be extended to apply to any substantially different condition thereof.'

Grants of servitudes should be drawn very carefully, and are construed *contra proferentem*. For example, one frequently sees a servitude right of access for 'pedestrian and vehicular' use. Does that include the right to drive cattle over the road? You might argue that the word pedestrian is derived from the Latin word for feet, and that cattle have feet, however that is not the ordinary meaning of the word. Further, the law of servitudes is drawn from Roman law, and it had three classes of servitude: *via* (the right to use the road for carriages drawn by horses or other beasts of draught); *iter* (allowing a person a right of way to pass over the land of another on horse or on foot); and *actus* (the right of use for carriages drawn by men, and for driving cattle), indicating a more precise distinction between the uses.

Servitudes should be used *civiliter* (i e with civility). The owner of the servient tenement is not under an obligation to maintain the ground, and should not obstruct the way. Where there is an agreement for the maintenance of a road, liability should be apportioned according to the extent of the respective uses.

7.20 The position with new houses is rather different. The builder will undertake, as part of the price of the house, to form the road to the appropriate council standard and to request the council to take it over, without it, of course, giving any guarantee that it will do so. (Provided the road is built to standard, a refusal to take over is virtually unknown.) Despite this partially incomplete work, the builder will nonetheless require the full price at the date of entry.

The builder should also provide a road bond. You may wonder why the purchasers should pay the full price before all work is complete. While payment is only made on completion of the house, the completion of roads is an exception, for it is useless to complete someone's road while there is work going on in the estate and the builder may have heavy plant using that road. A builder will normally complete all the houses in an estate, then finish the roads. The road bond covers the purchasers against the builder's insolvency in the intervening period between payment of the price and completion of the roads.

On the basis that good advice cannot be repeated too often, (1) the sellers' agents should obtain a letter as to roads from the appropriate council the minute the sellers instruct the sale (see JLSS Council Notes, October 1982 as corrected in Council Notes, November 1982) and (2) the purchasers and their agents should deal with such matters before completing missives, by personal observation, inquiry and survey.

7.21 Approximately the same position applies with the supply of water, gas, electricity, etc and with drainage. Most of us take these services for granted, but lawyers cannot do this, particularly when purchasing a property in a rural or even semi-rural area.

(a) Water. The appropriate authority will not necessarily run water into every house, especially those that are isolated, and the water may be drawn from a stream or well situated in someone else's land (*aquaehaustus*) and be carried from the mains to the house by a private pipe (*aqueduct*). Where this pipe crosses the land of another, make sure that there are clear servitude rights for running the pipe, and a right to gain access to the pipe if it requires maintenance.

In very rural areas the water system will be no concern of the appropriate board, and the conveyancer should ensure that the arrangement is adequate *tantum et tale* (both as to quantity and quality). Where the source is in someone else's land, make sure that the supply cannot be interfered with, and that the necessary servitude rights for pipes exist. Bear in mind the seasonal nature of water supply, even in Scotland.

(b) Gas, electricity and telephone. British Gas, Scottish Power, Scottish Hydro Electric and British Telecom will take care of the servitude rights (or wayleaves) for cables and pipes, under statutory powers, and these will not therefore concern the average conveyancer in the active sense. In the passive sense, however, note should be taken of wayleaves for cable and pipes leading to other properties, which must not be disturbed by digging, or obstructed in any way, e g by building over the wayleave area. Thus, for example, if you have a mains water pipe in your property, or a gas pipe-line, you would be well advised to know about these and to leave them well alone. Modern pipe-lines are sunk to a great depth, but the same cannot be said of Victorian pipe-lines.

(c) Drainage.   The position is as with water supply, but in reverse. In many rural areas drainage is not to a mains, but a private septic tank. It is a matter of survey to ensure that this tank is in order, and capable of treating the volume of waste generated by the household it serves. A properly constructed and maintained tank should do this without giving trouble. The local council should empty it from time to time. Again, if waste is piped through the land of another, the appropriate servitude rights must be seen to exist. There is, according to Professors Gretton and Reid (*Conveyancing* (2nd edn, 1999) para 13.02), a servitude of 'sinks' which covers this, although this is not one of the classic servitudes (although it perhaps should be).

In the case of a new house, all services will be (or at least should be) 'laid on'. Each house in a new estate will be transferred subject to a variety of servitude or wayleave rights, which may be expressed as follows:

'There is reserved to us and our successors as proprietors of the remaining area or piece of ground of which the feu forms part of a servitude right of wayleave for all necessary water pipes, sewers, drains, electricity cables, Post Office underground and overhead cables, field drains and whole other necessary pipes and cables passing through the feu and the feuars are prohibited from erecting any permanent construction on the lines of said water pipes, sewers, drains, electricity cables, underground and overhead communications cables and field drains if any within the feu and shall not do or permit to be done any act which may cause damage to said water pipes, sewers, drains, electricity cables, underground and overhead communications cables and field drains; and the feuars shall further be bound to allow all parties interested in said water pipes, sewers, drains and whole other pipes and cables right of access to the feu on all necessary occasions for opening up, uncovering, inspecting, maintaining, cleaning, repairing and renewing the same on payment of compensation to the feuars for any surface damaged which may be thereby occasioned; further declaring that there is reserved to us and our foresaids in all time coming a right to lay on, in or over the feu such water pipes, sewers, drains and whole other pipes and cables as we in our sole discretion shall consider necessary for the amenity of the feu and of the remaining area or piece of ground of which the feu forms part but that always on payment of compensation for the feuars for any surface damage which may be thereby occasioned.'

7.22   Every new house, or every new extension or alteration to a house, must carry the following permissions:

(a) planning permission from the district council under the Town and Country Planning (Scotland) Acts 1972 and 1977;
(b) building warrant from the district council under the Building (Scotland) Acts 1959 and 1970 and completion certificate;
(c) superior's consent (if applicable);
(d) the consent of any third parties *'tertii'* who may have a *jus quaesitum tertio* (i e a right given to a third party over land which is subject to a contract between the first and second parties only).

Planning permission and building warrants are often confused, perhaps because they cover roughly the same problems of decent building standards, and are obtained from the offices of the same council. They should not, however, be confused. They arise under different Acts and regulations, and are administered by different officials and committees. The existence of one does not in any way guarantee the existence of the other. Separate applications must be made for each.

Planning permission covers, very broadly, the appearance of an area, and the zoning of that area. If an area is zoned as residential, you would be very unlikely to get permission to build a factory there; but you would probably get permission to build a house, assuming all the other requirements of the Council, as to density, the suitability of the roads, etc, are met. Building warrant is given (again broadly) where a planned building complies with the building regulations as to materials used, space available, hygiene arrangements, fire precautions, ventilation, lack of dampness, etc. A completion certificate is granted when the building is complete to the building department's satisfaction, and only then may it be occupied. Failure to obtain these certificates can, in the worst cases, lead to an order being made to restore the land or building to its original condition.

Particular care should be taken with buildings of special historical or architectural significance, or which form part of a special townscape, and which are accordingly 'listed'. All alterations require listed building consent, and many owners may find the local councils and bodies such as Historic Scotland a bit pernickety. It is very pleasant to live in a listed building, until you come to alter it, when it can prove extremely expensive.

There is a dispensation contained in the Town and Country Planning (Scotland) Act 1972, s 84 to the effect that an enforcement action for breach of planning law is not enforceable after four years. It should be noted that this dispensation does not apply to a breach of building regulations. If obtaining permission or a completion certificate has been overlooked or forgotten, a retrospective warrant or certificate has to be obtained in cases of a serious breach. This can be extremely expensive, as the building work has to comply with current building regulations. Thus, even if a building was built in 1985, say, to comply with the regulations then, there is no guarantee that it would comply with the 1995 regulations. Alternatively, in less serious cases, the council may be prepared to issue a 'letter of comfort' covering the breach. An example of this, in a case where a completion certificate has not been obtained, might read:

'I would confirm that, following your application for confirmation of Completion, a survey of the above property has now been carried out. The purpose of this survey was to inspect the building operations referred to in the Building Warrant reference (number) and comment is therefore restricted to this. No responsibility for the condition of any concealed elements of the structure can be accepted.

Following inspection of the property, it has been ascertained, as far as is practical. that the operations detailed in the documents relating to the aforementioned Building Warrant, and any relevant amendment(s), have been completed. I can therefore confirm that this Authority shall take no action with regard to the absence of a Certificate of Completion relative to these operations.'

This letter is pretty qualified in its terms, and does not bind the council at all, nor does the council accept any liability, which might arise in the future, for building defects, but it may provide some comfort which should be acceptable to a purchaser. In truth, a completion certificate does not offer a great deal more protection, as it can be changed anytime.

Similarly, all building work should have the consent of superiors and third parties, if this is written in the titles. Great care should be taken with these rights, especially where you have a vigilant superior. Unless appeased, the superior may interdict the work. Third parties can also give trouble, as groups of people are very difficult to deal with.

Care must be taken with replacement windows, to ensure that (1) in a listed building they are compatible with the building and have council approval; (2) that they can be cleaned from the inside, unless they are at ground level; and (3) that they permit escape in case of fire. Practice varies from district to district, and if you are in doubt the matter should be discussed with the local council.

7.23   Where a sale is made by a person or persons on behalf of someone else, or in default of someone else, care must be taken to ensure that the power of sale is competent, and that it was properly exercised.

(a) Trustees.   Trustees have wide powers to sell, lease and grant securities over heritage under the Trusts (Scotland) Act 1921, s 4. The term 'trustee' includes (s 2): trustee *ex officiis* (namely trustees who are appointed by virtue of an office they hold, say a president and secretary of a bowling club, and who cease to be trustees when they demit office, giving way to the next incumbents automatically), executors-nominate, tutors, curators and judicial factors. This power of sale has now been extended to executors-dative by the Succession (Scotland) Act 1964, s 20. Further reference is made to the immunities at paragraph **7.12**.

(b) Creditors selling under a standard security.   The power of sale may be exercised among other remedies (see App V) when the debtor is in default. Appendix V also shows how such default arises, and the remedies that are available on default.

The CFR(S)A 1970, s 25 imposes a duty on the selling creditor to advertise the sale in a medium that is seen in the locality of the property being sold. Reference may be made to the more defined rules of advertising of a sale under a bond, referred to in paragraph (c) below; further, the seller shall take all reasonable steps to ensure that the price at which the sale is made is the best that can be reasonably obtained. The sale may either be made by private bargain (i e a sale normally concluded as outlined in previous chapters) or by public auction followed by articles of roup and a minute of preference stating the name of the successful purchaser and the offer made. The articles of roup and minute of preference have a similar effect to missives.

(c) Sellers under a bond and disposition in security.   Prior to CFR(S)A 1970 the rules of sale under a bond and disposition in security were strict, in that the sale had to be by public auction, and certain rules of advertisement had to be implicitly followed (see Halliday Report, paragraphs 107–118 for a critique of these rules).

These rules were relaxed by CFR(S)A 1970, ss 33 ff, but only to some extent. Thus, in terms of section 35(1), the sale may now be alternatively made by private bargain, for 'the best price that can be reasonably obtained'. A calling-up notice may take place two months after the date of service of notice, or such shorter period as may be agreed with the debtor and postponed creditors.

The CFR(S)A 1970, s 35 provides that a creditor in a standard security may sell either by private bargain or by auction, provided that the sale is advertised and all reasonable steps taken to ensure that the property is sold at the best price. The CFR(S)A 1970, s 36 imposes certain rules of advertisement which may be briefly summarised (under the *caveat* that a perusal of the Act is essential if you are involved in a sale) as follows:

(i)   Advertisements must be placed (1) if the property is in Midlothian in a daily paper published in Edinburgh; (2) if the property is in Lanarkshire (as it then was) in a daily paper published in Glasgow; (3) if the property is elsewhere in Scotland in a daily newspaper circulating in the district where the property is situated and in one newspaper (i e a local paper that may be weekly or twice weekly) circulating in the district and published in the county where the property is situated. (Note that the county system prior to local government reorganisation in 1973 still pertains: see App III.)

(ii)   When the sale is by public roup, one advertisement a week for three consecutive weeks must be made.

(iii)   When the sale is by private bargain, one advertisement a week for two consecutive weeks must be made.

These stipulations are the minimum requirements of law. The purchasers' agents must see copies of the advertisement certified as to date of publication by the newspaper publisher.

The final rule (CFR(S)A 1970, s 26), and one that can easily be forgotten, is that where a sale is by private bargain, the sale must be concluded within 28 days of the date of the second advertisement. This is taken to mean that missives must be concluded within the 28 days. If they are not concluded, the sale and every subsequent deed is invalid, so obviously this must be checked.

(d) Trustees in bankruptcy.   Trustees in bankruptcy should, in terms of the Insolvency Act 1986, s 338, be qualified insolvency practitioners, as should liquidators, receivers and administrators of limited companies.

Sequestrations commenced after 1 April 1986 are governed by a completely new code introduced by the Bankruptcy (Scotland) Act 1985 (B(S)A 1995). This provides, in summary, that an interim trustee in bankruptcy shall be appointed by the sheriff to preserve the estate, and he will be replaced by a permanent trustee who is elected by the creditors. The property vests in the permanent trustee on behalf of the creditors. The Accountant in Bankruptcy issues Notes for Guidance (printed as an appendix to Professor William McBryde's Commentary on the Act) which should be closely read by anyone practising in this field.

The interim trustee has no power to sell property. The decree in bankruptcy is registered in the Personal Register by the clerk of the relevant court (B(S)A 1985, s 14). The trustee cannot sell without the consent of the heritable creditors unless there are sufficient funds realised to pay off the heritable creditors, and the trustee cannot sell if a heritable creditor has intimated an intention to sell (B(S)A 1985, s 39). In the case of a sale of a family home (B(S)A 1985, s 40), the consent of the bankrupt's spouse (B(S)A 1985, s 40), or of the court if this is not forthcoming, is required. Inhibitions against the bankrupt need not be discharged (B(S)A 1985, s 31(2)). There is no requirement for any further sequestration orders to be lodged in the Personal Register.

Title to sell is deduced through the decree in bankruptcy from the last infeft proprietor to the purchaser, as with confirmation of a deceased person (see para **9.8**).

(e) A trustee under a trust deed.   A trust deed is a document signed 'voluntarily' by the bankrupt, without the necessity of a court order. The trustee grants the disposition, deducing title through the trust deed, which will have been registered in the Books of Council and Session.

(f) Liquidators of limited companies.   The deed to be granted here is in the name of the company and the liquidator, who signs on behalf of the company which now has no directors or secretary. As the conditions of the Companies Act 1985, s 36(3) (formerly CA 1948, s 32(4)) are not met, the signature must be witnessed. Title is deduced through the interlocutor ordering the winding up, if the liquidation is compulsory, and through the special resolution of the company, if it is voluntary. These documents should have been registered in the Companies Register as should the appointment of the liquidator.

Where the sale is by private bargain, as is usual, the consent of the creditors and of the Accountant of Court are not required (*Liquidator of Style & Mantle Ltd v Price's Tailors Ltd* 1934 SC 548) in the disposition. The powers of a liquidator are detailed in the Companies Act 1985, s 539 (formerly CA 1948, s 245) and include the power to sell, feu or otherwise dispose of property by public sale or private bargain.

In practice, the liquidation of a company is a matter of public knowledge, and is intimated widely in the *Edinburgh Gazette* and in newspapers which should be read by legal practitioners as part of their 'common knowledge', although in all cases of dealing with a limited company the searchers should be asked if there has been any liquidator, receiver or administrator appointed, or if the company has been struck off for failure to lodge documents. The question of the 'gap' between the appointment of a liquidator or receiver, and the printing of the advertisement is dealt with at paragraph **7.35**.

(g) Receivers.   In this case the floating charge should be carefully inspected to see that it has been properly executed and registered in the Companies Register within 21 days of its registration in the Land Register or Sasine Register (a requirement of CA 1985, s 410 and CA 1989, s 95). It should also be checked to see that it includes the property purported to being sold. The deed by the receiver runs in the name of the company and the receiver and is signed as with a deed by a liquidator.

(h) Administrators. This order proceeds upon a court interlocutor which is registered in the Companies and Personal Registers. Again, a disposition by an administrator runs in the name of the company and the administrator, and is signed by the latter.

Discharge of securities

7.24 Bearing in mind the valuable protection afforded by CFR(S)A 1970, s 41(1) (see para **7.13**) it is important to check discharges which have been recorded within a five-year period. You should therefore check (1) the details of the discharge—does it fully discharge the obligation that was created?; (2) the form of the discharge; (3) the execution of the discharge; and (4) the recording of the discharge.

As to the form of the discharge, the required forms are:

(a) *Bond and disposition in security.* (C(S)A 1924, s 29 and Sch K(3)). This is a very simple form of discharge, and contains no conveyancing description of the property or reference to burdens.
(b) *Standard security.* The form is provided in the CFR(S)A 1970, Sch 4 and Form F. Again this is a simple form.
(c) *Ex facie absolute disposition in security.* This covert security may be discharged in one of two ways:
  (i) traditional method—a disposition back to the owner of the subjects, which takes the form of an ordinary disposition but which sets out in the narrative that the original disposition to the lenders was truly in security of a loan of £X which has now been repaid, and it is now 'right and proper' that the subjects be reconveyed. The lenders grant warrandice only from their own facts and deeds;
  (ii) shorter statutory method—CFR(S)A 1970, s 40 and Sch 9 provide for a short form of discharge, analogous to discharges (a) and (b). This has the effect (on being recorded) of disburdening the land and vesting the land in the person entitled to it.

Generally, it makes little difference which method is used. One school prefers to discharge securities in the manner in which they were created (*unumquodque eodem modo dissolvitur quo colligatur*); the other school prefers the shorter modern method.

In addition to being discharges, a security may also be partially discharged on part payment, or restricted to any part of the land, thereby freeing the remainder for sale. (For the appropriate forms see CFR(S)A 1970, Sch 4, Forms C and D.)

Fences, walls and gables

7.25 As a general rule, fences, walls and gables that lie between the properties of two persons are owned to the centre line by each proprietor, with each proprietor having an interest in the other half. It is possible, however, that the wall is owned jointly, in which case the boundary of each property is the nearest outside face of the wall, and the wall is jointly owned and maintained. Obviously this must be closely checked from the deeds.

When there is no adjoining proprietor, the wall, fence or gable is usually owned and maintained solely by the houseowner. It may be provided, however, that at a future date when someone builds on the adjoining property and uses that fence, wall or gable then that person should refund one-half of the cost of building to the person who paid for it and become partly responsible for its maintenance.

When acting for purchasers of a house, particularly a new one, you should ensure:

(1) that the fences or walls are in conformity with the feuing conditions;
(2) the exact ownership of the fences or walls; and
(3) that there are no outstanding charges for formation or maintenance of mutual fences, walls or gables.

Rivers and lochs

7.26   Where a property is bounded by a non-tidal river, and there is no specification of the boundary, this is taken to be the middle line (*medium filum*) of the river. This includes the fishing rights, excepting salmon fishing which must be specifically transferred to the purchasers (see *McKendrick v Wilson* 1970 SLT (Sh Ct) 39). The same applies to non-tidal lochs. Care should be taken when purchasing a riparian property that the landowner has not retained a narrow strip of land between the property purchased and the loch or river. If this is the case, the purchaser is not a riparian proprietor and has no rights in the loch or river.

This should have been checked before missives were concluded but better late than never.

Use

7.27   Many houses carry feuing conditions that prohibit certain uses: trade or business or profession. If your clients wanted the house for any particular business use you should really have cleared this up before completing missives. Even if your clients do not have a business use in mind, still note the restriction and inform your clients of it, in case at some time they want to pursue a business from the house. They will, of course, require to get a waiver from the superiors or (if no such waiver is forthcoming at a reasonable price) from the Lands Tribunal under CFR(S)A 1970, s 1. Older, redundant uses are now omitted from a land certificate in land registration. Another restriction that can occur is on keeping pets, and this must be cleared up, or much distress can be caused.

Feu duty

7.28   Feu duty may be allocated or unallocated. As a general rule, in Glasgow at least, detached, semi-detached and terraced houses have allocated feu duties, and flats in tenements have a *cumulo* feu duty (as defined in CFR(S)A 1970, s 3(2)) apportioned informally, without the consent of the superior, over the various flats (see ch 18).

When the feu duty is allocated it may have been redeemed previously, either voluntarily (Land Tenure Reform (Scotland) Act 1974, s 4) or compulsorily on a previous sale (LTR(S)A 1974, ss 5 and 6). If not, it must be redeemed by the sellers now, and a feu duty redemption receipt produced to the purchasers' agents (LTR(S)A 1974, s 5). When a local authority is compulsorily purchasing the property, the acquiring authority should redeem the feu duty (LTR(S)A 1974, s 6).

It is a major, and often very dangerous, misconception that the redemption of feu duty extinguishes the feudal relationship. This can only be achieved by purchasing the superiority and consolidating it with the feu (or vice versa). Redemption is purely the extinction of an annual payment; it does not otherwise affect the superior/feuar relationship (see para **7.5**). Redemption does not extinguish land obligations, but these may, however, be extinguished *confusione* by consolidation. The two transactions should be distinguished clearly.

An unallocated feu duty need not be redeemed, but it is a prime duty of the purchasers' solicitors to ensure that the feu duty has been fully paid up to date, otherwise purchasers may find themselves responsible for arrears not only of their own unallocated share, but also of the *cumulo* feu duty.

Provisions are made to rid Scotland of feu duties in the Abolition of Feudal Tenure etc (Scotland) Act 2000, but these provisions are not yet in force.

Clause of pre-emption

7.29   This clause gives a person who has sold land or buildings the choice to repurchase the first time they are resold. The duty to offer the land back now affects only the first sale after the commencement of the CFR(S)A 1970, and after the offer has been made and refused one time the right lapses (Conveyancing Amendment (Scotland) Act 1938, s 9, as amended by CFR(S)A 1970, s 46).

The price at which the property is to be offered back is usually the amount of the highest offer received from other parties, although occasionally the contracting parties may fix another price (for example, a price fixed at the date of agreement) in the contract containing the pre-emption clause.

From the sellers' point of view, a valid clause of pre-emption is particularly irksome, especially if they know that the right is to be exercised (say by a local authority who sold the land, but have now decided that they would like it back). The sellers must nonetheless go through the deception of a bona fide sale to establish the market value. The prospective purchasers are put to the trouble of obtaining a survey and submitting an offer. Yet if the sellers warn the purchasers of the true position, the sellers will not get a good offer for the superior to match.

The sole remedy of persons who have a right of pre-emption, which has not been observed, is to seek a court order to reduce the disposition granted without the right having been observed, and all other deeds flowing from it (see *Roebuck v Edmunds* 1992 SLT 1055).

The right of pre-emption is another point that should ideally be cleared up before missives are completed. If it is found that missives have been completed and that a pre-emption clause has been overlooked, the sellers cannot give a valid title without offering the property back to the person entitled to benefit from the clause. If that person then accepts the offer, the sellers will not be able to fulfil their part of the agreement to the purchasers and will be liable in damages.

It should be mentioned that, while the clause of pre-emption is a nuisance, it now only operates between the two contracting parties, and is not a perpetual nuisance as is the case with other land conditions and will not be affected by forthcoming legislation. If people do not like it, they should not have contracted for it.

Clause of redemption

7.30   This clause is similar in effect to the clause of pre-emption, but in this case the original owners may call for the land to be resold to them at any time they choose, and not just when a resale takes place.

In deeds executed after 1 September 1974 a clause of redemption is exercisable only within 20 years of its creation (LTR(S)A 1974, s 12). (The reason for this rather unexpected provision is to prevent owners circumventing the restriction on creation of residential leases for more than 20 years, by selling property subject to a redemption clause and then redeeming it some time after 20 years have expired.) You will not therefore see a redemption clause after 1974, but be carefully aware of such clauses granted before 1974!

Limited time for feudalising a personal right

7.31   A deed may provide that it shall only be a valid warrant for registration for a certain time. This is to ensure that feu grants (especially) are recorded quickly and the rights of both parties made real. If this provision is not followed to the letter, and a deed is recorded despite the ever-watchful eye of the Keeper of the Register, then the registration and all that follows it are invalid.

Property bought subject to lease

7.32   Most houses are bought with vacant possession, but occasionally a house may be sold subject to a tenancy (colloquially 'with a sitting tenant'). Indeed a house may be sold to the sitting tenant (particularly local authority housing under the Housing (Scotland) Act 1987) (see ch 18). Where a house has a sitting tenant under the old Rent Acts the price will be accordingly abated where that tenant enjoys security of tenure. The value is (very roughly) around 50–60% of the value of the same house sold with vacant possession, but it depends on the circumstances (compare ch 18).

The intending purchasers of a house with a sitting tenant should realise what they are taking on: rent regulations, security of tenure, etc. The purchasers do not of course get 'vacant possession' and the sellers' warrandice must exclude the lease from its scope ('and we grant warrandice subject to the Lease between us and (etc)').

Moveable effects contained in missives

7.33   When the purchasers of a house buy furniture and furnishings with that house, the purchasers' solicitors should ask the sellers to confirm that they own these effects, and that there are no outstanding hire purchase, credit sale, leasing or other debts, which would mean that the sellers do not own the moveables they have sold.

National House-Building Council

7.34 Most builders are registered members of the National House Builders Council (NHBC), and this implies that a certain standard of work may be expected from the registered builder. When a new house is built by a registered builder, the council will issue an agreement and certificate of registration. Ninety per cent of new houses in Scotland are covered by this scheme.

In the first two years of the certificate the builder (whom failing, through insolvency or any other reason, the council) is bound to make good any defect arising from a breach of NHBC requirements. This does not include, however, fair wear and tear and damage caused by shrinkage of plasterwork, cement and wood, as the house has a considerable water content which dries out when the house is occupied.

After two years and up to ten years, the builder (again whom failing, the council) is bound to make good any major defects in the structure. In inflationary times, the 'top-up cover' options should always be taken. This means that the cover will increase progressively over the years to meet the cost of any repair that may be required.

The registration certificate transmits automatically from owner to owner but the purchasers should ensure that this certificate is handed over to them at settlement.

Small builders, particularly in country areas, may not be registered with the council. This implies no disrespect to most of them, as a good small builder may not find it worthwhile to join the NHBC scheme. In such a case, however, the purchasers should get a certificate from a qualified architect who is covered by indemnity insurance and who was involved in the building at all stages, that the house is complete (see **23.11**).

Dealing with limited companies

7.35 Most limited liability companies are reputable, especially public limited companies which have to submit to very rigorous scrutiny, although they can quite suddenly get into serious financial difficulties. Unfortunately, however, not all limited companies are reputable, and it should never be forgotten that the forming of a limited company is a method of escaping unlimited personal liability in the event of liquidation. In terms of the Insolvency Act 1986, s 214, personal liability for a company's debts may be placed upon directors of a limited company where, before the commencement of the winding up of that company, they knew or ought to have concluded that there was no reasonable prospect that the company would avoid going into insolvent liquidation. Such personal liability was placed upon directors in *Re Produce Marketing Consortium Ltd (in liquidation)* ([1989] 3 All ER 1), but this may only be cold comfort for a disappointed creditor.

Some extra formalities are therefore required when dealing with companies, unless you are dealing with a company of outstanding quality. Such a company might rather resent being treated like a company, with two £1 shares issued, which was floated yesterday. This is a matter of personal judgment in all the circumstances, but you can never be wrong to ask.

There are a number of questions you should ask when purchasing, or taking security, from a limited company:

(i)   Has the company been properly incorporated and constituted? You do not want to buy property from a company that does not yet exist. This information may be received by instructing the searchers to search in the Companies Register. Further, is the company's name absolutely correct?

(ii)   Is the company incorporated in this country, and as such subject to the Companies Act 1985, and other company legislation and safeguards? This applies particularly to companies registered in the Isle of Man, the Channel Islands, the Cayman Islands and Gibraltar, which can have very British names, without having the protection of British law.

(iii) Is the company properly registered, and has it been dissolved by the Register of Companies without formal liquidation in terms of CA 1985, ss 652, 653 (formerly CA 1948, s 353)? If you buy property from a dissolved company the disposition is invalid, and your only remedy is to petition the court for a restoration of the company to the Register. A search can be obtained from the Register of Companies certifying that the company has been continuously registered.

(iv)   Has the company power in its memorandum to do what it proposes to do? This has not been so crucial since the passing of the European Communitites Act 1972, s 9 (now CA 1985, ss 35 and 36), but it is as well to see the memorandum and articles of the company and to ensure that the action proposed is *intra vires* (within the power of the company as opposed to *ultra vires*). This is of particular relevance in land registration (see chs 13 to 16).

(v)   *Floating charges and receiverships.*   Floating charges show up in a search in the Charges Register. A receivership is public knowledge which a solicitor should know. There exists the slight difficulty (see *Gibson v Hunter Home Designs Ltd* 1976 SC 23) that a deed has been recorded adversely, affecting the company's property, or that the company is no longer solvent, and that these events have occurred so recently that they have not been included in the search or advertised. In practical terms, and it is a practical problem, a personal warranty by the company's directors may be obtained (although there may be some resistance to this from the sellers' agents) in the terms following (adapted from JLSS Workshop 1):

'We, John Smith and Jane Smith both of 173 Cathedral Street, Glasgow, respectively a Director and the Secretary of Smiths Reciprocating Sprockets Limited (hereafter called "the Company"), HEREBY CERTIFY and WARRANT after due and diligent enquiry:

(i)   that no deeds of any kind which are capable of being recorded in the Land Register in respect of or affecting the subjects of sale have been granted by the company other than as were disclosed in the Search (including Interim Reports in the Search) in the Companies Register exhibited to the said Messrs Campbell, Kinloch & Co, and

(ii) that the Company is solvent and no steps have been or are about to be taken by us or any third party to commence liquidation proceedings which would prejudice the validity of the Disposition of the subjects of sale now being granted to Steelhenge Property Co Ltd, or to appoint a Receiver or otherwise place the company in a position whereby it cannot execute and deliver to you a valid and unobjectionable title.

We further agree and acknowledge that in the event of Steelhenge Property Co Ltd incurring any loss, damage or expense as a result of any of the matters included in this certificate and warranty being untrue or proving to be unfounded we shall be liable personally and individually, and jointly and severally, to make good all such loss, damage and expense to Steelhenge Property Co Ltd.

Yours faithfully,'

In addition, a letter of non-crystallisation should be obtained from the floating charge holder.

> CALEDONIAN BANK
> Westport
> Edinburgh EH1

The Directors
Smiths Reciprocating Sprockets Limited
173 Cathedral Street
Glasgow G4

Dear Sirs,

173 Cathedral Street, Glasgow

As holders of a Floating Charge over the whole assets of Smiths Reciprocating Sprockets Limited, dated 2nd July and registered 14th July 1986, we hereby confirm that:

(1) As at that date we have taken no steps to crystallise the said Floating Charge, and we shall take no steps to crystallise the said Floating Charge within 21 days from this date, nor take any steps to impede the purchasers from obtaining a valid and marketable recorded title to the property specified in the heading of this letter.

(2) We have no objection to the sale of the above building by Smiths Reciprocating Sprockets Limited.

(3) We shall take no steps to deprive Smiths Reciprocating Sprockets Limited of right validly to convey the said subjects, provided that the Disposition thereof is recorded in the Land Register within 22 days of this date.

Yours faithfully,

Although there is still some uncertainty about this matter, this letter should meet the difficulties raised in the case of *Sharp v Thomson* (1994 GWD 19–1181), discussed in an article by Richard Leggett, 1994 SLG 99.

Adjudication titles

7.36 An adjudication may be granted against a person who either (a) does not pay a debt or (b) contracts to sell property under missives and then refuses or delays to transfer the property.

In case (a) the title given is a security title only, and the debtor may redeem within 'the legal', which is a ten-year period from the date of decree. Such a title should not be accepted by a purchaser until the legal has lapsed.

In case (b) the title is absolute and may be accepted by a purchaser or a lender in security.

A decree of adjudication is equivalent to a conveyance of lands, and the creditor (or 'adjudger' to give the proper name) completes title by recording the decree in the Personal Register, and then using the decree as a link in title to expede a notice of title which is recorded in the Register of Sasines.

Extracts

7.37 The original being locked up in Register House, an extract from the Books of Council and Session has always had exactly the same status as the original. Prior to 1970 a sasine extract would only be accepted with great misgivings and an insurance indemnity, as the original had been returned to the presenter.

The CFR(S)A 1970, s 45 now provides that a sasine extract shall be accepted for all purposes as sufficient evidence of the contents of the original.

One cannot, however, help having slight misgivings about accepting a title entirely made up of extracts!

Contracts of ground annual

7.38 This hybrid document, which perpetrated a legal fiction, was created to get around the restriction against owners of property in Royal burghs from granting feus, or where there was a restriction in a feu grant on the feuar sub-feuing part of the property. The granting of feus in burgage property became competent by C(S)A 1874, s 25. The provisions against subinfeudation were repealed by CA(S)A 1938, s 8, and it is no longer possible to create ground annuals (annual payments similar in form but not in nature to feu duties) by LTR(S)A 1974, s 2. The point of granting a contract of ground annual these days is therefore small, although the practice can still occasionally be found to preserve uniformity in selling off flats in a tenement.

Contracts of ground annual, however, contained land obligations and must still be referred to for this purpose. Further, an annual payment in perpetuity was created, which can or must be redeemed in the same way as an annual feu duty (LTR(S)A 1974, ss 4–6) if it is allocated. The form of the deed is a disposition by the granter ('creditor') to the grantee ('debtor') in return for certain obligations running with the land and the ground annual. In security of these obligations, the debtor then grants a disposition in security back to the creditor. The remedies of the creditor are more or less the same as those of a superior, including irritancy, which is the most important.

The contract of a ground annual is therefore both a transfer of land and a security deed—a clumsy deed that we can do well without, but which must still be treated with respect.

Power of attorney

7.39   A power of attorney is granted by a person who, for any reason (be it illness or absence abroad or any other reason), is unable to deal with his or her affairs either temporarily or permanently. This person is known as 'the constituent' and the power is granted in favour of another person or persons known as 'the attorney'. The important point is that the power must contain an exact specification of the act or acts that are permitted to the attorney. Unlike a will, no powers are vested in the attorney by law. Thus, if a power does not give the attorney power to sign a disposition of heritable property, for example, then no such power exists, and the power is valueless for that purpose. Obviously, therefore, where a deed is granted by an attorney, the conveyancer must ensure that the terms of this deed were permitted by the power.

A power of attorney may be either in general terms, empowering the attorney to do literally anything, or it may be in particular terms, empowering the attorney to do only one thing, such as to sell a house. An example of such a power is as follows:

> 'I, (name and designation), CONSIDERING that I am about to be absent from the United Kingdom and temporarily absent abroad and to facilitate the management and sale of subjects at (specify property to be sold), owned by me it is convenient that I should grant a Power of Attorney and having full trust and confidence in the integrity and competence of (name and design Attorney) THEREFORE I appoint the said (name) as my Attorney with full power to enter into any agreement for the sale of the said subjects and to sign all conveyances and other documents related thereto on my behalf and from the proceeds of sale to discharge any standard security or other form of security in connection therewith and to sign any documents related thereto; Thereafter from the net free proceeds of sale, to settle all expenses legally incurred in connection with the sale and generally to do whatever in his discretion my Attorney may think expedient for enforcing, carrying out and settling the said transaction; And I further grant to my said Attorney power to employ the firm of (name and design) to attend to the legal matters arising from the said sale; And I further authorise my Attorney to institute on my behalf, pursue to finality, defend, compromise, all and any suits or actions, disputes or differences arising from the execution of these presents or otherwise affecting me or my property; And I do hereby ratify and confirm and hereby promise to ratify, allow and confirm all and whatsoever my Attorney shall lawfully do or cause to be done in the premises in virtue hereof without prejudice always to my right demand just count and reckoning with me for the whole intromissions of my Attorney in terms hereof; And I declare that this Power of Attorney shall subsist until the same is recalled in writing; And I consent to registration hereof for preservation: IN WITNESS WHEREOF.'

A power of attorney may now be 'continuing', that is to say it continues after the constituent has become incapacitated. This has the tremendous advantage that a *curator bonis* does not have to be appointed, and the administration becomes much easier. On the other hand, it presents a temptation, for there is no real control over the attorney. For that reason the Law Society is very vigilant about solicitors who are appointed attorneys, and it is recommended that if an alternative person is available to act as attorney, then the solicitor should not be involved, except as agent for the attorney.

The Adults with Incapacity (Scotland) Act 2000 places all continuing powers of attorney under the supervision of the public guardian at Callander Park in Falkirk. Regulations have been made to ensure that these continuing powers are signed and used properly.

When a deed is signed under a power of attorney, it is signed by the attorney. The narrative of that deed may either (a) run in the name of the attorney narrating the power, and state in the testing clause that it is signed by the named attorney; or (b) run in the name of the constituent without mentioning the power, and then state in the testing clause that it is signed by the attorney on behalf of the constituent, by virtue of the power, which is then specified. Either method may be used, but in both cases the power of attorney must be produced with the deed to authorise the signature of the attorney.

Uninfeft granters of deeds

7.40   You do not need to have a recorded title (or 'be infeft') to grant many deeds, in terms of C(S)A 1924, s 13, which allows an uninfeft granter to grant certain deeds using a mid-couple or link in title (see para **7.14**). Certain deeds, by virtue of not being mentioned, do not come into this category. Among the most important are feu charters, feu dispositions, feu contracts, and deeds of conditions. If they are not granted by an infeft owner, they are inept, and the important conditions that they contain are not applicable. This is not a difficult mistake to make, but it can be an embarrassing and costly one.

The remedy is for the granter to expede a notice of title, record it, and the defect is cured by accretion. The damage may, however, be done by then.

7.41   These are some of the major points to be kept in view when examining and there are many more that could be mentioned! In a routine house purchase, however, there should not be too many other points which occur regularly. If you know of any that I have missed please do not hesitate to let me know.

Remedies for an unmarketable title

7.42   The purchasers are of course entitled to resile if presented with an unmarketable title, but we will presume that the purchasers and sellers are both keen to complete the purchase. There are many varied ways of reaching settlement, but the following should be considered:

(a) Disposition *per incuriam*.   If a disposition has a bad mistake in it, for example you sell the flat '1/right' instead of '1/left', which is probably the commonest conveyancing mistake, you can grant this form of disposition. It simply narrates that *per incuriam* you have sold the wrong flat, and then goes on to dispone the correct one. The use of the Latin tag hides the fact that it was done (literally) 'by mistake'!

(b) By skilful use of the Conveyancing (Scotland) Act 1874, ss 38 and 39 (now the Requirements of Writing (Scotland) Act 1995, ss 4 and 5). All manner of defects of execution and mistakes in the deed can be rectified by careful use of the provisions of these sections.

(c) By use of the Law Reform (Miscellaneous Provisions) (Scotland) Act 1985, s 8(1)(a). This useful provision of law allows a disposition to be rectified by the court if it does not reflect the agreement in missives.

(d) Positive and negative prescription. You should bear in mind that prescription cures all blemishes if it is appropriate.

(e) The Keeper's discretion. In land registration cases the Keeper has absolute discretion to record what he wants. Thus, for example, he keeps an 'elastic tape measure' for wrong measurements, which are not too wrong. Similarly he will turn a blind eye to other blemishes of title, which therefore disappear through not being shown on the land certificate. The only trouble is he will not tell you what he proposes to do, and turning a blind eye to something once does not mean that he will do it again. There is no doubt that judicious use of this power has made life much easier for conveyancers in operational areas for registration.

(f) The insurance indemnity. An indemnity policy can be taken out to cover a defect in title, which recompenses the purchaser if a claim arises from a third party. One insurance company advertises indemnity policies available against: absence of matrimonial affidavit, giving rise to a claim by a non-entitled spouse; *a non domino* disposition, where there is a claim by the true owner within the prescriptive period; failure to establish a link in title; lack of access rights; burdens imposed on the feu, and a possible claim by the superior when they have been contravened without having been discharged; discrepancies in the description of land and incorrect detailing of plans. A purchaser is not, however, obliged to accept an indemnity, as it does not render a title marketable. It is only an indemnity until prescription extends its healing balm.

(g) The *actio quanti minoris*. This remedy, which is now available automatically in terms of the Contract (Scotland) Act 1997, unless specifically excluded by contract, involves a reduction of the price where there is something wrong in the title of the subjects.

(h) *De minimis non curat lex*. ('The law does not care about little things'). Try and persuade the purchaser that no court would accept the objection to your defective title!

Chapter 8

NOTES ON TITLE, SEARCHES, REPORTS, OBLIGATIONS AND DRAFTS

'The Registers are public and so, in theory, anyone can search there. In practice, legal searches are done by firms of professional searchers, who guarantee the accuracy of their reports. Their services are generally swift, efficient and inexpensive, and they play a vital part in conveyancing practice. They offer searches in all the registers, including the Land Register. Register House staff provide searches in the Land Register, but not in the Sasine Register, except in connection with first registrations.'

(Conveyancing by Professors Gretton and Reid (2nd edn, 1999).

Notes on title

8.1 Formerly notes on title were a vital part of the conveyancing process. If a legal firm received a bundle of title deeds, a person (usually an apprentice) was set to noting title. This was a clause by clause analysis of all the deeds in the bundle. The object was to ensure that the title was a marketable one, that a report on title could be sent to the client setting out the salient points, and that observations on title could be sent to the other solicitor. The notes on title thus prepared were perused by a partner, or (more terrifying) by a senior conveyancing clerk, who approximated to a regimental sergeant-major in the army, and who did not spare the comments.

In former days the prescriptive period was longer (reduced from 20 to ten years in 1970) and thus a longer title had to be noted. Many of the modern dispensations did not exist. In particular, old deeds, referred to for descriptions or for the burdens they contained, were long, often handwritten in spidery writing, fragile, and of very doubtful hygienic quality. Yet every word had to be considered, and the deed analysed so that nothing was missed.

Finally when the transaction was settled, the notes were bound into a volume and indexed, for the benefit of succeeding generations.

With the almost universal adoption of registration of title, noting title is a much simplified procedure. The usual practice is to read through the land and charge certificates, and the reports, take from them the information that is required, and report accordingly to the client and to the other side raising observations. The certificates and reports are then photocopied and the copies retained on file, in case the property is resold before the present owner gets a registered title, or in case further observations as to title should be raised.

The Land Register system takes away the *caveat emptor* (buyer beware) responsibility of the purchasers' solicitor, and places it on the shoulders of the sellers' solicitor, and the Keeper, who is said to act as would a competent solicitor. Professional pride dictates, however, that the purchasers' solicitor does not send the Keeper a defective title, so the title should be examined fairly carefully, and that observations be made on any detected deficiencies before the title is sent to the Keeper.

Further, many of the matters that were formerly contained in a bundle of title deeds, are now contained in the certificates, with the property being clearly defined on an Ordnance Survey map, and the relevant burdens clearly printed, with all excess verbiage removed. Thus prohibitions on boiling glue and cudbear (whatever that is), lengthy directions as to how the road shall be built, when it has been built for years and is maintained by the local council, details of long-redeemed feu duties, and prohibitions against having grain ground anywhere but the local mill, feudal casualties (abolished in 1914), prohibitions against subinfeudation (abolished in 1874), and real warrandice (abolished in 1924) all are simply left out of the land certificate, and thus disappear forever. In the unlikely event of anyone being damaged by the omission, the Keeper will compensate them. Examples of such compensation being paid were where a land certificate in Glasgow omitted to mention a the right of third parties not to have an area of ground built on, and the third parties thereby suffered a diminution in value of their property; and where a land certificate in Lanarkshire failed to repeat the existence of a leasehold casualty (a quite different proposition from a feudal casualty) costing the person formerly entitled to enforce it a large sum of money, which the Keeper had to pay.

Examples of notes on title are given in previous editions of this book, but these are not reprinted in this edition as land registration has largely taken over from sasine registration in the intervening period. The need not to note title in any detail represents a considerable saving in work, for which a corresponding reduction of the fee is justified, as was foreseen by the Reid Committee and subsequent Keeper's reports.

Searches

8.2   The search or report from the searchers is an indispensable part of any conveyancing transaction (see the quotation at the head of this chapter). Conveyancers depend on the searchers, who mainly provide an invaluable service, although as in all human endeavour, mistakes can occasionally occur. Searchers carry a great deal of insurance against such an eventuality.

The search is found only in sasine registration, and for that reason, it is becoming very much less common. However, as the Keeper points out in his report for 2001–02, sasine registration remains competent for security transactions when the title is not land registered, as the deed is not granted for valuable consideration. Thus, principally through the growth in remortgage and refinancing transactions the number of sasine registrations remained pretty steady at 123,800 for the year. Thus, the requirement for an old search is not finished yet. Further the principles of searching are repeated in the modern reports 10A, 11A, 12A, and 13A.

In sasine registration the search has two aspects, or four where a company is involved: property, personal, charges and companies.

Property search (General Register of Sasines)

8.3   The search in the Property Register discloses a note of the salient details (parties, dates, and a brief description of the deed, together with the date of recording). The register is maintained at Meadowbank House, where originally the deeds were stored, but records are now mainly kept on microfilm, and deeds are registered with frame and fiche numbers, instead of volume and folio (i e page) numbers. This enables the deeds to be very quickly accessed. Indices are also kept of properties and persons transacting with properties, and these are extensively used by searchers in preparing searches.

The register may also be accessed through Registers Direct, which service is obtainable through the Marketing Department of the Registers (telephone: 0131 200 3946/7 or email: sales@ros.gov.uk).

The abridged details of all deeds registered in the Sasine Register are given: names and designations of parties, short details of the property, dates of signing and recording date. The search will not disclose the following details: deeds not recorded in this register, e g confirmations; servitudes informally created and not created by recorded deed; details of company liquidations, receiverships and administrations; leases not recorded, particularly short leases for less than 20 years which cannot be recorded; planning notices unless recorded; or old heritable securities kept alive by payments of interest.

Although financial details of securities and their transmissions are given in the search, property prices are not given. This information can be found from the deeds themselves or from another source, e g an index of property prices prepared from details in the register prepared by the Royal Institution of Chartered Surveyors.

A solicitor for a purchaser, or more importantly in post-registration days, a lender, should see a search in this register for a 40-year period. The reason for this lengthy search is that a security may have been created many years ago, and have been kept alive by payments of interest, which defeats the operation of prescription. It is thought that if you search back for 40 years, there will be some evidence of the existence of this security, which enables it to be dealt with (the security itself, an assignation, a restriction, a discharge or partial discharge).

One complaint frequently made against the Sasine Register was that the register was slow in preparation, thus leaving a significant gap between the most recent search available and the date of sale. In this gap period, an inhibition could be placed against the seller, and this would not show in the search available at settlement. This was the case with so-called 'double glazing' securities. A seller of the property would borrow money, and would sign, probably unwittingly, a standard security over the property. This security was then recorded in the gap period, and would not show up at settlement. When the search was finally made available, after settlement, the security would show up, and it would have to be dealt with (see *Beneficial Bank plc v Bennett* 1995 SCLR 284 and para 8.X).

Even worse, a dishonest seller could go to another solicitor, and say he had lost the title deeds. Extracts would then be ordered and a second sale of the property could be completed by the solicitor, in all innocence, in the gap period. Fortunately this was pretty rare.

In order to cut down the gap period, the Keeper introduced computerised presentment, to run as a trial, in tandem with the more traditional presentment book. This entails optical scanning of special presentment forms. If a search is requested in the computerised presentment book, it is much more up to date than a search in the traditional book. It is not, however, as yet, guaranteed by the Keeper. Nevertheless it is well worth requesting.

Personal search (Register of Inhibitions and Adjudications)

8.4   The Register of Inhibitions and Adjudications is regulated in terms of the Conveyancing (Scotland) Act 1924, although its origins are much more ancient. It is stated at section 44 of the 1924 Act to be a register of 'Inhibitions, Interdictions, Adjudications, Reductions and Notices of Litigiosity' which is a rather more explicit definition of the functions of this useful register. In short it gives details of any action taken against a person that would restrict their freedom to transact with their heritable property, on a voluntary basis. As any action of this nature would render a disposition or security granted over this property invalid, it is therefore important for any solicitor to consult this register in every purchase or security transaction involving the property.

8.5   (a) Inhibitions   An inhibition is an order of court which prevents the person inhibited from dealing with their property on a voluntary basis. The theory of this order is to preserve a debtor's estate.

An inhibition may be obtained in any action either (i) on the dependence of the action or (ii) in implement of a decree granted in the action. Although it is a Court of Session process, an inhibition may be obtained in a sheriff court action, if the sheriff gives leave to inhibit. Letters of inhibition may be obtained through the Petition Department of the Court of Session, and it is usual for a firm outside Edinburgh to use an Edinburgh agent to obtain these letters.

An inhibition on the dependence of an action may be obtained in any action of a pecuniary nature, and it means that the inhibition takes immediate effect although the action has not yet been heard. The court action then takes place, and if the defender is successful, the inhibition then is recalled. The only other method of recalling an inhibition is to lodge caution in court for the amount of the action. Unfortunately this process is often used by a creditor with a poor case, as a form of blackmail to bring a settlement. The debtors have their assets bound up for the length of the court action, which may be several years, and in any application for credit, the matter of the inhibition will be brought up. Bankers do not like their customers to be inhibited. It was held in *Karl Construction Ltd v Palisade Properties* 2002 SLT 312 that inhibitions or arrestments on the dependence, granted as a matter of course by sheriff clerks, were an infringement of human rights, under the European Convention. Thus warrant to inhibit on the dependence will now only be granted by a sheriff, who has heard why the action is considered necessary. If it turns out that an inhibition is raised unnecessarily, the person who raised it may be liable in damages. This should reduce the blackmail element.

An inhibition stops any transfer of or security over the debtors' property from being granted by the debtor. If, however, the debtor was under an obligation to grant the deed, it is however permissible to do so, despite the inhibition. Thus, if debtors had entered into missives the week before the inhibition, they would be under an obligation to grant the disposition, and would do so. Similarly, if the debtors entered into a loan agreement the week before, the obligation to grant the security would remain and be allowed. If, however, the obligations arose after the inhibition was placed, they are too late.

A purchaser should not, in any circumstances, accept a disposition where the granter is inhibited. The deed and everything that follows is invalid, and the title is utterly unmarketable. It is for this reason that it is so important to consult this register. If the debtors present a disposition granted under an obligation, prior to the disposition, to grant that disposition, that obligation must be proved to the creditor. If it is proved, the deed may be accepted. On this topic see the cases of *Newcastle Building Society v White* 1987 SLT (Sh Ct) 81 and *McGowan v A Middlemas & Sons Ltd* 1977 SLT (Sh Ct) 41.

When a warrant to inhibit on the dependence is presented at the Petition Department a preliminary acknowledgment of the arrestment is issued. A notice of this action must then be registered in the Personal Register in the form of the Titles to Land Consolidation (Scotland) Act 1868, Sch PP, This notice shall read: 'Notice of letters of inhibition (or of summons containing inhibition as the case may be), AB (design) against CD (design). Signeted (insert date of signeting).'

When the formal letters of inhibition are received, prepared in accordance with the Rules of the Court of Session 1994, these then are registered in the Personal Register. If these are registered within 21 days of the notice, then the inhibition is valid from the date of notice; if the notice is not registered the effective date of the inhibition is registration of the letters of inhibition; and if the letters are not registered within 21 days of the notice, then the notice becomes invalid and the whole matter must be recommenced. Obviously it is important to ensure that registration is made within 21 days, and for a purchaser or lender to make sure that this is done properly.

If the action is settled it will be a term of settlement that the pursuer shall withdraw the inhibition by a formal discharge, which is recorded in the Personal Register. Otherwise the inhibition may be recalled by the court, which is noted in the margin of the register. Further an inhibition prescribes after five years, and is of no further use unless it is renewed, which is thought to be rare. This prescriptive period should not be confused with the 10-year prescriptive period applicable to heritable deeds. We shall return to prescriptive periods under searching procedures.

Inhibitions cover only property owned by the debtor at the time of the inhibition. Property subsequently acquired (known as *acquirenda*) is not affected. Thus, if an inhibition is placed against A on 1 August, and A acquires property on 7 August, the inhibition does not affect the acquired property.

8.6 (b) Adjudications An adjudication is an active diligence which transfers heritable property to a person in implement of a court decree. It is not widely used, for an adjudication title may be redeemed within a ten-year period, known as 'the legal', and the property is unmarketable within the legal. In a recent case, gleaned from the tabloid press, a wife was granted decree of divorce with aliment payable by the husband. He paid nothing, and to add insult to injury he bought a house in Aberdeen, and installed his partner there. The wife found out and raised an action of adjudication, which was successful, in that the house was adjudicated to her.

A notice of adjudication requires to be lodged in the Personal Register in terms of Titles to Land Consolidation (Scotland) Act 1868, Sch RR, as amended by the Law Reform (Miscellaneous Provisions) (Scotland) Act 1985, Sch 2, para 5. This notice has the effect of rendering the property litigious from the date of registration of the notice.

8.7 (c) Reductions There may be objections to a deed because it was granted as a result of fraud, or essential error, or force and fear, facility and circumvention, undue influence, want of title, power to grant or of the requisite solemnities, or minority and lesion. In any of these cases the deed may be reduced, if the allegations can be proved. This makes the title, and all that flows from it, thoroughly unmarketable. Persons dealing with the owner will want to know if the title offered is about to be reduced, and will do so by looking in the register. They may see a notice in terms of Schedule RR, and obviously, again, this is vital information.

8.8 (d) Bankruptcies Bankruptcies in Scotland are regulated by the Bankruptcy (Scotland) Act 1985, as amended by the Bankruptcy (Scotland) Act 1993. The terms of these Acts replaced the Bankruptcy (Scotland) Act 1913, which, however, still governs bankruptcies arising before 1 April 1986.

Under the 1985 Act, the Accountant in Bankruptcy replaces the Accountant of Court. The Accountant's general function is defined in notes issued by the Accountant as 'the exercise of overall supervision of the administration of sequestrations and the conduct of those involved in that administration'. These notes, which appear in the *Parliament House Book* (W Green), should be carefully studied by all practising in this field.

Concerning conveyancing, the 1985 Act requires registration in the Personal Register of certain events affecting the capacity of the bankrupt, as follows:

(i)   a certified copy of the award of sequestration by the court (s 14(2)). The date of the order is the date of sequestration, and as it operates as an inhibition on the bankrupt's heritable property, the bankrupt loses control of the heritage from that date;
(ii)   a certified copy order of court refusing an award of seuestration (s 15(5)(a));
(iii) a certified copy order recalling an award of sequestration (s 17(8)(a));
(iv)   a certified copy of discharge of bankrupt (Sch 4, para 11);
(v)   a certified copy order deferring discharge of the debtor beyond the normal three-year period (s 54(7)).

These notices are registered to provide public notification of the event concerned, and the Register requires to be consulted for these notices. It should be noted that the normal period of bankruptcy is three years, and not five years, as was suggested by the Scottish Law Commission, to coincide with the short prescriptive period.

8.9 (e) English bankruptcies   These are governed by the Insolvency Act 1986. Where an English bankrupt owns heritable property in Scotland, an order for the adjudication of the bankrupt and appointment of a trustee is certified in the Petition Department of the Court of Session. This is then registered in the Personal Register.

The Personal Register is computerised and the information contained is more or less up to date. The computer also searches against all names which either look the same or sound the same as the one you are enquiring about. Thus, if you ask for a search against John Smith it will also search against Smyths and Smythes.

There are, however, limits to the computer's cleverness, which were exposed in the case of *Atlas Appointments v Tinsley* (1997 SC 200). A search was requested against Stephen John Tinsley, but it showed no entries against him. The software had, however, failed to pick up an inhibition against 'Steve Tinsley', although apparently the software would have picked up the inhibition in a search against 'S Tinsley'. This case shows the importance of asking for a search accurately against the person, and all known variants of the name.

Particular care must be taken over names derived from a foreign language, where the first name and the surname often appear in a different order from the established practice in this country.

Register of Charges and Companies Register

8.10   This register is only used when title is taken from a limited company, a public limited company or a limited liability partnership (LLP). The Register of Charges was established by the Companies (Floating Charges) (Scotland) Act 1961, s 6, was continued by the Companies (Floating Charges and Receivers) (Scotland) Act 1972, s 6, and the provisions of these Acts were then consolidated in the Companies Act 1985, Pt XVIII and the Insolvency Act 1986. Limited liability partnerships were established by the Limited Liability Partnership Act 2000, and the Limited Liability Partnerships (Scotland) Regulations 2001 authorised LLPs to grant floating charges.

Since 27 October 1961, the date of inception of the Register, it has been necessary for limited companies to lodge details with the the Register of Charges of all charges created by them, and secured over their assets. This includes such things as standard securities over heritable property; floating charges over any of the assets of the company, heritable or moveable, or both; debenture issues secured over company assets; and mortgages of ships and aeroplanes. Standard securities must first be registered in the Land Register or Register of Sasines, and a note of the date of registration should be received from the Keeper. From that date, you have 21 days to lodge particulars and a copy of the security with the Register of Charges.

If you fail to do this, the standard security then only ranks as an ordinary debt in competition with the liquidator. This is a great source of professional liability claims. You have been warned! The only remedies for a charge that has not been properly registered are (i) start again, but valuable time is lost; or (ii) petition the court to allow late registration, and be prepared for sarcastic remarks from the bench and your clients, and of course time has been lost, again.

The Register of Charges is not kept at Meadowbank House, but at Companies House, 37 Castle Terrace, Edinburgh EH1 2EB (www.companieshouse.gov.uk). Separate instructions for search are not however necessary, and instructions can be appended to a memorandum for search. Additionally it may be advisable to search fiches G and AR in the Companies Register. The former is a general register which gives information about the company, including, crucially, whether it has been put into liquidation, receivership, or administration. In that case you cannot deal with the directors.

Worst of all, this register may contain information which indicates that the company has been struck off the register for failing to lodge annual returns and other documents. In that case, you must petition to re-enrol the company, lodge all missing documents and pay the fees for these, ignore unconstructive comments from the bench, and deal with the Queen's and Lord Treasurer's Remembrancer (QLTR) at the Crown Office, to get the property back. On the company being struck off the register, it ceases to exist, and its property passes to the QLTR as *res nullius*. This is all very expensive and time consuming.

The AR fiche contains details of the directors and secretary of the company, and thus indicates who may, and who may not, sign deeds on its behalf. Companies should keep these details up to date.

Searching procedures

8.11   Property Register   It is usual to see a search for 40 years in the Property Register. The 40-year period is an arbitary one. It is thought that an old security over the property, which has not prescribed, because payments of interest have kept it alive, will show up—in some shape or form—in a 40-year search. It may be an assignation of the security, a partial discharge or restriction, a partial or total discharge, or a transmission upon death of the creditor.

If a 40-year search is not seen, and a security turns up, the purchaser's solicitor is responsible for clearing the register of the security. Further the indemnity policy restricts cover in these circumstances. If, however, a 40-year search is taken, and a security turns up later, the indemnity insurers will pay for the security to be cleared, because the solicitor took all reasonable steps to find out about this.

A seller's solicitor is only obliged to exhibit a 40-year search, and the purchaser's solicitor is only obliged to examine a similar search. If, however, a longer search is given, a quick look beyond the 40-year period is always justified. You never know what you will find.

8.12   Personal search   You should search against every party who had a right to the property in the ten-year prescriptive period. The search should be for a five-year period up to the date when each party sold the property. The reason for this is to ascertain whether the person was under an inhibition, or similar litigiosity (see para 8.4) which would prevent them from selling the property. In that case, the deed they granted, and all following it, are invalid, and the whole title is unmarketable.

Thus if you have the following situation:

A sold the house to B on 5 July 1995;
B sold the house to C on 6 November 1997;
C died and confirmation was granted to X his executor on 7 April 1998;
X sold the house to D on 10 August 1998.

You would then require to see a search in the Personal Register as follows:

Against A from 5 July 1990 to 5 July 1995;
Against B from 6 November 1992 to 6 November 1997;
Against C from 7 April 1993 to 7 April 1998 (date of confirmation);
Against X from 7 April 1998 (confirmation) to 10 August 1998 (sale).

8.13   Charges Register and Companies Register   These registers are only used where property is being acquired from a limited company, a public limited company or a limited liability partnership (LLP). The Charges Register was inaugurated on 27 October 1961 in terms of the Companies (Floating Charges) (Scotland) Act 1961, later amended by the Companies (Floating Charges and Receivers) (Scotland) Act 1972. The law is now consolidated in the Companies Act 1985, Pt XVIII and the Insolvency Act 1986. Limited liability partnerships are allowed by the Limited Liability Partnership Act 2000, and by the Limited Liability Partnership (Scotland) Regulations 2001, to execute floating charges.

The purpose of the register is to present an accurate picture of company borrowings on the security of their assets, which may be examined by any member of the public. Companies must lodge details of standard securities created over the heritable property, floating charges, secured over any assets of the company, heritable, moveable, or both, debentures secured on company property, and mortgages of ships and aeroplanes.

In the case of standard securites, the security is first registered in the Land Register or Sasine Register, as appropriate. Confirmation of the date of recording (or technically 'creation') is received from the Keeper. There are then 21 days from the date of creation for the company to lodge particulars and a copy of the standard security in the Charges Register. If this is not done within 21 days, the standard security is then not a preferential security over heritable property, and ranks only as an ordinary debt. The only options open are (i) to start the security process again, thus losing valuable time or (ii) to petition the court to allow late registration. The latter course will entail lost time and expense, to say nothing of unkind words from the bench and from the client. An action for professional negligence will probably ensue for recovery of losses. And there is little answer to this. You have been warned!

The register is not kept at Meadowbank House but at Companies House, 37 Castle Terrace, Edinburgh EH1 2EB (website www.companieshouse.gov.uk). Separate instruction for search are not however necessary. You simply add a note to the instructions requesting a charges and company registers search against the company involved.

It is usual to search the G and AR fiches as well. The former is a register of general information about the company, such as is it in liquidation, receivership or administration? Or, even worse, has it been struck off by the Registrar for failing to lodge annual returns or meet other requirements? In that case you will be dealing with a company that does not exist, and whose assets pass as *res nullius* to the Queen's and Lord Treasurers Remembrancer (QLTR) at the Crown Office.

In that event you will have to (i) petition the court for re-enrolment of the company; (ii) lodge all missing returns and notices; (iii) pay all outstanding fees; and (iv) deal with the QLTR to get the assets back. Again, an expensive and embarrassing process, accompanied by much ribaldry from the bench, who is only glad to have escaped from day-to-day practice, if this is what it means.

The AR return is culled from the annual returns of the company and other notices. From this you can find out who are the directors and secretary of the company and who are entitles to sign deeds on its behalf, and who are not. You can also find out from the Companies Register important facts such as the exact name of the company, for only that will do; and if the company is truly registered in Scotland. While this information may sound rather trite, it is very important to check.

8.14 Searching procedure Most of Scotland is now under land registration, but by no means all titles are land registered. In particular companies are long-term holders of property, and the necessity to register title on a sale of property seldom arises. If securities are granted, they are not treated as being for valuable consideration, and are thus not registered in the Land Register, but in the Sasine Register. The Keeper's Report for 2001/02 reveals that the amount of sasine registration deeds remained pretty steady at 123,800, largely as a result of remortgages by householders who did not have registered titles and refinancings by companies.

While sasine registration procedures are not being dealt with in this edition, it is expedient to deal with searching procedures when a new loan is being taken, as this is the major exception from the onward sweep of land registration. Thus, the lender to a limited company which is borrowing on its assets should see a search covering:

(a) in the Property Register a 40 year search;
(b) in the Personal Register against the borrower and predecessors in title in the prescriptive period for five years against each proprietor up to their date of sale or granting a security;
(c) in the Charges Register a search from the date of inception of the register (27 October 1961) or the date of the subsequent incorporation of the company;
(d) a search in the G and AR fiches against the company.

In the case of an unincorporated body or a person, only the first two steps are necessary.

Example

8.15   Q. Messrs Stacey and Tracey are acting for the Bank of Scotia, which is lending money to Weegy Widgets. The company owns heritable property over which it is granting a standard security to the bank. It is also granting a floating charge to the bank over all its assets, heritable and moveable. Draft a memorandum for search to the searchers.

A.

MEMORANDUM for SEARCH

Against

300 Polmadie Street, Glasgow G31 55XX

And against
Weegy Widgets having their Registered Office at
300 Polmadie Street, Glasgow

I.   Search in the Property Register against

300 Polmadie Street, Glasgow G31 55XX

For FORTY years to date of sasine Certificate (to disclose recording of Standard Security by Weegy Widgets Limited in favour of Scotia Bank Limited.)

II   Search in the Personal Register against

WEEGY WIDGETS LIMITED 300 Polmadie Street, Glasgow G31 55XX

For FIVE years to date of Sasine Certificate

II.   Search in the Charges Register

Against the said Weegy Widgets Limited from the date of inception of the register to date of sasine certificate

III.   Search in the G and AR fiches against the said Weegy Widgets Limited.

Notes:
1.   The searchers are asked to confirm that the the company searched against has not been struck off the register.

2. The searchers are asked also to search to the latest date in the Computerised Presentment Book.
3. Please send Interim Report and note of account to Stacey and Tracey, 130 St. Vincent Street, Glasgow.

In the event of a search being presented to Stacey and Tracey, they would prepare a Memorandum for Continuation of Search to bring the search up to the standard requested above.

The registers may also be accessed directly through Registers Direct, a service provided by the Registers of Scotland. To make further enquiries about this, and to enrol, contact the Marketing Department, telephone 0131 200 3946 or by e mail at sales@ros.gov.uk.

Reports

8.16 The system of land registration embodies the searching techniques out-lined above, with a more modern approach. If the land is not yet registered, and you are looking for a search report, you instruct it on a Form 10, and get in reply a Form 10A report. If you wish to continue the report up to the date of settlement, you use a Form 11, and get back a Form 11A report. If the land is already registered, you seek a search by a Form 12 and get back a Form 12A report, and the continuation is obtained by sending a Form 13, and getting a reply on a Form 13A.

There is no necessity to draft a memorandum, you merely complete a form, and many of your requirement will be met merely by completing the appropriate form. Thus, if you send a Form 10 you will get back a Form 10A which provides:

(a) a search in the Personal Register against the last owner for five years to the date of the certificate, and a similar search against other persons named by you, and designed (see para XX and the remarks therein);
(b) a list of deeds recorded within the ten year prescriptive period;
(c) a statement of securities within 40 years prior to the date of certificate and for which no final discharge has been recorded. This meets the difficulty mentioned in paragraph XX;
(d) a statement of discharge of securities within the five years prior to the date of certificate;
(e) deeds other than transfers or deeds creating or effecting securities recorded within the 40 years prior to the date of certificate. This covers any mis-cellaneous deeds such as planning agreements or tree preservation orders.

The details given are very short, such as 'Disposition to John Smith (date of recording).' An example of these Forms is given at the end of this chapter.

Letters of obligation

8.17 The Personal and Charges Registers are kept up to date, but the Land Register and the Sasine Registers both tend to be not entirely up to date, and there is a problem with the gap. This problem is discussed at paragraph **8.3**. Strenuous attempts have been made to cut down this gap, and these have been successful, particularly in land registration where the gap is only a few days. Nevertheless the problem remains, and it is a probably an endemic problem. It is met by the seller's solicitor granting a letter of obligation to the purchaser's solicitor.

8.18   The wording of the letter in a first registration is:

Dear Sirs

Subjects:

With reference to the settlement of this transaction today, we hereby:

1. Undertake to clear the records of any deed, decree or diligence (other than such as may be created by or against your clients) which may be recorded in the Personal Register or to which effect may be given in the Land Register in the period from   (date of last search report) to 14 days from the date hereof inclusive (or the earlier date of registration of your clients' interest in the above subjects) which would cause the Keeper to make an entry on, or qualify his indemnity in, the Land Certificate to be issued in respect of that interest; and
2. Confirm that to the best of knowledge and belief, the answers to the questions numbered 1 to 14 in the draft Form 1 adjusted with you (in so far as these answers relate to our clients or to our clients' interest in the above subjects) are still correct.
3. (If appropriate) We also undertake to deliver to you within 14 days of this date the duly executed Discharge of the existing Standard Security granted by our clients, with our Forms 2 and 4 thereanent and our cheque made payable to the Keeper for the registration dues thereof.

Yours faithfully

(Signed and Witnessed to be self proving)

8.19   The wording of the letter in a dealing of registered property is:

Dear Sirs

Subjects:

With reference to the settlement of this transaction today, we hereby:

1. Undertake to clear the records of any deed, decree or diligence (other than such as may be created by or against your clients) which may be recorded in the Personal Register to which effect may be given in the Land Register in the period from (date of last search report) to 14 days from the date hereof inclusive (or the earlier date of registration of your clients' interest in the above subjects) which would cause the Keeper to make an entry on, or qualify his indemnity in the Land Certificate to be issued in respect of that interest; and

2. Confirm that to the best of knowledge and belief, the answers to the questions numbered 1 to 8 in the draft form 2 (or 1 to 13 in the draft Form 3) adjusted with you (in so far as these answers relate to our clients' interest in the above subjects, are still correct.

3. (See para 3 in style above).

Yours faithfully

(Signed and Witnessed)

The main thrust of these letters is to make the sellers and their agents, jointly and severally, liable for correcting any defect in title which the Keeper raises, or any defect which shall arise in the gap period referred to above. The matter of joint and several liability is dealt with at paragraph XX.

8.20   The letter of obligation in a sasine registration reads:

Dear Sirs

Subjects:

With reference to the settlement of this transaction today, we hereby:

1. Undertake to exhibit/deliver to you within twelve months following the date hereof Searches in the Property and Personal Registers brought down to the date fourteen days after the date hereof in terms of the memorandum adjusted between us, which Searches shall be clear of any entry deed or diligence which is either prejudicial to the validity of or is an encumbrance upon the title of our clients and will disclose the Disposition or other deed in favour of your clients provided it is recorded in the Register of Sasines within fourteen days of the date hereof; and

2. Undertake to deliver to you within six months following the date hereof a duly recorded Discharge of (short details of security).

Yours faithfully

(Signed and Witnessed).

It should be noted that this letter covers only delivery or exhibition of a clear search, and does not guarantee the title in any way other than this. This is the primary difference between the two systems.

8.21   The joint and several obligation of solicitor and clients is established in the case of *McGillivray v Davidson* (1993 SLT 693). As the clients will probably have spent the money, and as the solicitor is covered by indemnity insurance, the purchaser will in all probability not trouble with the clients, and will raise the action against the solicitors (see also *Warners v Beveridge & Kellas* (1994 SLT (Sh Ct) 29). It should be noted that this case, which turned on a letter of obligation was contested by two firms of solicitors, with no reference to the clients.

8.22   These letters are known as 'classic' letters of obligation, and if an action is raised, the indemnity insurers will look charitably on the solicitor who has granted this, and who has made every effort to prevent a claim arising. On the other hand, there are 'non-classic' letters of obligation, which are heavily disapproved by the indemnity insurers.

These are guaranteed. Professor Robert Rennie in his article in 1993 JLSS 431 gives a list of 26 letters he has seen, where the solicitor has been obliged to produce things that cannot be guaranteed; for example a planning certificate, or a roads report, the contents of which cannot be predicted. The indemnity insurers will only grudgingly pay a claim that arises from any such obligation. Thus, if you oblige yourself to produce a clear roads report, and find you cannot do so, you should arm yourself with a few bags of asphalt and a road roller!

It is in order to grant an obligation to produce a discharge of a standard security. If you have repaid the loan, the creditor must give a discharge, and if, for some reason, you cannot get one, you can petition the court for a declaration that the debtor's obligation has been performed (CFR(S)A 1970, Sch 5, Form D, No 2).

Chapter 9

THE DRAFT DISPOSITION

'Staff in a Glasgow hospital were puzzled to read in a patient's notes that her inability to lose weight was due to her "love of Taggart on telly". A very interesting and specific case of couch potato-ism, they thought. Further enquiries of the doctor involved revealed that there had been a slip twixt dictaphone and typewriter. It should have read that her weight problem was due to "love of tagliatelle".'

(Tom Shields' Diary, *The Herald*)

9.1 There should not, in theory at least, be much difficulty in drafting the disposition of an established house. Unlike the drafting of a feudal grant of a piece of land cut out of a larger area, you should not have to worry about describing the land or creating lengthy and complex land obligations. This work should already have been done, and you simply have to refer to past deeds for these details.

The main attributes of a good draftsman are: (1) a fluency in written English; (2) a complete knowledge of the form of the deed and what should be found in the deed, and in what order; (3) in light of the quotation printed above, if dictating machines are used, clear diction.

No one can help you with the first attribute at this stage of your career, but I can remind you of the contents of a disposition. On the first point, incidentally, I have never understood why the disposition is such a travesty of English: full of obsolete terms, redundant words, and containing the grammatical solecism of being one long sentence, divided by semi-colons. I have expressed my views on this point already in 1975 JLSS 126 and 364 and over the years have not departed one iota from these. Fortunately there are signs that dispositions are becoming more 'user-friendly', but all I can say to the young lawyer at this stage is follow the conventional form now, and hope wiser ways will eventually prevail. A person with a sound knowledge of English should be able to write bad English as well as good! On this whole matter, see JH Sinclair *Drafting in Scotland* (2001).

If a draft deed is dictated or handwritten, please remember that the typist is not superhuman, and make your intentions crystal clear. Then carefully check the draft. The most dangerous examples are when a typist guesses, and *nearly* gets it right. Thus, a deed that said 'I grant drainage rise' instead of warrandice; and another which contained a restrictive covenant, not permitting a seller of a business to trade within one mile of a certain point—unfortunately the typist had not been able to read the writing, and had guessed at a distance of one metre!

Typing errors should not occur so frequently with word processors, and I would advise drafters of deeds to correct the drafts on the screen. Typists, however, do get tired and distracted, and that's when mistakes happen. The most common mistake is when a typist's eye jumps from a word on one line to the same word on a line below, and thus a chunk of the deed is missed out.

9.2 As with all deeds, there are four main parts:

(1) narrative clause;
(2) dispositive clause;
(3) ancillary clauses;
(4) testing clause.

In the case of a disposition, a fifth part (the warrant of registration) is added, except for deeds to be registered in the Land Register. In the Land Register it is not necessary to insert a warrant of registration, because LR(S)A 1979, Forms 1, 2 and 3 all contain a request to the Keeper to register the deed in the Land Register.

In a disposition the parts are made up as follows:

1   Narrative   (see paras **9.3** and **9.4**)

(a) Granter's name and designation
(b) Grantee's name and designation
(c) Any consenter's name and designation
(d) The consideration

2   Dispositive   (see paras **9.5** and **9.6**)

(a) Words of conveyance
(b) Any special destination required by the purchaser
(c) Description of the land
(d) Conveyance of the parts and pertinents
(e) Any excepted parts of the land, sold separately
(f) Land obligations affecting the land

3   Ancillary   (see paras **9.7** and **9.8**)

(a) Date of entry
(b) Deduction of title, if appropriate
(c) Assignation of writs (not now necessary)
(d) Assignation of rents (not now necessary)
(e) Obligation of relief (not now necessary)
(f) Warrandice
(g) Stamp duty certificate

4   Testing clause   (see paras **9.9** and **9.10**)

5   Warrant of registration   (see paras **9.11** and **9.12**)

The narrative

9.3   This clause should set out the reason for granting the deed and the names of the parties and the consideration. All the facts and circumstances affecting the liability of the instrument to stamp duty, or the amount of duty, shall be 'fully and truly set forth' (Stamp Act 1891, s 5).

(a)   The name and designation he, she or it had in a previous deed, for example:
    I, John Smith, Architect, residing formerly at 3 Talavera Street, Glasgow and now at 5 Salamanca Drive, Glasgow (where the grantee of the last deed has

changed address) *or* I, Mrs Jane Brown or Smith, Computer Programmer, residing at 6 Torres Vedras Road, Glasgow (formerly Jane Brown, University Student, residing at 8 Victoria Crescent, Glasgow) (where the grantee of the last deed was an unmarried female, who has now become married, adopted her husband's name and changed address) *or* We, Smith Limited, incorporated under the Companies Act and having our Registered Office at 100 Leipzig Road, Glasgow (formerly Brown Limited conform to Certificate of Change of Name granted by the Register of Companies on Fifth November Nineteen hundred and seventy three). (Where a limited company has simply changed its name it remains exactly the same company, but with a different name—just like a person who changes his or her name.)

(b/c) The consent would be taken of any person who has a contingent interest in the property, e g a liferenter, a person with a right under missives who has resold etc or most importantly these days, a non-entitled spouse under MH(FP)(S)A 1981 (see App IV.4). They and the grantees should be designated in the same manner as the granter.

(d) The consideration is either a sum of money in a normal sale; or 'for certain good and onerous causes' where it is a commercial transaction, but no price as such is paid (e g an old *ex facie* absolute disposition to a building society); or 'for the love, favour and affection that I bear for him/her' (e g in the case of a gift to a member of the granter's family).

Example of narrative clause

9.4

'I, John Smith, Solicitor of 23 Wilhelmina Street, Ayr, Executor Nominate of William McWilliam, late of 22 Juliana Street, Ayr, conform to Confirmation in my favour issued from the Commissariat of South Strathclyde, Dumfries and Galloway at Ayr on Tenth November Nineteen hundred and eighty five, and as such executor uninfeft proprietor of the subjects hereafter disponed IN CONSIDERATION of the price of THIRTY FIVE THOUSAND POUNDS (£35,000) paid to me as Executor aforesaid by JAMES LESLIE and LESLEY LESLIE, spouses, both of 23 Utopia Street, Glasgow, of which I acknowledge the receipt and discharge them.'

Notes: The granter is an executor and does not have a recorded title. The last name in the title was not his, and we must therefore explain why he is granting this deed of a property that apparently does not belong to him, and we must deduce his title under the Conveyancing (Scotland) Act 1924, s 3. The grantees of the deed are a married couple, and we shall therefore have to consider the special destination in the dispositive clause. We shall assume that in this case there is no consenter. The receipt and discharge is unnecessary, and may be omitted as delivery of the deed amounts to receipt of the price.

Dispositive clause

9.5 **(a) Words of conveyance.** You do not require to use these exact words, as long as you use words indicating the intention to transfer, but it is customary to say 'HAVE SOLD AND DO HEREBY DISPONE'.

(b) Special destinations.   Up until quite recently, it was quite common for the husband in a married couple to take the title to the family home in his (usually) name alone. This has been rendered more and more pointless by changed attitudes and consequent modern legislation, culminating in the Matrimonial Homes (Family Protection) (Scotland) Act 1981 (as amended). It is suggested therefore that nowadays the family home should be taken in joint names in all but the most exceptional cases.

There are however, two variants of this destination:

(i)   The house may be taken in the names of both spouses and the survivor. Thus, if one spouse dies, his or her share passes automatically to the other spouse without any further formality, as at the time of death. If the survivor sells the house, he or she simply grants the deed as survivor, and title need not be deduced through confirmation, although an affidavit would need to be granted certifying that the property is not a matrimonial home in relation to which a spouse of the seller has occupancy rights (see App II.1) and exhibited with a death certificate. It is also necessary to prove that the destination has been evacuated, and this is usually done by producing a death certificate of the spouse who has died.

(ii) Alternatively, the house may be taken in the name of both spouses, and their respective executors and representatives. Thus if one spouse dies, his or her share goes not automatically to the other spouse, but to the person entitled under the will or the laws of intestacy.

In the normal case alternative (i) is probably preferable, as it presents a quick and convenient method of giving the surviving spouse a title to the whole house. There may, however, be some convincing reason for not wanting this to happen, e g for inheritance tax purposes the estate of the surviving spouse perhaps should not be increased because he or she is already over the dutiable limit, and property should therefore be passed on to e g children.

In the case of two unrelated persons buying property jointly, they will possibly wish destination (ii) but the alternatives should be explained to them, and careful instructions taken, preferably in writing.

Where an engaged couple is purchasing, a survivorship destination is possibly not appropriate in case one party should die before the wedding takes place, and the whole house therefore becomes the property of the survivor. That might not be the wish of the deceased person. Again, explain and get instructions.

In all cases of special destinations to two or more persons, remember that effectively you are making a will for them of a substantial asset, and furthermore a will that they do not sign.

(c) Description of the land.   The words 'heritably and irredeemably' are surplusage, but are customarily inserted. The description starts with the words 'ALL and WHOLE'. Your description should be a valid reference to a prior full description, all in terms of the Conveyancing (Scotland) Act 1924, s 8 and Sch D. The Notes in Schedule D should be particularly studied by the conveyancer.

It is absolutely essential for a valid description to name the county in which the property is situated. The parish may also be mentioned, but this is not at all necessary. Please do not forget that conveyancing still operates on the old county system and not on regions and districts (see Apps III and IV.) The more modern-minded may want to put in the name of the new unitary authorities (see App V), but this is not required.

When a title has been registered it is enough to state the address, with postal code, and the registration number (e g GLA 123456).

(d) Conveyance of the parts and pertinents

'A grant of the lands of A is as extensive as a grant of the lands of A with the parts and pertinents.' (*Gordon* (1850) 13 D 1)

It is customary to insert here (even in Land Registration deeds) (a) the postal address of the house; (b) the heritable fittings and fixtures; (c) the pertinents, rights, privileges and all common rights; and (d) whole right, title and interest. None of these is necessary, except an exact postal address, which may clarify or supplement a faulty description, and supply a good common law description, if the statutory description is faulty.

(e) Exceptions.   If since the last deed was recorded, part of the garden has been sold for, say, road widening to the regional council, this area of ground should be excepted from the description.

(f) Land obligations.   Again it is customary to mention in the title deeds such words as 'BUT ALWAYS WITH and UNDER so far as valid, still subsisting and applicable, the real burdens, declarations, conditions, restrictions, obligations, servitudes and other affecting the plot of ground hereby disponed.' This practice overlooks the tidy definition of land obligations in CFR(S)A 1970, s 1, which includes all of these older words.

The reference to the earlier deed or deeds containing the land obligations affecting the plot of ground is governed by the terms of the Conveyancing (Scotland) Act 1874, s 32 and Sch H and the Conveyancing (Scotland) Act 1924, s 9 and Sch E. The rules of reference to the earlier deed are similar to those relating to deeds referred to for a description (see (c) above) and again the notes in the Schedules should be studied carefully.

If the title has been registered it is not necessary to narrate the writs referred to for burdens, as the details are contained in the land certificate. This makes a disposition of registered land a very short deed. It is ironic that as missives become longer and longer, the form of disposition becomes very much shorter.

Example of dispositive clause

9.6

'HAVE SOLD AND DO HEREBY DISPONE to and in favour of the said James Leslie and Lesley Leslie equally between them and to the survivor of them and to the Executor of the survivor (alternatively the ordinary destination—"equally between them and to their respective executors and assignees whomsoever") ALL and WHOLE that plot of ground lying in the County of Ayr containing Eighty four decimal or one thousandth part of an acre or thereby Imperial Measure, being the plot of ground described in, and delineated and marked Plot III on the plan annexed and signed as relative to Feu Charter by Millhaugh Development Company Limited in favour of Gregor McGregor dated Third and recorded in the Division of the General Register of Sasines applicable to the County of Ayr on Tenth both days of July Nineteen hundred and fifty three, together with (One) the dwelling house known as 22 Juliana Street, Ayr and other buildings and erections built on the ground; (Two) the fixtures and fittings therein and thereon; (Three) the pertinents, rights and privileges including common rights (if any) pertaining to the said plot of ground; and (Four) my whole right, title and interest present and future in and to the said plot of ground as Executor foresaid; BUT ALWAYS WITH and UNDER so far as still valid, subsisting and applicable the real burdens, declarations, conditions, restrictions, obligations, servitudes and others specified in (First) Feu Contract between Alpin McAlpine and another of the one part and Hugh McHugh of the other part dated First and subsequent dates of January and recorded in the said Division of the General Register of Sasines on Third February Eighteen hundred and eighty four; and (second) Disposition by Jon Evans and another the Trustees of Evan Evans in favour of Millhaugh Development Company Limited dated Third and subsequent dates and recorded Twenty fourth all days of June Nineteen hundred and fifty two; and (third) the said Feu Charter by Millhaugh Development Company Limited on favour of Gregor McGregor dated and recorded as aforesaid;'

Note: I have drafted this clause in the traditional manner. It should not be taken as being to my liking, but the great thing for a young lawyer is to plagiarise slavishly at the start of their career, and to innovate later!

The much simpler description of registered land would be: 'ALL and WHOLE the plot of land at 22 Juliana Street, Ayr KA 7 4HR registered under title number AYR 12345'. And that's it.

Ancillary clauses

9.7   *3(a) Date of entry.*   This is simply the date on which the control of the house changes hands. If a date of entry is not inserted in a formal deed of this nature, the court will supply one—generally the next term date of Whitsunday or Martinmas. Please note that this does not apply to missives where no date of entry is stated.

3(b) Deduction of title.   If this is appropriate (as it is in this case because the granter is an executor and not the person who appears in the search as the last recorded owner) the deduction is made after the entry clause in terms of C(S)A 1924, ss 3 and 5 and Sch A. This relates back to paragraph **9.3(a)**. The deduction of title is made through a link in title as defined by section 5. In this case it is a confirmation. Other examples of links in title are defined in this section as being 'any statute, conveyance, deed, instrument, decree or other writing whereby a right to land ... is vested in or transmitted to any person'.

(a) English probate or letters of administration which have similar effect respectively to our confirmation nominative and dative.
(b) A will was used prior to the Succession (Scotland) Act 1964 rather than confirmation which then related only to moveable items. A will may still

be used as a link but this is not in any way recommended (see Opinion of the Professors of Conveyancing 1965 JLSS 153 and notes issued by the Law Society 1966 JLSS 84).

(c) A signed but unrecorded disposition which is not correct in form may be used by a grantee as a link in title when he conveys the property (e g A sells to B and gives him a disposition which cannot be recorded because there is a mistake in form. B then resells to C and grants the disposition as uninfeft proprietor deriving right through the unrecorded disposition which is a link in title).

(d) The decree in bankruptcy granted by the court in favour of a trustee in bankruptcy.

(e) An Act of Parliament may be used as a link. Thus when property was vested in the pre-1973 Corporation of the City of Glasgow, the property either passed to the City of Glasgow District Council or to Strathclyde Region, for their separate functions, in terms of the Local Government (Scotland) Act 1973. If either of these bodies wished to sell that property, they would have done so as uninfeft proprietors and deduced title through the 1973 Act. With the passing of the Local Government etc (Scotland) Act 1994, which introduced new units of local government, these provisions also apply. Thus, if an old tramway depot is sold, Glasgow City Council would grant a title deducing their title from the Corporation through the Region to the City Council to the purchaser.

3(c)(d)(e) Assignation of writs (assignation of rents/obligations of relief).   A great deal of substantive law lies under these three headings, but the practical conveyancer can hide behind the Land Registration (Scotland) Act 1979, s 16, which makes it no longer necessary to insert these clauses. Statutory meanings are provided in section 16 which are imported into the deed instead and these are quite sufficient, unless something different from the statutory meaning is required. As this is unlikely in an average house sale, I shall not deal further with these clauses.

3(f) Warrandice.   This is the undertaking by the granters to recompense the grantees for any loss they may suffer through the granters' want of title or their actings, past and future.

In the case of executors or trustees, who act in a purely fiduciary capacity and without personal interest in the property, a lesser degree of warrandice is competent—warrandice from their own facts and deeds only. This means that the trustees or executors have not done, nor will do, anything to prejudice the grantees' enjoyment of the land. The executors or trustees do not, however, personally guarantee the title, and that guarantee is carried instead by the beneficiaries under the trust estate, expressed in the words 'and we bind the executry/trust estate under our charge in absolute warrandice'. Please note therefore the warrandice to be granted by executors. If executors mistakenly grant absolute warrandice, they will be held to this (*Horsbrugh's Trustees v Welch* (1886) 14 R 67).

The competent warrandice for an individual proprietor granting warrandice in his own right is 'I grant (absolute) warrandice'. In the case of a trustee or executor: 'I grant warrandice from my own fact and deed only and bind the trust estate under my charge in absolute warrandice'. In the case of a gift the competent warrandice is 'I grant simple warrandice', which means that the grantee takes the title as it stands, but the granter will not grant any future deeds which might prejudice the right given to the grantee.

3(g) Stamp duty certificate.   Stamp duty, at the time of writing, is 1% of the whole price, if it is £60,001 or over, and 3% over £250,000 and 4% over £500,000. If the purchasers do not need to pay stamp duty of 1% (or 3% or 4%) on the whole consideration, there must be a certificate in the disposition stating that the consideration does not exceed £60,000 or £250,000 or £500,000. In addition, from 30 November 2001 properties in Disadvantaged Areas where the consideration does not exceed £100,000 are exempt from Stamp Duty but dispositions relating to such properties still need a certificate stating the consideration does not exceed £250,000. The deed is then stamped accordingly.

It is also necessary to certify that the deed is not one of a series of deeds, designed to escape or mitigate liability for duty. Thus, for example, if a house was worth £61,000, the stamp duty on the deed is £610. One might consider then selling the property in two halves, each of £30,500, and thus escaping duty. But this is part of a larger transaction or of a series of transactions, and as such not permissible. The certificate reads:

> 'And I certify that the transaction hereby effected does not form part of a larger transaction, or of a series of transactions, in respect of which the amount or value or the aggregate amount or value of the consideration exceeds Thirty Thousand pounds.'

Moveable property included in the sale is not subject to stamp duty, so the sensible thing in the above case is to find £1,000 of moveables in the sale, and to reduce the price to £60,000, and to certify the price accordingly. This produces a saving of £610. A stamp duty mitigation certificate should, however, be truthful and not used to achieve a tax evasion (consider *Saunders v Edwards* [1987] 2 All ER 651, 1 WLR 1116, CA). Tax evasion, which is a criminal offence, should be distinguished from tax avoidance, which is perfectly all right, as each person has the right to arrange their affairs so as to pay the legal minimum of tax.

3(i) Consent to registration (for publication and preservation).   This clause need not be inserted in a disposition as this registration is administrative and not in any way prejudicial to the granter. Registration for execution is however prejudicial to the granter, and must be specifically consented to by the granter (see App I.27). This is not normally required in a simple deed of transfer such as a disposition, with no continuing obligation, although it may occur in a bilateral deed with continuing obligations such as a feu contract or lease. The consent to registration clause can therefore be safely left out in this case.

Example of ancillary clauses
9.8

> 'With entry as at the Fifteenth day of January, Nineteen hundred and ninety three; which subjects were last vested in the said William McWilliam, late of 22 Juliana Street, Ayr, whose title thereto was recorded in the said Division of the General Register of Sasines on the Third day of March Nineteen hundred and Seventy nine and from whom I acquired right by the Confirmation hereinbefore mentioned; and I grant warrandice as Executor foresaid from my own facts and deeds only and I bind the

Executry Estate under my charge in absolute warrandice; and I certify that the transaction hereby effected does not form part of a larger transaction or of a series of transactions in respect of which the aggregate amount or value of the consideration exceeds Sixty Thousand pounds: IN WITNESS WHEREOF'.

Testing clause

9.9 A space is left for the testing clause which is of course inserted after the deed has been signed. The testing clause is a record of the date of execution, and the names and designations of the witnesses. The testing clause should also be used to correct any mistakes that may have occurred. Such mistakes should be referred to in the testing clause. The substantive law in this matter is voluminous and should be studied. (See the Requirements in Writing (Scotland) Act 1995, s 5).

Apart from these uses the testing clause should not be used as a means of varying the terms of the deed (*Chamber's Trs v Smiths* (1878) 5 R (HL) 151). While the testing clause appears above the subscription it is well known that in point of time it is inserted after a signature and is merely a record of this. Any further provision to the deed is not therefore authenticated by signature.

Example of testing clause

9.10

'IN WITNESS WHEREOF these presents typewritten on this page are signed by me as Executor foresaid at Glasgow on the Third day of January Nineteen hundred and ninety in presence of Pearl King Secretary in the employment of Messrs Wylde, Lyfe, Solicitors of 170 Tiree Street, Ayr.'

Warrant of registration

9.11 The warrant of registration is a direction to the Keeper of the Register of Sasines authorising him to register the deed in the appropriate register. Before a real right can be acquired by registration, it is essential that the person acquiring the right shall be named and identified in the writ and/or the warrant of registration. In the normal case, the disponee will be identified in the writ, and need only be named, but not designed, in the warrant. If there has been a change in designation this should be narrated in the warrant. The warrant is signed by the solicitors for the purchasers, or by the parties acting on their own behalf. No one else may sign this (Solicitors (Scotland) Act 1980, s 32). This is the crux of the solicitors' monopoly.

In deeds to be registered in the Land Register, a warrant of registration is not necessary.

Example of warrant of registration

9.12

'REGISTER on behalf of the within-named JAMES LESLIE and LESLEY LESLIE in the REGISTER for the COUNTY of AYR.

Solicitors, Ayr, Agents.'

9.13   In accordance with the General Regulations of the Law Society, Table of Fees, para 7(1) it is the duty of the solicitors for the grantee or obligee to the deed to draw up that deed. Special cases of exception are contained in paragraph **7(2)**, or the Tables, the most important of these being the feu writs which are drawn by the granter's agent.

9.14   All of these remarks apply only to Dispositions in Sasine Register transactions or in First Land Registrations. The Disposition in Land Register dealings is very much simpler. (See para **14.5**).

Chapter 10

THE FINAL STEPS BEFORE SETTLEMENT

'I knew my days were numbered when I was warming up behind the goal at Parkhead and one of our fans shouted "Kinnaird, we like the poll tax more than we like you!"'

(Paul Kinnaird of St Mirren)

10.1 The purchasers' agents have now:

(a) examined title (in sasine transactions and first registration and the land certificate in registered land transactions);
(b) approved, or revised the draft memorandum for (or continuation of) search in sasine transactions or the appropriate form in Land Register transactions; and
(c) drafted the disposition.

The purchasers' solicitors therefore return the title deeds to the sellers' agents, with these drafts. When doing so, they ask any questions that may arise from examination of title and request the sellers' agents to explain or rectify any defect.

10.2 On receipt of these papers, the sellers' agents:

(a) Send the appropriate form to the searchers and ask for a report which brings the search down to date.
(b) They obtain any further writs or papers that the purchasers' agents may reasonably require and which may not be digested in the land certificate. If the writs required are not in their possession, they obtain these either by borrowing them from the firm who hold them (e g the agents for the builder of the estate). The fee payable to the firm holding the writ is given in the Table of Fees, ch 1, para 5(4). Alternatively it may be easier, quicker and cheaper to obtain an extract from the General Register of Sasines, or the cheaper and quicker 'quick copy'. A quick copy is a photocopy made in the Register, but, unlike an extract, uncertified as correct by the Keeper's staff.
(c) Answer the queries made as best they can.
(d) Revise the draft disposition and return it to the purchasers' agents with the interim report and answers to questions.

10.3 The purchasers' agents then have the draft disposition 'engrossed' (or typed) and return the engrossment with the draft to the sellers' agents. The sellers' agents compare the draft with the engrossment, and if it is in order they send the disposition to the sellers for signature. If the property is in the name of one spouse only, the non-entitled spouse should consent to the disposition to renounce the right, or the right should otherwise be renounced (see App I and App II, Forms 2 and 4 for the appropriate style).

10.4   The purchasers' agents consider whether or not they are satisfied with the title position and with the answers given to their queries. They write to their clients setting out the salient features of the title and may warn the purchasers about any obtrusive conditions (particularly about any prohibition against trade, keeping animals, cutting down trees etc). They further appraise the purchasers of any financial commitment that may arise in the future. The clients should not, however, be swamped with inessential and confusing information. What is inessential or confusing obviously varies from case to case; broadly speaking a minimum of useful information will usually satisfy a residential purchaser, but a commercial purchaser may want a detailed report.

If anything is amiss in the title, and for present purposes we shall assume that it is not, the clients' instructions must be taken as to dealing with this, both at this stage and indeed at all stages of the transaction. If the purchasers' solicitors and their clients are not reasonably satisfied as to any important point, it must be cleared up before settlement takes place.

10.5   We must consider the financial arrangements to be made at settlement. The sellers prepare a state for settlement which is the sellers' account to the purchasers, and this is approved by the purchasers' agents. It should reflect the following items:

(a) The price of the house and the price of any moveables included.

(b) In non-domestic properties the apportionment of local rates.   First of all, a short explanation of local government financing is required. The bulk of local government spending is funded by central government, but the remainder has to be raised locally. This was formerly done entirely from local rates, which were collected by regional councils, both on their own behalf, and of their constituent districts. The new local government structure from 1996 is shown in Appendix IV.

Every five years (the quinquennium) a valuation is made of every item of heritable property, except agricultural land which is exempt. The official government valuer ('the District Valuer') analyses rental evidence of all commercial property, which is only one element in the calculation of individual rates bills. Much dissatisfaction was expressed at the fact that rates in the south of England are invariably much lower than those fixed for similar properties in Scotland. Scottish and English rates are now being equalised, but this is a lengthy and complex process. Rating tends to be a rather specialised subject confined to valuation lawyers and surveyors.

The rates of the property are apportioned on a daily basis as at settlement. The rating year runs from 1 April in each year until 31 March in the next year. Thus if the purchase date is, say 15 November 1994, the sellers pay the rates for 229 days, and the purchasers pay for the balance of the year to March 1995, i e 136 days.

10.6   Meantime in domestic properties rates had been replaced by the community charge, otherwise known as the 'poll tax'. This was not a charge on properties but on persons who lived in properties, on the basis that if a person used a council service, then they should pay for it, and that the whole burden should not fall on property owners. While the reasoning behind this proposition was quite sound, you could not have called the charge controversial—at the end of the day, nearly everyone hated it. It was, therefore, replaced on 1 April 1993 by the council tax, which remains in effect, and while it is unloved, as is any tax, it is seen as being reasonably fair.

Houses are valued as at their market value on 1 April 1991 or at their building date, or date of significant alteration, and are placed in bands A to H according to value, band A being the value up to £27,000 and band H being the value over £212,000. There are various exemptions: students, student nurses, youth training trainees, apprentices, and persons under 18. This gets the tax away from socially divisive 'can't pay, won't pay' argument that existed with the poll tax.

As at the date of settlement a notice of the change of ownership should be sent to the appropriate council, who will apportion the tax between the sellers and the purchasers.

Feu duty

10.7   Where an allocated feu duty is still payable in respect of the house, the sellers are under a duty to redeem the feu duty as at the date of sale (see LTR(S)A 1974, s 5). Where, however, the feu duty is not allocated, there is no compulsion upon the sellers to redeem the portion of the *cumulo* feu duty, and the payment must therefore be apportioned between the parties as at the date of settlement.

As a quite general rule, apportioned feu duties are most commonly found in tenements, and the factor normally collects this sum along with the other outgoings, and will undertake the apportionment of the feu duty between purchasers and sellers.

Feu duty is in almost all cases paid at Whitsunday (15 May) and Martinmas (11 November) in each year. Unlike most payments, it is payable in arrears, i e the payment from 11 November to 15 May is payable on 15 May.

The purchasers should see a current receipt for the *cumulo* feu duty payable to the superior, as the liability for payment of arrears could fall on the purchasers if they have not been paid.

Common charges

10.8   Where a flat in a tenement building is sold, the factor should be asked by the sellers' agents to apportion the common charges for maintenance of the building between the parties (see Form issued by the Property Managers Association Scotland Ltd at para **17.11**). This can be done when the factor is informed of the change of ownership by the sellers' solicitors. In modern practice it is usual for the factor to ask an incoming owner for a deposit to meet future charges. This deposit is set against these charges.

Factors are very wary about instructing repairs, let alone paying tradesmen without having received money from the owners well in advance. The reason for this is that they have incurred huge debts, paying tradesmen in the past, and which have not been repaid. The case of *David Watson Property*

Management v Woolwich Equitable Building Society (1992 SLT 430), which held that a heritable creditor who has taken possession of a house on the default of the borrower, is not responsible for common charges which the borrower had failed to pay, amply illustrates this point. Although *David Watson* possibly excuses purchasers from having to pay the sellers' common charges debts, it is the invariable practice for the purchasing solicitors to see a recent common charges receipt.

Interest

10.9 When settlement takes place properly on the agreed date of entry, the question of interest does not arise—that is to say when the full purchase price is paid by the purchaser and the property is made available with the disposition, the titles and the keys. Where, however, one party or the other cannot meet their obligation, the question of interest arises.

Example. Mr and Mrs A contract to sell their house to Mr and Mrs B for £50,000 as at 16 December 1994. For some reason personal to them Mr and Mrs B cannot pay this sum at 16 December. Their building society loan may have been held up, or the proceeds of the sale of their own house may not yet have come through. What do Mr and Mrs B do?

The position at law is that the purchasers are obliged to pay the price at the date of entry, failing which they are in default, and the obligation can be enforced by the sellers. Thus at law (*ex lege*) the sellers may raise an action of implement, including a crave for interest at the legal rate, which is currently well below what the sellers would have to pay their bank if they take an overdraft to cover the lack of money received from the purchasers.

Additionally, interest runs only from the date of warranting the action, and not from the date of entry, unless the parties have entered, or enter into an agreement to the contrary. But the parties may agree (*ex pacto*) that a different provision shall apply (see para **4.8** and *Lloyd's Bank v Bamberger* 1994 SLT 424) and that interest at a stated rate shall apply if there is a delay or default by the purchasers. If no such agreement is made, there must be doubts as to whether overdraft interest can be demanded by the sellers without entry being given in return, on the basis of a statement in *Erskine* III, 3, 79 to the effect that the sellers cannot gain interest as well as enjoy the 'fruits of the property'— whatever these may be (see *Thomson v Vernon* 1983 SLT (Sh Ct) 17 discussed by Professor D J Cusine, 1983 JLSS 273).

If the sellers are unable to settle on the date of entry, there is no obligation upon the purchasers either to take entry or pay interest (see *Bowie v Semple's Executors* 1978 SLT (Sh Ct) 9). If, however, the purchasers wish to take entry they may do so on consigning the price on deposit receipt with a bank. This is in terms of *Prestwick Cinema Co v Gardiner* (1951 SC 98). When the money is on deposit receipt neither party has control over it without the consent of the other. While this may seem to be a very convenient arrangement, it is spoiled as a practical remedy by the extremely poor rate of interest offered by banks on deposit receipt.

The most practical solution to this reasonably common problem is for the purchasers to ask their bank for a 'bridging loan', that is to say, a short-term loan, usually given on the basis of the probability of the borrower receiving funds on a certain future date. Thus the purchasers can say to their bank: 'Our building society loan is coming through next week and we'll repay you then'. It should be emphasised that bridging loans are expensive and should only be taken on a short-term basis; further the bank may ask for an 'arrangement fee' for arranging the loan which may make these loans unattractive, save in an emergency.

Banks are not, however, so keen on lending against a payment on an uncertain future date; for example, if the purchasers are still selling their own house and have not found a buyer yet, their bank may not be willing to provide 'the bridge'. Banks like their loans to be short term and repayment to be certain, unless they make a specified arrangement as in a 'personal loan'. This provides for regular payments to account, and the banks charge more handsomely for a personal loan.

If the purchasers cannot therefore get a bridging loan, or if the parties decide it is unnecessary, a possible arrangement is for the purchasers to pay the sellers what money they have in return for possession, and for interest to run on the balance at an agreed rate until settlement. This rate of interest might be the rate that would have been payable by the purchasers to their building society. This of course is not necessarily recommended, as it is fraught with danger, but in many circumstances it would be unreasonable for the sellers not to co-operate with such a request, and to insist on implement of the contract strictly. When both parties agree to this, the sellers get a good rate of interest on their money and the purchasers get possession of the house although they have technically been in breach of contract. What has happened is that the contract has been partially reconstructed by agreement. This is a common feature of conveyancing practice—an unsatisfactory provision of law is altered by contract as in the law of tenement, passing of risk and mineral reservations, all of which are discussed in this book.

This agreement can, however, run deeper. (See Professor A J McDonald 'A Question of Interest' 1980 JLSS 103; Professor J M Halliday 'Delay in Settlement' 1981 SLG 68; and Professor Noble 'Delays in Settlement' 1984 JLSS 116, which contain a comprehensive review of the law.) The legal arguments on this matter are so complex that there is every reason for the conveyancer to seek to avoid such a dispute by:

(a) inserting a suitable '*ex pacto*' clause in missives to cover delays (see para **4.8(a)**);
(b) ensuring that the buyers have made satisfactory financial arrangements;
(c) choosing a sensible and realistic date of entry; and
(d) keeping the transaction running on schedule until settlement.

10.10 The sellers who receive an interest payment without deduction of tax should account for this in their next tax return. They should, in turn, issue a tax receipt for the payment to the purchasers, who should use (if applicable) this to claim tax relief on the payment. Similarly when a bridging loan from a bank is taken, the bank should issue a certificate of interest paid for tax purposes. Interest payments made to persons resident overseas should be made after deduction of tax by the person paying interest, and that person should account to the Inland Revenue for the tax deducted, because the Inland Revenue has no power of collection once the money has left the country.

10.11 When the state of settlement has been agreed and entry is near, both solicitors should ensure that they are ready to settle, and that there are no loose ends which could cause settlement to be postponed. In particular the purchasers' solicitors should ensure that they have received sufficient money from the purchasers to enable them to settle. They should at this stage also render their fee and get this settled while the clients still depend on the solicitors. This may sound cynical but the lawyers have by this time earned and deserve their fee, and any lawyers will tell you sad stories of highly grateful clients who have become quite the opposite when faced with a bill. I shall however deal with the question of fees in the next chapter.

The purchasers' cheque should therefore be given to the solicitors in plenty of time for it to be cleared through the purchasers' bank. This cannot be stressed sufficiently. A solicitors' cheque from clients' account is treated like cash, because of the strict rules (Solicitors' Account Rules) that solicitors shall ensure that at all times they have enough in their clients' bank account to meet the total amount that the firm is due to clients (irrespective of any money owed to the solicitors by clients). If, therefore, solicitors issue a cheque, and then are informed that the clients' cheque paid to the firm has not been met by the clients' bank, the solicitors may not order the firm's own bank to refuse payment of the firm's cheque. The loss in other words is the solicitors' and any attempt to shift that misfortune to the sellers may amount to professional misconduct. This point is brought home in a statement by the Law Society contained in 1981 JLSS 357 which is worth repeating verbatim in view of the importance of the matter.

'A solicitor acting for a purchaser in a conveyancing transaction has a duty to ensure either that he has cleared funds in his clients' account for the settlement of such a conveyancing transaction or that any cheque which he has received for his client will be met by the paying bank. There is a principle that a cheque drawn by the solicitor acting for a purchaser on his client bank account and handed over in settlement in a conveyancing transaction to the solicitor acting for the seller should not be stopped except in exceptional circumstances.

Such exceptional circumstances would arise in the event of circumstances amounting to breach of contract on the part of the seller, as for example when the purchasers are unable to receive vacant possession or if the subjects have been destroyed (and these circumstances are contrary to the terms of the missives) or in the event of a postal settlement where the disposition which is delivered contains a defect in execution.'

In this unfortunate event the purchasers' solicitors would be well advised to inform the Law Society before they stop their cheque.

Golden Rule: always make sure you have cleared funds in your bank on settlement date, and before you write a cheque on the clients' account.

Chapter 11

THE SETTLEMENT, FEEING-UP
AND TIDYING-UP

'We find it rather difficult to offer an estimate of the amount of time which would be saved by the solicitor (in a system of land registration) as this will vary with each transaction, but in general our view is that there will be an average saving of about one-third of the time which a solicitor spends on a similar transaction under the present system. But this is not the only element which enters into the assessment of solicitors' fees and on the whole we think a reduction of 25 per cent on the present scale of fees should be achieved in transactions in land the title of which has been registered.'

(*Registration of Title* (Reid Report) (Cmnd 2032, 1963) para 149)

'People of the same trade seldom meet together, even for merriment and diversion, but the conversation ends in a conspiracy against the public, or some contrivance to raise prices.'

(Adam Smith *The Wealth of Nations* Vol Ii, Bk 1, ch 10, Pt II)

'Eight Austrian banks were found to be involved in the "most shocking" cartel ever uncovered by the European Commission. The banks' bosses met frequently at a Vienna hotel to fix charges and rates. The Commission levied fines of 124 million euros. Three banks are preparing to appeal (against the fines, not the charges).'

(*The Economist*, 15 June 2002)

11.1   The sellers' and purchasers' solicitors should arrange a time and place for the settlement. Except in unusual circumstances the rule is 'the cheque goes to the disposition'—that is settlement takes place at the sellers' solicitors' office. Both parties should make a check list of what they require for the settlement:

Sellers	Purchasers
Keys	Cheque (As with the letter of
Signed disposition	obligation opposite, make sure that
Detail of signatures	this is signed by a partner of the firm
Title deeds or land certificate	in good time—the inexperienced
Signed letter of obligation and draft	lawyer leaves this until the last
for comparison	moment, and then finds everyone is
Feu duty redemption receipt	out to lunch.)
Any other papers to be delivered	
State for settlement and draft for	
comparison	

If it is not convenient for the sellers to hand the keys in to the solicitors, as is often the case, they may be left with a third party, e g the selling estate agent. Then when the sellers' solicitors have the cheque, they telephone the third party and ask them to release the keys to the purchasers.

11.2   The cheque is exchanged for the disposition, letter of obligation, land certificate, keys, the receipted state for settlement and any other papers. Please note that this ceremony amounts to delivery of the disposition, in its technical sense.

Ideally settlements should be done face to face, so that the cheque and the disposition are exchanged at the same time. This was the traditional manner of settlement, but many settlements nowadays are carried out by post or courier, owing to constraints of time. To get round the difficulty of the cheque or the deed reaching the other solicitor before the other part is returned, and being misused, the sender of the cheque or disposition writes a short letter to the other solicitor saying: 'We enclose the cheque/disposition and settlement papers, which please hold as undelivered until you dispatch the disposition and settlement papers/cheque to us.' This is a request that mirrors the obligation in missives and must be adhered to, as delivery is postponed until the event happens.

11.3   Alternatively the price may be 'telegraphed' from the buyer's solicitor's bank account to that of the seller's solictor. This, of course, entails in the buyer's solicitor having cleared funds in their clients' account, and a certain amount of careful planning. Incidentally do not assume that a telegraphic transfer will be an instant transfer—the process sometimes takes several hours. Banks do not like to explain why this should be so.

11.4   The sellers' solicitors then bank the cheque and pay any outlays (such as estate agents, advertising accounts and their own fees). They then send the balance to the sellers with a statement of their outlays.

11.5   Other loose ends may remain.

Redemption of feu duty.   Although the terms Part II of the Abolition of Feudal Tenure Etc (Scotland) Act 2000 provide that that all feu duties will be compulsorily redeemed, after the appointed day, the appointed day has not yet been fixed. In addition many feu duties in Scotland will have been redeemed on sale, or voluntarily, under the provisions of the Land Tenure Reform (Scotland) Act 1974. Ideally any feu duty allocated over the property being sold should be redeemed, where necessary, under LTR(S)A 1974, s 5, before the transaction is settled, and the receipt handed over at settlement. The sellers may not however be in funds to do this, so the letter of obligation may contain an obligation to redeem and produce the receipt within (say) 14 days. This is an acceptable obligation to give, for fulfilment of the obligation is totally within the solicitors' control.

The redemption is then made by the solicitors from the proceeds of the sale. The basis of redemption is the feu duty factor one month before the date of redemption, plus payment of all arrears. The price paid is therefore:

(Annual feu duty x feu duty factor) + arrears = redemption price

The feu duty factor is worked out on the basis of the price of 2½% consolidated stock (2½% consols) as its middle price on the appropriate date. On 19

June 2002 the price of 2½% consols was £48.20 per £100 of stock. If, therefore, you wanted to redeem a feu duty as at that date, you would notionally give the superior enough money to buy consols to provide an income of £10 (ignoring all purchase costs). This would be £400 of stock costing (4 × £48.20) = £192.80. The feu duty factor is therefore £192.80 divided by 10 = £19.28.

This provision applies only to allocated feu duties, and not to feu duties that are unallocated, but are only apportioned, as in many tenement buildings. The provisions of the Abolition of Feudal Tenure etc (Scotland) Act 2000 will apply to both. Therefore, in the not too distant future we should see an end to feu duties, at last.

Common charges. These are charges levied upon proprietors in respect of maintenance of common property, mainly in flats. It was decided in the House of Lords case of *David Watson Property Management v Woolwich Equitable Building Society* (1992 SLT 430) that the liability for common charges, that were unpaid by a former owner, did not pass to a creditor who had taken possession. From the reasoning in the case it would also seem likely that the liability for unpaid common charges also does not pass to a purchaser, but in practice a prudent solicitor will require to see an up-to-date receipt for payment of common charges, to be fully satisfied, and to curtail further argument. This should be requested when the factors are asked to apportion the common charges between purchasers and sellers.

11.6 The sellers' agents make sure that the sellers' home insurances are cancelled, and that refund of premium is obtained for the remainder of the insurance year, and that all advertising is cancelled, if not already done.

11.7 After settlement the purchasers' solicitors complete the testing clause, have the deed stamped (for rates see para **3.17**) and then send the deed to be registered in the Land Register, together with the deeds being sent in support of the registration, a cheque for registration dues and LR(S)A 1979 Form 1/2/3 as appropriate and Form 4 in duplicate. Before the deeds are sent to the Keeper, these should be carefully checked to avoid a deed being returned by the Keeper. Make sure that the Form 1/2/3 is signed at the bottom of the first page by a partner of the firm.

The deed then goes through the registration process at Meadowbank House and is fairly carefully checked. If there is anything wrong—for things that do go wrong, see the annual report by the Keeper—Register House will either send the deed straight back to you in serious cases (e g forgetting to sign a form or not recording within a time limit (see para **7. 31**), or a defective form of deed) or telephone you in less serious cases to see what you want done (e g a small mistake in the testing clause or an unauthenticated erasure of a minor nature).

11.8 The land certificate is duly returned having been registered, together with the deeds sent with the application. The purchasers' solicitors should check that there is no restriction of indemnity contained in the land certificate, and that the land certificate contains no mistakes. In the latter case, the certificate is returned to the Keeper for correction. Having satisfied themselves, the purchasers' solicitors discharge the letter of obligation (usually by writing the word 'implemented' on it and dating and initialling it) and return it to the sellers' solicitors. The file is then checked for loose ends, for useful papers to be retained, and is put away.

11.9   The land certificate and the charge certificate, if appropriate, are now in the hands of the purchasers' solicitors. They should report this to the purchasers and ask for instructions as to safekeeping of the land certificate, which is the property of the clients subject to any right of lien the solicitor may have. If a lender is involved, the land and charge certificates are sent to the lender in terms of their instructions (see App I.58). If there is no lender involved, should the solicitors keep the land certificate or the purchasers' bank, or the purchasers themselves? The first two courses are preferable. 'In the tin box under the bed' is not to be encouraged, but it is the clients' choice.

In the case of the now redundant title deeds these should be sent to the purchasers telling them that the land certificate is now the title, and that the old deeds are redundant, and you are sure that the purchaser would like these for historical or sentimental reasons. The purchaser may decline with thanks, in which case the old titles may be discarded, but it is useful to ask the local archivist first, to see if the deeds are of any value to the archivist.

Finally do not forget that if the fees have not been paid, the solicitors have a lien over the title deeds until payment. It is recommended (1984 JLSS 198) that conveyancing files be kept for ten years, or at least until the property is successfully resold.

Feeing-up

11.10   You have done the work and you are worthy of your fee, but the question is how much?

Fees were fixed by Law Society scales until 1985 when, under intense pressure from free traders, the Law Society was forced to abandon these fixed charges based on the value of the property. The weakness in scale fees was that they encouraged 'price fixing', placed low fees on small property transactions, which were often the most work-intensive, and high fees on large property transactions, which were often the least work-intensive. It should be noted, however, that estate agents, architects, surveyors and indeed the government can still charge fees based on the value of the property.

In place of scale fees the Law Society in 1985 issued a set of guidelines which should be followed:

(1)   The fee shall be fair and reasonable to both the solicitor and the client.
(2)   The fixing of every fee is a balanced judgment rather than an arithmetical calculation.
(3)   The solicitor should keep detailed records in respect of work carried out (i) to ascertain total time and (ii) to justify the fee fixed if need be.
(4)   The fee may consist of charges for detailed items charged at the current unit rate (unit rate for 2002: £9.85) recommended in the General Table of Fees.
(5)   Alternatively the solicitor may charge according to circumstances, taking into account the seven factors following:
    (a)   the importance of the matter to the client;
    (b)   the amount or value of any money or property involved;
    (c)   the complexity or difficulty or novelty of the question raised;
    (d)   the skill, labour, specialised knowledge and responsibility involved;
    (e)   the time expended;
    (f)   the length, number and importance of any documents prepared or perused; and

(g) the place where and the circumstances in which the services are rendered, including the degree of expenditure required.

(6) It is important to establish an hourly charge rate for each fee earner in the firm.

(7) Once hourly charge rates have been set, the first step is to determine the product of the rate charges and the time expended. The result should then be appraised to see if it is reasonable to the client.

(8) The fee may contain an element which reflects all other relevant factors as set out in regulation 4 of the General Table of Fees.

(9) There may be factors producing a negative weighting, e g property of small value or very routine work.

(10) The practioner should then 'step back' and take an overall view to check if the fee thus fixed is fair and reasonable.

(11) Where a solicitor does business which is fairly standard, the solicitor may prepare his or her own table of fees for such work, but it must be prepared in conformity with these guidelines.

(12) Where a first registration of land is induced, some additional weighting is normally appropriate, but negative weighting is appropriate in dealings in a registered interest.

(13) Before embarking on business involving sale or purchase of property, the enquirer is entitled to know the approximate cost in fees and outlays.

Fees should, therefore, be charged at a rate to enable your firm to reflect the work done, to reflect the resources used (your time at university and training, office rental, stationery, equipment, cost of indemnity insurance, responsibility, continuing legal education, and so on) and to make a decent profit, to make the whole exercise worthwhile.

The unit rate (in 2002: £9.85 for six minutes) may seem very high, but reflect on the following—I go to the hairdresser who has me out of the door in about six minutes, because it is an increasingly small job. For this he charges me £6, which is not significantly below the unit rate, and the hairdresser doesn't have to keep detailed accounts, files, records of haircuts made, title deeds, computers, a huge staff, and a large office and is not subject to the attentions of various regulatory bodies.

As a rule of thumb, you can perhaps look at the old scale of fees, and see what would have been allowed, although these fees are probably on the high side for modern conditions, bearing in mind the remarks of the Reid Report, in 1963, quoted above. Also bear in mind that to open a file and a cash card and to vet the client for money laundering and general financial reliability will probably cost a minumum of £100, before you do very much.

The effect of competition should always be borne in mind—many firms, who had what they considered 'dripping roasts', are now having to quote competitively for the provision of these legal services, which they formerly considered as a job for life. This is of course, in general, a good thing, although it may seem a fairly mixed blessing to those firms. Even large firms have to submit to 'beauty parades' at which they have to make a competitive presentation of services offered and fees charged to firms for whom they have worked for years. A sad story was related in *The Times* recently of a London firm who worked at minimum cost to set up the new Tate Art Gallery in London, involving the critical financing of the project. At a subsequent beauty parade, their services were not accepted.

Estimates should be pretty accurate, although one cannot prepare for the unexpected, and a loophole should be left here. Value added tax is not, however, unexpected, and should be fully reflected in the quotation. The Ombudsman in his report for 1993 had some fairly tart comments about certain estimates of fees that had been scrutinised by him, and to which reference is made.

The best distilled wisdom in this feeing-up process is contained in guideline number 1: the fee shall be reasonable to both the client and the solicitor. A fair fee to the solicitor covers the overheads of the practice, and a reasonable profit margin. (For a further discussion on this topic, please see an excellent article by Brian Allingham 'Conveyancing: The profit motive' 1992 JLSS 439.) It should also be remembered that the level of your fees depends on what your competitors are charging.

11.11   Unless otherwise stated in the missives, each of the parties pay their own fees to their own solicitors. It used to be the case that builders insisted on buyers of new houses paying both the builders' and their own fees. This was not, however, popular, and the practice was scrapped. The builders' legal fees are now, therefore, presumably included in the price of the house!

11.12   Value added tax at 17.5% is currently payable on all legal fees. Value added tax is not, however, chargeable on recording dues in the Land Register (although if you order an extract deed from the Keeper, VAT is payable on that charge) or stamp duty. Value added tax is also payable on Land Register reports. For the position of VAT on land prices (if applicable in a minority cases of tenanted land) see *Jaymarke Development Ltd v Elinacre Ltd* (1992 SLT 1193).

11.13   In addition a loan fee is payable, which is based on the principles enumerated in paragraph **11.10.** Where the same lawyers act for the borrowers and the lenders, less work would be involved, and the fee would presumably be smaller than if completely different solicitors acted for the lenders, and had to go through the title of new. Under the old Table of Fees the reduction in fees was from scale fee based on the amount of the loan to 40% of that fee. Value added tax is payable on these fees, but there is no stamp duty on security documents.

Recording dues or Land Registry dues are payable for the recording of the security. If, however, the security is presented at the same time as the conveyance to the purchaser, only a nominal charge of £22 is payable.

11.14   Some specimen costs of house sale or purchase

Price	Stamp Duty (Purchasers only)	Registration Fees (Land or Sasine Registers)
Up to £10,000	Nil	£22.00
Up to £20,000	Nil	44.00
Up to £30,000	Nil	66.00
Up to £40,000	Nil	88.00
Up to £50,000	Nil	110.00
Up to £60,000	Nil	132.00
Up to £70,000	£700	154,00
Up to £80,000	£800	176.00
Up to £90,000	£900	198.00

Up to £100,000	£1000	220.00
Up to £200,000	£2000	440.00
Up to £250,000	£2500	
Up to £400,000	£4,000	550.00
Up to £500,000 (3%)	£15,000	600.00
Up to £1,000,000 (4%)	£40,000	900.00
Exceeding £ 5,000,000	£200,000	£7,500

Notes:

1   A separate charge may be made for completion of missives, arranging loan, redemption of feu duties etc. (See Regulation 21.)
2   A charge may also be made for posts and incidents which is normally about 10%. (See Regulation 14.)
3   The seller will also incur dues of property enquiry and other searches and Land Register reports.
4   The table above is for illustration only and the current Law Society Table of Fees and unit rate should be consulted, also the Stamp Duty Rates and Fees in the Department of the Registers of Scotland (Amendment) Order 1990.
5   Land and Sasine Register fees are now identical at all levels and are contained in Table 'A' of Registration Fees.
6   The Finance Act 2001 introduced an exemption from stamp duty applicable to property in disadvantaged areas. These areas are specified by postal codes in Schedule 3 of the Stamp Duty (Disadvantaged Areas) Regulations 2001.

11.15   Loan fees

Loan of £	*Registration Fees* *Land and Sasine Registers* £
20,000	22.00
30,000	33.00
40,000	44.00
50,000	55.00
60,000	66.00
100,000	110.00
200,000	220.00
300,000	250.00
400,000	275.00
500,000	300.00
1,000,000	450.00
in excess of £5,000,000	3,750.00

Notes:

1   Loan fees are quoted in Table 'B' of Registration Fees. There is no stamp duty on loan documents.
2   In the case of endowment loans the fee may be increased as extra work is involved.
3   Where a security is recorded together with a disposition in favour of the borrower, the dues of recording the standard security are £22.

4   All data is believed to be correct at date of publication but as these figures are liable to frequent change they should be treated as illustrative only. Recording dues are not generally subject to annual upward revision. The apparently automatic rise in house prices has had the effect of increasing the level of dues.

11.16   Land Register report fees (as at October 2002)

Form 10	£ 22.70
Form 11	13.60
Form 12	22.70
Form 13	13.60
Form 14 (to ascertain if subjects are registered or not)	22.70
Form P16 Report	22.70

Chapter 12

BORROWING ON HERITABLE PROPERTY

'Most bankers dwell in marble halls
Which they do to encourage deposits
And discourage withdrawals'

(Ogden Nash)

'I spent a lot of money on booze, birds, and fast cars. The rest I just squandered.'

(George Best)

12.1   We have assumed to date that the sellers are not repaying a loan, and that the purchasers are not taking a loan on the new house. In fact, most transactions are aided by loans, but the main bulk of the work has already been done, and a discharge or a new security does not present any great difficulty, provided you have followed the scheme of things so far.

12.2   Most loans are made by banks or building societies, or former building societies that have become banks but which have not yet attained full banking status. Local authorities also lend, particularly in purchases of public sector housing, if they have the money available. Broadly, however, the procedure is the same whoever the lender may be. I shall refer to mortgage lenders as 'lenders' and the customer as the 'borrower'. Lenders are now represented by a central body called the Council of Mortgage Lenders, who issue a handbook detailing the practices of the various lenders, and issuing standard forms. The Council's office is at 3 Savile Row, London W15 3PB. The Mortgage Lenders' handbook can be downloaded from the Council's website (www.cml.org.uk), and it should be studied carefully.

12.3   Generally, a lending institution will permit the solicitors acting for the purchasers to act also on their behalf in domestic transactions providing that the solicitors are on their approved 'panel'. This means a substantial saving in work, and thus in fees to be paid by the purchasers.

If the institution insists on using solicitors chosen by them, and some will, especially in commercial transactions, then two solicitors become involved in doing the same work and in examining the same title. This fee to the lenders' solicitors is payable by the borrowers, as well as their own solicitors' fee, all in terms of CFR(S)A 1970, Sch 3, standard condition 12. If the purchasers' solicitors also act for the lender, they are entitled to charge (a) a fee for the purchase and (b) a fee for the loan, based on the principles stated in paragraph **11.10**.

12.4   When a lending institution instructs the purchasers' solicitors to act for it as well, the solicitors may do so, provided there is no conflict of interest. If a conflict arises, the solicitors must then decide which party to represent. In all probability they will represent the purchasers, who are their clients and will return the papers to the lenders. The lenders will then instruct another solicitor.

It should be particularly noted that a solicitor acting for both borrower and lender must provide the same information to each client. They must not reveal information to one client, e g as to prices paid for the property, and not to the other. This was clearly established in the case of *Mortgage Express v Bowerman & Partners* ([1996] 2 All ER 808). If solicitors find that they are in possession of information that is clearly detrimental to one of the parties, they are under a duty to reveal it to the other party. If they feel unable to do so, they must then withdraw from acting for one, or even both, of the parties.

12.5   Where solicitors are acting for more than one borrower, and the security is being given by the borrowers, jointly and severally, it is the responsibility of the solicitors to ensure that all persons signing the security understand the extent of the security, and where appropriate the solicitors must recommend that the individuals take separate legal advice. In particular, where a wife is asked to sign a security over the family home, in support of her husband's business, it is mandatory to ensure that both parties obtain separate advice as to the extent of the obligation, from at least another partner in the firm.

12.6   This duty is clearly established in the House of Lords decision of *Royal Bank of Scotland plc v Etridge (No 2)* ([2001] 4 All ER 449). This case is an appeal from the English Appeal Court, who had laid down very strict conditions for solicitors acting in such a situation. The House of Lords moderated these somewhat in a long and complex judgment which may be summarised as follows:

- The solicitor who is to advise the wife, must explain why the meeting is being held, and the consequences of signing the security. Needless to say the husband should not be present at the meeting, and the lawyer should explain matters to the wife in non-technical language.
- The solicitor should be satisfied that the wife wishes the solicitor to advise her.
- The solicitor should be satisfied that there is no possible conflict of interest.
- The solicitor should explain the documents and what legal effects these might have.
- The solicitor should also explain the risks involved.
- The solicitor should obtain from the lender detailed information as to the husband's accounts with the lender, and his application for a loan.
- The solicitor should state what debts are being guaranteed and their amount.
- The solicitor should explain that the amount of debt and the terms may change, with or without reference to the wife.
- The solicitor should discuss with the wife her own financial means and the husband's means.
- The solicitor should explain to the wife that she has a choice in the matter, and establish that she wishes to proceed.

- The solicitor should check that the wife wishes the firm to write to the lender confirming that she has been given legal advice.

Naturally this advice will not always apply to a wife, but until now it has in all the cases involved: see *Smith v Bank of Scotland* (1997 SC (HL) 111), *Broadway v Clydesdale Bank plc* (2001 GWD 14–552), *Forsyth v Royal Bank of Scotland* (2000 SLT 1295).

12.7 Assuming that the same solicitors act for the purchasers and for the lenders, the following steps should be taken by the solicitors.

(a) The purchasers' solicitors receive and carefully peruse the lenders' instructions. After examining title, they draft a standard security and assignation of life policy (if it is an endowment mortgage).
(b) They have the standard security (and assignation if required) signed by the borrowers. In the event of the title standing in the name of one entitled spouse only, a form of consent of the loan has to be signed by the non-entitled spouse (see MH(FP)(S)A 1981). Naturally, the advice given in paragraph 12.6 also applies to the signing of the form of consent. They send the report on title, and certificate that it is in order, to the lenders and request the loan cheque. This should be done in good time for settlement (allow three to five days, shorter if the lenders will telegraph the money).
(c) The standard security should be sent to the Keeper of the appropriate register at the same time as the disposition. A notice of assignation of the life policy to the lenders should be sent in duplicate to the assurance company who issued the policy, to create a real right in the lenders. ('The assignation itself is not a complete valid right until it be orderly intimated to the debtor': Stair III, 1, 6.) One copy of this should be receipted by the assurance company ('the debtor' in Stair's words) and put with the assignation in the title deeds. The lending institution will in virtually every case insure the property in its own name 'as heritable creditors' and in the purchasers' name 'as proprietor in reversion', from the time it receives the report on title (see CFR(S)A 1970, Sch 3, standard condition 5).

    The purchasers' solicitors need not worry further about this. This insurance cover will be for reinstatement value, and should also be index-linked to increase annually with building costs. It is possible for the borrowers to obtain alternative quotations from other insurance companies, provided they are not on a fixed–interest contract, and considerable savings may be made in this way.
(d) When the titles are all in the hands of the solicitors they should then send these to the lending institution and receive their receipt. Some building societies, however, like to receive the other titles before the disposition and the standard security are returned from the record. It is a matter of reading the instructions.

Golden Rule: read the instructions carefully.

12.8 When property is sold and there is an existing security created by the sellers, the sellers' solicitors will (as above) probably be asked to act for the lenders in its discharge. In that case, the solicitors should do the following:

(a) The sellers' solicitors inform the sellers' lenders of the sale, and obtain the title deeds on loan.
(b) The sellers' solicitors inform the lenders of the sale, and the date of entry

and repayment. They ask what is the amount required to redeem the loan on that date. They draft the discharge and send it to the purchasers' solicitors for revisal.

(c)   On return of the discharge, they have the principal discharge engrossed and signed by the lenders, who return it to be held as 'undelivered pending repayment of the loan'.

(d)   The sellers' solicitors hand the discharge over at settlement, with the testing clause complete and the warrant of registration signed by the sellers' solicitors. They also give the purchasers' agents Forms 2 and 4 which are sent to the Keeper asking that the discharge be recorded, and a cheque for the appropriate fee. The letter of obligation is enlarged to include delivery of the duly recorded discharge within (say) 14 days of the recording date. The purchasers' agents send these documents to the Keeper with the disposition and a cheque for the fee together with the purchasers' standard security to their lender. All are recorded at the same time in the order: (i) discharge, (ii) disposition and (iii) standard security.

(e)   When the discharge is returned by the Keeper, this is sent to the purchasers' solicitors, who are asked to discharge the letter of obligation to that extent.

12.9   If the lenders insist on their own solicitors acting, a rather cumbersome 'three-cornered' settlement has to be arranged. This involves the lenders' solicitors handing over the cheque in return for the disposition, standard security, land certificate and letter of obligation from the purchasers' solicitors, which the purchasers' solicitors obtain from the sellers' solicitors, by presenting a cheque for the purchase price. This is, of course, dependent on the lenders' solicitors' cheque being produced. Alternatively this whole process can be conducted by post. The exact ramifications of this complex process depend on the circumstances of each transaction and are, unfortunately, only learnt by experience.

12.10   The interest rate on money borrowed for house purchase generally fluctuates with the level of interest rates on the money market. These rates are all geared around the Bank of England base rate, and rise and fall in conformity with it. The base rate is fixed by a committee of the Bank of England largely for fiscal reasons, which have little to do with supply and demand, and everything to do with world markets, and the fluctuations are quite unpredictable.

The only borrowers who are not affected are those who took out a 'fixed-rate' mortgage in the past. If such a fixed-rate contract can be obtained, it has seldom proved a mistake to take advantage of it. Fixed-rate mortgages are generally not now available, unless they are fixed for a limited period of time. They are still thought to be a good investment, although nobody knows where interest rates are going to go in the next few years. Borrowers can also obtain 'cap and collar' loans, which fix a minimum and a maximum rate of interest that can be charged on the loan.

When taking out any loan, whether over heritable property or otherwise, the borrower should clearly differentiate between 'flat rate' and 'annual percentage' (APR). The APR is the true yardstick of the cost, and must be prominently displayed in all promotional material. *The Independent* (7 October 1989) told the story of a building society which had (quite inadvertently) breached the advertising rules on this topic. The society had offered loans at an interest rate of 12.75%, which was the annual flat rate, and the advertisement also stated that the APR was 13.7%. The latter being the true rate of interest, the amount of interest payable in a year would be the amount borrowed at 13.7% rather than the amount borrowed at the flat rate (12.75%).

The Consumer Credit Act 1974 requires that the flat rate not be given greater prominence than the APR, for the flat rate, while being mathematically correct, is misleading. The reason for this is that the flat rate is applied at times which distort the amount payable. In some cases this distortion is quite dramatic, and before the coming into force of the 1974 Act it was formerly the practice of less reputable lenders to quote a low flat rate to attract investors. This rate was then applied in such a way as to provide a huge APR, which was not of course revealed. An example of the difference between flat rate and APR can be seen in advertisments for credit cards, where the flat rate appears quite reasonable (say 1½% a month) but the APR is actually nearer 30%.

12.11   Against the cost of a home loan must be set the considerable subsidy offered by the Treasury in tax allowances. Thus interest on the first £30,000 of a genuine home loan can be offset against the top slice of a person's income, and there is no capital gains tax on the sale of one's principal residence. The figure of £30,000 (restricted in 1994–95 to 20 per cent and in 1995–96 to 15 per cent) has applied for many years. Capital gains tax is, however, payable on the sale of a second home or on investment properties. If you own two or more houses you must nominate which is to be your 'main private residence' and the exemption, which may be a generous one, can only be obtained on the sale of that house. You can change your election, if your circumstances change (e g you retire to live in what was your holiday house). Generally speaking, however, you are not otherwise allowed to change your election, and certainly not in such a way as merely to avoid paying tax.

Even when capital gains tax is payable it is relatively light in comparison to income tax. The tax is payable on a 'chargeable gain' on disposal of an asset, which is defined to include land and buildings. To compute the gain on which tax is payable, you deduct from the disposal consideration (a) any incidental expenses in connection with the original acquisition, (b) any incidental expenses in connection with the disposal and (c) any 'enhancement' expenditure, that is the cost of capital improvements (e g building costs) as opposed to expenditure of a 'revenue nature' (e g decoration and maintenance).

Further, an annual exemption may be deducted from the amount of the gain, provided this has not been applied to other gains. Any gains made before 31 March 1982 may be ignored, as only gains made after that date are taxable.

Finally, an indexation allowance is applied to the amount of the gain, to strip out part of the gain that is due to the effect of inflation on the price, as opposed to the pure profit made on the sale. The indexation indices are based on the retail price index, which reflects the rate of inflation monthly.

Example   Mr and Mrs Smith bought a holiday house in January 1983, at a price of £20,000. Their total expenses on purchase amounted to £1,000, including surveyor's and lawyer's fees and outlays. They immediately spent £10,000 on building a kitchen extension. In August 1988 they sold the property for £50,000. They spent £250 on advertising the sale, and £1,000 on legal and other sale expenses. What is their taxation liability on this sale? (The retail price index in January 1983 was 82.61, and in August 1988 it was 107.90.)

Cost of house	£20,000
Add	
Enhancement Expenditure	10,000
Legal and Survey Costs	1,000
Total cost	£31,000
Add	
Indexation £31,000 $\times \dfrac{(107.9-82.61)}{82.61}$	9,490
TOTAL COST	£40,490
Proceeds of sale	£50,000

Less		
Cost as above	£40,490	
Advertising	250	
Legal and other fees	1,000	
Annual exemption 1988/89	5,000	
		£46,740
CHARGEABLE GAIN		£ 3,260

(Tax is payable on the chargeable gain at income tax rates on Mr and Mrs Smith's top slice of income.)

12.12   An average lending by a lender will normally be 2½ or 3 times the joint incomes, but this depends very much on the circumstances and to a large extent a lending that the borrower can clearly afford.

There are basically ten methods by which borrowers may repay a loan. The repayment figures, which are given for illustrative purposes only, are based on a male, non-smoking, aged 35 next birthday, borrowing £40,000 over a 25-year term. The interest rate applicable when these quotations were obtained was 6.75% gross. A more attractive rate could have been obtained in 2002, but these figures are valuable for comparative purposes:

(a) Repayment of capital and interest method.   By this method a sum is paid monthly to the lenders throughout the life of the loan. This may either be calculated on a varying payment or a level payment basis. Where the former is chosen, the payments start as relatively small and increase annually, presumably in line with the borrowers' ability to repay. When the latter method is chosen, the payment remains fixed throughout the life of the loan. In either event, part of the payment is interest and part is capital. The ratios of income to capital fluctuate throughout the term of the loan—at the start of the loan, the interest is high, but steadily falls. About two-thirds through the life of the loan the ratio of interest payment to capital repayment is roughly equal; and thereafter the capital repayment content of the monthly sum becomes progressively greater than the interest content. At the end of the loan, the payments are almost entirely composed of capital being repaid.

Tax relief on mortgage interest payments was slowly whittled away and finally cancelled in 2000. At one time when interest rates were high (15% or so) this relief was critical to the whole house purchase structure, but is now offset by lower interest rates.

A mortgage protection policy should be effected to cover the risk of the borrower dying before the loan is repaid. This is considerably cheaper than an endowment policy, because it only pays out if the borrower dies during the loan period, and the sum payable decreases every year of the loan. The monthly cost of this loan on the above assumptions, would be £276.00, on which tax relief can be obtained. A mortgage protection policy is quoted at £12.31.

(b) Endowment repayment method. The borrowers take out an endowment policy for the amount of the loan to mature on the date that the loan comes to an end. This policy is assigned to the lenders (although not all lenders insist on this now), who repay their loan from the proceeds on repayment and hand over any balance to the borrowers. Thus, if the borrowers borrow £40,000 over 25 years, the policy is on their joint lives for £40,000 and matures in 25 years. The maturity value (see below) is paid to the lenders to repay the loan. Throughout the life of the loan the borrowers pay only interest and repay no capital. If one of the borrowers does not live to the end of the loan term, the proceeds of the policy are then used to repay the loan, and the survivor gets the house free of heritable debt.

Three variations are available:

(i) **Low cost endowment, level premium.** The monthly premium is £77.77, and monthly interest of £230 approximately is payable to the lender. The monthly premium on the insurance policy are also payable. While this is attractive in terms of outlay, the snag is that the low cost endowment policy may not repay the full amount of the loan on maturity. If we assume a 6% per annum growth in the fund, there would be no excess fund at maturity.

(ii) **Low cost endowment, low start premium.** The monthly premium starts low at £44.72, but rises in year four to £89.44. Again monthly interest of around £230 is payable to the lenders, and the monthly premium on the insurance policy is also payable. Assuming, again, 6% growth in the fund, there would be no excess fund at maturity.

(iii) **Full endowment.** You get what you pay for. The monthly premium is £147.00, which is much higher than the other two methods, but the fund at maturity will pay a sum of £47,400 to the borrower, after repayment of the loan, assuming 6% growth. Again the borrower must pay interest of around £230 a month to the lender and the monthly premium to the insurance company.

In all these endowment cases, if the borrower had the misfortune to die during the loan period, the mortgage protection policy would pay out the balance of the loan, and the beneficiaries would get the house free of debt.

In recent years there has been considerable criticism directed at endowment loans, simply because in a time of comparatively low inflation, and bad investment conditions, the excess amounts payable to borrowers have sometimes been non-existent, and in some cases the policies have not paid out enough even to repay the loan. The answer is to pay bigger premiums, and the policies should always be kept under review, and topped up when required.

There is no tax relief on the premiums payable on endowment policies, which is another complaint. Life companies also have to pay tax on income earned and capital gains tax on investments sold at a profit, all of which have combined to make endowment loans less attractive.

(c) Pension mortgage.   This method is only available to the self-employed, or to those employees who have, say, personal consultancy fees on which they pay Schedule D income tax, or to employees who are not members of an occupational pension scheme. The government has, however, widened the qualifications for personal pensions, not always with happy results.

By this method the borrowers take out a personal pension plan, and the loan is repaid from the fund accumulated at date of retiral, the balance being used to purchase an annuity which will provide a pension for the borrowers. There are enormous tax advantages here; the premiums paid come off the top slice of the borrowers' income, and when the pension is claimed, any lump sum payable is tax free. The only difficulty is that a pension plan cannot be assigned in security, as can an endowment policy. A low cost life policy is therefore taken out, providing only basic life cover, and is assigned to the lender. Life policies no longer attract tax relief since 14 March 1984, but this policy is written under the Income and Corporation Taxes Act 1970, s 226A which is an exception and does still attract tax relief.

On the above assumptions, and assuming that the borrower is to retire at age 60, when the loan of £40,000 is complete, the borrower pays interest to the lender, and £161.07 net of basic tax to the pension provider, as well as the life cover. Assuming a growth of 7% in the fund, the loan will be repaid at age 60, and the borrower will get a pension of £9,890. Again in recent years this method has been criticised mainly because of poor investment conditions, the comparative lack of inflation, and the lamentable performance of some pension providers.

(d) Individual savings account (ISA) or personal equity plan (PEP) method.
(ISAs replaced PEPs, but are approximately similar in effect. Existing PEPs continue, although new ones cannot be taken out.) An ISA or PEP mortgage is similar in principle to an endowment or pension mortgage, and is repaid on an interest-only method, with the capital being repaid at the end of the term. Instead of paying life insurance premiums (other than on a simple protection policy (see para **12.12(a)**) you pay instead into an ISA or PEP. ISA funds may be invested in stock exchange securities or cash or other investments.

Thus, on the same assumptions as above, a borrower would pay interest of £230 approximate to the lender, £62.58 to the ISA provider, and pay for a mortgage protection policy. At the end of the loan period the loan would be repaid, but assuming 6% growth in the fund, there would be no surplus payable to the borrower.

(e) Over 60 or equity release plan.   This is suitable for homeowners over age 60, who enjoy living where they are, and don't want to move to a smaller house, but would appreciate having extra capital. They may borrow up to 25% of the value of their house, and make no repayments until the house is sold. The interest is accumulated to the capital sum owing, although if the appreciated sum exceeds 75% of the value of the house at any time, a repayment may be called for. The impact, however, on any housing benefit or other state benefit received by a pensioner should be taken into account. There have been some very adverse developments with these loans, and the advice of Help the Aged should be obtained if this is contemplated. Prior to the property slump of the early nineties many elderly people, especially in the south, were tempted into granting equity-release mortgages on their properties. The funds thus released were then invested in bonds, giving, supposedly, a good income. The bonds fell in value, as did the value of the houses, and thus the borrowers lost out twice, often with dire consequences. This method, therefore, requires careful consideration.

(f) Interest only schemes.   The borrower pays only interest to the society, and is left to work out the best method of repayment. This could be from an inheritance, the lump sum paid from a pension plan, the benefits of a share option scheme, the proceeds of assurance policies, or any combination of these.

(g) Fixed interest loans.   A fixed rate is offered for, say, two years, after which the loan reverts to the market-rate interest. These should not be confused with the old fixed-rate loans, which lasted the whole term of the loan, and gave some lucky people an extraordinary bargain.

(h) Discounted rate loans.   First time buyers are given a discount for the first year or two of their loan.

(i) Cap and collar loans.   Fixes a maximum and a minimum rate of interest for the loan for a given term.

(j) Foreign currency loans.   When interest rates in this country were high, it was tempting to borrow money in another country at a much lower rate. The snag with this was that if the foreign currency (e g Swiss franc) continued to appreciate against sterling, the borrower was repaying the loan at a worse (for the borrower) exchange rate. This method should really only be used by the financially sophisticated, and, even then, with care. The recent strength of sterling against other currencies has, in any event, made it less attractive.

12.13   Insurance to cover payment of premiums in a period of ill health or redundancy should also be considered by the borrower.

12.14   Formerly, tax relief could be claimed on mortgage interest. When mortgage interest rates were high, this relief was crucial to many people. It was cancelled in 2000, but is offset by lower rates of interest. This makes your self assessment tax form slightly less complicated.

12.15   Which method should be chosen? This is entirely a matter of circumstances. The following points may be considered.

(a) Expense.   While lenders were pretty cagey about the endowment method originally, they now promote it quite widely. Over the years this method soared in popularity, but is now on the wane, as it is thought that the expenses are too high, and there is no tax relief on premiums. The monthly repayment to the lenders is lower, because no capital is repaid, but the borrowers must pay the assurance policy premiums. The endowment method is therefore slightly more expensive in the average case, but this depends on the amount of the loan and the ages of the borrowers.

(b) Tax relief. Tax relief on mortgage interest payments is no longer competent, so this does not confer any advantage to any one method.

(c) Life cover. The endowment method has the advantage of providing automatic cover on the borrowers' lives; where capital repayment is used the borrowers' lives should be assured separately by the mortgage protection policy. An additional advantage in using the endowment method is that this valuable life cover is provided.

(d) Taxation in the fund's hands. Pension funds pay no capital gains tax on disposal of assets. Life assurance schemes receive income on a tax-deducted basis and pay capital gains tax on disposals. PEPs are in between—receiving income on a net basis, but paying no capital gains tax. The effects of these factors on the fund available at the end of the day should be considered.

Thus in summary, the endowment method is possibly better where a person is likely to stay a long time in the house, and the capital repayment method is possibly better for someone who intends to change in three or four years. A young couple may prefer the slightly cheaper capital repayment method at the outset. Self-employed people are probably better with the pension fund method.

While certain conclusions may be drawn from these figures, I should stress that every case should be looked at on its own merits, and no one method is automatically better than the others. It is essential that the best advice be taken. It is not axiomatic that a lender which is tied to one life office is giving the best advice, even although the office is a good one. Bear in mind that no one has to take a policy from the same source as they receive a mortgage, although it may well be convenient to do so. Solicitors are not permitted to be tied agents (see ch 1) and they must seek competitive quotations. Some solicitors will do this through Solicitors Financial Services Limited.

12.16   All loans over heritage must, since 29 November 1970, be constituted by a standard security (CFR(S)A 1970, s 9(3)). The law of standard securities is contained in Part II (ss 9 to 32) of the 1970 Act.

A standard security may either be in terms of CFR(S)A 1970, Sch 2, Form A or Form B. Form A is used where the personal obligation and the details of the loan are contained in the standard security, and is widely used by building societies. Form B is used where the personal obligations and the details of the loan are contained in a separate unrecorded document, and is widely used by banks in housing loans, or by 'commercial' lenders, e g loans in connection with trade (brewers, garage, etc) and large loans over office and factory buildings, where the parties are not anxious to make the details public.

12.17   The Conveyancing and Feudal Reform (Scotland) Act 1970, Sch 2, Form A is made up as follows:

Names of granters
Personal obligation ('Hereby undertake to pay')
Name of lender
Amount of loan

Interest and repayment details
Grant of standard security
Description of property
Incorporation of standard conditions and incorporation of any variations
  (see CFR(S)A 1970, ss 11 and 16)
Warrandice
Consent to registration for execution
Testing clause
Warrant of registration (unless land is registered)

12.18 The Conveyancing and Feudal Reform (Scotland) Act 1970, Sch 2, Form B is made up as above, but omitting the personal obligation, the amount of the loan, the interest and repayment details, and the consent to registration for execution. These are contained in a separate unrecorded bond or minute of agreement. In commercial loans this document may also carry heavy variations of the standard conditions, and trading conditions (e g in a brewer's loan). A loan to an individual from a bank will probably also be secured by this method.

12.19 Where a life policy is assigned in security, the age of the policy holder should be proved to the assurance company and 'age admitted', by producing a birth certificate for the policy holder. The solicitors should also ensure that with a new policy, the first premium has been paid and the policy is therefore in operation, and that with an old policy, the premiums are up to date and the policy not invalidated in any way.

12.20 Do not forget to intimate the assignation to the assurance company at its chief office or chief Scottish office, as shown on the policy, if this is required by the lenders. This is done by sending a notice of assignation in duplicate, one copy of which is receipted by the company and returned.

12.21 It is unwise to 'chop and change' with endowment policies. Most of the premiums in the first two years are used in the company's expenses and commission and the surrender value is liable to be very small (if any). Beware of unscrupulous agents who 'churn' policies, that is when they are arranging a new loan they advise the borrower to surrender existing policies, and take out new ones. This can be a very expensive business.

If a life policy has to be surrendered, the surrender value offered by the life office can be very disappointing. If a policy is well established, it can have a substantial surrender value, and it is certainly worth investigating if it can be sold more advantageously at an auction. A firm of auctioneers in London, Foster & Cranfield, run regular specialised auction sales for assurance policies and reversionary interests generally, and there are numerous other companies who buy well-established endowment policies. You are almost guaranteed to get more from them than from the meagre surrender values given by the assurance companies.

12.22 Discharges, partial discharges, and restrictions are discussed at paragraph **7.21**. While it is assumed that the borrowers will want to discharge the loan when it has been repaid, the smart thing may be to leave it undischarged with a balance of £1 owing. The advantage of this is that the building society will continue to look after the insurance of the property, and if a loan, say to extend the house, is required in the future, the expense of creating new security documents is avoided. The society will be quite happy with this arrangement as they will keep the insurance commission, if the policy is brokered by them. It may be prudent to check that the insurance premiums being charged by the Society are competitive.

12.23   It is, of course, quite permissible for the lenders to assign your loan to someone else, simply by granting an assignation in terms of CFR(S)A 1970, Sch 4, Form A. The borrowers' consent is not required, and the assignation is simply intimated to the borrowers. This is a useful way for the lenders to raise money, and was used by Glasgow District Council, for one, when it assigned a large number of loans to the Trustee Savings Bank. The consideration for the assignation was £4,774,727, and the deed was recorded in the Register for the County of the Barony and Regality of Glasgow (Book 14657 Folio 54) on 23 May 1985. Commercial lenders are quite used to such transactions, known as 'selling the loan book' to raise money for whatever purpose. Such transactions should not affect the borrower at all, and the expenses involved are not paid by the borrower, unlike other expenses in connection with the loan.

12.24   Where a loan is a high proportion of the purchase price, the lenders may insist on the borrowers providing an indemnity policy. Thus, if the sale price does not cover the loan, the policy provides the shortfall. There is generally a single premium payable at the time of making the loan, and as this premium is usually substantial, the purchasers should be clearly advised of the liability. If the borrowers default, the indemnity insurers pay out the sum due to the lenders. The unredeemed portion of the sum owing under the standard security is then assigned in subrogation to the insurance company, who may then pursue the borrowers, using the personal obligation contained in the standard security. The debtor, while paying the premium, generally has no rights at all under an indemnity policy, and it is understood that some lenders will not even make these policies available for inspection by debtors.

12.25   A small proportion of loans go sour every year, and, in these cases, the lender has to consider the enforcement of the loan conditions. When the Mortgage Rights (Scotland) Act 2001 was passing through Parliament, it was said that an average of 6,000 repossession actions were raised in Scotland every year, from which 5,400 decrees were granted, and 2,000 properties were repossessed. In England the court may suspend such orders, but , as was pointed out in the case of *Halifax Building Society v Gupta* (1994 SLT 339), no such power to suspend existed in Scotland. Further consideration of the 2001 Act will be given at paragraph 12.31.

12.26   The contract between lender and borrower is contained in the standard conditions of the loan. While the lenders may have made a huge loan over the property, the borrowers remain the owners, and the standard conditions are meant to make sure that the borrowers do not imperil the security of the lenders. Otherwise if the lenders have to sell the property, they may not get back their original investment.

12.27   The standard conditions are in summary: Variable condition (V); Non-variable condition (NV); and Partially non-variable condition (PNV).

(1) (V) Debtor to keep property in good and sufficient repair.
(2) (V) Debtor to complete buildings and make alterations only with creditor's permission.
(3) (V) Debtor to observe conditions of title, pay feu duty, and observe requirements of law (i e local authority notices etc).
(4) (V) Debtor to deal with planning notices.
(5) (V) Debtor to insure property for 'market value', to pay premiums, and use proceeds as directed by the creditor. Market value is almost universally changed to replacement value, especially in older buildings built with traditional materials and workmanship. In that case the replacement value may be in excess of the market value.
(6) (V) Debtor shall not let the property without the creditor's consent. In practice this means that the creditor will ensure that steps are taken to prevent the tenant from getting security of tenure.
(7) (V) If the debtor does not perform his duties, the creditor may do them, at the debtor's expense.
(8) (V) Calling up—if the creditor wants to terminate the loan, he may serve a calling-up notice, and if the loan is not repaid within two months, the debtor is in default.
(9) (V) Default—if the debtor does not comply with a calling-up notice, or a default notice, or the proprietor is insolvent, the debtor is in default and the creditor may exercise the remedies given by CFR(S)A 1970 (see App VI).
(10) (V) Rights of creditor on default (see App VI).
    (a) Remedies outwith Act (V)
    (b) Sale (NV)
    (c) Entering into possession (V)
    (d) Letting (V)
    (e) Granting leases (V)
    (f) Repair, reconstruction and improvement (V)
    (g) Foreclosure (NV)
(11) (PNV) Redemption—the debtor may redeem the loan on giving two-months' notice of intention. The two-month period is variable, but the remainder of this condition is non-variable. This provision was intended to stop people being tied up indefinitely in unattractive loans. However, it proved unsuitable to commercial lenders and the condition itself was varied by the Redemption of Standard Securities (Scotland) Act 1971.
(12) (V) The debtor is liable for the expenses of the security, any discharge or partial discharge or restriction of the security. The debtor is not responsible, however, for the expenses of the assignation of the security to a purchaser.

12.28 The creditors can, and frequently do, vary the conditions, but they cannot touch the ones that are non-variable (i e sale and foreclosure, and, partially, redemption).

12.29 If a debtor receives a calling-up notice or default notice but does not comply with it respectively in two and one months, the debtor is in default. The debtor is also in default if the propreitor of the subjects becomes insovent, bankrupt, or goes into liquidation. Finally the creditor can ask the sheriff court for power to exercise the remedies, and if this is granted, the debtor is in default.

12.30   When the debtor is in default, the creditor may exercise the remedies contained in CFR(S)A 1970, Sch 3, standard condition 10, and in tabular form in Appendix V. The most noticeable remedy is sale, which must be advertised and which must be for a fair price (see *Rimmer v Usher* 1967 SLT 7 and CFR(S)A 1970, s 25).

12.31   As was pointed out by Parliament, this is very creditor-friendly law. Once the debtor is on the slippery slope, there is very little to save them. Most reputable lenders would give a debtor a chance, if they met them half way, but not all lenders are reputable. Accordingly the Mortgage Rights (Scotland) Act 2001 gives the debtors a lifeline. If the debtors are heading towards default, an action may be raised to request the court to suspend proceedings, to allow the matter to be straightened out. Under CFR(S)A 1970, s 2(2), the court shall bear four things in mind:

(a)   the nature and reasons for the default;
(b)   the applicant's ability to fulfil the obligations within a reasonable time;
(c)   any action taken by the creditor to assist the debtor;
(d)   the ability of the applicant, and any other person living in the security subjects, to find other suitable accommodation.

12.32   It is too early to say whether MR(S)A 2001 achieves its aim. We do not know yet if it is a genuine social improvement or merely a time-wasters charter.

12.33   Further details on standard securities are available in *Standard Securities* (2nd edn 2002) Douglas J Cusine and Robert Rennie.

Chapter 13

FIRST REGISTRATION

'The Land Register for Scotland is a State guaranteed register of title to interests in land. Registration of a property for the first time in the Land Register results in the creation of a Title Sheet. The Title Sheet defines precisely the property on the Ordnance Map and also gives details of current registered owners as well as charges and burdens upon properties. The accuracy of the Title Sheet is guaranteed by the State and indemnity is payable for loss suffered as a result of an error or inaccuracy in the Register.'

(The Keeper's Report 1993–94)

First registration

13.1   The basic scheme of a transaction is similar to a transaction in sasine registration, with the addition of certain steps characteristic of land registration. This chapter should be read with reference to the timetable at the start of the book, and to the specimen transaction contained in Appendix II. It should also be read with reference to the following land registration forms:

Form 1   (Pink) and Notes—Application for first registration
Form 4   (White) and Notes—Inventory of writs
Form 6   Land certificate
Form 10   Application for report prior to registration
Form 10A Keeper's reply to Form 10 application (similar to a search)
Form 11   Application for update of Form 10A
Form 11A Continuation of the report contained in Form 10A (similar to an interim report on search)
Form 14   Application for report to ascertain whether subjects are registered or not
Form P16   (White)—Application to compare a boundary description with the Ordnance map

13.2   The offer in Appendix I is basically used in all transactions but only covers the obligations in a first land registration not for a subsequent dealing of registered land or for a sasine transaction. The form of offer for all three should otherwise be basically identical.

'In exchange for the price the seller will deliver a duly executed disposition in favour of the purchaser and will exhibit or deliver a valid marketable title together with a Form 10 Report brought down to a date as near as practicable to the date of settlement and showing no entries adverse to the seller's interest, the cost of said report being the responsibility of the seller. In addition, the seller, at or before the date of entry and at his expense, shall deliver to the purchaser such documents and evidence as the Keeper may require to enable the Keeper to issue a land certificate in the name of the purchaser as the registered proprietor of the whole subjects of offer and containing no exclusion of indemnity in terms of section 12(2) of the Land Registration (Scotland) Act 1979: such documents shall include (unless the whole subjects of offer only comprise part of a tenement or flatted building) a plan or bounding description sufficient to enable the whole subjects of offer to be identified on the Ordnance map and evidence (such as a Form P16 Report) that the description of the whole subjects of offer as contained in the title deed is *habile* to include the whole of the occupied extent. The land certificate to be issued to the purchaser will disclose no entry, deed or diligence prejudicial to the purchaser's interest other than such as are created by or against the purchaser, or have been disclosed to, and accepted by, the purchaser prior to the date of settlement.'

You will note that the obligation is similar to a sasine obligation in that a marketable title and a valid disposition are to be produced, and the main differences from a sasine obligation are (1) the search drops out and is replaced by a Form 10A report; and (2) there is an extra obligation upon the sellers to provide 'such documents and evidence including a plan' as may be required to satisfy the Keeper and enable him to issue a land certificate with the full state guarantee, without any qualification. This is a clause characteristic of land registration which keeps the sellers' solicitors 'on the hook', and ultimately responsible for the quality of the title presented for registration (see para **13.9**).

13.3   As soon as instructed the sellers' solicitors should (as well as obtaining roads certificates, planning certificates, matrimonial homes affidavits, planning permissions, building warrants, completion certificates, superiors' permissions (if required), timber treatment guarantees, replacement window guarantees, and any necessary links in title as before), send a copy of any deed plan they have from the titles together with a Form P16 asking the Keeper to compare the plan with the Ordnance Survey map. The title deeds should also be scrutinised to ascertain whether there is any obstacle to a successful sale, such as an obtrusive land obligation or a clause of pre-emption. If the title is registered there will be a land certificate; if not the assumption is that the title is not registered, but there may be some reason for a land certificate not being with the titles. If in doubt the Form 10A report will clarify this (see para **13.6**). My remarks as to the quality of plans should be noted (see para **12.2(h)**).

13.4   The Keeper will reply to Form P16 in one of the following ways:

(1) *'The subjects are not identifiable on the Ordnance map.'*   In this case there is a serious problem, and if missives have not been concluded, the seller should be advised to withdraw the subjects from sale while this is cleared up. If this is not clarified before registration the Keeper may restrict his

indemnity so as not to cover loss suffered through this defect in title. For this reason the Form P16 report should be ordered before a sale is made, but this is not always possible with an impetuous seller. In practice this reply may not necessarily be difficult to overcome—the plan may be 'floating', i e it is not related in any way to adjoining geographical features, and the land could be situated anywhere. This can be easily corrected by the insertion of necessary details, such as streets or geographical features.

(2) *'The boundaries of the subjects coincide with those on the Ordnance map.'* This is the answer you hope for, and if you get it, you can proceed without worry.

(3) *'The boundaries do not coincide with those on the Ordnance map. Please see print herewith.'* This indicates a minor, but material, discrepancy, which will have to be cleared up. It does not, however, go to the root of the sale as does Answer 1.

However, failing this discrepancy in the boundaries being clarified, the Keeper would have to give a qualified indemnity, because of the uncertainty of the boundaries. This is contrary to the obligation in the missives (see para **13.2**). This matter is clarified in the article by the Deputy Keeper in 1995 JLSS 15 which states:

> 'If the comparison confirms that the Ordnance map is correct and there is a discrepancy between the legal extent and the occupied extent, what will require to be done will depend on which extent is the greater. If the legal extent is greater than the occupied extent and the latter is contained wholly within the former then, if the purchaser is prepared to accept a title to the occupied extent, the Keeper should be informed of this when the application is made and he will process the application accordingly. The second additional question provides an opportunity to do so. Where, however, the occupied extent exceeds the boundaries of the legal extent, remedial conveyancing will be necessary and should be completed before application for registration is made.'

13.5 If the discrepancy is not major, the Keeper will provide this answer, but will not deal with the matter until the deed is presented for registration. In all likelihood the discrepancy will then be dealt with informally under the Keeper's discretion, or by using the mythical—but indispensable—'elastic tape measure'. However, where the discrepancy cannot be overlooked, the boundaries may have to be set out in a section 19 agreement, signed by the adjoining proprietors. This agreement reads, in skeletal form, and each such deed will depend on the individual circumstances of the case, as follows:

> 'WE, Proprietor 1 (name and design and specify title) and Proprietor 2 (name and design and specify title) CONSIDERING that the boundary (state circumstances) of the subjects belonging to me the said (Proprietor 1) shown on the said Plan first referred to does not coincide with the mutual boundary depicted on the current Ordnance Survey map (specify map) AND FURTHER CONSIDERING that the parties hereto are satisfied that the said mutual boundary is correctly shown on the Ordnance Survey of which a print has been annexed and subscribed as relative hereto;

> therefore it is agreed between the parties hereto as follows (state
> agreement); and the parties hereto bind and oblige themselves and
> take their respective successors and assignees bound and obliged
> to accept the said mutual boundary as defined in terms hereof: IN
> WITNESS WHEREOF (Testing Clause).'

A warrant of registration is put on the deed for each proprietor, unless one
already has a registered title. As the deed is usually prepared on the
occurrence of a first registration on one or other property, the agreement is
recorded in the Sasine Register prior to the land registration, and the
appropriate correction is carried onto the land certificate.

A Form P16 report will not be provided by the Keeper for a flat in a
tenement, and should not therefore be requested.

13.6   Further before missives are concluded, the sellers' solicitors should send
a Form 10 to the register, which is 'an application for report prior to registration'.
The Keeper responds with an LR(S)A 1979, Form 10A report which is equivalent
to a sasine search. The Form 10A report also contains a definitive statement as
to whether the title has been registered or not, if, for some reason, this cannot
be deduced from scrutiny of the title deeds (see para **13.3**).

Alternatively a Form 14 report can be obtained to ascertain whether a title
is registered or not ('application for report to ascertain whether or not subjects
have been registered'), but this contains nothing the Form 10A report does not
contain. The main purpose of a Form 14 report is where the enquirer has no
knowledge of the subjects or the state of the title. The sellers' solicitors should
ideally not, of course, be in this position. This is to some extent, it is admitted,
a counsel of perfection—but often the first time solicitors know a house is to be
sold is when an offer lands at their reception with a 12-hour time limit for
acceptance!

13.7   When missives are complete the sellers' solicitors send to the
purchasers' solicitors the following:

(a) The title deeds being sent to the Keeper (detailed at para **13.15**). It is not
     necessary to send any other deeds, including the search, although this
     may be helpful.
(b) Draft letter of obligation for approval.
(c) Any other relevant documents such as roads certificates, property enquiry
     reports, building warrants and completion certificates, guarantees, links
     in title, and matrimonial homes consents.
(d) A Form 10A report with a draft Form 11.
(e) A Form P16 report.

13.8   The draft letter of obligation is in terms similar to:

> With reference to the settlement of the above transaction today, we
> hereby (1) undertake to clear the records of any deed, decree or
> diligence (other than such as may be created by or against your
> clients) which may be recorded in the Property or Personal
> Registers, or to which effect may be given in the Land Register in
> the period from*   to†   inclusive (or to the

earlier registration of your clients' interest in the above subjects), which would cause the Keeper to make an entry on, or qualify his indemnity in the Land Certificate to be issued in respect of that interest; and (2) confirm that, to the best of our knowledge and belief, as at this date, the answers to the questions numbered 1 to 14 in draft Form 1 adjusted with you (in so far as the answers relate to our client or to our clients' interest in the above subjects) are still correct.

*Insert date of certificate of Form 10 (or Form 11) report.
†Insert date 14 days (or such other period as may be agreed) after settlement.

This letter of obligation is signed and adopted as holograph. This letter keeps the seller 'on the hook' and is the letter of obligation called for in the offer printed at Appendix I.11. It is also a 'classic' letter of obligation (see App I.18(b)).

Due to the Requirements of Writing (Scotland) Act 1995 it is no longer necessary to sign offers and acceptances 'adopted as holograph'.

13.9 The Form 10 asks the Keeper to provide the following details:

(a) A search in the Register of Inhibitions and Adjudication against the party(ies) last infeft for five years to date of certificate, and any other parties interested (e g their building society or other parties who have disposed of the house within the past ten years).
(b) A list of deeds recorded within the prescriptive period (see para **7.10**).
(c) A statement of securities within 40 years prior to the date of certificate and for which no final discharge has been recorded (see para **7.24**).
(d) A statement of discharge of securities within the five years prior to the date of certificate (see para **7.13**).
(e) Deeds other than transfer, or deeds creating or affecting securities recorded within the 40 years prior to the date of certificate (any miscellaneous recorded deeds).

13.10 If there is a significant time gap between obtaining the Form 10A report and settlement this report should be brought down to a date nearer settlement by sending a Form 11 to the Keeper for a more current report (Form 11A). This simply continues the Form 10A report. It may be tempting to delay the ordering of a Form 10A report until a date near settlement, and to save a little money on a Form 11A report, but this is playing with fire, as the Form 10A may disclose something prejudicial that you should have known much earlier.

The Keeper will normally reply to reports within two days, or for a small additional charge will fax the report. An almost instant reply can be obtained by faxing requests for reports, and requesting a faxed reply.

13.11 The purchasers' solicitors look through the title and the contents of the Form 10A report, which is equivalent to a search, and will prepare their observations on title, revise the draft letter of obligation, draft discharge of the sellers' security, and return these to the sellers' agents. They also send back the draft disposition they will have drafted, which is drawn in exactly the same manner as one for unregistered land but contains no warrant for registration (a much simpler form is used for subsequent transfers) and drafts of Forms 1 and 4. The sellers' solicitors approve these and then return them.

13.12   Form 1 ('the pink form') is an 'application (to the Keeper) for first registration'. The Keeper requires the applicant for registration to answer (as at 2002) 14 questions, which are self-explanatory (except for two). These questions should be answered truthfully. You are asking the Keeper to guarantee a title, and the Form 1 is therefore like an insurance proposal, and is therefore to be completed in the utmost good faith.

Forms 1, 2 and 3 are (i) a request for registration; (ii) a form of proposal for insurance; and (iii) a list of questions that every conveyancer should be asking anyway, and as such, a valuable aide-memoire.

As with other forms, notes and directions are given for completion. The form itself and the notes are quite self-explanatory, and more or less straightforward, but it might be mentioned that the purchaser has to supply the following information to the Keeper of the Land Register:

(a) a short description only of the subjects to which the deed being registered relates; that is an identifiable postal address, rather than a full conveyancing description;

(b) the full name of the person granting the deed (i e the seller) or the party last infeft if it is not the granter. Thus, if John Smith owned the property, but has died, and his executors were granting the deed without having made up a recorded title, the purchasers' solicitors would insert the late John Smith's name here, as the person last infeft;

(c) the name and address of the grantee (i e purchaser) who is applying for registration;

(d) the price;

(e) the purchasers' solicitors sign the application on page one 'I/We certify that the information supplied in this application is correct to the best of my/our knowledge and belief and apply for registration in respect of Deed No   in the Inventory of Writs (Form 4)'. This certificate and signature are equivalent to the warrant of registration placed on sasine dispositions, but not necessary here;

(f) the presenting solicitors' name, address reference and FAS number (for financial accounting purposes).

13.13   Further in Form 1, Pt B a number of questions must be answered, most of which are self-explanatory, but three only require further explanation:

No. 3.   'Is there any person in possession or occupation of the subject or any part of them adversely to the interest of the applicant?'

Here the applicants' solicitors should give details of any tenancy under a lease or any tenant who may have acquired security of tenure.

No. 5(c).   'Are there any over-riding interests affecting the subjects or any part of them which you wish noted on the title sheet?'

An 'over-riding interest' is defined by LR(S)A 1979, s 28(1) as including (in summary) a right or interest over land of lessee under a lease which is not a long lease who has acquired a real right by virtue of possession; a crofter or cottar; the proprietor of the dominant tenement in a servitude; the Crown or other authority under an enactment which does not require the recording of a deed in the register to complete the right; the holder of a floating charge, whether crystallised or not; a member of the public in respect of a public right of way or *regalia majora*; any person having a right which has been made real other than by registration. This definition does not include properly constituted land obligations which are covered in the schedule of burdens, p 4 of the form. Section 28 would seem to refer principally to minor public services, rights of way acquired by prescription, etc.

No. 7.   Where any party to the deed inducing registration is a company registered under the Companies Acts can you confirm:

(a)   that it is not a charity as defined in s 112 of the Companies Act 1989 and
(b)   that the transaction to which the deed gives effect is not one to which s 322A of the Companies Act 1985 applies.

This question refers to the ultra vires doctrine (within the company's powers), which used to be applied strictly, but is not so important nowadays, except for (a) where the company selling property is a charity and (b) where the company is transferring property to its directors. In both cases the power to transfer property in these circumstances must be seen to exist.

The questions asked in Form 1 are helpful to solicitors and Keeper alike. For solicitors, they present a check list of questions that should be asked of the sellers' solicitors (e g where the deed inducing registration is in implement of the exercise of a power of sale under a heritable security—have the statutory procedures necessary for the proper exercise of such power been complied with? Yes/No). From the Keeper's point of view, it helps him to identify any problem at an early stage.

13.14   On Form 1, p 4, you are required to state what heritable securities (if any) affect the property. Please note this covers only existing securities transferred with the property, and not any new security created by the purchaser which are dealt with as a dealing in registered land and by use of a Form 2 (blue) for the security. Similarly you are also required to state the writs concerning the property which state land obligations.

13.15   The other form to be completed by the purchasers at this stage is Form 4 ('inventory of writs relevant to application for registration'). Again the notes relative to this form require careful study, and most particularly one should note the definition of 'relevant deeds and documents'.

The Keeper does not require all the writs of the property, no matter how old or obsolete, through the acting of prescription. He does require:

(a)   a sufficient progress of titles including the deed inducing registration and unrecorded links in title;
(b)   all prior writs containing rights or burdens affecting the land;
(c)   a feu duty redemption receipt (if applicable);
(d)   any existing heritable securities and related deeds;
(e)   a deed outside the prescriptive progress which contains a plan;
(f)   Form P16 (see para **13.4**)—this report must now be returned to the Keeper;
(g)   matrimonial affidavits, consents or renunciations, as appropriate;
(h)   any other relevant document.

13.16   On receipt of these documents from the purchasers' solicitors, the sellers' solicitors should then:

(a) if not already done, send the Form 10 in *duplicate* and Form P16 to the Keeper, and send the resulting reports to the purchasers' solicitors;
(b) revise and return the purchasers' solicitors' Forms 1, 4 and draft disposition;
(c) answer any title queries and obtain anything further required by the purchasers (cf para **10.2**).

13.17   The purchasers' solicitors then have the disposition engrossed and return it to the sellers' solicitors for signature, with the draft for comparison, and blank form of particulars of signing and witnesses. Forms 1 and 4 are typed in principal form. Everything is prepared for settlement as before.

13.18   At settlement the sellers' solicitors hand over in exchange for the price:

(a) the signed disposition, draft and particulars of signing;
(b) Form P16 report;
(c) letter of obligation (in terms of para **13.8**). They also exhibit the draft letter of obligation to the purchasers' solicitors to enable them to check the principal;
(d) the title deeds and any other relevant papers;
(e) the receipted state for settlement;
(f) Form 11A report, which brings down the report to a date as close as possible to settlement. This should be applied for by the seller at least three working days before settlement. Sellers' solicitors who have applied for, but not yet received, a Form 11A report at settlement, may obtain a telephoned or faxed report from Register House, at a small fee. This allows the sellers' solicitors to grant a letter of obligation with an easy conscience (para **13.8**).

13.19   The purchasers' solicitors then send off to the Keeper:

(a) Forms 1 and 4, the latter in duplicate;
(b) the disposition;
(c) the various documents specified in 13.15.

The Keeper checks off the deeds against the Form 4, and acknowledges receipt by returning the duplicate Form 4, which also bears the new title number and the date of the registration, both of which can be regarded as conclusive.

   The purchasers' solicitors then settle up the odds and ends of the transaction as they would have under the old system and answer any questions the Keeper may have.

13.20   Assuming that everything is in order, the Keeper will send out in due course a land certificate, Form 6, which discloses the following:

(a) Registered number of the title.
(b) Statement of indemnity.   'Subject to any specific qualification … a person who suffers loss as a result of any of the events specified in s 12(1) of the above [1979] Act shall be entitled to be indemnified in respect of that loss by the Keeper of the Registers of Scotland in terms of that Act.'

(c) **Section A—the property section.** A description of the property and a coloured plan based on the Ordnance Survey scale 1:1,250 for densely populated urban areas; 1:2,500 for less densely populated urban areas and farms; or 1:10,000 for hill farms, mountains and moorland.

(d) **Section B—the proprietorship section.** The name and designation of the proprietor, the date of registration (i e when the real right was created), the price and the date of entry.

(e) **Section C—the charges section.** Details of charges affecting the property whether previously existing or created by the proprietor. There is also a separate charge certificate (Form 7, see para **16.2**).

(f) **Section D—the burdens section.** A verbatim note of all land obligations affecting the property, in so far as still relevant and existing. The Keeper discards what he considers all irrelevant information: such as narrative and ancillary clauses; descriptions; old and useless burdens, such as details of roads that have long since been formed; and retains only the relevant ones. The Keeper is walking a tightrope in this respect, for what may be considered to be irrelevant, may turn out to be painfully relevant (see leasehold casualties) and the Keeper will be responsible for any loss in respect of lost rights (see ch 21).

13.21 When the purchasers' solicitors receive the land certificate, they should read it to confirm it is in order and then discharge the letter of obligation (assuming that all other items on it have been met) and return it to the sellers' solicitors.

13.22 This wonderful document completely takes the place of the title deeds, and can be brought up to date in future, as and when required. If it is lost an office copy can be obtained from the Keeper who prepares this from the title sheet. You can, in theory at least, tear up all the title deeds—but before you do so remember (1) it is better to keep them until the first sale, just in case there has been a mistake that has been overlooked; (2) they belong to the owner of the house who may very well want to keep them; and (3) the deeds may have archival interest to the local archivist who should be allowed to see any old documents before they are shredded.

13.23 If the purchasers sell the property in the course of registration, a difficult situation arises. The Keeper can be requested to return the title deeds, but this only delays the registration. Alternatively, the Keeper prefers to supply photocopies of the title deeds, but this is an expensive and time-wasting procedure. The Keeper in a circular to the profession suggested that, if there is any likelihood of the property being sold before registration is complete, the applicants' solicitors should take photocopies of the deeds presented before sending them. This is not very satisfactory either. This problem has become less acute as registration delays have decreased.

In any event, when the sellers' solicitors do get the title, or photocopies of them, they are sent to the purchasers' solicitors, and in all other respects the transaction proceeds as a normal dealing of a registered interest (see ch 15).

13.24 Armed with the land certificate and after a great deal of hard work, the lawyer's job is now a great deal easier. In summary, it might be said that the main difference between this transaction and a sasine transaction is that there is a greater burden on the sellers' solicitors in a land registration transaction. If they do not ensure that the papers presented to the Keeper are in order, they will have to rectify these sooner or later, under the terms of the letter of obligation. The purchasers' solicitors are essentially the 'middlemen' between the sellers' solicitors and the Keeper.

Chapter 14

THE DEALING

'Once a property is registered, subsequent transfers are much simpler to effect, thus providing scope for lower conveyancing costs.'

(Keeper's Report 1993–94)

14.1 A dealing is a second registration and subsequent registrations of the same subjects, together with a transfer of a part of a registered holding (see ch 15), securities, discharges or other deeds granted affecting the subjects, at any time after, or contemporaneously with, the first registration (as opposed to part of the subjects only).

14.2 The land registration forms which I refer to in this chapter are:

Form 2 (Blue) Application for registration of a dealing
Form 4 Inventory writs
Form 6 Land certificate
Form 12 Application for report over registered subjects (similar in purpose to Form 10 in a first registration)
Form 13 Continuation of Form 12 (similar to the Form 11 in a first registration).

14.3 The missives are completed exactly as previously, in the compendious form, which includes the obligation for dealings in land:

'In exchange for the purchase price there will be delivered a duly executed disposition in favour of the purchasers and there will be exhibited or delivered to the purchasers

(i) a land certificate (containing no exclusion if indemnity under section 12(2) of the Land Registration (Scotland) Act 1979), (ii) all necessary links in title evidencing the sellers' exclusive ownership of the subjects of offer and (iii) a Form 12 report brought down as near as practicable to the date of settlement and showing no entries adverse to the sellers' interest. The cost of said report shall be the responsibility of the purchasers.

In addition, the sellers will furnish to the purchasers such documents and evidence as the Keeper may require to enable the interest of the purchasers to be registered in the Land Register without exclusion of indemnity under section 12(2). The land certificate to be issued to the purchasers will disclose no entry, deed, or diligence prejudicial to the purchasers' interest, other than such as are created by, or against the purchasers, or have been disclosed to and accepted by the purchasers prior to the date of settlement.'

The sellers' obligation is thus to provide a valid disposition, a clear title in the form of a land certificate without restriction of indemnity, and clear searches in the shape of Form 12 and 13 reports.

14.4   The land certificate is sent to the purchasers' solicitors together with:

(a) a draft Form 12 (not a Form 10 which is applicable only prior to a first registration). Form 12 is a report over registered subjects;
(b) any other certificate (e g planning and roads), affidavits, links in title etc that may be required;
(c) draft letter of obligation.

The title deeds, of course, need not be sent as they are replaced by the land certificate.

14.5   The purchasers' solicitors inspect the various sections of the land certificate. This is a matter of comparative simplicity, because the land certificate contains all relevant information that would have previously required to be extracted from the title deeds. Everything now is nicely printed in a central document, and you do not have to hunt through a mass of spidery handwriting, on crumbling paper, to discover the land obligations affecting the land. This makes it all the more imperative that you read the land certificate very carefully—there are no excuses available if you do not.

The purchasers' solicitors also draw up a draft disposition. This document is simplicity itself, because you need only state the postal address of the property and the number of the land certificate, which provide a sufficient description. You do not require a traditional conveyancing description, nor need you mention the deeds referred to for the land obligations they contain. The disposition thus becomes a very short document. It is perhaps paradoxical that as missives have got longer and longer, the disposition, which is still the primary deed of transfer, has shrunk to almost nothing.

The disposition need contain only the following:

(a) narrative clause—granter, grantee, and consents, and the consideration;
(b) dispositive clause—words of transference, destination of grantee, postal address of subjects, and land certificate number;
(c) ancillary clauses—date of entry, warrandice, stamp duty mitigation certificate (if appropriate);
(d) testing clause.

A sample disposition might therefore read:

I, Allister McAllister (design) in consideration of the price of
FIFTY NINE THOUSAND NINE HUNDRED POUNDS (£59,900)
paid to me by JAMES MEIKLE (design) HEREBY DISPONE to the
said James Meikle and his executors and assignees ALL and
WHOLE the subjects 3 Miller Drive, Paisley, Renfrewshire,
registered under Title Number   ; with entry on Thirty first
October Nineteen hundred and ninety four; and I grant
warrandice; and I certify that the transaction hereby effected does
not form part of a larger transaction or of a series of transactions
in respect of which the amount or value or the aggregate amount
or value of the consideration exceeds sixty thousand pounds: IN
WITNESS WHEREOF (Testing Clause)

Note: There is no reference to burdens, no parts and pertinents and no warrant of registration.

14.6 Form 2 (blue) and Form 4 are filled up in accordance with the printed form of instructions. This Form 2 is substantially the same as Form 1 (pink) (see para **14.8**), and nothing further need be added in this respect. The draft Form 2 is returned to the sellers' solicitors for approval together with:

(a) draft letter of obligation, duly approved;
(b) draft Form 12 (application for report over registered subjects) duly approved;
(c) the draft disposition;
(d) the land certificate and other papers sent by the sellers' solicitors;
(e) draft Form 4 (inventory of writs).

14.7 The sellers' solicitors revise the disposition and return it to the purchasers' solicitors, who in turn have this document engrossed and send the typed deed and draft back to the sellers' solicitors for signature by their clients. The draft disposition is also returned for comparison purposes.

14.8 The sellers' solicitors send Form 12 to Meadowbank House or George Square, as appropriate, for a Form 12A report which they exhibit to the purchasers' solicitors. The latter should satisfy themselves as to the sufficiency of the report, as with an interim report in preregistration procedures. If there is a significant time gap between obtaining the Form 12 report and settlement this report should be brought down to a date nearer settlement by sending a Form 13 to the Keeper for a more current report, observing a three-working-day period.

14.9 Settlement duly takes place and the disposition, Form 2 (duly signed), Form 4, land certificate and such other papers as are required (see para **13.13**) are sent to the Keeper. In due course the land certificate is returned, with the purchasers' name inserted in the proprietorship section. The letter of obligation, which is in the terms following, is returned to the sellers' solicitors.

> With reference to the settlement of the above transaction today, we hereby (1) undertake to clear the records of any deed, decree or diligence—other than such as may be created by or against your clients—which may be recorded in the Personal Register in the period from*   to†   inclusive (or to the earlier registration of your clients' interest in the above subjects) and which would cause the Keeper to make an entry on, or qualify his indemnity in, the Land Certificate to be issued in respect of their interest; and (2) confirm that, to the best of my knowledge and belief, as at this date the answers to the questions numbered 1 to 8 in the draft Form 2 adjusted with you (in so far as these answers relate to my client or to my client's interest in the above subjects) are still correct.

*Insert date of certification of Form 12 report, or if a Form 13 report has been instructed, the date of certification of that report. If there is a significant time gap between obtaining the Form 12 report and settlement, the report should be brought down to a date nearer settlement by sending a Form 13 to the Keeper, who will return a more up-to-date report.

†Insert a date 14 days (or such other period as may be agreed) after settlement.

14.10   The land certificate and other relevant papers are kept carefully either by the client, or as instructed by the client. If the land certificate is misplaced, an office copy can be obtained from the Land Register (see para **15.7**). If a land certificate is irretrievably lost, a substitute one can be requested from the Keeper. The Keeper is, however, reluctant to issue one unless satisfied by due inquiry and certification that every reasonable effort has been made to locate the land certificate, which accordingly can be viewed as irretrievably lost, as distinct from misplaced.

Chapter 15

SOME OTHER REGISTRATION PROCEDURES

'As regards turnround times for Transfers of Part, in the last Report it was reported that the legal profession had intimated, through the Joint Consultative Committee of the Agency and the Law Society of Scotland, its preference for the current policy of attempting to ensure conformity with the legal extent and the fenced position as picked up by the Ordnance Survey. The continuation of this policy means that turnround time is an inappropriate measure of performance and the sole measure is output. In that respect output exceeded intake by slightly over 6%.'

(Keeper's Report 1993–94)

Application for registration of a transfer of part of registered holding

15.1   This procedure is similar to that under chapter 14 ('blue form' procedure) which refers to the transfer of an entire landholding. Thus if A bought a house in 1993, registered the title, and then resold the house in 1999, the proper procedure is the 'blue form' procedure. If, however, a builder bought a two-acre field in 1993, registered the title and then sold off the field in 20 plots with houses, then the appropriate procedure for each house purchase is 'yellow form'.

Again the yellow form is largely similar to the pink and blue forms (Forms 1 and 2) and there are similar official notes for its completion. The transaction will follow the same course as a 'blue form' transaction (see ch 14). The disposition, however, is slightly different, as the proper conveyancing description must be prepared for the plot of land being split off the larger, registered, subjects.

If you refer to the sample disposition of 3 Miller Drive, Paisley, in paragraph **14.5**, and then assume that part of the (presumably large) garden is being sold for the building of a small house, then the disposition would read along these lines:

'I, JAMES MEIKLE (design) in consideration of the price of £X paid to me by JEREMIAH JONES (design) HEREBY DISPONE to the said JEREMIAH JONES and his executors and assignees ALL and WHOLE that plot of ground in the County of Renfrew containing one-tenth of an acre Imperial Measure delineated and shown within the boundaries coloured red on the plan annexed to this Disposition; being part of the subjects registered under Title number REN   . (Thereafter insert any new land obligations relating to the new holding: the date of entry; warrandice; stamp duty clause; and testing clause.)

Considerable difficulties in registration are caused by builders lodging estate plans with the Keeper, of proposed building estates, and then not adhering to them. This is not done maliciously, it's just that it's easy to draw a site plan in the office, but hard to mark out the site accurately on the ground, and the boundary markers are often misplaced, or run over by a bulldozer. The fence is then placed in a position different from the site plan, and this is the boundary that is picked up by the Ordnance Survey when it maps the site. For this reason the Keeper will take some time to produce a land certificate, as it will be necessary to obtain an Ordnance map of the estate, and to see that all the land certificates in the estate are consistent with each other.

Charges over land under registration procedures

15.2   The first thing to point out is that if you frame a new security over unregistered land without a transfer of ownership for valuable consideration in an operational area, this security is registered in the General Register of Sasines, which continues to run in parallel with the Land Register. Thus, for example, if A has a loan from Y building society, but discharges this and creates a new security in favour of Z building society, then both of these deeds are registered in the General Register of Sasines. Similarly if A dispones a half interest in his house to his spouse for 'love, favour and affection', that is not a valuable consideration and the disposition is registered in the General Register of Sasines. If, however, you buy a house for valuable consideration in an operational area, you must register the title (pink form) and register any simultaneous or subsequent security, using the blue form procedure (Form 2).

You will see that the notes for the blue form say that this form is to be used among other things for:

(a) standard security over the whole of the interest;
(b) standard security over part of the interest in one registered title;
(c) discharge of a registered standard security (a discharge of an unregistered security will be registered in the General Register of Sasines).

The standard security is sent to the Land Register, with a blue form and the land certificate, and any existing charge certificate (which is prepared by the Keeper to conform with Form 7), and any other writs which may be necessary (such as links in title, but see explanatory notes for fuller details).

The charge thus created is entered into section C of the land certificate (the charges section). A charge certificate (Form 7) is also prepared, which is made to agree with the title sheet. The certificate certifies that the lender is a registered creditor in the heritable security on the date of registration. The standard security is also annexed to the charge certificate. Where a limited company is creating the security, a copy of the certificate of registration of charge in the Register of Charges (which is mandatory under the Companies Act 1985, ss 410ff) should be sent to the Keeper within 21 days of the registration of the standard security in the Land or Sasine Registers. Where separate solicitors act for the lender, as is usually the case, a letter of obligation is given to them by the borrowers' solicitors in the following terms:

(a) *First registration or purchase of registered interest with immediate grant of a standard security*

'With reference to the settlement of the above transaction today, we hereby undertake to deliver to you within twelve (or as appropriate) months of this date a Land Certificate issued by the Keeper of the Registers of Scotland in favour of our clients, showing the interest of our clients as registered proprietors of the above subjects, which Land Certificate shall be unaffected by any deed, decree, or diligence—other than such as may be created by or against your clients—given effect to in the Land Register in the period from*   to†   inclusive, or to the earlier date of registration of clients' Standard Security over the above subjects, and further will disclose the Standard Security granted in favour of your clients; provided that it is presented for registration in the Land Register within fourteen days of this date.'

*Date of certificate 10/11/12/13.
†Fourteen days after settlement.

'Further we (1) undertake to exhibit to you along with the said Land Certificate all deeds, documents and other evidence which were submitted to the Keeper in support of our clients' application for registration of their interest as heritable proprietors of the above subjects; and (2) confirm that, to the best of our knowledge and belief, as at this date the answers to the Questions numbered 1 to 8 in the draft Form 2 adjusted with you—in so far as these relate to our clients or to our clients' interest in the above subjects—are still correct.

We further undertake to exhibit to you within fourteen days of this date the duplicate Form 4 lodged with our clients' application for registration with the Keeper's acknowledgment thereon.§

Yours faithfully,'

§Where purchasers' solicitors lodge the purchasers' application with the Keeper; or where there are two lenders, one of whom will present that application.

(b) *Where borrower is already registered proprietor of the interest to be secured*

'With reference to the settlement of the above loan transaction today, I hereby (1) undertake to clear the records of any deed, decree, or diligence—other than such as may be created by or against your clients—which may be recorded in the Personal Register or to which effect may be given in the Land Register in the period from*   to†   inclusive (or to the earlier date of registration of your clients' interest in the above subjects) which would cause the Keeper to make an entry on, or qualify his indemnity in, the Title Sheet relating to my clients' interest in the above subjects; and (2) confirm that, to the best of my knowledge and belief, as at this date the answers in Questions numbered 1 to 8 in the draft Form 2 adjusted with you—in so far as these answers relate to your client or to my clients' interest in the above subjects—are still current.

I further undertake on behalf of my clients, to deliver to you within two months a clear Search in the Companies and Charges Register in terms of the Memorandum adjusted between us down to the date occurring twenty one days after today's date.

Yours faithfully,

*Insert date of Form 12/13 report.
†Insert date fourteen days from settlement.

Form 5—Application for noting an over-riding interest or for entry of discharge of an over-riding interest or of additional information

15.3   An over-riding interest is defined in s 28(1), which is the definition section (see para **13.13**). Reference should be made to this subsection, but the interest is generally an interest in the land concerned, enjoyed, by a third party, and not constituted by a deed recorded in the General Register of Sasines. Some examples given are:

(a) the interest of a lessee under a long lease, provided that the leasehold interest has not been registered in the Land Register. On registration the interest ceases to come within the definition of an over-riding interest;
(b) the right of a crofter under the crofting legislation;
(c) the dominant tenement in a servitude;
(d) a public right of way.

Such over-riding interests are generally to be notified to the Keeper on the pink, blue or yellow forms as appropriate, and they are noted on the title sheet. Any interest or discharge of an interest not thus notified, should be notified on Form 5, in terms of the Land Registration (Scotland) Rules 1980, r 13.

Form 8—Application for land or charge certificate to be made to correspond with the title sheet (Land Registration (Scotland) Rules 1980, r 16)

15.4   Where a certificate has been in existence for some time, without any dealings taking place, the Keeper may be requested in a Form 8 to bring it up to date with his title sheet.

Form 9—Application for rectification of the Register (Land Registration (Scotland) Rules 1980, r 20)

15.5   Where it appears to any party that there is a mistake in the land certificate, however trivial or however fundamental, the Keeper may be requested to rectify this mistake. Reference is made to LR(S)A 1979, s 9.

Form 14—Application to ascertain whether or not the subjects have been registered

15.6   This form may be used in the course of a normal transaction but it is more usual to obtain this information from the relevant part of the Form 10. (see para **13.6**.)

Form 15—Application for an office copy of a land certificate or charge certificate or any part of one of these

15.7   An office copy of the title sheet kept by the Keeper may be requested if a land certificate is in constant use or is misplaced. The office copy may be of the whole title sheet or any part of it, or of any document referred to in it. If a land certificate is irretrievably lost, see the comments in paragraph **14.10**.

Rectification of boundaries

15.8   When the boundary disclosed on the deed plan and the boundary shown on the Ordnance Survey plan do not agree, as will happen from time to time, an agreement in terms of LR(S)A 1979, s 19, may be signed by the parties concerned and registered. This agreement should also contain a plan showing the agreed boundary. The agreement is registered in the Land Register, in the case of registered interests, or in the Sasine Register, in the case of unregistered interests (for style, see para **13.5**).

Legal and occupational extents of boundaries

15.9   Forms 1, 2 and 3 pose the question: 'Is there any person in possession or occupation of the subjects or any part of them adversely to the interest of the applicant?' The main purpose of this question is to elicit whether legal and occupational extents correspond, and whether there may be a competition in title with, e g a neighbour.

Long leases

15.10   The transfer of an interest which is held under a long lease is also a registerable event. A long lease is defined in LTR(S)A 1974, as being a lease over 20 years' duration. In practice, many commercial leases will be for a long period, because only by registering a lease may a security over that lease be created. The LTR(S)A 1974, s 12, also prohibited the creation of leases of residential property for a period exceeding 20 years. This is therefore a matter principally for commercial leases, although a pre-1974 residential long-lease may still be registered, if it hasn't been already. Similarly an assignation of a registered long-lease, or a sublease, or a subunderlease, or a standard security over any part of the property contained in the registered lease, may be registered.

If an unregistered long-lease has less than 20 years to run, but its length was originally over 20 years, it may still be registered. Thus (writing in 2002) a lease for a 25-year period, granted say in 1987, may still be registered although it has only a life of a further ten years. The registration of a long leasehold interest proceeds in exactly the same way as the registration of a right of ownership, although one must apply for the registration of an assignation etc, and not of a disposition.

Obtaining guidance from the Keeper

15.11   The Keeper and his staff are very helpful, and are willing to discuss any problems that you may have. If it is a general question, ask the group services for the appropriate division at Edinburgh or George Square, Glasgow, but if it is a specific question, ask for the appropriate county register, and specify the title number, or the property involved. The telephone numbers are: Meadowbank House, tel: 0131 659 6111; and George Square, tel: 0141 306 4424. See also the Registers of Scotland website, which contains a lot of useful information: www.ros.gov.uk.

In return the legal profession owe consideration to the Keeper's staff. In particular, you should:

(a) Not bombard the Keeper with stupid or hypothetical questions. The story goes that the stupidest question ever asked was 'does a title in Paisley have to be registered?'
(b) Fill in the correct forms carefully and accurately. Do not forget to sign applications for reports and registration. Check all writs carefully before sending them—that they are properly signed, stamped, completed, and that the testing clauses are in order.
(c) Send duplicates of forms where these are specified.
(d) Check that you have up-to-date forms.
(e) Obtain quick copies of deeds that you do not have. Do not expect the Land Register to obtain these itself, just because it is in the same building as the Sasine Register. It will not, as this would impose an intolerable extra workload. Keep copies on file of all important deeds sent to the register, in case a resale is necessary before the land certificate is sent.
(f) Make sure that if you have a note that the Keeper has already seen a common title in connection with another earlier application, quote that title number to the Keeper.
(g) Pay fee notes promptly. Since the passing of the Land Registers (Scotland) Act 1995 it is important to remember to send a cheque for registration dues with the application.

Part three

TRANSFERS OF SPECIAL SUBJECTS

Chapter 16

TRANSFERS OF SUPERIORITIES

'One of Jersey's leading lawyers is using an obscure feudal title, which has been in his family for years, to try and win legal control of a £1 billion development site on the island.

Tradition says that the rights extend as far as the seigneur could ride his horse into the sea at low tide. Mr Falle is asserting that the feudal rights over the foreshore, which boasts the island's main power station, a fuel farm, and a large area of reclaimed land, include ownership.

If Mr Falle wins, the States—the island's parliament—has been advised by lawyers that he would own everything built on the land in perpetuity.'

(*The Times*)

16.1   Scotland and the Channel Islands remain the last bastions of feudalism in the civilised world, and as long as they do, we shall be subjected to picturesque medieval claptrap and blackmail by title raiders, that is to say purchasers who buy these titles solely to squeeze out of the carcass what they can get. Their reasons for doing so are narrated at paragraph **16.11**. Hopefully the Abolition of Feudal Tenure etc (Scotland) Act 2000, which has received the royal assent, but has not yet been brought into operation, will spell an end to the feudal system so far as Scotland is concerned. The operative date of the Act depends on the passage through Parliament of the Title Conditions (Scotland) Bill, which was introduced in Parliament in June 2002, but this is a long and complex Bill, and it may take until 2003 or 2004 to declare the appointed day.

16.2   Until AFT(S)A 2000 becomes operational, lawyers will have to deal with superiority estates. Section 1 of the 2000 Act provides that 'the feudal system of land tenure, that is to say the entire system whereby land is held by a vassal on perpetual tenure from a superior is, on the appointed day, abolished'. Section 2 of the 2000 Act declares that the estate of the *dominium utile* shall cease to exist, and shall forthwith become the ownership of the land. Also abolished are superiority rights, including the power to interfere with the enjoyment of the land by the owner. However, until the appointed day conveyancers will have to deal with superiors and superiority rights. Having said that the position is considerably eased by the fact that the ridiculously disproportionate action of irritancy of the feu was abolished from 9 June 2000, and no longer can superiors take back the feu, without compensation after an infringement of any of the feuing conditions.

16.3   Until the appointed day it is still marginally attractive to own superiority estates, although they will become worthless on the appointed day.

16.4   We have to date dealt with the transfer of title of a reasonably average detached house. You will have noticed that there are four main parts of the sale:

(a) negotiation;
(b) completion of missives;
(c) examination of title and transfer to title;
(d) settlement.

The same pattern can be distinguished in the transfer of a number of special kinds of subjects, although obviously there are differences of emphasis depending on the nature of the property involved.

Superiorities

16.5 When land is completely in the ownership of the superiors, they are said to own the *dominium plenum*. If they sell it, or any part of it, they may either:

(a) sell the *dominium plenum* or any part of it without dividing it into different strata of ownership (generally known as a 'freehold' conveyance, which will become the norm after the appointed day); or
(b) sell the *dominium plenum* wholly or partially into two strata of ownership: the superiority (or *dominium directum* or direct ownership) which the seller retains, and the feu (or *dominium utile* or useful ownership) which is sold to the purchaser.

16.6 When a sale is made by the landowners either of the *dominium plenum* or of the *dominium utile*, the method of sale is similar to the method already outlined in this book. In (a), an offer to purchase or sell is made, and accepted. A disposition is then prepared, agreed and signed and delivered. The disposition is granted subject to any land obligations the sellers may wish to impose. Please note that a disposition is the competent deed for this transfer, because it is a transfer, pure and simple, and nothing is created. If it was this would require a deed of creation.

In (b) however, two new strata of ownership in the same property are created (the superiority and the feu), and this requires a deed of creation. An agreement to sell and buy is negotiated and a feu disposition, or feu contract or feu charter is prepared by the sellers' solicitors (this is the normal rule: see Table of Fees, reg 7(2)) agreed, signed and delivered. These three deeds are deeds of creation and are generally referred to as 'feu writs' or 'feu grants'. They actually create a superiority and a feu out of a whole and single owner-ship and confer different rights and duties on the parties to them.

16.7 Once a superiority has been created it can be bought and sold in the same way as a feu (to the sale of which the foregoing chapters have been devoted). The competent deed is a deed of transfer (a disposition) and not a deed of creation or feu grant. Nothing in this case is created.

Sales of created superiorities are relatively uncommon, but do occur from time to time, even though they are now of limited life. In the past, superiorities were bought as a sound perpetual investment, both for the feu duties payable annually, and for the chance of an occasional fee for granting a waiver of a land obligation, e g the prohibition of using a house for certain commercial purposes (see *Howard de Walden Estates Ltd v Bowmaker Ltd* 1965 SC 163). The price payable for the sale of a superiority is negotiable. As a rule of thumb it was generally about 20 times the annual feu duty, but this very much depends on the negotiating powers of the parties, and the circumstances. At time of writing it is doubtful if you could achieve this price, or anything like it, which raises the spectre that dispossessed superiors may have a valid claim for expropriation of their property under the European Charter of Human Rights, Protocol 1, in that the value of the property has been removed. We shall just have to wait to see what happens.

In addition, the owners of a feu may wish to purchase their superiority and consolidate the superiority and the feu in terms of C(S)A 1874, s 6 and Sch C and C(S)A 1924, s 11 and Sch G.

16.8   Purchase of the superiority should not, however, under any circumstances be confused with redemption of the feu duty under the terms of LTR(S)A 1974, ss 4 to 6, which is merely a cancellation of a monetary payment as opposed to an extinction of the right to enforce land obligations.

A firm of English property owners bought the superiorities of a number of houses in Bearsden from the builders. They then wrote to the various feuars offering 'to extinguish the feuduty at a price of ten times the annual rent [sic] together with contribution of £35 towards legal costs and expenses'. If the firm had really been intending to sell the superiority and grant a disposition of the superiority to the feuar, then this would have been a fair offer, for a certain amount of legal work is involved. But the firm appears to have become hopelessly muddled between feu duties and English ground rents, and was not sure if it intended to redeem the feu duty or sell the superiority. If it intended the former there is of course a simple procedure for this, and indeed an inalienable right to the feuar to require a redemption. Redemption is made at a variable multiplier of the feu duty (around 11 or 12 times the feu duty on November 1994: see para **7.28**) and no legal fee is payable to the superior for this.

16.9   A sale of the superiority is not a sale of a right of possession, thus many of the clauses in an offer for the feu are inapplicable. The offer is a very simple document making no mention of planning, roads, affidavits, moveable property included, rateable value or maintenance. The form of disposition of a superiority of land is very similar to a disposition of the feu of the same land, and indeed the unwary may be tricked. The only sure sign of a superiority disposition is the warrandice clause which reads:

'And I grant warrandice subject to the current feu rights, but without prejudice however to the rights of the grantee to quarrel or impugn the same on any ground not inferring warrandice against me.'

16.10   A sale of the *dominium plenum* or undivided ownership of land is effected again by a disposition, which is little different from a disposition either of a superiority or a feu. In fact the only way you can truly distinguish a disposition of the *dominium plenum* from a disposition of the feu is by reference to the title of the granters, to see what they own and to ensure that the disposition transfers these rights intact.

16.11   Most superiorities have now passed into institutional hands (pension funds, assurance companies, friendly societies) who regard them as a sound rather than a spectacular investment. The benefits of buying estates that have largely been feued off are:

(a) a high income return from feu duties;
(b) a regular flow of feu duty redemptions in terms of LTR(S)A 1974, ss 4 to 6 (see para **7.28**);
(c) payments from granting waivers of feuing conditions;
(d) a likelihood that little pockets of land in the estate have been left unfeued, and thus still belonging to the superior. Such pockets may be of considerable value nowadays. (Consider the pension fund that recently sold a small stretch of private road to a builder for access—price £35,000!)

Title raiders are now buying estates that have been largely feued off, and picking the carcasses clean. Consider the profitable operation of a title raider in the Aberdeen area, who discovered that the estate he had bought had formerly gifted land to the county council for the building of a school. Incredibly a formal title to the land had never been taken, presumably because people in those days thought that once land was owned by a county council it would never revert to private hands. The council built the school, and houses for teachers, which houses latterly became unnecessary, and the council sold them off. The council could, of course, produce no title in their favour, and gave each purchaser a disposition by the council backed by an insurance indemnity.

The title raider, who had obviously done his homework, then pounced, claiming that the land was still his. Further the houses were his, because what is built in the ground belongs to the ground (*aedificatum solo solo cedit*). He was right of course; the insurance company paid up, and there were red faces all round. The title raider said that he was not punishing the houseowners, he was punishing solicitors who had not noticed this loophole, and insurance companies who must accept an element of risk! For another example of a title raider's activities, see *Hamilton v Grampian Regional Council* (1995 GWD 8–443), where it was held that the closure of a school, built on land given by the superiors, operated as a statutory irritancy, and the land reverted to the superiors.

Incidentally the building of houses on ground you do not actually own is a risky business, as the Scottish Office found out. In anticipation of an oil boom on the west coast, which never came, they bought land at Portvadie in Argyll and built a deep harbour there. They also built a splendid village for the expected workforce, which also never arrived, called Polphail. Unfortunately they did not acquire the land, which was believed to be in the ownership of a company registered in the Netherlands Antilles. Meanwhile the village became a rotting eyesore on what used to be one of the most beautiful parts of Argyll, and no one can do anything about it. It is understood that it has now been sold, although I have no details of how the title difficulties were breached.

This should be compared with, but not confused with, the activities of the people who try to exercise leasehold casualties (see ch 21) which were another unwelcome survival from another age, which have now been removed by the Leasehold Casualties (Scotland) Act 2001. These casualties should not, however, be confused with feudal casualties, which were abolished by the Feudal Casualties Act 1914.

Chapter 17

SALES AND PURCHASES OF FLATS IN TENEMENT BUILDINGS

'The "broom cupboard" sold in the summer of 1987 for £36,500 wasn't just an estate agent's fanciful description of a small studio flat but a real life former broom cupboard which was converted into a 9 ft by 7 ft "town flat" in a building close to Harrods. It had no cooking facilities and was marketed as a weekday residence for "the professional who likes to eat out".'

(*Daily Mail*)

'It would assist the members of the [Property Managers] Association greatly if the [legal] profession could ensure that purchasers of property are made fully aware of their obligations in terms of the deed of conditions and counselled to keep for future reference the copy deed of conditions which their solicitor sent to them.'

(Letter from James A Millar, Secretary of the Association, 1994 JLSS 445)

17.1 A tenement of flats in separate ownership is to some extent an alien concept in Scots law, in that the owner of a flat owns only a slice of air space surrounded by walls, ceiling and floor, and not the ground. There is also the question of the ownership of the structure of the tenement. The position in Scots law (where not amended by agreement) is fully summarised by Professor Kenneth Reid in 18 *Stair Memorial Encyclopaedia* paras 227–251. General information on tenements, in Glasgow at least, can be found in Frank Wordsall's superb book *The Tenement, A Way of Life* (Chambers, 1989).

Briefly, the common law of tenement provides that each flat owner should own and maintain the parts of the tenement nearest their own flat. Thus, the top flat owners are the owners of the roof above them, and the ground floor flat owners are the owners of the ground below them. The owners of each flat own the walls which bound the flat, and the floor and ceiling to the centre of the joists, and the common passage and stairs are the property of all owners. While this may appear perfectly logical in theory, it doesn't really work in practice. Thus for example, if there is a storm and some roof tiles are blown off, water will eventually penetrate the roof beams. An expensive repair is urgently called for, otherwise the water will percolate through the building to the detriment of all owners. Yet the cost is borne only by the top floor owners and, if it is prohibitive, they may neglect the repair.

It is, therefore, more practical to have as much of the tenement in mutual ownership as possible, with repairs being paid for by all owners in the tenement, in order that the structure is kept in good order and repair at the expense of all owners.

17.2 When missives for the first sale of a flat in a tenement building have been completed, a disposition is prepared in favour of the purchasers, as with any other sale. The property transferred is (a) the ownership of the flat itself and (b) a fractional right to the commonly-owned parts of the building. These common parts are, as a general rule, the solum, foundations, outside walls, gables, roof, attic, chimneyheads (but not the pots), the entrance, close, staircase, hatchway to the roof, rhones, gutters, all pipes, wires and sewers, the back garden ground and the walls surrounding it, the coal cellars and the street back lane and pavement in so far as not maintained by the regional council. In more modern buildings these common parts may be extended to such common property as landscaped gardens, car-parking areas, door entry-systems, lifts and television aerials and satellite dishes.

There then follow the burdens and land obligations applicable to the ownership of the flats in the tenement, which are outlined in paragraph **17.4**.

17.3 If the owners of a tenement building, which is currently in their sole ownership, decide to dispose of the flats individually, there are two approaches to the problem:

(a) the burdens can be detailed at length in every single disposition of every flat. This creates an enormous amount of repetitive work, and does not necessarily ensure uniformity, as a disposition granted in 1975 may vary from one granted in 1980, by accident or design. If therefore a dispute arises as to, say, common maintenance you may have to inspect every disposition granted to ascertain the true position;

(b) preferably, therefore, advantage should be taken of the provisions of C(S)A 1874, s 32, which permits a deed of conditions to be granted setting forth the burdens at length. This deed is granted before the first sale is made and the deed is registered in the Register of Sasines or Land Register. That deed is then simply referred to in future dispositions for the burdens it sets out. This deed is not one of those referred to in C(S)A 1924, s 3, and the granter must therefore have a registered title ('be infeft'). In terms of LR(S)A 1979, s 17, the burdens become real as soon as the deed of conditions is recorded, unless section 17 is specifically disapplied, in which case the burdens (as was the case before the 1979 Act came into force) only become real when a flat is conveyed to another person. A disapplication of this kind may be appropriate when the tenement owners wish to reserve the right to change conditions in the future, but it is thought that the circumstances where this might happen are pretty limited.

17.4 The standard deed of conditions is still that prepared between the wars by the Royal Faculty of Procurators in Glasgow, although this is now a bit dated in its phrasing. This deed sets out a precise pattern of common ownership and maintenance, and its clauses may be summarised as follows:

Preamble. This sets out the name of the granter and the description of the property in question. It states that the granter wishes to set forth the burdens and conditions applying to each flat, which are as follows:

One. The common parts of the building are defined (see para **17.2**).

Two.   It is declared that these are to be held in common for the use and benefit of all proprietors, and kept in good repair.

Three.   Only the flats themselves and their fixtures and fittings are to be in individual ownership, and the owners shall keep them in good condition, for the benefit of all.

Four.   The small garden plots at the front are usually given in ownership to the owners of the ground floor flats, unlike the back gardens which are in common ownership.

Five.   The coal cellars are, as appropriate, distributed among the various owners.

Six.   The feu duties and ground annuals are apportioned (not allocated usually: see para **7.28**) among the various owners.

Seven.   There is to be a common insurance policy against loss by fire, storm, impact, property owners' liability, and so on. The amount of the insurance is to be decided on by the proprietors of the building in meeting (see **Eight**) and the premium apportioned among the owners in the same way as the other common charges (see **Ten**). This is very much preferable to each flat having its own insurance, or not as the case may be. Experience shows that 'seamless' insurance cover of the building is infinitely easier to handle in the event of damage to the whole building. The alternative is to have various insurers, with varying liabilities, haggling over the reinstatement. (Note the further comments on insurance at para **17.8**.)

Eight.   Any owner in the building may at any time call a meeting of owners on seven days' notice. A quorum for the meeting is fixed in the deed. The owner of each house has one vote. The meeting (if properly constituted) can order repairs, renewals or redecoration, make regulations for the preservation and enjoyment of the building (e g stair cleaning) which regulations are binding on all owners, whether they agree or not, decide insurance details, and appoint or dismiss factors and fix their remuneration.

Nine.   The factors, when appointed, shall exercise these powers on behalf of the owners, subject to any limit of expenditure set by the owners.

Ten.   The expenses of maintaining and repairing the building are divided amongst all owners (contrast the common law position: see para **17.1**). If all the houses are of equal size, the repair costs are divided equally. If the houses are not of equal sizes, or if there are shops in the building, the common charges are generally divided in the ratio the rateable value of the flats bears to the rateable value of the whole building. This is generally taken as the rateable value when rates were last charged on domestic properties, but this may present a problem when there have been extensive alterations.

Eleven.   The factors are empowered to collect all proportions of feu duty, ground annual, insurance premiums, expenses and their fees from the owners and to pay accounts incurred on behalf of the owners.

Twelve.   If one proprietor feels that certain work should be done, but cannot get the approval of a majority of the proprietors, that proprietor may refer the matter to arbitration (see **Nineteen**). If the arbiter sanctions the repairs, this decision is then binding on all owners, whether consenting or not.

Thirteen.   Any owner who is aggrieved by a decision of a meeting, may appeal that decision to the arbiter, who is generally someone appointed by the local sheriff court, or by the dean of the local legal faculty.

Fourteen.   No houses are to be subdivided or used for trade purposes or for schools, or for the teaching of music—especially, for some reason, singing! Each flat shall be used as a house for one family only.

Fifteen.   There is a prohibition against keeping hens and pigeons, and any other animal to be kept should not constitute a nuisance, as determined by the other owners in the building—this time without there being recourse to arbitration.

Sixteen.   The top floor owners are not permitted to build storm or attic windows, lest this should weaken the communally-owned roof.

Seventeen.   No owner shall put up notices outside the building or decorate the interior differently from the commonly-agreed scheme of decoration, nor make structural alterations.

Eighteen.   Each owner shall allow the other owners in the building and their tradesmen access to their houses for the purpose of repairing common parts of the tenement which can only be reached by entering privately owned property. If this is a reciprocal obligation, there can be no logical objection to it, otherwise it can make work, particularly to ceilings and floors, very difficult.

Nineteen.   All disputes arising (except under **Fifteen**) are referred to arbitration and the arbiter's decision is binding. The arbiter may take skilled advice and apportion the costs of the arbitration as considered appropriate.

Twenty.   These burdens are declared to be real burdens to be referred to in all future conveyances.

17.5   If you are involved in preparing a deed of conditions for a building firm, say, you will probably find that the owner has nominated the first factors, whose appointment should subsist until all the flats are sold, when the owners may make their own decision. It would be advisable for you to liaise closely with the factors in the preparation of the deed, as the factors will probably want rather more modern conditions relating to their powers. They will, for example, want a fairly realistic deposit or float from the owners to ease their cash-flow problem. Factors do not like to order repairs and then wait endlessly to get paid for them. When an owner sells, the factor will deduct the amount of any outstanding accounts from that owner's float, and refund the balance on sale of the property.

17.6 When an offer to purchase a flat is made to the owner, the offer should include not only the flat itself but also the common rights of property. When describing the flat, great care must be taken—'left' and 'right' are ambiguous words. Thus, if I am standing inside the building looking at you on the street, I will think I am in the leftmost flat. You on the other hand will think I am in the rightmost flat, and in a way we are both correct. It is always preferable to use compass points. Similarly floors tend to be numbered in different ways, so you should say 'first floor above street or ground level'.

It may also be stated in the offer that 'the liability for the maintenance of the tenement shall be assessed on an equitable basis' (see para **17.4,Ten**) and 'that the conditions regulating the rights and obligations of the proprietors are normal for a tenement property and contain nothing unusual or unduly onerous'. In particular, when the purchase is of a top-floor flat, careful solicitors will require evidence that the maintenance of the roof is shared by all proprietors in the building, and not just by the two top-floor proprietors. To satisfy themselves they will have to read through every disposition of parts of the tenement, unless there is a deed of conditions. Where there is no deed of conditions, this may entail reading through all dispositions granted in the tenement to see that each flat has a liability for roof repairs. As these statements are very much a matter of opinion, the sellers' solicitors may simply send you the titles referred to for burdens, and invite you to satisfy yourself within a certain time limit. This is quite a reasonable suggestion.

17.7 In the case of flats, the clauses referring to local authority notices and orders tend to apply more readily to flats than to houses standing in their own ground. For an example of the dangers lurking see the property certificate printed at paragraph **17.16**.

The most obvious danger is that there may be a repairs notice, requiring the houseowner to rectify the defect within 28 days, in terms of the Housing (Scotland) Act 1987, s 108. Worse still, there may be a closing order under section 114 of the same Act, or a demolition order under section 115. Section 108 corresponds to and replaces the Housing (Scotland) Act 1969, s 24, and still tends to be referred to as 'a section 24 notice', as everyone knows what that means. Section 24 notices were served fairly liberally, in Glasgow at least, to enable maximum grants to be obtained for the refurbishment of tenements, but the incidence of these has dropped away.

Where such a notice is revealed by a letter from the council, you should check: (a) does it prejudicially affect the property? (if it does, you should take advantage of the provision in missives, and suggest to your clients that they rescind, and save themselves a lot of problems); (b) has the necessary work been done and paid for? (if it has, you should see that the notice is withdrawn); and (c) if the work has been done, but not paid for, part of the purchase price should be placed on deposit in joint names at settlement and used to pay the account when it is received.

17.8 Insurance presents a constant difficulty in tenements, and most tenements are believed to be substantially under-insured, simply because the proprietors will not agree to realistic values. It is perhaps understandable that a person who bought a flat for £20,000 should find an insurance valuation of £50,000 simply extortionate. Yet the larger valuation is probably justified because it is a reinstatement value: the cost of repairing the damage, which can be very expensive in tenements built of traditional building materials. The *Golden Rule*, as ever, is 'fire insurance is cheap—it is always better to be over-insured than under-insured'. Again do not forget the doctrine of 'average': if there is partial destruction (e g your kitchen goes on fire) and you are under-insured, the insurers may determine that you were carrying a proportion of the risk yourself, and pay out only part of the claim, leaving the remainder with you.

Check if there is a common policy over the whole tenement—a good idea as it provides 'seamless' insurance—but if the common policy for the tenement seems to be on the low side, persuade your clients to take out extra insurance. Also, lenders on the flat may not wish to accept a common policy if it is too low, and will insist on instructing their own insurance.

17.9 Traditionally the interest of a new owner of a flat should be endorsed on the common policy, as should the interest of a lender. You write to the insurance company and ask 'to endorse the interest of James and Mary Bloggs as proprietors and the Black Country Building Society as heritable creditors *primo loco*' on the policy. In modern practice, however, this is too unwieldy and policies are taken in the name of the factors on behalf of all owners and heritable creditors of flats in the tenement and it is not then necessary to notify a change of ownership to the insurance company.

17.10 The factors will submit an account to owners half-yearly at Whitsunday and Martinmas, detailing the payments made on their behalf (including repairs to the common parts, insurance premiums, ground burdens, cleaning expenses, fees etc) and dividing these among the owners in the proportions set out in the deed of conditions. When a flat changes hands, the factors will apportion the account between the sellers and purchasers around the date of entry. The sellers' portion is then deducted from the float and the balance is refunded. The purchaser is, of course, required to pay a float to the factor to cover future expenses.

The agreed reference to the House of Lords in the case of *David Watson Property Management v Woolwich Equitable Building Society* (1992 SLT 430), indicates that when a lender repossesses a house on default of the borrower, then there is no obligation on the lender to recompense the factor for expenses incurred by the factor prior to default. This has caused considerable difficulties for factors, as the same reasoning could be applied to arrears incurred by a normal seller. A prudent conveyancer should insist on having confirmation from the factor that common charges have been paid to the date of entry.

17.11 Blocks of flats built in recent years have beeen built to a far higher specification than the traditional tenement. The deeds of condition should reflect this, and regulate the use, maintenance and repairs of lifts, landscaped gardens and amenity areas, garages, car parks, common television aerials and satellite dishes.

It is, therefore, recommended that when a sale is agreed, the sellers' agents should write to the factor in terms similar to:

The Property Managers Association, Scotland, Limited

To Solicitors

Please complete and send this Form to the Property Factor on completion of Missives of Sale of Flat, Shop etc. in tenement property.

COMMON FACTORS PRO-FORMA

DETAILS OF CHANGE OF OWNERSHIP

FOR THE APPORTIONMENT OF COMMON CHARGES

FOR PROPERTY FACTORED BY:–Messrs Brittain & Brown

ADDRESS OF PROPERTY:–23 Dundee Street, Glasgow

FLAT POSITION:–1st Floor North

NAME OF SELLER:–Euphemia Flange

SELLERS' SOLICITORS:–Messrs Edwards & Bennett, Glasgow

DATE OF ENTRY:–16th December 1994

SELLERS' NEW ADDRESS:–per solicitor

_____

NAME OF PURCHASER/S:–Mr & Mrs FitzHenry
PURCHASER/S SOLICITORS:–Messrs Kyle & Strathdee, Glasgow

_____

Information required by Sellers' Solicitors   Please tick as required
Please send

(1) details of Common Insurance Policy

(2) copy of last cumulo Ground Burdens Receipt

(3) copy of last Common Charges Receipt.

The factors are also requested to confirm that no substantial work has been instructed but not yet done.

17.12 To prevent argument, it is usual to provide in missives (see App I.12, cl 5) that the cost of any work instructed or done before the date of entry, is the responsibility of the seller or the purchaser may, if this is not the case, rescind without penalty. The factors (above) are requested to provide details of any such work. Where the work is major this, of course, may be a matter of negotiation between the parties.

17.13 When the title of a flat being sold requires to be registered in the Land Register, the procedure is little different from that for a detached house. The most important difference is that you do not apply for a Form P16 report, even in a first registration, as the Keeper will not issue these for flats or buildings with 'a shared solum'.

17.14 The principles outlined in this chapter also apply to large houses that are being horizontally divided and to 'four-in-a-block' houses, which are known in Glasgow as 'cottage flats' for some reason. In such cases there will, however, be a garden to divide into separate ownership (it is unusual to put the whole garden into common ownership) and a right of access over the garden ground to each house must be reserved, usually by making the paths into common property. There should also be a servitude right in favour of the upper house over the garden on the lower house, permitting ladders to be placed for window cleaning and other maintenance.

17.15   The collector's department should also be advised on the change of ownership in order that the council tax may be apportioned around the date of entry between purchaser and seller. A form for this purpose is available from the appropriate council.

17.16   Example of a property certificate

SUBJECTS: 64 MILLION DOLLAR COURT, GLASGOW
Date of Certificate: 1/10/94   Property Certificate No. 999/999
COMBINED DISTRICT AND REGIONAL SEARCH

With reference to your recent enquiry regarding the above noted please find detailed below information gathered from Searches of the publicly available records from the District Council Departments of Planning, Building Control, Environmental Health and Housing, together with the Regional Departments of Planning, Roads, Water and Sewerage. Searches are from January 1986 onwards.

DISTRICT SEARCH
Town and Country Planning (Scotland) Acts as Amended and associated Planning Legislation

Policies
1. The subjects lie within a Land Use Policy Area zoned for Mixed use, as defined by Glasgow Central Area Finalised Draft Local Plan Approved May 1991.

Proposals
2. There are no proposals by the District Authority under the Town and Country Planning (Scotland) Acts which would affect the subjects.
   However, please note that the subjects lie in close proximity to the following sites, identified as having opportunity for development, as defined by Glasgow Central Area Local Plan, Finalised Draft May 1991:
   Site 9, City Halls, Candleriggs/Albion Street–Refurbishment for leisure/cultural use;
   Site 10, Former Cheesemarket, Albion Street/Walls Street–Refurbishment/redevelopment for residential/retail/office use;
   Site 16, Former Goldbergs Store, Candleriggs–Redevelopment/refurbishment for residential/retail/office use (consent granted, see application no. 02848/91 below);
   Site 17, Property at Bell Street/Candleriggs/Trongate–Redevelopment/refurbishment for residential/office use.

Planning Applications
3. Please note the following Planning Applications which may have relevance with regard to the subjects:

01020/88	Demolition, redevelopment and conversion of commercial premises to provide private housing development comprising 117 flats, shops, car parking, landscaped courtyard, formation of vehicular access and external alterations at site on Wilson Street. Approved on conditions 21 April 1989.
02114/88	Demolition of building, erection of 30 flats (including 2 shops and 2 offices), formation of basement car-park, conversion of workshops/offices to 16 flats, use of warehouse as art gallery (including photographic studio and conference room), shop, restaurant and extension of licensed restaurant, at 62–100 Albion Street/51 Bell Street/25–27 Blackfriar Street/5–19 Walls Street. Approved on conditions 31 October 1989.
01148/90	Demolition of existing buildings and erection of 5-storey building comprising retail units at ground and first floor, with residential on 2nd, 3rd and 4th floors in the form of 54 flats, with basement servicing and car parking and landscaped courtyard area at 14–54 Glassford Street/17–57 Hutcheson Street/63–69 Wilson Street. Approved on conditions 22/3/91.
00718/91	Demolition behind retained facade including complete demolition of 96 Trongate with erection of new facade and building. Construction of extension to facade on Candleriggs and use of ground floor for retail use and upper floor offices, at 76–104 Trongate. Approved on conditions 25 June 1991.
02848/91	Partial demolition of listed buildings (facade retention), demolition of buildings within the conservation area, refurbishment of remaining buildings

and new build infill to provide 97 residential flats, offices, shops, leisure centre, landscaping and basement car parking, at the Goldbergs Building (3–69 Candleriggs, 5–33 Wilson Street, 106–122, 124, 132 and 142 Trongate, 44–74 Brunswick Street). Approved on conditions 10 January 1992.

461/94   Use of former market hall as shop with associated internal and external works at, 80 Albion Street/Walls Street. No decision, application registered 24 February 1994.

Designations, Directions, Notices or Orders

4. Subjects listed as a building of Special Architectural or Historic Interest — No
5. Subjects situated in a Conservation Area — Yes
   The subjects lie within Glasgow Central Conservation Area.
6. Subjects affected by Article 4 Direction — Yes
   The subjects are affected by an Article 4 Direction, which has the effect of removing permitted development rights. Within the designated Glasgow Central Conservation Area planning permission is required for the following Classes of Development (Town and Country Planning (General Permitted Development) (Scotland) Order 1992 As Amended):–
   Class 7–The erection, construction, maintenance, improvement or alteration of a gate, fence, wall or other means of enclosure.
   Class 9–The stone cleaning or painting of the exterior of any building or works.
   Class 14–The provision on land of buildings, moveable structures, works, plant or machinery required temporarily in connection with and for the duration of operations being or to be carried out on, in, under or over that land or on land adjoining that land.
   Class 15–The use of land (other than a building or land within the curtilage of a building) for any purpose, except as a caravan site or an open air market, on not more than 28 days in total in any calender year, and the erection or placing of moveable structures on the land for the purposes of that use.
   Class 27–The carrying out on land within the boundaries of a private road or private way of works required for the maintenance or improvement of the road or way.
   Class 28–The carrying out of any works for the purposes of inspecting, repairing or renewing any sewer, main pipe, cable or other apparatus, including breaking open any land for that purpose.
   Classes 30, 31 and 32—(relating to Development by Local Authorities).
   Classes 38, 39, 40, 41 and 43—(relating to Development by Statutory Undertakers).
   Class 67–(relating to Development by Telecommunications Code System Operators).
7. Subjects situated in a Site of Special Scientific Interest — No
8. Subjects situated in an Area of Special Advertisement Control — No
9. Subjects affected by a Tree Preservation Order — See below
   The subjects are not affected by a Tree Preservation Order. However, please note that within a Conservation Area it is an offence to fell or lop any tree without notifying the District Council Planning Department six weeks before it is intended to carry out the work.
10. Subjects affected by an Enforcement Notice — No
11. Subjects affected by a Stop Notice — No
12. Subjects affected by a Breach of Condition Notice — No
13. Subjects affected by an Execution and Cost of Works Notice — No
14. Subjects affected by a Waste Land Notice — No
15. Subjects affected by the location of an Ancient Monument — No

Other Legislation

16. A Search has also been carried out for Orders, Notices, Declarations and Agreements under the following Acts:– — Outstanding

Public Health (Scotland) Act 1897

Section 20(1)   Notice requiring Removal of Nuisance — No

Clean Air Acts 1956/68 [as amended by the Clean Air Act 1993]

Section 18(1)   Subjects situated within a Smoke Control Area — Yes

Building (Scotland) Acts 1959/70 [as amended by the Housing (Scotland) Act 1974]

Section 10	Work without warrant or in Contravention of Conditions of Warrant	No
Section 11	Requirements for an existing Building to conform to Building Standards Regulations	No
Section 13	Dangerous Buildings	No

Civic Government (Scotland) Act 1982

Section 87(1)	Statutory Repairs Notice	No
Section 87(3)	Emergency Repairs Notice	No
Section 90(5)	Lighting of Common Stairs etc Notice	No
Section 92(6)	Cleaning and Painting of Common Stairs Notice	No
Section 95(2)	Private Open Spaces Notice	No
Section 96(1)	Statues and Monuments Notice	No

Housing (Scotland) Act 1969

Section 24	Compulsory Repairs Notice	Yes–see below

Housing (Scotland) Act 1974 [as inserted by Section 10 of the Housing (Financial Provisions)(Scotland) Act 1978]

Section 14(A)	Improvement Order	No
Section 44	Agency Agreement/Voluntary Grant	No

Housing (Scotland) Act 1987

Section 88	Improvement Order of Houses Below Tolerable Standard	No
Section 89	Housing Action Area for Demolition Declaration	No
Section 90	Housing Action Area for Improvement Declaration	No
Section 91	Housing Action Area for Demolition and Improvement Declaration	No
Section 106	Improvement or Repair Agreement (Agency Agreement/Voluntary Grant)	No
Section 108	Compulsory Repair Notice	Yes—see below
Section 114	Closing Order	No
Section 115	Demolition Order	No
Section 157	Management Order relating to House in Multiple Occupation	No
Section 160	Multiple Occupancy Management Code Works Notice	No
Section 161	Works Notice relating to House in Multiple Occupancy	No
Section 162	Notice requiring Provision of Fire Escape	No
Section 166	Overcrowding Direction Notice	No

Housing (Scotland) Act 1969 and 1987

Action has been taken under Sections 24 and 108 of the above Acts in respect of the subjects. SPH Property Search have written to City of Glasgow District Council for further information and will advise accordingly.

REGIONAL SEARCH

Town and Country Planning (Scotland) Acts as Amended and associated Planning Legislation

17. There are Policies, Proposals and Recommendations of relevance to the subjects as noted in the Consolidated Strathclyde Structure Plan, corrected edition 1991 as approved by the Secretary of State and as revised by the Written Statement 1990 Update with modifications approved by the Secretary of State on 10th September 1992.

   The Written Statement of the 1992 Update of the Strathclyde Structure Plan was approved on 26th May 1994. The Update deals with the balance of supply and demand for private housing land in the period 1992–99.

   The Structure Plan recommends (Recommendation R2, R3b, R3c) that Glasgow city centre be designated a *Renewal Area*, requiring action in the fields of housing, derelict and degraded land, and planning blight both to improve employment opportunities and maintain the process of renewal.

Roads (Scotland) Act 1984

18. The road and footway ex adverso the subjects have been taken over and are maintained by the Regional Authority.

19. The subjects lie approximately 500 metres from the proposed Townhead-London Road Link as defined by Strathclyde Transport Policies & Programmes No.8 1992–97. This scheme involves 0.6km of dual 3-lane 11.0m carriageway with Special Road Status and 1.1km dual 2-lane 7.3m (All Purpose) carriageway including a tunnelled section between Cathedral Street and Duke Street. The scheme will improve accessibility between the motorway network and the eastern side of the City Centre and the East End by providing more direct connections to Ingram Street/George Street and Gallowgate/London Road. The Link Road will result in traffic relief to High Street and Castle Street and enable environmental improvements to be achieved in the area between the Cathedral and Strathclyde University precinct, and at Glasgow Cross. The scheme will ease congestion in the Townhead section of the ring road and will be of substantial benefit to buses in the north east of the Central Area. Please note that as amended by the Transport Policies and Programmes TPP No.8A this scheme is now not included in the 1993–98 Roads Capital Programme.

Sewerage (Scotland) Act 1968

20. A public sewerage pipe which is maintained by the Regional Authority lies ex adverso the subjects.

Water (Scotland) Act 1980

21. A public water pipe which is maintained by the Regional Authority lies ex adverso the subjects.

Notes:

1. This enquiry does not consider whether all necessary consents have been obtained. Purchasing agents are advised to obtain the necessary documentation from the vendors.

2. The information contained in this Certificate is based on public record information and is accurate 3 days prior to issuing the Certificate.

Signed

Stirrat Park Hogg

[SPH Property Search is a division of Stirrat Park Hogg,
Chartered Town Planners, 113 St George's Road, Glasgow G3 6JA
Greater Glasgow Tel: 0141 353 2680 Glasgow District Tel: 0141 353 2681
Fax: 0141 331 2425]

Chapter 18

PURCHASING OF PUBLIC SECTOR HOUSING

'I believe that right to buy sales will remain very attractive to many tenants. On average the weekly mortgage payments to buy a house under the right to buy legislation, at current interest rates, could be only £2–£3 a week greater than the average standard rent. Home ownership is within reach of many thousands more households.'

(Lord James Douglas-Hamilton quoted in *The Herald*)

18.1   A right to tenants to purchase the house they are occupying was given by the Tenants' Rights Etc (Scotland) Act 1980 as amended by the Tenants' Rights Etc (Scotland) Amendment Act 1984. This legislation has been consolidated in the Housing (Scotland) Act 1987, Pt III (ss 44–84). Prior to 1980, however, some local authorities were prepared to sell their housing stock to tenants voluntarily, and such sales proceeded in the manner already outlined, for private sales, in prior chapters. Not all local authorities by any means were prepared to do this, and the main 1980 Act introduced a right for the tenant to buy, whether the local authority consented or not. The amending Acts merely circumvented certain difficulties that had arisen from the objection of recalcitrant councils.

The 1987 Act also introduced a statutory procedure for sales under the Act, and this only is dealt with in this chapter.

18.2   The procedure is fully detailed in the Housing (Scotland) Act 1987, which should be carefully studied before undertaking a transaction in this area. The application to purchase must be made on an official form which is available from the local authority concerned, with '*Notes for Guidance to Tenants on the Completion of the Application*'. A helpful booklet 'Your Right to Buy Your Home' is also available from The Scottish Executive Environment Department, Victoria Quay, Edinburgh EH6 6QQ.

18.3   Tenants who have occupied a publicly provided house on a secure tenancy for at least two years have a right to purchase such housing provided by:

(a) a local authority council, under the Local Government etc (Scotland) Act 1994, or as a successor to the New Town development corporations;
(b) Scottish Housing, formerly Scottish Special Housing Association;
(c) housing corporation;
(d) a registered housing association, which in many cases will take over the responsibilities from local councils from 2002.

Also included are a variety of other authorities, the most important being, a housing co-operative, a police authority, a fire authority, the prison service, the armed forces, a health board, the Forestry Commission, a State hospital, the Commissioners of Northern Lighthouses, HM Coastguard, the United Kingdom Atomic Energy Authority, the Ministry of Defence, and any other authority prescribed by the Secretary of State by order.

18.4   There are three kinds of occupation for the two-year period which the authority must take into account: (1) a house occupied by the applicant as tenant (in one case, a person who was in prison was held to be 'in occupation' of the house); (2) a house occupied by the applicant as husband or wife of the tenant; and (3) a house occupied by the applicant of which one or both of the applicant's parents were tenants.

18.5   Houses which are subject, not to a tenancy agreement, but a service agreement requiring the occupier to occupy the house for the better performance of the occupier's duties, and which must be surrendered on termination of the employment (e g houses in parks) are not included, as there is no secure tenancy (see *Naylor v Glasgow District Council* 1982 LTS/TB/129). Further a house which is provided with certain services (e g sheltered housing for the elderly or infirm) is not susceptible to purchase in terms of the 1987 Act.

18.6   The tenant who is qualified to purchase should first complete the official application and send it to the authority concerned by recorded delivery, keeping a copy. When the form is received the authority will arrange for the house to be valued by the district valuer, who is the official government valuer for a number of such purposes including assessment of gross annual values and valuation for capital transfer tax. Alternatively the valuation can be made by another valuer, nominated by the landlord and accepted by the tenant, so the valuer should be informed of any such improvements at the time of inspection.

18.7   The authority concerned should issue an offer to sell within two months of the application, or a notice of refusal if it considers the applicant not to be qualified to purchase for any reason (e g if it is not a secure tenancy, or is sheltered housing, is specially designed for use by the elderly, or if it is required by an islands council for educational purposes). A notice of refusal may be referred to the Lands Tribunal by a disgruntled applicant, and the tribunal may order the authority to make the offer if it is satisfied that this should be done.

18.8   The offer to sell should then be checked to see that it contains the subjects intended. The authority should sell all rights possessed by (see *Annott v Midlothian District Council* 1982 LTS/TR/191). The offer should also stipulate the valuation made, the discount applied to the valuation, and the price thus reached. Further the offer may contain conditions stipulated by the authority. Any of these matters can be referred to the Lands Tribunal. For examples of decisions on unreasonable conditions, see *Clark v Shetland Islands Council* (1981 LTS/TR/599, 598, 597, 594, all summarised in 1984 JLSS 469), and *McLeod v Ross and Cromarty District Council* (1981 LTS/TB/150).

18.9   The time limits here are quite crucial. If the tenant is satisfied with the offer, an acceptance should be sent within two months. If the tenant needs a loan from the selling authority, the time limit in that case is only one month. If the authority will not alter conditions to which the applicant objects, the applicant may refer the matter to the Lands Tribunal, the time allowed being one month, starting from a date one month after the tenant wrote to the authority asking it to amend the offer to sell.

18.10   If the authority does not issue an offer to sell within two months of the application to buy, the matter may be referred to the Lands Tribunal which will investigate the matter, and which may, in the last resort, issue an offer on behalf of the defaulting authority.

18.11   When the valuation of the house has been agreed, a discount is then deducted in respect of the application being made to purchase by a secure tenant. It is, incidentally, a general principle that a tenanted house should be sold at a discount, because vacant possession can be given to no one but the tenant. The basic discount after two years' occupation is 32% and the discount rises by 1% for every year's tenancy to a maximum of 60%. In the authority's discretion a period of occupation prior to a break of between 12 and 24 months may be taken into account. The reason for the break should be stated on the application.

In the case of a flat, the basic discount is 44% of the value, rising by 2% each year to a maximum of 70%. A flat is defined as 'a separate and self-contained set of premises whether or not on the same floor, forming part of a building from some other part of which it is divided horizontally'. This definition includes the traditional tenement and 'four-in-a-block' type of houses, as well as high-rise flats.

18.12   When agreement has been reached, and missives concluded, the transaction then proceeds, as previously outlined, to settlement. The applicant has a recorded title and may sell at any time thereafter. However, there is a financial penalty if a sale is made within three years of purchase. If a sale is made within one year of purchase, all discount is refundable, and this figure then decreases by $33\frac{1}{3}$% a year until it reaches nil at the end of the third year. The purchaser grants a standard security over the property in favour of the authority for the amount of the discount plus interest, which security ranks second to any security granted by the purchaser in respect of a loan to purchase the property. If the purchaser then defaults on repayment of the discount, or part of it, the authority may then enforce its security. On the expiry of the three-year period, it is not necessary to record a discharge of the security, as the security is discharged by operation of statute. If the owners insist on receiving a discharge, they will be expected to pay the legal discharge fee of the council.

18.13   If an application is made by one person only, a valid consent must be received from any non-entitled spouse, although the title may of course still be taken in joint names. Similarly if there are any other joint tenants, who are not included in the title, their consents must also be given.

18.14   If the tenant requires a loan to purchase, application to lending institutions should be made as in the normal case, but if two refusals are received, the authority is under an obligation to provide a loan based on the applicant's income and other circumstances. Please remember that in these circumstances there is only one month for acceptance of the offer to sell (see para **18.9**). Applications for loans therefore should be made as soon as the application to purchase is submitted, for time is very tight. As mentioned in paragraph **18.12**, the standard security in favour of the lender has the first ranking. Finally, if the authority does not offer a loan sufficient for the purchase to be made, the tenant may on payment of £100 reserve an option to purchase the house at the price currently fixed at any time within two years of the date of the original application to purchase.

18.15   In the past, there have been many complaints about long delays in processing applications, which were caused by a variety of reasons: title difficulties, in many cases councils had never completed the conveyancing formalities after compulsory purchase of land for building, staff shortages, and huge numbers of applications. This, fortunately, has settled down now.

18.16   When a house which was bought from a public authority in this manner is resold, the procedure is exactly the same as with any other house. If the house is disposed of within three years of its acquisition date, however, it is necessary to repay the discount (or part of it) and obtain a discharge of the standard security signed to protect the discount (see para **18.12**). Acquisition and disposal are defined respectively as the date on which the purchaser and the council complete missives.

18.17   While this scheme has proved to be very attractive to many, there are certain matters to be made clear to a potential purchaser. The new owner, in particular, will become responsible for repairs and insurance of the property, and should be advised of this new liability. In the case of high-rise flats particularly, repairs may be higher than expected, as recladding of the building or expensive lift repairs may be needed. While the former tenant pays only a small proportion of the account, it may nonetheless be a lot of money in real terms.

Further, many local authority houses were built of suspect materials and by unsatisfactory methods, which might give rise to a high level of repairs. The valuer's report will issue a warning where this is the case, and the purchaser must then decide whether to proceed or not. For an example see the case of *Forsyth v Scottish Homes* (1990 GWD 10–558).

18.18   In the case of *Clydebank District Council v Keeper of the Land Register* (1992 LTS/LR/1) the Lands Tribunal found that in terms of H(S)A 1987, ss 72 and 73 the sale of the subjects by an executor terminated the liability to repay to the council a proportion of the statutory discount on the purchase price of a house, and that the Keeper had acted correctly in cancelling the entry in the Land Register relating to the standard security for the amount of the discount. The missives had been concluded on 13 August 1990, the owner died in February 1991, and the disposition was registered on 5 November 1991.

18.19   There has now been introduced the complex rent to mortgage scheme, which allows tenants to buy their homes for a weekly outlay roughly equivalent to the rent paid. The rent to mortgage (RTM) scheme divided the purchase price into two lump sums: the initial capital payment (ICP) and the deferred financial commitment (DFC). The value of the house is discounted in the same way as in the right to buy (RTB) scheme, but the discounts are 15%

less. Thus for a house the minimum discount is 17% going up by 1% a year to a maximum of 45% after 30 years' tenancy. In a flat the similar figures are 29% minimum; 2% a year increase; 55% maximum.

The ICP is normally financed by a building society or bank or other financial institution loan (loans from the landlord are not available), and the tenant becomes the owner on paying this, and as such is responsible for insurance and maintenance. The DFC does not have to be repaid until the house is sold or the owner dies. The rent is reduced to 90% of the present rent.

In as much as the former tenant becomes the owner on payment of the ICP, no rent is now payable and the owner is responsible only for the mortgage payment and the insurance and maintenance of the property. The DFC is payable on the sale of the house, or the death of the tenant turned owner. The monthly outgoings should thus be approximately equal, and the rent is transferred to a mortgage payment.

18.20   Where elderly people are the tenants, they will be helped sometimes by younger relatives. This is, of course, in order, but the position of the younger relatives must be protected. Some authorities will allow the young relatives to appear on the deeds, in the destination clause, and you should enquire if this is possible. If not, the older persons should make wills in favour of the young relatives, to protect their position against other relatives, with preferential or equal claims on the estates, who have not been involved in the purchase. The only trouble with that plan is that wills are revocable, and it may be preferable to set up a trust with the older persons as liferenters and the younger relatives as fiars. In addition the older persons can grant a standard security over the property to the younger relatives, to protect their interest. This standard security would rank third, behind (1) a security to a commercial lender; (2) the discount security, for three years; and (3) the security to the younger relatives. The solicitor should be expected to give the best advice as to which course should be followed. Certainly there is a probable cause of action if the interests of the younger relatives are not protected in some way.

Where the original landowner, who sold the land to the council for building, retained a right of pre-emption, the question arose in several cases: did that right of pre-emption have preference to the right to buy available to the tenant? It was decided, on appeal, that it did not. (See *Ross and Cromarty District Council v Patience* 1997 SLT 463.)

Chapter 19

SALE AND PURCHASE OF BUSINESS

'How the price (360p a share) was finally arrived at reflects precious little credit on the Low board and its advisers . . . it is not the job of any board to recommend to its shareholders one opening offer (225p a share) which, within weeks, proves to be £100m less than that bidder is actually willing to pay for the business.'

(Alf Young, *The Herald* (discussing the sale of Wm Low to Tesco in 1994))

19.1 I think that I should first of all explain what this chapter sets out to do, and what it does not set out to do. I have reproduced at the end of the chapter a simple offer for a small retail business. My main effort will be to show that such a business is simply a collection of assets, bound together by the goodwill of the business, and that the sale of the business is really only a transfer of the various assets, with certain safeguards built in for the purchasers.

I shall ignore businesses run as limited companies, for such organisations are outwith the scope of this subject. I shall merely leave the topic with the suggestion that the differences between a small retail business and, say, British Petroleum, is one of scale. I know that I shall be accused of over-simplification, but both businesses are collections of assets, and whereas the small business's transport is represented by one bicycle, BP's transport is represented by a hundred super tankers, five hundred petrol tankers, ten thousand cars, and so on. When either business is sold, these assets are valued and the total forms part of the price to be paid by the intending purchasers.

19.2 The assets of a business are: heritable property (whether owned or leased), stock-in-trade, trade fittings and fixtures, work-in-progress (but not particularly with retail businesses), money owing, vehicles, trade name, trade marks, copyrights, patents etc, and any licences of franchises owned by the business. All of these assets are wrapped up in the goodwill of the business. The liabilities of the business, which are deducted from the valuation of the assets, are basically money owing to suppliers, employees, the taxman, and so on. And lastly, we have the people of the business, who are probably an asset in a good business and a liability in a bad business, but not always so.

Heritable property

19.3 The property of the business is valued by a surveyor, and the offer should make the usual stipulations for the purchase of heritage; that is date of entry, clauses dealing with heritable and moveable property, clauses dealing with property enquiry certificates and outstanding notices, and so on. It should be remembered that there are certain statutory requirements for commercial property, particularly the Health and Safety at Work Acts, and the offer should stipulate that all requirements under these Acts have been met, particularly fire requirements, otherwise the purchasers may be faced with making extremely expensive alterations. Where the property is leasehold, the lease will be valued bearing in mind, among others, these considerations: (a) remaining life of the lease; (b) rent being charged; (c) frequency of rent reviews and the terms of the rent review clause; (d) use permitted by the lease; (e) planning position of the property; (f) restrictions of assigning and subletting; (g) general fairness of the lease to the tenant; and (h) location and trading prospects of the site.

Precaution should be taken that there are no outstanding liabilities to the landlord for, e g rent and dilapidations of the property (the cost of restoring the property to the condition it was in when it was first let). As well as receiving permission from the landlord for the assignation of the lease or sublet, a certificate should also be received from the landlord confirming that there are no outstanding liabilities, and that the proposed use of the property is approved.

Stock-in-trade

19.4   This is valued, at cost except in the case of old or slow-moving stock, by agreement of the parties. If so wished, a valuation can be made by a person specialising in stocktaking, with the account being divided equally between the parties. The stocktaking should obviously be done as near to the date of sale as possible, at a quiet time, perhaps in the evening or on a Sunday afternoon.

Trade fittings and fixtures

19.5   These include counters, scales, cash registers etc. Some of these items are expensive to buy and may be on hire purchase or other credit arrangement. This should be clarified in the offer to buy, and if the item is owned by a finance company, arrangements for the transfer of the item should be made subject to the amounts still payable under the contract. It should be carefully noted that VAT is payable on secondhand trade fittings and fixtures. Thus, if a price is quoted for these, without mention of VAT, it will be taken to mean that the price is VAT inclusive. With VAT at $17\frac{1}{2}\%$ the VAT content is 7/47ths of the total. The purchasers should therefore get a receipt from the sellers showing the VAT content, in order that they may claim this as an input on their own return.

The purchasers of a business relying largely on telephone orders, will also want to acquire the telephone number(s), and to make sure that the telephone company has not withdrawn the number, as happened with Atlantic Telecom, which went into liquidation, and withdrew all its numbers.

It is as well that the offer shall contain a fairly tight condition about the working order of any central-heating, refrigeration, air-conditioning or other mechanical plant, and the liability of the sellers to pay for any repairs. To avoid bad feeling, the purchasers should inspect the mechanical equipment concerned, and arrange for the sellers to pay for any necessary repairs, before parting with any money. The contractual position should, however, also be preserved.

Work-in-progress

19.6   This refers particularly to business people like solicitors or builders who do work and get paid at the end of that work. If the business is transferred while the work is continuing, a valuation should be made of the work done but not yet paid for, and that forms an asset of the business.

Money owing to the business

19.7   The debts owing to the business are generally retained in the ownership of the sellers, who collect them as and when they can. If the sellers are emigrating or retiring, however, this may not be appropriate, and the purchasers may take these over. The purchasers should then pay the sellers for this asset, and it should be remembered that the debts should be assigned to the purchasers, and the assignation intimated to each debtor, both to satisfy the technical rule that 'the right of a creditor in a debt is fully transferred by an assignation followed by an intimation' (Gloag *Law of Contract* (2nd edn, 1929) p 74) and to let the debtor know who the creditors are. The intimation can simply be printed on the account when it is rendered. A simple statement requesting the debtor to pay the account to the assignee should suffice.

Similarly the purchasers of a business, who take over the collection of the debts, can have the benefit (or liability) of any court actions in which their predecessors were engaged, or the benefit of any court decrees that they hold. There is a businessman in Edinburgh who specialises in buying causes of action from people, and then fighting the cases himself. This is a simple way around the monopoly of lawyers to appear in court cases.

The valuation of the debts of the business should reflect the likely outcome of the cases they have started.

Vehicles

19.8   Vehicles being taken over are valued at date of sale, by reference to *Glass's Guide*, a trade publication containing current values. These figures will probably have to be obtained through someone in the motor trade. Again care must be taken to ensure that there is no outstanding debt on these vehicles, or alternatively that the debt is allowed for in the price.

Trade name

19.9   Some trade names are beyond value and form a very valuable part of the business; others are of very doubtful value, and may be changed on takeover. Where an individual or partnership or limited company trades under a name that is not its own, details of the ownership of the trade names must be disclosed on letterheads and by a notice displayed in the place of business. This provision of the Business Names Act 1985 (formerly Companies Act 1981, ss 28 to 30) replaces the provisions of the Registration of Business Names Act 1916, which provided for such names to be registered in the Register of Business Names. That useful register is now discontinued, although an unofficial register is kept privately.

It should be noted that neither the old nor the new register conferred any right of ownership in a name, as was mistakenly thought. The old register was in fact designed to reveal the name of enemy aliens who might be trading under assumed names when anti-German feeling was at its height during the First World War. Unchallenged ownership of a trade name can only be acquired by use, and both registers provide the useful information as to when a name was first used.

A trend emerged in the 1980s for companies to take over other companies whose principal assets are their strong brand names (e g Rowntree Mackintosh, which was in turn taken over by Nestle—the company had some very strong brand names, e g Smarties, KitKat, and Polo). This led to some companies placing a valuation on their brand names in their balance sheet (eg Guinness). Some doubt of the value of brand names emerged in the 1990s, when first Marlboro, a strong brand name, began to discount its goods because of competition from 'own name' brands. The notion grew that the public was in fact paying extra for the brand names, and this led to supermarkets introducing 'own name' brands which were packaged similarly to branded goods, but which sold for rather less. This was exemplified in the 'cola war' of 1994, when Sainsbury's eventually had to repackage its cola, so that it would not be confused with a well-known brand. This is a problem that will continue.

Intellectual property

19.10   A small retail business is unlikely to own any patents, designs, trade marks or copyrights, but a small electronics business, for example, might own all four, and be completely dependent on their existence. For example, Dyson own the patent of the method for their cyclonic cleaner, the design of the machine, the copyright of the packaging and instruction manual, and the trade mark of the name. They protect their intellectual property rigorously, as a number of cases against competitors have shown.

It is important, therefore, to check (a) that the sellers own the right to the particular intellectual property, (b) that the rights are validly registered, (c) their remaining years of life and the date of renewal in the case of a trade or service mark, (d) that they are properly assigned and intimated, in the case of trade marks and patents, to the appropriate registrar. The specialist advice of a chartered patent agent should probably be sought, as a mistake in this direction could be catastrophic. In addition intellectual property in overseas countries should be protected as well.

Licences and franchises

19.11   Many businesses depend almost entirely on a licence or franchise for their existence. There is little point in buying the business unless you can be sure the licence or franchise can be transferred to the purchasers. The purchasers may, therefore, wish to insert a suspensive condition making the purchase dependent on getting a transfer of the licence or franchise. The commonest example of the former is a hotel or shop licensed to sell alcohol, and of the latter, a business which owns a franchise outlet of one of the franchise companies (e g McDonalds, Dyno-Rod, Pronuptia, Pancake House, Holiday Inns etc).

An application for transfer of licence must be made to the licensing board set up by each council under the Licensing (Scotland) Act 1976. These boards meet quarterly, and an application for transfer must be submitted before the last date for submission, which date is intimated in the local press (usually a month before the board meets). The offer should therefore, unless circumstances dictate otherwise, be suspended in action until a day or two after the next licensing board meeting, or any adjournment of it (*Tarditi v Drummond* 1989 SLT 554).

If there are to be objections, which are fairly rare to transfers unless the transferee is of doubtful character, the purchasers will be told well in advance, and are given a chance to meet the objections. If no such indications are received, the parties can get on with arranging the formalities of the licence being transferred.

The purchase of a business which depends on a franchise will depend on the consent of the franchisers, who will probably prove extremely fussy about the ability of the purchasers to run the business, and pay for the supplies. Please remember that the franchisers, and other franchisees, will lose heavily if one of the franchises is badly run, especially in the case of a food shop.

Various other activities require a licence, e g road haulage, post offices, bookmakers and so on. The rules for the transfer of these licences are quite complicated, and specialist advice should probably be sought. In addition the Civic Government (Scotland) Act 1982 provides that metal dealers must have a licence. The same Act also provides that each council may adopt a licensing system for any of the following activities: the operation of taxis and private hire-cars, secondhand dealing, boat hire, street trading, private markets, operation of places of entertainment, late-hours catering, window cleaning, and sex shops. Requirements vary widely from area to area and enquiries should be made of the appropriate council when dealing in any of these areas.

Incidentally, if you think that my spelling is a bit variable I would refer you to Bill Bryson *Troublesome Words*: 'Licence, License. In British usage the first is the noun, the second the verb—"a licence to sell wines" but "licensed premises". In America "license" is preferred for both noun and verb.'

Franchises are licences privately granted authorising the licensee to use the business style of the licensor. See articles by the author on the topic in Scottish Law Gazette, March 1985, p 7 and June 1986. Note the case under Article 85 of the Treaty of Rome where international franchises were considered and broadly ratified (under conditions) by the European Court (see *Pronuptia de Paris GmbH v Pronuptia de Paris Irmgard Schillgallis* (1986) CMLR 414).

Goodwill

19.12 Goodwill has been defined as 'the probability that the old customers will revert to the old place' (*Crutwell v Lye* (1810) 17 Ves 335 at 346 per Lord Eldon). But perhaps it is something more prosaic as suggested by Dr Samuel Johnson remarking on the sale of Thrale's Brewery in 1781: 'We are not here to sell a parcel of boilers and vats, but the potentiality of growing rich beyond the dreams of avarice.'

Goodwill is the only asset so far that cannot be precisely valued, and its valuation will vary widely from case to case. To some extent it will also vary with the purchasers' opinion as to whether it is a good business that can be extended, or it is a poor business that will require an investment of time and money to bring it round. You must always be careful, especially in small businesses, of highly personal goodwill that will simply disappear when the sellers leave. Customers or clients of a business are often resentful of having their custom being taken for granted, and sold like a pound of butter, as Saatchi and Saatchi discovered when they bought, in the 1980s, an advertising agency in the United States for $450m. Almost immediately they lost the three main clients of the business and consequently $300m of annual billings. You will probably wish to discuss this valuation with an accountant who will base a valuation largely on past figures, which is as good a basis as any, but a shrewd business person will have a sixth sense for the value of the goodwill.

Generally speaking, people do return to the old place despite a change of ownership, unless they are antagonised, or the takeover is too radical for their tastes. Goodwill was treated as heritable property for stamp duty purposes (until the Finance Act 2002), and must be included in the disposition of the property, and the duty paid.

With no particular apologies I would mention that Saatchi and Saatchi had more troubles in 1994–95, when the founder of the business (Maurice Saatchi) was effectively sacked. He has set up a new business, and taken many clients with him. This underlines the dangers of a business where the only real assets are the goodwill and the staff. Please remember that both can simply walk out of the door. I will deal with this further under 'people'.

Value

19.13   The valuation of a business is part art and part science. An accountant will work it out almost exactly, but a good businessman will pay less, and a fool will pay more. All in all it is a matter of negotiation (see quotation at head of chapter). You can pay an asset valuation, but what value is there in a pile of assets which produce a loss every year or which need replaced largely? A multiplier of income is probably a fair starting point for negotiations. Another starting point, and probably a more accurate one, is what it would cost your clients to set up a similar business, taking into account the initial losses your clients would probably suffer.

People

19.14   As I indicated earlier, a business is largely at the mercy of its employees. A good business which is being sold will probably have high calibre employees whom the purchasers will wish to retain. A bad business may have been brought to its knees by its employees, and the purchasers are unlikely to feel a great compulsion to inherit these liabilities.

Good employees may be hard to retain. They may feel upset at the business being sold over their heads, and the owner disappearing with a large sum, representing their unrewarded hard work. They may even decide that they could do the same thing, and will leave to start up their own businesses. Apart from advising on and drawing up service contracts, there is not much the solicitor can do here. It is more of a personnel management exercise, or 'golden handcuffs' to give them their vulgar name—that is a good reward to stay faithful to the employer.

If an employee is under contract for a number of years, and the employers are afraid that the employee is going to be disruptive and unco-operative, yet they are unwilling to cancel the contract, and let the employee immediately move to another firm, taking their secrets and customers with them, they can give the employee 'gardening leave', i e pay the employee to do nothing for a period, at the end of which the customers will have forgotten them. Unhelpful staff are rather easier to lose, but the rights conferred on them on redundancy or dismissal under the various Employment Acts may make this an expensive exercise for the purchasers.

It is no longer competent to provide in the sale agreement that the sellers shall dismiss employees before takeover, and pay their compensation, in order that the purchasers may re-engage only such of those as they wish to keep (see Transfer of Undertakings (Protection of Employment) Regulations 1981 and various cases under these regulations). Formerly a clause would normally be put into a contract to the effect that the purchasers of a business would require the sellers to terminate all contracts before the sale and the sellers would deal with the employees' redundancy and unfair dismissal claims. The purchase would then re-employ such employees as might be required, as new employees without accumulated rights.

Under TU(PE)R 1981, this process is no longer possible. The rather poor drafting of these regulations originally caused considerable speculation as to their meanings, and at one stage the Scottish and English Employment Appeal Tribunals managed to find different interpretations of the same United Kingdom regulations. The matter was put beyond doubt by the House of Lords case *Litster v Forth Dry Dock and Engineering Co Ltd* (1989 SLT 540, [1989] IRLR 161, HL). In this case, employees had been dismissed by the receivers of the business an hour before the transfer of the business took place. The Court of Session held that the employees were not therefore (as stated in the regulations) 'employed immediately before the transfer', and therefore did not transfer to the purchaser's business.

The House of Lords held that the Court of Session had erred in this literal interpretation of regulation 5(1), which would allow the transferor of a business to dismiss employees a short time before the transfer becomes operative. Where the transferor is insolvent, as Lord Keith of Kinkel (a Scottish judge in the House of Lords) pointed out, this would leave the employees with only a worthless claim for unfair dismissal against the transferor. Lord Keith continued by saying that the European Court, in a number of decisions and particularly in *P Bork Internationals A/S v Foreningen af Arbejdsledere i Danmark* ([1989] IRLR 41), had ruled that where employees have been dismissed by the transferor for a reason connected with the transfer, at a time before the transfer takes effect, then the employees are to be treated as still employed by the undertaking at the time of the transfer. Thus, as Lord Templeman further said, the courts of the United Kingdom are under a duty to follow the practice of the European Court by giving a purposive construction to EC directives, and to regulations issued for the purpose of complying with the directives. The meaning of the term 'purposive construction' is that the purpose of the relevant directive is not thwarted or evaded. (For a discussion on this topic see the article by Roderick Mackenzie in Property Law Bulletin 1994, p 7.) A clause, therefore, which purports to require the sellers of a business to dismiss all employees before transfer, and to be responsible for the employees' claims, is not competent.

Employees dismissed will also generally be entitled to a redundancy payment (see *Anderson and McAlonie v Dalkeith Engineering Ltd* [1984] IRLR

429). Consultations with workers' representatives must take place before any transfer, with a view to reaching agreement about changing conditions, and the Directive for Informing and Consulting Employees, which is about to be adopted in the United Kingdom, requires employers to inform and consult employees representatives when they propose to make 20 or more workers in one workplace redundant. This must be taken seriously. Vendors of a failed scottish business were fined £750,000 when they failed to consult workforce representatives, and this is not an isolated instance.

It has to be said that most businesses and mergers result, sooner or later, in job losses—whatever pious intentions are expressed at the time of the happy event. The effect can hopefully be achieved by natural wastage, but the purchasers of a business who intend to trim the workforce should bear these provisions in mind, should consult and inform, and should adjust the price to be paid in accordance with the potential liability for redundancy and unfair dismissal payments that are acquired with the business.

What of the departing sellers? Hopefully they will have made enough to enjoy a well-earned retirement, but whether they have or not, they should be subjected to a restrictive covenant to prevent them from returning to business to compete with the purchasers. The covenant should be neither too loose to stop the sellers from competing unfairly, nor too tight to be declared unenforceable by the courts (see *Scottish Farmers Dairy Co (Glasgow) Ltd v McGhee* 1933 SC 148, and many subsequent cases on the topic).

Lastly, some other terms in use in this area of practice include:

'Golden hello'—where an employee is induced to change jobs by a 'head-hunter' (recruitment agent) the employee is usually rewarded by an additional incentive. This is to cover the danger of the employee moving from a job for life, only to find that things are not working out, and thus having to leave. This happens frequently.

'Golden parachute'—an executive has a contract which provides extra rewards in the event of a hostile takeover of a firm, leading to dismissal.

'Poison pill'—a company makes provisions for certain things to happen in the event of a hostile takeover, which will make the company less attractive to a purchaser.

19.15   The question of creating a monopoly situation under the Fair Trading Act 1973, or of falling foul of Articles 85 and 86 of the Treaty of Rome, relating to the creation of monopolies or the abuse of a dominant position, should always be borne in mind. From October 1990 the European Commission alone is responsible for vetting all cross-border mergers where the companies concerned have a joint turnover of 5 billion euros, unless three-quarters of the total turnover is earned in one member state. Where these conditions are not fulfilled, the national authorities, such as the Competition Commission, have jurisdiction. This has the effect of clearing up the confusion where a merger might face vetting both in Brussels and by a national body. While these provisions are relevant mainly to large companies, they could also apply where two quite small companies merge, and thereby control a quarter of the home market. If there is any doubt about this, the Office of Fair Trading and the appropriate office in Brussels should be consulted.

19.16 The sale agreement should, where necessary, call upon the sellers to grant warranties that the situation is as they have stated. The purchasers will also do 'due diligence', i e a thorough inspection of company records, which may cut down the need for elaborate warranties. Warranties may not be very effective unless there are also indemnities to cover them. For this reason agreements for the sale of large companies are very lengthy and complex, there being alone about 30 different kinds of tax liability that may arise after the sellers have received their money. This is, however, outwith the scope of this work, and is dealt with in other specialist publications.

19.17   Offer of a business—contract to be completed by acceptance

Messrs Talle, Darke & Hansom,
Solicitors,
33 Watson Street,
INVERNESS

6 November 2001

Dear Sirs,

On behalf of our client Mr Art Sidewright ('the purchaser') we hereby offer to purchase from your client Mr Humphrey MacKerrell ('the seller'):

(1) the shop property at 44 Angus Avenue, Inverness together with all the heritable fittings and fixtures therein;
(2) the goodwill of the business of Fishmonger and Poulterer carried on therein by the seller under the name 'Seafresh';
(3) the fittings and equipments hereinafter specified; and
(4) the non-perishable stock-in-trade;

and that at the price and on the terms and conditions following:

1.   The price for the heritable property shall be FIFTY THOUSAND POUNDS (£50,000) STERLING payable as at the date of entry aftermentioned. The price for the goodwill shall be SEVEN THOUSAND POUNDS (£7,000) STERLING payable as at the date of transfer aftermentioned.
2.   The seller will sell as at the date of transfer and at the price of THREE THOUSAND POUNDS (£3,000) STERLING to the purchaser the whole trade fixtures and fittings, trade utensils and equipment which shall include counters, refrigerators, cash registers and scales. By acceptance of this Offer the seller warrants that there are no hire purchase or credit sale agreements, diligences, liens or charges of any kind affecting any of these moveable items, and that the title of the seller thereto cannot be reduced or affected at the instance of third parties. It is further understood that this price is inclusive of Value Added Tax and that the seller will account for this and will hand over a valid receipt to the purchaser within two weeks of payment of the price.
3.   The purchaser will take over the non-perishable stock-in-trade of the business as at the date of entry and transfer, at a price to be agreed between the parties. Failing agreement the Valuation

shall be referred to a neutral Valuer to be agreed between the parties.

4. The date of entry to the heritable property and the date of transfer of the goodwill and other subjects of sale shall be at the commencement of business on Thursday, 28 December 2001.

5. The following conditions shall apply with reference to the heritable property:

(a) It is understood that the Rateable Value is £2,800 and that the share of the ground burdens apportioned on the subjects does not exceed £2.50 per annum. It is understood that the property is liable for one-eighth of the common charges of the whole tenement in which it is situated. The current rates, ground burdens and common charges and other outgoings will be apportioned as at the date of entry.

(b) In exchange for the price the seller will deliver a valid Disposition of the shop premises in favour of the purchaser or his nominees, and will deliver or exhibit a valid marketable title with Searches in the Property Register for not less than Forty years and in the Personal Registers for the prescriptive period showing clear records.

(c) It is understood that the minerals are included in the sale only in so far as the seller has right thereto.

(d) It is understood that there are no burdensome or unusual conditions, servitudes or wayleaves affecting the subjects and that there are no Orders affecting the subjects under the Town and Country Planning (Scotland) Act or the Public Health Acts or other Acts or any Notices or Orders by the the Local Authority or other authority affecting the subjects. Full Planning Permission for the present use has been granted and not revoked.

(e) It is understood that there are no conditions of Title which would prejudice the free use by the purchaser of the premises for trading purposes.

(f) It is understood that the premises meet the requirements of the Offices, Shops and Railway Premises Act; Health and Safety at Work Act and all other statutory provisions applicable thereto and that a Fire Certificate has been issued and not withdrawn or revoked.

(g) It is understood that the roadway ex adverso the subjects of sale and the sewer service the same have been taken over and are maintained by the Local Authority.

(h) The subjects of purchase shall include the refrigerated cold store, and the refrigeration system, all thermostats, pipes, plant, valves, pumps, time clocks, laggings, and vents. It is understood that the purchaser or his engineer shall be entitled to inspect the said equipment in the week before the date of transfer, and satisfy himself that it is in full working order. In the event of any repair being necessary, the purchaser shall be entitled to withhold a reasonable part of the price pending execution of the required repairs.

[The purchaser may also wish to insert other clauses for heritable property, such as a clause dealing with local authority notices et cetera.]

6. The following conditions shall apply with reference to the sale of the goodwill.

(a) The seller will be entitled to the whole sum due in respect of sales of stock prior to the date of transfer and be liable to meet the cost of all stock ordered and delivered to the shop prior to that date.

(b) The seller will maintain the business as at present between the date of acceptance of this Offer and the date of the transfer but shall not order stock for delivery after the date of transfer without the consent of the purchaser.

(c) All outgoings of the business shall be apportioned as at the date of transfer, and the seller will be entitled to all book debts owing to the business prior to the date of transfer, and will be responsible for their collection. The purchaser will assist the seller to collect such book debts, but without recourse to legal proceedings.

(d) The seller shall indemnify the purchaser against all liabilities whatever of the business incurred or arising in connection with the business transactions carried out prior to the date of transfer.

(e) The Books of Account relating to the business shall become the property of the purchaser on the date of transfer, but they shall for a period of six months thereafter be open to the inspection by the seller or his agents at all reasonable times for entries relating to the period prior to the date of transfer and twenty-one days thereafter.

(f) The seller will not in any way carry on directly or indirectly (unless with the written consent of the purchaser) within one year after the date of transfer and within one mile of 44 Angus Avenue either on his own account or as a partner with, or in the name of, or as a servant or agent to any person or persons, firm or company, the business of Fishmonger or Poulterer within the said area.

7. The whole subject of Offer will be maintained by the seller in good condition and repair to the date of entry and transfer and adequately insured against fire, theft and other usual risks to the said date.

8. The purchaser shall be entitled to take over all telephonic and telegraphic equipment, and any telephone numbers presently used by the seller. The seller warrants that asll accounts for telephonic services have been paid up to date, and that there are no proposals to withdraw any of the telephone numbers purchased with the business.

9. This Offer is for immediate acceptance only.

Yours faithfully,

SHORT, FATTE & UGGLY (signed by a partner of the firm, and witnessed)

Notes :
1. From this point completion of the contract will be reached by exchange of letters until all points are resolved and *consensus in idem* has been reached.

2. The total consideration for the business does not exceed £60,000 and therefore there is no stamp duty payable. As it is a marginal case, however, the Inland Revenue may demand evidence that the valuations of the property are correct.

3. The property is situated in Inverness, and the purchase in 2001 is therefore under Sasine Register procedures. From April 2003 the sale would be under Land Register procedures. The only real difference that this would make is that the condition 5 (b) would refer to the rather longer Land Register obligation.

4. Stamp duty is no longer payable on sales of goodwill (Finance Act 2002).

Chapter 20

ASSIGNATIONS OF LEASES

'During the course of the year the Agency made a total of 18 payments, totalling £62,779.96 in respect of indemnity claims. Of this amount over £55,000 was paid out in respect of 3 claims, 2 of which were a result of omissions from, or misleading information in Agency reports, and the third was in respect of leasehold casualties omitted from the title sheet.'

(Keeper's Report 1992–93)

20.1 In certain areas it was traditionally the practice to grant long leases (or tacks to use the old Scottish term) of property, rather than feudal rights. The lease would usually be for a period of 99 or even 999 years, or in one case noted by the Scottish law Commission, 9,999 years. If you buy a leasehold property with some 800 years of the lease to run, it may seem little different from a feu, but it is quite a different concept, and there are certain differences of emphasis. The most obvious difference is that you never own the property, and the lease will come to an end one day, no matter how remote that day may be.

Thus certain unfortunate tenants on Seafield Estates, in the north east, were faced with losing their houses simply because their leases were about to expire, and they were being asked to pay substantial sums to buy houses that they had considered as their own. It is perhaps difficult to understand why this miscomprehension had arisen, but that is the way things stand, and no statutory relief was offered. Presumably these unfortuante people will now have had to pay for what they considered, however wrongly, to be 'their' houses. They should have been told, or perhaps were told, but chose not to hear, that if a lease is granted, the tenant is only entitled to occupy the property for the term of the lease, and that anything that is built on the land belongs to the owner of the land. Perhaps they got confused with the security of tenure provisions under the Rent Acts, but these apply to relatively recent leases.

20.2 It is perhaps also unfortunate that advantage was not taken of the provisions of the Long Leases (Scotland) Act 1954, Pt I, which allowed such tenants to convert their leases into feus on a small payment to the landlord in compensation. Sadly the benefits of that Act ceased to be available after 1 September 1959, and have never been renewed.

The model village of Eaglesham in Renfrewshire was largely let on long leases by the Earl of Eglinton, who had, however, to sell the village some years later to make up for his disastrous losses when he staged a jousting tournament at his castle on one of the wettest days apparently ever remembered. The rentals charged were one or two old shillings per house, with the only notable condition being a requirement on the villagers to pay for a piper for the Earl when required. The successors to Eglinton Estates were happy enough to convert their leases into feus, and will, I believe, still do so, if asked by anyone who has not yet done so. Not so Seafield Estates, who rest on the contracts signed by their predecessors.

20.3   When a leasehold property is sold, the land is not sold, merely the right to occupy it for a certain number of years. A disposition is not therefore the competent deed, it is an assignation of the lease in the form provided by the Registration of Leases (Scotland) Act 1857, Sch A.

An assignation of lease takes this form:

'I, (*name and address of seller*) IN CONSIDERATION of the price of (*price*) paid to me by (*name and address of purchaser*) of which price I hereby acknowledge the receipt HAVE SOLD and DO HEREBY ASSIGN to the said (*purchaser*) the tenant's right and interest to and in a Tack (*specify details of the Tack*); and further I assign in so far as necessary my title thereto which is recorded (*specify Register and date of registration*); Together with (first) the parts privileges and pertinents of the Leasehold rights hereby assigned; and (second) my whole right, title and interest present and future therein; WITH ENTRY as at (*date*); And I grant warrandice (*Stamp Duty clause if appropriate*) : IN WITNESS WHEREOF'

Similarly if money is borrowed on the security of the long lease, the competent security was a bond and assignation in security, in terms of Schedule B to the 1857 Act. Nowadays, of course, in terms of CFR(S)A 1970, s 9 it is competent to grant a standard security over any interest in land, including a leasehold interest.

It should, however, be made perfectly clear that, as a practical matter, no institution will lend money over a leasehold property of which the lease has only a few years to run as this does not constitute a reasonable security, nor over an unregistered lease.

20.4   Purchasers acquiring a lease should be satisfied that the landlord's title to the land is a good one, and therefore that the lease is competent. Further, all assignations of the lease should be checked as if these were normal dispositions. A search over the lease (not over the property which is a distinctly separate interest) should also be seen. Searches over both lease and property can of course be requested, but the sellers of the leasehold interest may not be willing to produce the latter which is not really their concern.

20.5   It was a requirement of the Leases Act 1449, s 18, that to qualify for the protection of that Act, the tenants must enter into possession of the land. This had the effect that a lease could not be used as security for money borrowed. This difficulty was circumvented by the Registration of Leases Act 1857, s 1, which provided that a probative lease for a period of 31 years or more might be registered in the General Register of Sasines, thereby giving the tenants a real right. Any lease of less than 31 years was regarded as not being of sufficient importance to be so registered, but LTR(S)A 1974, Sch 6, has reduced that qualification period to 20 years.

Conversely, however, LTR(S)A 1974, s 8, forbids the creation of future leases of residential property for periods exceeding 20 years. It is thus unlikely that residential leases will be registered any more, and the remarks that follow on registration would therefore seem to apply mainly to commercial leases.

20.6 It should be noted, however, that it is still competent to register long residential leases created before 1974 which have not yet been registered. If the lease is in an area which has been declared operational for land registration, the lease or a transfer of it for value must now be registered in the Land Register. The forms and procedures used are as for dispositions of feudal property (see chs 7 and 9).

20.7 The advent of land registration has thrown up another difficulty with long leases that was not appreciated before, and which is fully discussed by Colin Miller in his paper 'Conveyancing: Points to ponder', Law Society PQLE Papers of Missives and General Conveyancing Course, February 1985. Miller points out that the Keeper of the Land Register has taken the view that it is not, and never has been, competent to use a deed of conditions to regulate leasehold property, on a strict reading of C(S)A 1874, s 32. Further the Keeper takes the view that it is not competent to impose land obligations by reference in an assignation or partial assignation of a lease, as would be the case with a disposition. Any such obligations referred to in an assignation are therefore incompetent, and would be only personal obligations upon the tenants, and that the only safe way to proceed in such transactions is to set forth at length the conditions of title in each and every assignation—something which has never apparently been done.

20.8 The Law Reform (Miscellaneous Provisions) (Scotland) Act 1985, s 3, however, provides that it is retrospectively competent to impose conditions and make stipulations by reference to a previous deed which upon recording in the Register of Sasines or registration in the Land Register become binding upon singular successors of the tenants. Miller also points out that this piece of retrospective legislation is to cure difficulties raised by the Keeper, but it does not seem to apply to deeds of conditions.

20.9 An unexpected feature of long leases which cropped up in the last few years (note the quotation at the head of this chapter), has been the incidence of leasehold casualties. It should be explained that casualties were double payments of feu duty or rent which occurred every nineteenth year, or on the sale of the property. Feudal casualties were abolished in 1914, by the Feudal Casualties (Scotland) Act 1914. Unfortunately, however, this Act did not cover leasehold casualties. It had been generally assumed that these had been cancelled by the 1914 Act, or had otherwise dropped away, but this has not turned out to be the case.

A leasehold casualty is an additional payment of rent occurring on certain events. An example of this is as follows:

> 'As also to pay to the said (Landlord) and his successors
> proprietors of the said subjects or his or their assignees the sum of
> twelve pounds of additional rent for the first year's possession at
> the entry or succession of every heir to the said subjects and one
> full year's rent or value of the said subjects including all buildings
> erected or to be erected thereon according to the actual value
> thereof at the time for the first year's possession or entry of every
> assignee or singular successor and that within a year and a day
> from the date of the heir assignee or singular successor succeeding
> or acquiring right or possession or of the right or possession
> opening to or devolving upon him, her or them;'

You will note that I have underlined the part dealing with full year's rent or value, which is the critical part, it being claimed that this is intended to reflect inflationary changes, although at the time of the granting of the lease, inflation was not really known to any extent.

On the basis of this clause the landlord made a claim for a payment of several thousand pounds, on the basis of the 'full year's rent or value' being the amount of the rateable value on the property. In this case a member of the Keeper's staff had omitted the leasehold casualty from the land certificate, presumably believing it to be a matter that had then become redundant—this being several years ago, when virtually everyone would have thought similarly. It turned out not to be, and a claim was received from the landlord for the loss of the casualty payment, and was paid.

It is understood that there are many such casualty rights throughout Scotland, and that 'title raiders' were buying estates and enforcing these casualty rights. They were, of course, totally within their legal rights to do so, if the clauses supported them and were specific.

What was wrong was the legal position. These payments should have been abolished in 1914 together with feudal casualties, they caused much distress, and they were finally laid to rest by the Leasehold Casualties (Scotland) Act 2001, which makes such payments unenforceable.

Chapter 21

COMMERCIAL LEASES

'Lease Terms: The building is being offered to let on the basis of a 25 year full repairing and insuring lease with upward only rent reviews at five yearly intervals. The incoming tenants will be responsible for the landlords' legal expenses together with stamp duty and VAT incurred in connection with the grant of the lease.'

(Developer's Circular)

'A leading City (London) law firm is being sued for £7.5 million over a blunder allegedly made in drafting a guarantee. The action is being brought ... on behalf of 2,700 investors ... who complain that because of the guarantee they are only receiving a third of the rent promised.

The main purpose of the guarantee was to ensure that even if the buildings were not let, investors would still receive rental income for the first five years. In the event the guarantee failed to do the one thing it was supposed to do—protect the investors in the event of the developers of the building, who promised to pay the rent, going bust.'

(*Financial Mail on Sunday*)

21.1 The modern commercial lease is a repairing, renewing and insuring lease (RRI); that is, these obligations are placed on the tenants by agreement. This is a basic practice which has become customary (see quotation above). Whatever else you may be able to negotiate with the landlord, you are very unlikely to be able to negotiate out of this stipulation.

21.2 The modern commercial (or full repairing, renewing and insuring lease) is a formidable creature, and was, until recently, entirely unmoderated by any statutory relaxation of its strict terms, with the exception of the modest security of tenure given by the Tenancy of Shops (Scotland) Acts 1949 and 1964. The contents of such a lease are entirely governed by negotiation between the parties. The terms are fixed usually by the landlord, and agreed by the tenants. There are none of the safeguards of security of tenure, and of compensation payable on outgoing afforded to tenants in England by the string of Landlord and Tenants Acts 1929 to 1988.

There was enacted the Law Reform (Miscellaneous Provisions) (Scotland) Act 1985, which protected tenants from an irritancy arising from late payment of rent, as in the case of *Dorchester Studios (Glasgow) Ltd v Stone* (1975 SLT 153). It also protected the tenants from an irritancy relating to non-monetary breaches of the lease. At section 5 it produced the most bizarre legal animal yet. Burdened and benefited proprietors, entitled spouses and non-entitled spouses, to name but four recently created legal animals, are fairly clearly definable legal concepts, but the concept of a 'fair and reasonable landlord' who 'in all the circumstances of the case' would not have terminated a lease, is vague beyond belief.

In his annotations of the 1985 Act, Professor Joseph Thomson says that 'it is to be hoped that the uncertainty surrounding "the fair and reasonable landlord" test will not be the occasion for protracted litigation'. This approach was tried successfully in *Lothian Chemical Co Ltd v City of Edinburgh District Council* (1995 GWD 4–197).

21.3   But what are fair and reasonable landlords? It could be argued that the landlords are merely attending to their duties on behalf of their investors, and it is right and proper that the landlords should follow a consistent management philosophy, and that they should not let the tenants away with too much for the sake of their investors, and indeed, for the sake of the tenants themselves. Alternatively, you could argue that fair and reasonable landlords are benign characters, not getting too upset about minor breaches of the rules, and turning a blind eye to breaches of the conditions of leases; but if a tenant neglects an essential repair, the whole property may suffer, and that is not being a fair and reasonable landlord at all.

21.4   And if LR(MP)(S)A 1985 does not create a matching concept of a 'fair and reasonable tenant' can we perhaps invent one? Tenants who always pay their rent in time, perform the various other obligations posed by the lease, are good traders and attract customers to the development, are an example of this. These tenants are otherwise known as a 'good covenant', and needless to say are a highly sought-after commodity. A good covenant can more or less dictate terms to the landlord, within the restraints mentioned above, whereas a lesser covenant has to take more or less the terms the landlord dictates.

21.5   Thus, when we have negotiations for a lease, much depends on the respective bargaining powers of the two parties. You may have two kinds of negotiation: (a) competitive, or win/lose, negotiation where one party is intent on imposing its will on the other party, and if it does not succeed in any respect, it will simply stop negotiations; and (b) co-operative, or win/win, negotiations where both parties are prepared to concede certain points to the other, and, without breaking the basic pattern of the leasing scheme, the landlord is prepared to allow certain deviations from it.

The former pattern of 'negotiation', which is less common nowadays, because leases that are too strict have proved to be counter-productive when they come to a rent review, requires the lawyer to do little more than to report to the client on the possible impact of the conditions imposed, and to outline the costs involved, which are liable to be extensive. But if we take the second possibility, of co-operative negotiation, it is here that the skilled leasing lawyers come into their own. Wit is pitted against wit, each striving to get the best deal for their clients, and at the end of the day both should feel that they have done a good job for their clients. You can take satisfaction that you have acted like good lawyers should, instead of like an unskilled office junior, whose only job is to take the bad news to the client.

21.6   What then, in sensible negotiations, are some of the major points that good lawyers should be looking for? First of all the lease should be clear and comprehensible, not repetitive or ambiguous, in a logical order, with an index and side-headings, and have a clear definition section at the beginning. Solicitors for both parties should keep their clients continuously informed of the progress of negotiations. You may feel that this is unnecessary, as the client does not understand what is going on, but it is very important to keep the client informed, in this sphere of law as all others. This is as much a matter of self-protection as anything else.

21.7   The rent payable is a matter for negotiation; the tenants should not necessarily be expected to accept the landlord's first figure. You will be kept advised on this, as on other matters, by a competent surveyor. Whether or not value added tax is payable on the rent is a competent matter for negotiation. Basically, to a VAT-registered company, whether or not it pays VAT on the rental is neither here nor there, because it can claim it back, and the only loss is that it had to pay the tax rather earlier, with a cash-flow benefit to the landlord, and detriment to the tenants. Where tenants are not VAT registered, as with a bank or other financial institution, it is distinctly detrimental to have VAT imposed, as it is just a straight 17½% rent increase, which cannot be reclaimed. As such companies are generally good covenants, however, some solution can usually be found with co-operative negotiation.

21.8   Machinery for reviewing the rent must be established. Landlords are entitled to have the rent adjusted to cover the fall in the value of money, but the tenants should not yield completely to the landlord. This is purely a matter for negotiation—the length of the review break and so on—but there are important drafting considerations too. There should be resisted by the tenants any attempt to impose a condition that any restriction on use shall be disregarded on a rent review (see para **21.12**). On the other hand, the tenants should insist on the insertion of 'disregards' for rent review purposes of the tenants' occupancy and the goodwill the tenants have created, and of improvements made by the tenants. It is bad enough to improve someone else's property, without having to pay additional rent in respect of those improvements.

21.9   While on a longish lease it is quite acceptable that the tenants shall pay for repairs, there should be excluded repairs of latent defects that were not reasonably foreseeable at the outset of the lease, and which not even a competent survey of the premises would have revealed. These defects seem to arise mainly in the much-maligned buildings of the 1960s when, as it turns out, all sorts of dubious materials were used and poor building practices followed. Asbestos and concrete which dissolved ('concrete cancer'), cladding which separates from the building, and high alumina cement are among the most likely building materials to cause latent defects.

21.10   The insurance provisions should be fair, and if in doubt the insurances of the property should be checked over by a broker. While the tenants can be reasonably expected to pay premiums, and while the landlords can fairly expect also to instruct the insurances, care should be taken that all risks that need to be covered are in fact covered, and that those that are not requiring cover, are not. The premiums should also be competitive, and the risks should be insured with a sound company. The position as to destruction of the property, and the insurance provisions against it, should be fair to the tenants. Ideally the tenants would want the Scottish law of *rei interitus* to apply, as in the case of *Cantors Properties (Scotland) Ltd v Swears & Wells* (1980 SLT 165), and to be able to abandon the lease in the event of destruction of the property, but it is now fairly well established that the landlord will wish to contract out of this provision. An unwelcome recent development has been the need to instruct cover against terrorist damage, and as one never knows where or when this may occur, comprehensive cover against this scourge must not be neglected. In the mainland United Kingdom, the government will not compensate for terrorist damage.

21.11   As heritable securities are generally taken over registered leases, the lending institutions will generally want clauses contained in the lease which will protect their interests in the event of an irritancy, or bankruptcy or liquidation of the tenants. These clauses will rarely be resisted by landlords, as the 'muscle' of financial institutions is hard to resist, and also because they would simply cease to lend if they lost their security in the event that the tenants became insolvent, or failed to pay their rent in time. It should be borne in mind that no security can be created over a lease that is not registerable, that is to say with a lease period of 20 years or less, as opposed to a lease for a period greater than 20 years, but which has less than 20 years of that period left to run.

21.12   The tenants must ensure that every contemplated use of the premises is allowed by the lease, and is permitted under town and country planning legislation. The tenants should ensure that not only does this permission exist, but is applicable to the whole length of the lease, and is not personal to another party. If planning permission is to be obtained, the lease should be made subject to the permission being obtained, and in terms acceptable to the tenants. Further the solicitors for the tenants should ensure that the use contemplated is acceptable in terms of the title deeds and that there are no restrictions which would adversely affect the use proposed by the tenants. From the landlords' point of view, restrictions on other uses should not be disallowed by the lease, lest this should affect the level of rent to be fixed on review, on the basis that the restriction makes the lease hard to transfer, and therefore of less value. If a restriction on use is imposed, this should not be stated in the lease to be disregarded on a future review of the rent, as the impact on the rent payable could be quite dramatic.

21.13   The tenants' solicitors should also inspect the title deeds, as if the property was being purchased, and searches should be obtained to show that the landlord truly is the owner of the property and that there are no securities over the property, or if there are that the consent of the security holder to the lease is obtained. The consent of the superior, or of any head landlord, to the proposed lease arrangement and to the proposed usage of the property should be obtained, if required. The same care should be taken when leasing a property, as when purchasing it, in seeing the appropriate planning and building certificates and any permission required from the superior.

21.14   Details of the landlords' management charges should be obtained and be seen to be reasonable. Where, as the modern practice is, a shopping development contains, say, an ice rink, the tenants should not incur any share of the charges involved in running the rink.

21.15   From the tenants' point of view, there should not be too severe restrictions on assigning and subletting the lease. In addition, the tenants should be assured that in the event of an assignation of the lease being allowed that the original tenants are released from any further liability under the lease. In England there is a doctrine of privity, which imposes this liability on the original leaseholder. There have been distressing cases in England where the original tenant has retired, and sold his lease to a purchaser of the business. A few years later the new tenant cannot meet the rent, and under the doctrine of privity of contract, the original tenant is asked to pay. Landlords may well try to impose this concept to Scotland by negotiation and by inserting a joint and several liability on the original tenants and all assignees. It should be resisted, as the consequences for the original tenants can be very considerable.

From the landlords' point of view, it is also desirable to have a fair degree of freedom to assign or sublet, as if the lease is unduly restrictive in this regard, this too may have a detrimental effect on the level of future rent reviews. Landlords will, reasonably, wish to ensure that a future tenant is as good a covenant as the old tenant.

Generally, throughout the lease the tenants should be protected against any temptation on the landlords to spend the tenants' money freely, and safeguards should be built in that all expenditure should be incurred 'reasonably'. Further, the ascertainment of what is reasonable spending, and what is not, should be referred to an arbiter.

21.16 The tenants should be allowed quiet possession of the whole subjects of lease, provided that the terms of the lease are adhered to. The tenants should also reserve such rights over adjoining areas of ground, belonging to the landlords, as may be required, particularly from the point of view of access, and support of buildings, and for the leading of services to the premises leased.

21.17 It is certainly reasonable that the tenants should keep the subjects decorated, in a lease of any length. This obligation should not be too onerous, however, nor should it be inappropriate. If the tenants have a particular 'house style' the lease should not be framed in such a way as to be inimical to this. Also the tenants should not accept an out-of-date decoration clause, which requires them, e g, to paint the woodwork with 'three coats of oil-based paint' and to apply distemper to the walls. Just try and get oil paint and distemper in your local supermarket!

21.18 The landlords may attempt to get personal guarantees from the directors of a company to a lease in favour of a limited company, if it is considered that the covenant of the company is not good enough, and that the company is not financially secure. This is a perfectly acceptable practice, and is not unfair. Having said that, the tenants' solicitors should automatically resist the attempt, but if the tenants are a small or newly established company, it is not unreasonable for the landlords to protect their own interests if the tenant company is quietly dissolved at the first sign of trouble. What is important from the guarantor's point of view is that it is released when the tenants assign the lease, and that it be kept informed of any aberrant practices by the tenants which, if continued, might lead to an irritancy of the lease, such as slow payment of rent. A time limit on the guarantee may also be included.

21.19 The lease should specify the landlords' fixtures, bearing in mind that fixtures brought onto the premises may be deemed to have become heritable by the operation of the rule in *Brand's Trustees v Brand's Trustees* ((1876) 3 R

(HL) 16) and *Scottish Discount Co Ltd v Blin* (1986 SLT 123). As should be the general practice disclosed in a number of conflicting cases following *Winston v Patrick* (1981 SLT 41), central-heating and ventilation plant should always be inspected before taking over premises, to ensure that they are in good working order.

21.20   The tenant should be taken bound in the lease to keep the premises well stocked, in order that the landlord may exercise a right of hypothec over moveables in the tenanted premises. Further the tenants should be bound to trade continuously throughout the terms of the lease, because there is nothing more depressing than an empty shop, even though rent is being received (see *Highland and Universal Properties Ltd v Safeway Properties Ltd* 2000 SC 297).

21.21   Lastly, after a long recital of the obligations of the tenants, all of which must be paid for by the tenants, the expenses of preparation of this document by the landlords' agent are fairly and squarely placed on the tenants' shoulders. Of course, you may console the tenants by saying that if they did not pay for these now, they would only have to pay for them in the future in the form of an increased rent, for in this world there is no such thing as a free lunch. The tenants will probably reply that while they admit that, were the case otherwise, the payment would probably be spread over a number of years. I would suggest that the tenants' solicitors attempt to limit these expenses at the outset, and tell the clients what they must expect to pay.

Better still, if you can negotiate out of paying the landlords' expenses at all, you should enjoy the gratitude of the clients. It really comes down to curbing the free spending of your clients' money, and your clients should not be expected to pay a very fancy price for a long, word-processed lease.

Be sure to warn the tenants at the outset of the negotiations of the cost of all this: stamp duty, recording dues, landlords' expenses, management charges, VAT, your expenses, as well as the first rental payment due in advance, and the fitting out costs. If you fail to do this you may find that the tenants seek to make a saving of the only thing under their control, and delay to pay your fee!

21.22   These are only some of the major considerations of negotiation and drafting a lease. No practitioner in this field should be without a copy of M J Ross and D J McKichan's invaluable *The Negotiating and Drafting of Commercial Leases in Scotland* (2nd edn, 1993).

Chapter 22

SITE ASSEMBLY

'The next step was to buy all the land as quietly as possible. The site stretched for a quarter of a mile between the underground stations at Warren Street and Great Portland Street, along the north side of Euston Road, which until the 18th century had been the northern boundary of London ... an area which Joe Levy (property developer) extravagantly describes as "a derelict bloody den of disease".

Joe Levy was forming a consortium of estate agents. He knew that if his firm alone were to attempt to buy from all the many different owners, freeholders, leaseholders, and subleaseholders, his intention might become apparent and there would be two great dangers. Owners might dream up an exaggerated idea of the value, to him, of their properties, or some small time property dealers might compete against him in order to hold him to ransom. In either case his ultimate profit on the redevelopment could either be slimmed down or wiped out entirely.'

(*The Property Boom*, Joseph Marriott, on the redevelopment of the Euston station site)

22.1 Commercial conveyancing is reasonably similar to domestic conveyancing, in that the same sort of documentation applies. There the similarity ends because commercial conveyancers handle huge sums of money, deal probably with several lenders, floating charges, ranking of securities, and go into other esoteric matters like leverage (borrowing) and mezzanine financing (a debt half secured by a security over the borrowers' assets and half by shares in the borrowing company). A good commercial conveyancer should, however, have a sound grounding in the basics of domestic conveyancing, and then the other bits can be grafted on.

While I feel that this chapter will introduce many basic concepts of commercial conveyancing, I should, however, stress that this chapter makes no claim to be anything but introductory, although I hope that it will be usefully so.

22.2 First it is important to note that the conveyancing aspects of commercial deals do not differ radically from domestic conveyancing. There are the four main stages: (1) negotiation; (2) missives; (3) examination of title; and (4) settlement. The real difference lies in the fact that the lawyer in a commercial transaction must liase with a number of other people, and know fairly well what each is attempting to do. It should be remembered that it is the lawyers who must complete the evidence of the agreement, with their own signature on the missives, and therefore they must be amply satisfied that everything leading to the agreement seems to be in order.

I shall turn to the these aspects later, but first it may be useful to look at some of the metaphorical creatures in the metaphorical jungle of commercial conveyancing.

The landowner

22.3   The first persons with whom we must deal are the persons who own the land, and who are now being stalked by the developer. In most cases the developer will wish to acquire the landowner's interest absolutely, and the landowner will then be paid and will disappear. Developers do not like third parties to have any interest in their developments, as such interests may prove awkward at a future date. Some landowners, however, will not sell their land, but will grant a 'ground lease' to the developer. This lease will be for a long number of years and will require the developers to build the building and to pay a ground rent to the landowner. The developers then sublease the building to the tenants, and their profit is the difference between the two rentals (known as the profit rental), less, of course, the expenses of development.

The landowner will enjoy an annual rental income, probably increasing regularly, and at the end of the lease period, the land and buildings will revert to the landowner, or more probably to unknown descendants. This right is known as a 'reversion'.

As such arrangements tend to be for a period exceeding the normal lifespan, one may assume that in the intervening period the developers (who are not long-term investors) will have sold the reversion to a pension fund or similar body, which invests in the long term. The developers will then move on to the next development, or to a well-padded retirement. The small landowner is unlikely to reach such an agreement with a developer, and only powerful and experienced landowners are likely to reach such arrangements. For the rest, it is the case of a lump sum in their hands, and off to the Bahamas.

The developer

22.4   The developer is the person who makes the whole thing happen; the co-ordinator, profit maker, and let it not be forgotten, the risk taker. The developer runs considerable risks and will not get profit for several years and in return expects a substantial return. A sensible developer will employ a team of experts. They include:

(a) The lawyer: The lawyer completes all the documents and in such role should be the key adviser in the development. No detail should escape the lawyer's notice, for all may have a vital bearing on the documentation and, indeed, in any disputes that may follow. The lawyer should clearly establish the brief before commencing: is the lawyer engaged merely for clerical functions, or to provide commercial expertise? It is, I understand, a common source of liability claims when the lawyer thought that the job was to supply clerical services, but in fact the developer expected to be provided with commercial development expertise as well. When I talk of lawyers here I mean solicitors, but of course an advocate may also be called in at any stage to advise, or indeed may have to be. The lawyer is also responsible for the site assembly, where the development is made up of several parcels.

(b) The valuation surveyor: A valuation surveyor (as opposed to a quantity surveyor who provides a quite different service although belonging to the same professional body: the Royal Institution of Chartered Surveyors) is the expert on the price of land—the price at which it may be bought, and the price at which the development may be rented to provide the maximum return to the developer.

(c) The architect: The architect's primary task is to design and supervise the building of an attractive and useful development which conforms to all the requirements of the planning and building authorities. The architect may also provide useful advice on planning and environmental aspects, in conjunction with a planning consultant or otherwise.

(d) The planning consultant: The planning consultant and architect will negotiate with the council planning department, bearing in mind the requirements for a successful development, and also that it is unlikely that this can be completed nowadays in the teeth of opposition from the planning department. The planning position wished by the developer should be a material, suspensive, condition of purchase. The architect and the planning consultant will also deal with various bodies, such as Historic Scotland and the Civic Trust, who will wish an input of any development involving buildings of significant interest, or if there are archaeological considerations.

(e) The environmental consultant: The environmental consultant will advise on the environmental audit to be carried out before purchase, and the carrying out of the required cleaning of a contaminated site. This process is referred to as 'best available treatment at not excessive cost' (BATNEC). The environmental consultant may come from any discipline, but most probably will have a planning, surveying, scientific, or engineering background. An environmental audit should be made a material condition of purchase, and be the subject of a suspensive condition.

The purchase of land should be the subject of a suspensive environmental clause, along the following lines:

'The purchasers shall receive, in respect of the site, ground support and geotechnical survey reports (all including soils and minerals survey reports and a site survey report in terms satisfactory to them) in which regard the purchasers will be the sole judge and whose judgement shall not be challengeable.

The purchasers will also carry out an environmental audit to allow them to satisfy themselves no dangerous or deleterious substances have been used on, disposed of, dumped, released, deposited or buried at the site and that the site is not adversely otherwise affected by the terms of the Public Health (Scotland) Act 1897, Control of Pollution Act 1974, Environmental Protection Act 1990 (all as amended or varied or substituted from time to time) or any other legislation concerning the protection of human health or the environment or the treatment or disposal of dangerous substances.'

(f) The accountant: The accountant will give advice generally on financial matters and particularly on the many complex taxation problems that may arise. The accountant is also responsible for due diligence reports on any companies bought as part of the site assembly.

(g) The civil engineer: Initially the engineer will take test bores and will assess the ground conditions both for contamination and building purposes. The engineer will sink test bores to make sure that the ground is sufficiently stable to support the building envisaged. No contract should be entered into by the developer without it being made a material, suspensive, condition that if test bores, or environmental audit, prove unsatisfactory, the developer may withdraw. The potential cost of making an unstable site suitable for building is horrific. After the site has been assembled the engineer may well work with the architect to ensure the structural safety of the building, and other matters like lift shafts.

In addition a mechanical engineer will be called in to assess moving plant, such as lift machinery, heating and air conditioning plant, and so on. It is a significant aspect of modern buildings that they are largely controlled by machinery.

(h) The quantity surveyor: The quantity surveyor will again work with the architect. Broadly the architect will produce plans of the building and the quantity surveyor will prepare bills of quantity, which specify what work is to be done, and materials used, and these will be handed out to potential tenderers for the building work. A good quantity surveyor should be able to provide an accurate estimate of the costs of the building.

(i) The insurance broker: The insurance broker will advise on all insurance aspects from the first acquisition of property, through the building work, until the tenants are in possession of the new building. This covers an enormous range of potential insurable risks.

(j) The financier: The developer will have to buy the land, pay substantial professional fees, and then pay the cost of the building before any significant return is received. Temporary financing will therefore be necessary, and no doubt some form of security over the ground will also have to be given.

The planning and building departments of the council

22.5   The obtaining of a building warrant is relatively simple, provided the various complex building regulations are followed. This can be safely left to the architect, quantity surveyor and builders. Planning is much less simple as other considerations enter, particularly aesthetic and political considerations, which should quite properly enter, but which do not make life any easier, as they are imprecise and unspecified.

Thus the developer may find that the substandard building that is to be demolished is, in fact, a little-known work of someone famous, and that listed building consent is required, and various preservation societies are opposed to the development. The co-operation of a planning department is most important, without it being necessary to concede all their points. Basically these departments are reasonable to deal with, and they will not block a useful development—one which provides 'planning gain', in the form of cleaning up an eyesore or providing jobs etc—and which increases rates income. The council, possessing compulsory purchase powers as it does, may prove to be vital.

There was an example in Glasgow of the council saving a major development by compulsorily purchasing a small piece of land in disputed ownership, which dispute was preventing access to the development. There are also numerous other examples of councils helping the developer by stopping up streets or closing rights of way, and so on. As a quid pro quo for help rendered, the council may enter into an enforceable agreement with the developer under of the Town and Country Planning (Scotland) Act 1972, s 50. Thus the parties might agree that while the developer is building on the site anyway, something else, e g a public toilet, shall be built, thereby saving the council expense. The 'section 75 agreement' (formerly a section 50 agreement) is enforceable and can be recorded or registered.

An example of a very simple agreement of this kind follows:

Section 75

WHEREAS the first party are planning Authority for the   in terms of the Town and Country Planning (Scotland) Act 1972; AND WHEREAS the second party are the heritable proprietors of ALL and WHOLE that piece of ground part of the farm and lands of in the Parish of and County of   and comprising the south-east part of the field or enclosure?   numbered on the Ordnance Survey Map of the said County of   all as the said piece of ground is delineated and coloured red on the plan annexed and subscribed as relative hereto;

AND WHEREAS an application has been made to the first party by the second party for permission to erect a dwellinghouse on the said area of ground outlined in red on the plan annexed and executed as relative hereto;

AND WHEREAS the first party are disposed to grant the said planning permission subject to the second party entering into an Agreement with the first party in terms of Section 50 of the Town and Country Planning (Scotland) Act 1972; THEREFORE the parties have agreed and do hereby agree as follows, videlicet:–

(First) The second party hereby undertake that the dwellinghouse to be erected on the said subjects outlined in red on the said plan shall be used in all time coming by a person connected with or employed in agriculture and the dependents of any such person;

(Second) The second party further undertake that the said dwellinghouse shall not be sold in all time coming other than to a person so employed in or connected with agriculture;

The parties hereby agree that in the event of any disputes or differences of opinion arising as to the provisions of these presents or the interpretation thereof, such disputes or differences shall be referred to the Secretary of State for Scotland, or such other person or persons as may be nominated by him, and the decision of the Secretary of State, or his nominee as the case may be, shall be final and binding; But the provisions contained in this clause shall be without prejudice to the right of the first party to enforce these presents or any provision thereof or any condition of the planning permission to be granted in respect of the said dwellinghouse against the second party or anyone deriving title from him;

The second party hereby obliges himself to meet the recording dues of this Agreement and any other outlays and administrative expenses incurred by the first party in connection herewith;

The parties hereby grant consent to registration hereof for preservation and execution as well as for publication.

There was an important litigation in England under almost identical provisions in the English Town and Country Planning Act. The case, known as 'the Tesco Witney case' was reported at [1995] 1 WLR 759. It concerned a planning application by Tesco for a development of an 'out of town' store at Witney in Oxfordshire. Tesco's application was accompanied by an offer to build a by-pass road around the town, which was not particularly near the proposed store. This was a major planning gain for a council, as it would save them some £5 million. Tesco did not get the permission, as the Council decided that the road was not sufficiently connnected with the proposed development. The Reporter appointed by the Department of the Environment agreed. The case was then considered by the House of Lords, who in long and carefully considered judgments dismissed the appeal.

As a result of this case, and the general feeling that planning permission was being bought in many cases, the Department of the Environment and the Scottish Office issued circulars dealing with planning agreements. The Scottish version is to be found in Scottish Office Circular 12.1996, and is indispensable reading for anyone concerned with such agreements.

The demolishers

22.6　The demolishers level the site for the builders. The developer should ensure that the price charged for this service reflects the value of any reusable material on the site, e g tiles, steel, wood, copper etc.

The builders

22.7　The builders are obviously in charge of building work. It is important that they do their work properly and promptly, under the supervision of the architect. The building contract is in standard form and should provide that the builders shall pay a penalty for every day late in completion. This should, of course, be a genuine estimate of loss incurred through lack of use, and consequently rental or deemed rental, it must not be merely punitive. Conversely, a bonus may be payable to them if they finish the work early.

Examples of typical, if simplified, clauses are given below:

Penalty (or properly 'liquidate damages') clause.　The parties bind themselves and their respective representatives whomsoever to implement and fulfil the whole terms of this agreement, each to the other, under a penalty of £X sterling (or £X per day) to be paid by the party failing, to the party observing or willing to observe his part, and that over and above performance.

Force majeure.　The sellers shall not be responsible for prevention or delay in production transport to and delivery into the XY Terminal, storage in the XY Terminal, loading into trucks from XY Terminal, transport to place of delivery of the goods, or any part thereof, whether in country of origin, in XY, in the country of delivery or in transit, occasioned by any executive or legislative act done by or on behalf of any government, act of God, war, blockade, hostilities, strike, lockout, riot, or civil commotion, combination of workmen, breakdown of machinery, fire, floods, earthquakes, or any other causes whatsoever beyond the reasonable control of the sellers or the producer. Sellers shall advise buyers if delivery is prevented or delayed by any such cause and sellers have the option either to cancel the contract or to extend the delivery period by such times as is required to effect delivery.

Arbitration.　Any difference or question that may arise between the partners or their representatives or creditors or trustees in bankruptcy as to the meaning of the terms of this agreement, or as to the rights and liabilities of the parties to the agreement, or in the winding up of the partnership, or any other matter or claim relating to or arising out of the partnerships or any affairs thereof, whether during its subsistence, or after its termination, is hereby referred to the arbitration of (here state a person's name or an office-bearer who shall choose an arbiter); (if the arbiter's decision is to be final state here 'the terms of the Administration of Justice (Scotland) 1972 section 3 are hereby excluded from this agreement to arbitration').

Mediation. The parties attempt in good faith to resolve through negotiation any dispute arising out of or relating to the contract. If a dispute shall arise which cannot be resolved between the duty manager and the supervisor, the chief executives of the parties shall attempt in good faith to resolve the dispute. They shall meet within 5 days of the date (the 'breakdown date') of failure of the duty manager and supervisor to resolve the issue and if they are unable to resolve the issue within 10 days of the breakdown date either party may request to resolve the dispute through mediation conducted by a mediator appointed by the Law Society of Scotland by sending a written request to that body with a copy to the other party. The mediation procedure shall be determined by the appointed mediator in consultation with the parties. The fees and expenses of the mediator shall be borne equally by the parties. If the dispute has not been resolved within 14 days of the commencement of the mediation hearings or if no mediation has been commenced within 30 days of the breakdown date the provisions of this clause shall be of no effect.

Whether a dispute is resolved in court, by arbitration or by mediation is the question to be met by the parties. It is as well to think of this at the outset, when the parties are on co-operative terms, rather than when a dispute breaks out and they cannot even agree the time of day. Each has its merits, but, on the other hand, court proceedings are perceived to be expensive and too bound up in archaic rituals. Arbitration should be quicker and cheaper, but too often degenerates into a court without gowns. Therefore mediation would seem to be the ideal answer, but the concept has not fully caught on in Scotland yet, although it is enthusiastically used in the United States, and increasingly in England, at the instigation of the Lord Chancellor.

22.8 The letting agents These may be the same people as the valuation surveyors mentioned earlier, but not necessarily. They obtain tenants for the building. A really clever developer with a good development may 'pre-let' it, that is let it out before it is even complete. This will obviously make the developer's life much easier.

22.9 The tenants They provide the income which should reward the developer's efforts. Once the development is let, the developer will want as little to do with tenants as possible, and accordingly all maintenance and other obligations are passed to the tenants (see ch 21). The only obligation remaining upon the developer then will be to ensure that the rent cheques arrive promptly.

22.10 The fund The development is now complete, and let. The developer is drawing rents. Developers, as a class, are not collectors of rent. They prefer to develop, sell, and move on to the next development.

On the other hand a good building, full of responsible tenants, all on full repairing leases, and subject to frequent rent reviews and an eventual reversion, presents an admirable investment opportunity to a pension fund or life assurance company with plenty of money to invest in solid investments, providing a good return, safety, and increasing rents. The developer therefore sells on to one such, and is happy. The acquiring fund is also happy for it has a sound investment with an attractive yield and prospects of increases. Further, if the leases are properly drawn up, it need never trouble itself with the tenants and can safely leave a managing agent in charge of the building— at the expense of the tenants naturally!

22.11   The development   Having identified, I hope, the principal players, I would now like to look at the various problems which may face the developer. In the exercise at the end of the chapter, I have sought to provide examples of some of the simpler problems that face the developer.

It is implicit in the developer's job that a messy collection of buildings and pieces of land are acquired and bit by bit a site is assembled for development. This technique is known as 'site assembly' and perhaps the simplest example of this is to be found in the game of Monopoly. You may remember that if you own Fleet Street you can demand a substantial rent; but if you also acquire The Strand and Trafalgar Square, you have all the reds, and the rents double. You can then start developing the site, and by the time you have built hotels, the rents are enormous. This is of course a simplification, but I hope you will see the point.

In real life the process is obviously much more complex. Sites have to be assembled laboriously, subject to many conditions of purchase and usually without letting anybody know that the process is going on. If the secret is released, prices will inevitably rise, and as the acquisition is nearly complete, the persons with the 'ransom strip' can demand almost anything they want, as they can otherwise block the development. For this reason the developer has to work in a cunning and covert fashion. Property and interests in property have to be acquired bit by bit, a property here, the landlord's part of a lease there (to await the termination of the lease). Businesses or property companies must be bought for their property content, and be run both to divert suspicion and to provide the developer with a bit of income. Properties must be bought in name of nominees or associated companies.

The properties have to be bought subject to suspensive conditions— conditions that suspend the implement of the agreement until the conditions are met—such as a grant of planning permission or the transfer of a licence, or satisfactory test bores or environmental audit (see para **23.4**).

At all time natural caution must be tempered with stealth and it may be that buildings may have to be bought without planning permission, as an application for this might reveal the master plan. Here careful advice on planning is certainly necessary. The duty of the lawyer in site assembly is to obtain for the developer a good and clear title to the entire development, with all third-party interests, so far as possible, eradicated.

22.12   The negotiations with the planning authorities do not primarily concern the lawyer, and I shall pass over these, as I will pass over the building of the property. The next problem is therefore to let the building to good tenants. It is a lucky developer who can get a single tenant for the whole development, and most have to be content with a number of tenants, and the standard lease of the development must therefore allow for multi-ownership.

The whole concept of ownership of commercial property subject to tenancies is, as I have attempted to point out, to shift the entire responsibility for the buildings to the tenants. Thus the practice has grown up in commercial leasing for the leases to be on a full repairing, renewing and insuring basis. Because of the immense power and ability of developers to choose their tenants at leisure, this is generally accepted practice.

22.13　There follows a fairly simplified example of a successful site assembly, which hopefully will show some of the problems that can arise.

You act for a Mr John Buzz, who has been engaged in property development on a small scale for several years. He now informs you that he wants to put through a larger development which will, if successful, provide a sum of money which will enable him to retire. For some months now Mr Buzz has quietly been acquiring a block at the corner of Sardinia Terrace and Lombardy Street (see Plan A attached) which is in a rather run-down part of town, but which is nevertheless near a lot of housing. Mr Buzz has accordingly entered into a tentative agreement to build a supermarket on the cleared site and then to let this to Prontomart Ltd, a well-known national supermarket chain (see Plan B attached).

Furthermore, assuming that everything else goes to plan, Mr Buzz has an understanding with the Long Life Assurance Company Ltd that it will buy the developed and tenanted site as an investment of pension funds, and will therefore then become the landlords of Prontomart. This will provide Mr Buzz with a sizeable sum which will enable him to retire in some comfort. There are, however, a number of problems to be overcome, and you are asked to provide general or specific advice on these.

(1)　Referring to Plan A, which shows the existing site, you will notice that there is at the corner of Sardinia Terrace and Lombardy Street a plot of ground with two large trees. These trees are the subject of a Tree Preservation Order under the Town and Country Planning (Scotland) Act 1972, s 58. However, they overhang Lombardy Street, and the falling leaves in autumn make the road slippery. Furthermore, the roots are intruding under Number 1 Sardinia Terrace causing difficulties in the foundations. Advise Mr Buzz as to the possibility of his being allowed to remove these trees legally, and substitute a landscaped area. (Hint: TCP(S)A 1972, s 58.)

(2)　The bottom floor of the house at Number 1 Sardinia Terrace is a shop which is tenanted by a Mr Hammer. Mr Hammer is opposed to the development as, he says, he will not be able to obtain a new shop property at an equally advantageous rent. Further, he says that the new supermarket will ruin his business anyway. Has Mr Hammer any security of tenure? (Hint: Tenancy of Shops (Scotland) Act 1949.)

(3)　Between Numbers 2 and 3 Sardinia Terrace, there runs a right of way to the public park. This is quite extensively used by children from the nearby school as a way to the swings. Mr Buzz wants to build over this right of way, and is quite prepared to provide an alternative route. Can Mr Buzz have the right of way closed? (Hint: TCP(S)A 1972, ss 203 ff.)

(4)　The public house, the Dog and Ferret, has two full-time employees, Ron and Fred (known to the clientele as Fido and Ferdie), whose belligerent and unhelpful attitude has ensured that over the years the public house has not

PLAN A

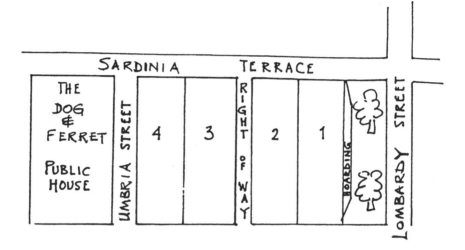

PLAN B

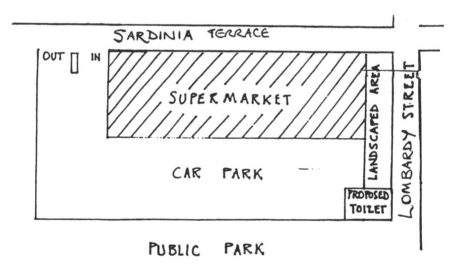

been very successful. Can Mr Buzz ask the seller to dismiss Ron and Fred before Mr Buzz takes over, and, if not, what are Mr Buzz's liabilities in this matter to Ron and Fred? (Hint: see para **19.14**).

(5)   The superiors are the Diamond Insurance Group, and the title conditions are that the houses shall be used as houses for the occupation of one family only. Some years ago a minute of waiver was granted over Number 3 Sardinia

Terrace, permitting this to be used as a private nursery school. It has, in fact, never been used as such. Mr Buzz has told the Diamond Insurance Group of his plans, and they have refused to allow the property to be used for the building of a supermarket. Advise Mr Buzz. (Hint: CFR(S)A 1970, s 1.)

(6)   The planning department of the district council has told Mr Buzz that if it grants planning permission for the supermarket it would 'very much like' if he would build a public toilet in the position shown on Plan B, while he is building the store. If he agrees to do this, can that agreement be binding on Mr Buzz and his successors? (Hint: see TCPA 1997, s 75.)

(7)   Advise Mr Buzz on his liability for: (a) stamp duty, (b) capital gains tax, (c) income tax on rental income received prior to the development being started, and (d) value added tax on the sales made in the public house and on any commercial rents received. (Hint: see taxation textbook.)

(8)   Advise Mr Buzz in general terms on the terms of the lease to be granted by him to Prontomart Ltd. (Hint: see ch 22.)
    The entire law of landlord and tenant is, therefore, completely replaced by the terms of the lease. Unlike in England there is no statutory interference with this process, barring the relatively mild security of tenure provisions of the Tenancy of Shops (Scotland) Act 1949 and the prohibition of automatic irritancies contained in the Law Reform (Miscellaneous Provisions) (Scotland) Act 1985. There is thus no security of tenure beyond the terms of the lease, no machinery for fixing fair rents, and no compensation for improvements made by the tenant. The lawyer for the tenant must therefore proceed with great care and try to get some sort of safeguard for the tenant if at all possible.
    The entire topic of commercial leasing is a complex one, and is dealt with in a general manner in chapter 22, but for a fuller discussion I can confidently refer you to M J Ross and D J McKichan *Negotiation and Drafting of Commercial Leases in Scotland* (2nd edn, 1993). Any lawyer who embarks on commercial leasing without reference to this book is either very good or very foolish.

Chapter 23

BUYING FROM A BUILDER

'Despite the land rush last year saw 17,330 new housing starts in Scotland—a 22% increase on the previous year (1993) and a figure which outperformed every other UK region.

It has been estimated that some 5,000 acres of land in Glasgow is derelict—some 9% of all the land within the city boundary ... a higher spend on decontamination and site preparation would unlock new sites, strengthen urban communities and ease the pressure on the green belt. And we would not need so many motorways.'

(Stewart McIntosh: *The Herald*, 1995)

23.1 We have until now been discussing the purchase of 'secondhand' housing. Your clients may well wish to buy a new house, and the procedure is similar, but there are some very important differences; for a start, the purchasers usually have almost no bargaining power, other than the power to try another building site, and have to sign a printed missive, produced by the builder. This document is not susceptible to any alterations, other than very minor ones. The terms of this agreement favour the builder, not unnaturally, and it behoves the solicitor to make sure that the settlement takes place on the date when it is agreed, otherwise strict penalties are incurred.

23.2 Before entering into an agreement, the purchasers should ensure that the houses are not built on an environmentally unsound site. This may sound rather dramatic, but there have been numerous instances of builders, even in good faith, building on sites which latterly turn out to be heavily contaminated. Builders are encouraged to build on 'brownfield' sites which have been used for other purposes. Such sites can frequently be contaminated by a number of very nasty substances such as asbestos, petroleum, arsenic, explosives, radioactive substances, and chrome, or have been subjected to mining or quarrying, or waste tipping. It is estimated, by Landmark Information Group Ltd, who provide information about contaminated sites, that there are about 35,000 potentially contaminated sites in Scotland. It should be said that local authorities are now much more vigilant in giving planning permission for contaminated sites, and generally will not grant planning permission if the site is environmentally unsound. The following case, however, was cited in a pamphlet entitled 'Buyer Beware!' published by Friends of the Earth:

'57 families were evacuated from a housing estate in Portsmouth. The families were given 24 hours to leave their homes after dangerous levels of asbestos were found in air and soil samples. The houses had been built on a former Ministry of Defence landfill site. The landfill had been covered with clean topsoil to prevent contamination but the capping proved inadequate.'

Potentially contaminative uses of the land are as follows: agricultural, extractive industry, energy industry, production of metals, production of non-metals and their products, glass-making and ceramics, production and use of chemicals, engineering and manufacturing processes, food processing industry, paper, pulp and printing industry, textile industry, rubber industry, infrastructure, waste disposal, gas work sites, landfill sites, metal industries, sewage works and sludge tips, chemical works, docks and wharfs, tar, oil and petroleum depots, scrap yards, tanneries, railway sidings and depots.

Even when the site appears to be an attractive 'greenfield' site, it should be remembered that it may have been used for some other purpose in the past, particularly in wartime. The history of 'brownfield' sites—that is sites that have been previously occupied—should always be carefully checked.

The builders should be able to provide sufficient evidence of the prior uses of the land, or treatment that has been done to the site, but if they do not, certain information as to past uses can be obtained from the local library, or from asking a specialist surveyor or environmental consultant to investigate the history of the land. The conveyancer may also be able to shed some light from the title deeds, but the ironic aspect of land registration is that the whole purpose of the land certificate is not to give the history of the title. Therefore, if you wish to find out who owned the site in years gone by, investigations have to be made in the old Sasine Register.

If your clients cannot be satisfied as to the prior uses of the site by the information given by the builders, or from their own enquiries, they are better not to purchase. The purchase may prove to be an unpleasant one, and the house may eventually turn out to be unsaleable, or in exaggerated cases, explode through a build up of methane gas. Prospective buyers should also make enquiries about any history of flooding in low-lying areas. A 'home envirosearch' can be obtained from Landmark Information Group Ltd which gives a 500 metre search, discloses former uses, gives coal-mining areas nearby and subsidence risks, and gives details of flood risk and overhead transmission lines or pylons. This report currently costs £39 including VAT, and if the purchaser has any lingering doubts, that is money well spent.

23.3   The typical builders' missive describes a property, and the description of the property should be checked, and in particular the boundaries of the property. In land registration areas, considerable difficulty has been caused to the Keeper by properties not being laid out as they were stated to be in estate plans submitted to the Keeper prior to sales. For this reason, land certificates of new houses are often delayed until all the land certificates in the site are prepared, so that they can be fully consistent with each other. The plan of the house should not be a standard estate plan, with the relevant house coloured in—this is not sufficient for land registration, and remember that the whole country will be subject to land registration by April 2003.

The standard for descriptions is stated in an article by Alistair Rennie, the Deputy Keeper, in the January 1995 JLSS 16, where it is suggested that the appropriate obligation should read:

'In exchange for the price the seller will deliver a duly executed disposition in favour of the purchaser and will exhibit or deliver a valid marketable title together with a Form 10 Report brought down to a date as near as practicable to the date of settlement and showing no entries adverse to the seller's interest, the cost of said report being the responsibilty of the seller. In addition, the seller, at or before the date of entry and at his expense, shall deliver to the purchaser such documents and evidence as the Keeper may require to enable the Keeper to issue a land certificate in the name of the purchaser as the registered proprietor of the whole subjects of offer and containing no exclusion of indemnity in terms of section 12(2) of the Land Registration (Scotland) Act 1979: such documents shall include (unless the whole subjects of offer only comprise part of a tenement or flatted building) a plan or bounding description sufficient to enable the whole subjects of offer to be identified on the Ordnance map and evidence (such as a Form P16 Report) that the description of the whole subjects of offer as contained in the title deed is *habile* to include the whole of the occupied extent. The land certificate to be issued to the purchaser will disclose no entry, deed or diligence prejudicial to the purchaser's interest other than such as are created by or against the purchaser prior to the date of settlement. Notwithstanding the delivery of the disposition above referred to this clause shall remain in full force and effect and may be founded upon.'

Builders' solicitors may be reluctant to give such an obligation, but this is the standard of information that should be provided in every case.

23.4   The price is stated, and the date of entry is given, not as a precise date, but as the date on which it is certified as complete. A small deposit may be payable upon signing of missives, which deposit is subtracted from the final purchase price. It is generally provided that the settlement shall be by telegraphic transfer, and if the purchaser fails to make payment, interest is payable at a commercial price on the balance outstanding. After a certain time the contract may be brought to an end by the builder. No partial payment of the price is generally permitted, and the keys are not available until full settlement is made. Let me remind you at this point, that the expression 'telegraphic transfer' does not indicate any sense of urgency from the transferring bank.

23.5   The offer states briefly the principal feuing conditions, such as reservation of minerals, use of the house and garden, formation of roads, fencing, provisions as to the ownership, use and maintenance of open amenity spaces, reservation of servitude and wayleave rights for mains services, and the usual obligations of the seller in sasine and land register transactions. To avoid disputes arising this selection of conditions is stated to be 'without prejudice to the generality': which is that the conditions to be included in the feu grant shall be 'in conformity with similar titles given off on this and other of (the builders') estates and will be subject to a deed of conditions containing such conditions as (the builders) consider appropriate for the preservation of amenity'. A deed of conditions is prepared in terms of the Conveyancing (Scotland) Act 1924, s 9, and lays down the standard conditions for the whole estate. The feu grant can, therefore, be kept relatively short, because it refers to the deed of conditions for the conditions contained.

23.6   The builders will usually apply for and warrant that necessary planning permissions, building warrants and the like have been obtained, but will not give an obligation to produce these. Furthermore, the superior's consent should also be obtained, particularly where an older building has been knocked down or converted, as there may be an old feuing condition that is inconsistent with the modern use.

The builders, however, give an obligation to produce a completion or habitation certificate from the local authority. Settlement should not be made until this is exhibited, and the transfer from builder to purchaser is available for delivery. (See *Gibson v Hunter Home Designs Ltd* 1976 SC 23 for a case when it was not, and the terrible consequences that flowed from this failure, both for the purchaser who lost the house and the money, and for the legal profession generally.) The cases of *Sharp v Thomson* (1997 SC (HL) 66) and *Burnett's Trustee v Grainger* (2000 SLT (Sh Ct) 116), (the decision of the sheriff principal was successfully appealed to the Inner House in a judgment of 15 May 2002 reported on the website http:/www.scotcourts.gov.uk), indicate the great importance of the solicitor sending a conveyance to the register immediately.

23.7   The builders will reserve the right to vary the building materials to materials of a similar specification, in accordance with the circumstances, without affecting the price.

23.8   All extras on the building price, such as additional fittings to the basic specification, should be carefully checked, as should all discounts and incentives offered, in order that the purchasers may comply with the conditions for obtaining these.

23.9   The provision of searches in the Sasines Register is similar to the normal obligation, but the builders will not continue the search to disclose any security created by the purchasers. In land registration cases, the obligation is the same as is normally given.

23.10   The builders will give a probable completion date, but they will not warrant this, nor pay any sort of damages if this date is not met. Thus a penalty clause and a force majeure clause are not appropriate, which would force the builders to pay damages if the house is not ready by a certain date ('penalty clause'), but exempting the builders for any failure caused by certain events such as war or strikes (force majeure clause).

23.11   Larger builders are usually members of the National House-Building Council, and as such offer a buildmark certificate to cover the house against defects arising over a ten-year period (see para **7.34**). A small builder may not be a member of the NHBC, which implies no disrespect, in which case a certificate of inspection will be produced from the independent architect who supervised the development, stating that the development is complete in accordance with the plans. The architect should possess full indemnity insurance cover, in the event that a mistake is made.

The Council of Mortage Lenders, in the *CML Handbook*, suggest a certificate be given in the following terms:–

PROFESSIONAL CONSULTANT'S CERTIFICATE TO CERTIFY
A NEW HOUSE

I certify that:

1. **I have visited the site at appropriate periods from the commencement of construction to the current stage to check:**
    (a) progress
    (b) use of materials, and
    (c) conformity with structural drawings, specifications and building regulations.

2. At the stage of my last inspection on . . . . the property had reached the stage of . . . .

3. So far as could be determined by each periodic visual inspection, the property has been constructed:
    (a) to a satisfactory standard, and
    (b) in general compliance with the approved structural drawings and specifications and/or building regulations

4. I was originally retained by . . . . applicant/builder/ developer in this case. I am aware that this certificate is being relied upon by the first purchaser . . . . of the property and also by . . . . (name of lender) when making a mortgage advance to the purchaser when secured on this property. I confirm that I have appropriate experience in the design and/or monitoring of the construction or conversion of residential or commercial buildings.

(Followed by details of consultant and indemnity insurance.)

23.12   When a purchase is made from a large builder, a 'package' is being bought and stamp duty is payable on the total price of the heritage, less any moveable items included.

When a plot is bought separately, and a house is then later built on it, stamp duty is broadly only payable on the purchase of the land. Thus, if a plot is bought at £20,000 and a house is then built on it at a price of £50,000, stamp duty would only be payable on the price of the plot. As the current threshold for stamp duty is £60,000, there is therefore no stamp duty, instead of £700, which would have been payable if the items had been purchased simultaneously. This useful device must not, however, be used artificially, and the Stamp Office has produced a statement of practice (SP 10/87 of 22.11.87) restating the Inland Revenue's views on this matter.

A further complication arises with the introduction of the 3% (over £250,000) and 4% (over £500,000) stamp duty bands, when the stamp duty may be collosal, and the temptation to avoid it even greater. The Inland Revenue have recently warned that in suspected cases of the price being understated, they will expect to see full valuations of items excluded from the total price, to reduce the consideration below a certain threshhold.

In the purchase of a new house each party will generally pay their own fees, but certain builders may offer incentives, including a contribution to the purchasers' fees. This should be carefully checked.

APPENDICES

Appendix I

A FIRST REGISTRATION IN THE LAND REGISTER IN 2002

Sale of 3 Miller Drive, Inveraray 2002

1. File Note of telephone conversation between Henry Pink, partner, and John James, client, 1 March 2002

Attendance on telephone with Mr. James. Noting that he is moving to London, and that he wanted us to sell his house at 3 Miller Drive, which we had bought for him a few years ago.

Offering to market the property for him, but noting that a colleague was interested in the house, and would probably buy it. Quoting a fee of £350 plus VAT and outlays. Explaining that as a seller he did not pay stamp duty, but that if he is buying in London, this may be a substantial problem. He said that some lawyers were advertising that they would do conveyancing for £250 plus VAT and outlays. Explaining that you get what you pay for, but that we would drop the fee to £300 plus VAT and outlays. He seemed quite pleased, and I said we would send a written estimate. (Engaged 10 minutes)

Notes: 1. This conversation perhaps explains the professional difficulty encountered in Chapter 1. The fee being charged will hardly yield a profit at all, if the job is done properly.

2. Inverary is in Argyllshire, which became operational for land registration from 1 April 2000

2. Letter from Henry Pink to John James (1 March 2002)

**42 Registration Row
Glasgow**

1 March 2002

John James Esq.
3 Miller Drive
INVERARAY
PA 32 5XX

Dear Mr. James

3 Miller Drive, Inveraray

I refer to our telephone conversation today and now annex a written estimate for work to be done in connection with your sale at a price of, say, £100,000.

This is in accordance with my telephone estimate today. As this is a sale, there is no stamp duty payable by you, and the only other outlays are on the various reports and registration dues of the discharge of the standard security.

I hope that this will be in order, and I shall be pleased to have your instructions.

When replying could you please let me know if you are married?

Yours sincerely

Henry Pink

Fee Quotation:

Fee for doing all work in connection with the sale by John James of the house a t 3 Miller Drive, Inveraray at £100,000, including Discharge of the Standard Security granted to Black Country plc (formerly Black Country Building Society)

Fee	£300.00
VAT thereon	52.50
OUTLAYS	
Registration of Discharge	22.00
Property Enquiry certificate – estimate	75.00
Form 10 and 11 reports – estimate	36.30
Form P16 -estimate	22.70
Coal Mining Report	15.00
TOTAL	£533.50

1. This proposed fee is for a normal transaction involving the normal amount of work. In the event of the work required involving more than normal time or being of an unusually complex nature, the proposed fee may require to be increased. You will be advised of any such development in the course of transaction.
2. Outlays are estimated on current rates.

Notes: 1. In his Report of 1995 the Legal Services Ombudsman was most emphatic about the need for accurate fee estimation. The lawyer is the first to expect this service from other providers!

2. An escape clause should be left, in case the transaction goes wrong, through no fault of the conveyancer, thus causing considerable extra work which would not normally be expected, or included in the quotation.

3. Letter from John James, client, to Henry Pink, partner, 2 March 2002

Dear Mr. Pink

Thank you for your letter. Your estimate is quite acceptable and I shall be obliged if you will act on our behalf. I am pretty certain that Lachie MacLachlan will buy the house, and he has been to see it. If I want the property put on the market, I shall tell you.

Yes I am married. I married my wife Agnes in August 1995. Do you not remember, you were at the wedding? Why do you need to know anyway? Does my marriage present any difficulty?.

Yours sincerely

John James

Note: Ouch!

4.   E.mail Henry Pink to administrator Veronica Vanbrugh 2 March 2002 and her reply

Please see letter from Mr.James. Why did you not remind me that I was at his wedding? HP.

Reply:

I was still at school in August 1995. Regards. Veronica.

Note: The efficient Veronica, who Mr. Pink is extremely lucky to keep, was formerly a Secretary, but the firm does not have private Secretaries any more.

5.   E.mail Henry Pink to Wendy Robertson, trainee, 2 March 2002.

Wendy – please take over this transaction. It is a first registration in Inveraray. We bought the house for Mr. James, in the good old days of Sasine Registration. I suppose this is not now competent? You know all about Land Registration, having studied it at University, and will be able to do the transaction. HP.

Note: Mr. Pink, of course , knows all about Land Registration He is merely passing routine work down the chain, as all professionals must now do. He will of course keep an eye on Wendy Robertson's work, for which he is ultimately responsible. Please note that older lawyers will expect trainees to be fully conversant with all developments in the law, rightly or wrongly.

6.   E.mail Wendy Robertson to Henry Pink 3 March 2002

Thank you for sending me the stuff about Miller Drive, Inveraray. I have written to ask for the title deeds and to Mr. James and to the Local Authority for the required property Enquiry Certificate, and for a Coal Mining Report, and for the appropriate P.16 and form 10 reports. WR

6 (a)   Application for P.16 Report

REGISTERS OF SCOTLAND
Executive Agency

· p r o p e r t y **REPORTS** s e r v i c e
FORM P16

APPLICATION TO COMPARE A BOUNDING DESCRIPTION[1] WITH THE O.S. MAP

Applicant's Reference	HP/WR/Jame.123

County	Argyll

From

Brown, Jarvie & Walker
42 Registration Road
Glasgow
G1 3XX

Telephone No.	0141 204 123X

FAS No.	7777

FAX No.	0141 204 432X

O.S. Map grid reference (if known)	

I/We apply for the boundaries of the subjects
POSTAL ADDRESS

Street No.	3	House Name	

Street Name	Miller Drive

Town	Inveraray

Postcode	PA32 5XX

(1) Described below
(2) Delineated on the plan annexed } to be compared with the O.S. Map.

1. The bounding description must sufficiently define the extent of the subjects to enable the Keeper to identify them on the O.S. Map, by supplying:

(a) a plan with boundaries of stated lineal dimensions or boundaries which can be measured from an adequate scale appearing on the face of the plan, the position of the property being tied by stated measurements to road junctions or other features which are depicted on the O.S. Map, or

(b) such a plan, together with a postal address, but without the position of the property being so tied to features which are depicted on the O.S. Map, or

(c) a written description which includes measurements and refers to adjoining subjects by name or street number and not by the name of the owner, together with a postal address.

2. Delete (1) or (2) is applicable

Signature: ....   Date: ....

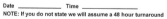

Users Identifier

FOR RESULTS SEE OVERLEAF>

DIARY SERVICE:

Please state date and time you require report

Date _____ Time _____
NOTE: If you do not state we will assume a 48 hour turnaround

Meadowbank House, 153 London Road, Edinburgh EH8 7AU
www.ros.gov.uk DX 555338 EDINBURGH 15 reports@ros.gov.uk
Tel: 0845 6070162 Fax: 0131 479 3651/3683/3667

Published by everyform

· p r o p e r t y REPORTS s e r v i c e ·
FORM P16

FOR OFFICIAL USE

RESULT OF COMPARISON OF BOUNDING DESCRIPTION WITH THE O.S. MAP

1. The subjects are not identifiable on the O.S. Map.
2. The boundaries of the subjects coincide with those on the O.S. Map.
3. The boundaries do not coincide with those on the O.S. Map. Please see print herewith.

Signature: ....   Date: ....

NOTES

1. THE ABOVE INFORMATION HAS BEEN ISSUED IN RESPECT OF THE SUBJECTS DESCRIBED OVERLEAF. IT DOES NOT NECESSARILY REPRESENT THE SUBJECTS PRESENTLY COMPRISED IN THE TITLE.

2. PLEASE ENSURE THAT THIS FORM ACCOMPANIES ANY APPLICATION FOR FIRST REGISTRATION OF THE SUBJECT DESCRIBED OVERLEAF.

Users Identifier

Published by **everyform**

6 (b)   Application for a Form 10 Report

REGISTERS OF SCOTLAND
Executive Agency

· p r o p e r t y **REPORTS** s e r v i c e ·
FORM 10

(Land Registration (Scotland) Rules 1980 Rule 24(1))

APPLICATION FOR A REPORT PRIOR TO REGISTRATION OF THE SUBJECTS DESCRIBED BELOW

Note: No covering letter is required and an existing Search should not be submitted.
VAT Reg No. GD 410 GB 888 8410 64

Please complete in DUPLICATE and in BLACK TYPE

From	FOR OFFICIAL USE
Brown, Jarvie & Walker **42 Registration Road** **Glasgow** **G1 3XX**	Report Number Date of Receipt Search Sheet Nos. Fee

County	**Argyll**	FAS No.	**7777**

Applicant's Reference	**HP/WR/Jame.123**	FAX No.	**0141 204 432X**

Telephone	**0141 204 123X**	FAX response required (X here)	

POSTAL ADDRESS OF SUBJECTS

Street No.	**3**	House Name		Street Name	**Miller Drive**

Town	**Inveraray**	Postcode	**PA32 5XX**

OTHER:

Description of Subjects	**Detached house of above address**

The above subjects being	edged red on the accompanying plan, 2
	~~being shown within the boundaries described below~~ 3

I/We apply for a report

(1) on the subjects described above, for which an application for registration in the Land Register is to be made, from

(a) the **REGISTER OF SASINES** and

(b) the **LAND REGISTER** stating whether or not registration of the said subjects has been effected [4]

1. Delete if inapplicable
2. A plan need not be attached if a verbal description will sufficiently identify the subjects
3. Describe by reference to a writ recorded in the Register of Sasines
4. If the subjects have been registered, the Keeper will supply an Office Copy of the Title Sheet only on specific request.

Faxed applications should not be followed up by a written request and may not be accepted if a plan is included.

DIARY SERVICE:

Please state date and time you require report

Date _____ Time _____
NOTE: If you do not state we will assume a 48 hour turnaround

User Identifier

Meadowbank House, 153 London Road, Edinburgh EH8 7AU
www.ros.gov.uk DX 555338 EDINBURGH 15 reports@ros.gov.uk
Tel: 0845 6070162 Fax: 0131 479 3651/3683/3667

Published by **everyform**

·p r o p e r t y **REPORTS** s e r v i c e ·
FORM 10

and (2) from the Registers of Inhibitions and Adjudications for 5 years prior to the date of Certificate against the Register of Inhibitions and Adjudications, viz.

| 1. Surname(s) | James | Forename(s) | John |

| Address(es) | 3 Miller Drive, Inveraray PA32 5XX |

| 2. Surname(s) | James | Forename(s) | Agnes |

| Address(es) | 3 Miller Drive, Inveraray PA32 5XX |

| 3. Surname(s) | | Forename(s) | |

| Address(es) | |

| 4. Surname(s) | | Forename(s) | |

| Address(es) | |

| 5. Company/ Firm/ Corporate body | |

| Address(es) | |

| 6. Company/ Firm/ Corporate body | |

| Address(es) | |

NOTE: Insert full names and addresses of the persons on whom a Report is required.

Signature: _____   Date: _____

User Identifier

Note: Many of the Letters which follow are absolutely standard in their form, and in a modern office they will be available from the firm's database. This means a tremendous labour saving.

7. Letter from Brown Jarvie & Walker to Black Country plc (3 March 2002)

The Mortgage Manager
Black Country plc
Black Country Buildings
STOKE-ON-TRENT

HP/WR/JAME 123

Dear Sir

Mr. John . James
Roll No. XY 1234567/A

Please note that we are to act for Mr. James in the sale of his house at 3 Miller Drive, Inveraray.

Please let us have the title deeds to enable us to process the sale. We shall let you know the details of sale as soon as possible.

Please also let us have a suitable form of Discharge, following your recent conversion to a public company.

Yours faithfully

Brown Jarvie & Walker

Note: The Black Country Building Society was one of the first Building Societies in the world. A few years ago it amalgamated with the Midlands Building Society, but recently the members voted to demutualise. This meant that the Building society became a PLC, the directors were paid more money, and the account holders each got 150 shares of the PLC. Everybody seems to have won, but please bear in mind that there is no such thing as a free lunch, and someone is going to have to pay – probably investors, who will get less interest, and borrowers, who will pay more interest. The change of status means that in the Discharge the PLC will have to deduce title from the old society, in whose name the security stands.

8. **Letter from Brown Jarvie & Walker to John James (3 March 2002)**

John James
3 Miller Drive
INVERARAY

PA32 5XX

HP/WR/JAME .123

Dear Mr. James

3 Miller Drive, Inveraray

Thank you for your letter of 2 March.

In reply to your query, Mrs. James' name does not appear on the title, but she has an occupancy right in the house which will require to be released to effect a sale.

We propose that she will consent in the Disposition to release the occupancy right, and we shall contact you about this soon.

Can you please let us know if there have been any alterations to your house which would require permission from Argyll Council, or the Superior, or both,and let us have any certificates of such permission.

Yours faithfully

BJW

Notes: 1. This polite and businesslike letter should get around any embarrassment about Mr. and Mrs. James' wedding.

2. A separate consent to the sale can also be obtained, and it is signed before a Notary Public. It is probably easier to have the consent contained in the Disposition, because this deed is recorded, and there is then no danger of it being lost, as can all too easily happen with a separate consent, unless it is registered in the Books of Council and Session or the Sheriff Court Books. For the various forms see Appendix II.

9   (a) Letter from Brown Jarvie & Walker to Argyll and Bute Council
3 March 2002

The Chief Executive
Argyll and Bute Council
Kilmory
LOCHGILPHEAD

PA31 8RT

HP/WR/JAME123

Dear Sir,

**John James
3 Miller Drive, Inveraray**

In connection with a sale of the above property we shall be obliged if you will provide us with a certificate that (a) there are no outstanding orders or notices over the property and (b) that the roads footpaths and sewers have been taken over and are maintained by your Council.

We enclose a cheque for £XX in payment of your fee in this respect.

Yours faithfully

BJW

Notes: 1. These certificates have been applied for in plenty of time, but the great art is (a) to apply in enough time to get certificates before settlement and (b) not to apply too early, so that the purchasers may reject the certificates as being out of date. Great care must be exercised in this respect, especially if the sale is going to be lengthy process.

2. The appropriate authority and correct address and current fee should always be checked with the Law Society website **www.lawscot.org.uk** or with the appropriate authority. You will need a registration number to access the Law Society website, Conveyancer's section. If you do not send the correct fee, all the papers will simply be returned to you, and that is at least a week wasted, which may be critical.

9   (b) Letter from Brown Jarvie & Walker to Coal Authority 3 March 2002

The Coal Authority
Mining Reports Office
200 Lichfield Lane
Berry Hill
MANSFIELD
Nottinghamshire
NG18 4RG

HP/WR/JAME123

Dear Sirs

**Mr. John James
3 Miller Drive, Inveraray, Argyll**

In connection with a sale of the above property, we shall be obliged if you will let us have a Coal Mining Search over the property.

We enclose cheque for £XX in respect of your fee in this matter.

Yours faithfully

BJW

Notes: 1.   There is no point in asking Mr. Pink about this. Older practitioners tend to get very hot under the collar, and tend to splutter about "wasted money" where these reports concern properties that are obviously not in a traditional mining area. Wendy Robertson may not have consulted the list of mining areas, for which reports are required, and which appear in a Law Society list, which is printed in the Appendix to Professor Rennie's book on Mineral Law. The point is that coal mining can have taken place virtually anywhere, and this report is an important feature in guarding the conveyancer's back against any negligence claims, if the house suddenly slips down a subsidence hole.

2.   Again the current fee should be checked against the Law Society website.

10   (a) Property Definition Report – all in order

11   (b) Form 10A Report – all in order

Note: These reports should be checked for any nasty surprises before they are sent to the purchaser's agent. Nothing is apparent, so the sellers are now in a position to conclude missives, when an offer is received.

11   Letter from Mair & Kildare to Brown, Jarvie & Walker (5 April 2002)

Mair & Kildare,
Solicitors,
35 Magister Street,
PAISLEY PA1 4ZZ.

5 March 2002

Messrs Brown, Jarvie & Walker,
Solicitors,
42 Registration Row,
GLASGOW G1 3XX.

DX GW500

DEAR SIRS

On behalf of our clients, Lachlan and Jean MacLachlan of 3 Glenlivet Road, Glasgow, (hereinafter called 'the Purchaser') we hereby offer to purchase from your client Mr John James the heritable proprietor, (hereinafter called 'the Seller') the subjects comprising the dwellinghouse known as and forming 3 Miller Drive, Inverary; together with (one) the whole parts, privileges and pertinents; (two) the whole common, mutual, and exclusive rights of property; (three) all necessary rights of access; (four) the heritable fittings and fixtures; (five) the central heating system; and (six) the Seller's whole right title and interest in and to the said subjects (hereinafter called the subjects), which term shall include any part of the said subjects), which term shall include any part of the said subjects; and that on the following terms and conditions:

1. The price will be ONE HUNDRED THOUSAND POUNDS (£100,000) (hereinafter called 'the price'). The price will be apportioned between the heritable property (£98,500) and the moveable property included in the sale (£1,500). The price shall be payable on the date of entry.

2. Entry to and vacant possession of the subjects will be given on 18th April 2002 (hereinafter called 'the date of entry') or such other and earlier date as may be agreed between the contracting parties.

3. (a) The price shall include the following specific items, whether heritable or moveable in character, as viewed by the Purchaser:

    the carpet in the dining room, the refrigerator, two electric fires in the hall and dining room, the hob and split level oven, all non-carpet floor coverings, all curtain rails, rods and pelmets, all door handles and door knobs, all light flexes, bulbs and bulbholders and ceiling roses, all fluorescent light casings, the door bell and burglar alarm system, all decorative panels, mirrors, shelves, cabinets, towel rails, furniture shelves, fire surrounds, other units and accessories to the extent that the foregoing are presently attached or fixed to the floors, ceilings or walls, all stair clips, rods and eyes, all gas fires, storage heaters, fireplaces and grates, all fitted units, cupboards, sinks, water closets, baths, showers, bidets, and other sanitary ware, all built in wardrobes and cupboards, all television and radio aerials and satellite dishes, all venetian, roller, and other blinds, all central heating systems and plant, all plants, trees, shrubs, stock and ornaments in the garden and common areas generally, all boundary walls, fencing, and gates, and garages, garden huts and outhouses.

(b) It is warranted that the said items belong absolutely to the Seller and none is subject to any hire purchase, leasing, loan or other similar agreement.

The said central heating system, burglar alarm system and any electrically operated and/or mechanically operated items among the said items will be in good working order on the Date of Entry.

4. The seller will inform the Council Tax Office of the change of ownership.

5. As at the Date of Entry there shall be no allocated monetary ground burdens exigible from the Subjects. Any unallocated burdens exigible from the Subjects do not exceed £10 per annum.

6. (a) The minerals are included in the sale or alternatively there are adequate rights of support and adequate provisions in the title of the Subjects for compensation for subsidence and/or any damage to the surface of the Subjects or any buildings comprised therein caused by or arising from mineral workings past present or future.

(b) There are no unduly onerous conditions or restrictions in the title of the Subjects and the title conditions have been adhered to. There are no conditions in the said title which restrict the present use of the Subjects. There are no unimplemented building or feuing conditions (other than those of a continuing nature).

(c) There are no servitudes, wayleaves or rights in favour of third parties affecting the Subjects.

(d) There are no overriding interests (as defined by the Land Registration (Scotland) Act 1979) affecting the Subjects.

7. (I)   The Seller warrants that as at the Date of Entry and as at the date hereof:

   (a)   there are no notices, orders, proposals or others served or intimated by the relevant local authority or any other authority under any public, local or other statute (or regulation, order or other thereunder) affecting or likely to affect the Subjects;

   (b)   there are no outstanding notices, orders, undertakings or others issued by or given to the relevant local authority or any other authority or body in respect of repairs, renewals, improvements, demolition or other works to the Subjects;

   (c)   the Subjects are in an area zoned for residential purposes in the Development Plan; they are not affected by any planning schemes or redevelopment proposals at the instance of or contemplated by the relevant local authority; they are not listed as being of Special Architectural or Historic Interest and they do not lie within a Conservation Area;

   (d)   the roads, footpaths and sewers ex adverso the Subjects have been taken over for maintenance by the relevant local authority and there are no road widening or other road proposals affecting the Subjects; and

   (e)   the Subjects are adequately served by a mains water supply and mains drainage and sewerage systems.

   (II)   Written evidence of the foregoing will be exhibited or delivered to the Purchaser on or prior to the Date of Entry.

   (III) If the matters warranted herein are not as stated, the Purchaser shall be entitled, but not bound, in their sole discretion, to rescind without penalty from the missives of which this offer forms part ('the Missives').

8. If any alterations or other works have been carried out to the Subjects for which Planning Permission or Building Warrant would have been required, all necessary Planning Permissions, Building Warrants and Completion Certificates will be delivered on the Date of Entry together with the Superior's consent or waiver if such consent or waiver was required. The Seller warrants that all works have been carried out strictly in accordance with such Planning Permissions, Building Warrants and Superior's consent or waiver.

9. The Seller warrants that the Seller is not aware of any applications or proposed applications for Planning Permission

or Building Warrant in respect of other subjects in the vicinity of the Subjects in respect of which the relevant works have not been completed at the date hereof. If the Seller becomes aware of any such applications prior to the Date of Entry the Seller shall notify the same to us forthwith and the Purchaser shall at the Purchaser's option have ten working days to resile from the Missives by notice in writing to the Seller's Solicitors if such application would adversely affect the Purchaser's use and enjoyment, or the value, of the Subjects.

10. (a) If any Specialist treatments have been carried out to the Subjects, the Seller warrants that such treatments have been carried out by reputable tradesmen and a valid guarantee in terms acceptable to the Purchaser exists and will be delivered along with the relative survey report at the Date of Entry. Further the Seller will execute and deliver at the Date of Entry a valid assignation of all rights under such guarantee.

    (b) If double glazing, replacement windows, central heating or a burglar alarm system have been installed in the Subjects then the Seller will deliver at the Date of Entry any guarantee in respect thereof and will, if requested by the Purchaser, execute and deliver at the Date of Entry a valid assignation of all rights under such guarantee.

11. The Seller will maintain the Subjects and the specific items hereinbefore mentioned in their present condition (fair wear and tear excepted) until settlement of the transaction on the Date of Entry. The risk of damage or destruction to the Subjects or any part thereof and the specific items hereinbefore mentioned will remain with the Seller until settlement of the transaction on the Date of Entry. If the Subjects or any part of them are destroyed or materially damaged on or prior to the Date of Entry or if there is any material deterioration or change in the Subjects between the time when they were viewed by the Purchaser and the Date of Entry, the Purchaser will be entitled to resile without penalty.

12. At the Date of Entry the Seller will in exchange for the Price:–

    (a) deliver a duly executed disposition in favour of the purchaser and will exhibit or deliver a valid marketable title together with a Form 10 Report brought down to a date as near as practicable to the date of settlement and showing no entries adverse to the Seller's interest, the cost of said report being the responsibility of the Seller. In addition, the Seller, at or before the date of entry and at his expense, shall deliver to the Purchaser such documents and evidence as the Keeper may require to enable the Keeper to issue a land certificate in the name of the purchaser as the registered proprietor of the whole subjects of offer and containing no exclusion of indemnity in terms of section 12(2) of the Land Registration (Scotland) Act 1979: such documents shall include (unless the whole subjects of offer only comprise part of a tenement or flatted building) a plan or bounding description sufficient to enable the whole subjects of offer to be identified on the Ordnance map and evidence (such as a Form P16 Report) that the description of the whole subjects of offer as contained in the title deed is habile to include the whole of the occupied extent. The Land Certificate to be issued to the Purchaser will disclose no entry, deed or diligence prejudicial to the Purchaser's interest other than such as are created by or against the Purchaser, or have been disclosed to, and accepted by, the Purchaser prior to the date of settlement.

Notwithstanding the delivery of the disposition above referred to this clause shall remain in full force and effect and may be founded upon.

(b) If the Seller is a Company:–
 (i) exhibit or deliver clear Searches in the Company Charges Register and Company files against all limited companies (or other corporate bodies) interested in the Subjects within the prescriptive period brought down to 22 days after the company or companies concerned ceased to be infeft in the Subjects. In the event of such Searches disclosing any Floating Charge currently affecting the Subjects, there will be delivered to the Purchaser on the Date of Entry a Certificate of Non-crystallisation of such Floating Charge granted by the holders thereof. Such Searches so far as against the Seller, after being brought down as aforesaid will be delivered to the Purchaser not later than two months after the Date of Entry;
 (ii) deliver to the Purchaser a letter signed by two of the Directors of the Seller in terms of the draft letter set out in Schedule 1 hereof.

13. Notwithstanding delivery of the said Disposition (and except as otherwise hereinbefore provided), the missives shall remain in full force and effect for a period of two years from the date of delivery of the said Disposition and thereafter only insofar as they are founded on in any court proceedings which have commenced within the said period.

14. The Seller will provide such reasonable evidence as shall be satisfactory to us in all respects that as at the Date of Entry there are no subsisting occupancy rights under either the Matrimonial Homes (Family Protection) (Scotland) Act 1981

(as amended) or the Family Law (Scotland) Act 1985 prejudicial to the Purchaser or the nominees of the Purchaser affecting the Subjects. Any spouse of the Seller shall sign the Disposition hereinbefore referred to giving consent to the dealing implemented by the delivery of the said Disposition.

15. The Seller warrants that the Subjects are not affected by any transfer of property order under the Family Law (Scotland) Act 1985.

16. The Seller will, prior to the Date of Entry, disclose his new address to the Purchaser.

17. If the subjects are a flat in a tenement, the following conditions shall apply:–

   (a) The said dwellinghouse forms part of a tenement and the usual parts of the said tenement are held in common by all of the proprietors thereof, including without prejudice to the foregoing generality the roof, outside walls, the foundations, the solum on which the said tenement is erected and the back green or court thereof. The cost of maintenance, repair and renewal of the common parts is borne in equal shares by all of the proprietors of the said tenement. The common charges will be apportioned between the Purchaser and the Seller as at the said Date of Entry.

   (b) The Seller will be liable for the cost of all common repairs instructed or undertaken prior to the Date of Entry whether completed or not. The Seller warrants that there are no common repairs in contemplation, or under tender but not yet instructed.

18. This offer is open for acceptance unless sooner withdrawn until 10am on Friday 8th March 2002 and if an acceptance has not been received by us by then this offer shall be deemed to be withdrawn.

Yours faithfully,

MAIR & KILDARE

Witnessed

M & K

Schedule 1

To: Messrs Mair & Kildare,
     Solicitors,
     35 Magister Street
     Paisley   Date:

WE,   both Directors of
Limited ('the Seller') hereby certify and warrant after due and
diligent enquiry (i) that no deeds of any kind which are capable of
being recorded in the Register of Sasines or Land Register in respect
of or affecting
('the Subjects') have been granted by the Seller other than as are
disclosed in the Search (including Interim Reports on Search) in the
Sasine Register or Land Register exhibited to you as Solicitors for
('the Purchaser') (ii) that no Floating Charge, Debenture or other
security document which is capable of being registered in the
Companies Charges Register has been granted by the Seller other
than as are disclosed in the Search (including Interim Reports on
Search) in the Companies Register exhibited to you and (iii) that the
Seller is solvent and no steps have been or are about to be taken by
us or to the best of our knowledge and belief by any third party to
commence liquidation proceedings which would prejudice the
validity of the Disposition of the Subjects now being granted to the
Purchaser or to appoint a Receiver or otherwise place the Seller in a
position whereby it cannot execute and deliver to the Purchaser a
valid and unobjectionable title.

We further agree and acknowledge that in the event of the Purchaser
incurring any loss, damage or expense as a result of any of the
matters included in the foregoing certificate and warrant being
untrue or proving to be unfounded we shall be liable personally and
individually, and jointly and severally to make good all such loss,
damage and expense to the Purchaser.

                                                            M & K

Note: This is an optional Directors' Warranty letter, which may be used if the
Seller is a limited company, which is not the case here. If so, this letter should
be referred to in the missives as in 12(c).

Notes: (1) This is a pretty good example of the standardised wordprocessor
offer, which has the advantage of being better looking than an offer with a
photocopied schedule of conditions, of being quickly prepared, and of
covering a lot of eventualities. On the other hand, parts of the offer are
inappropriate (eg the large parts covering a company seller and the sale of a
tenement). Care must be taken with such offers, as they are dynamite in the
wrong hands – for instance I recently saw a residential offer being used for a
commercial property, for which it was quite inappropriate. If you are using
such an offer, it should not be issued uncritically.

(2) The offer stipulates that the purchaser be informed of any material development to adjoining subjects. Of course, one has no rights to a view, unless one owns the land over which the view is, but the purchaser does not want to buy a house in a nice settled area, only to find that it becomes a building site after the move takes place.

(3) The selling company clause is inappropriate, as is the tenement clause. It is the seller's decision whether they will be deleted or not – it is probably better to delete them, just in case a problem arises.

(4) Note how labels are attached to everyone and anything at the outset of the offer. This is perfectly sound drafting practice, and avoids tiresome repetition and possible mistakes, which is commendable. Note, however, the labels should be clear and self explanatory – eg 'Seller', 'Purchaser' and so on. Avoid jargon words like 'party of the first part' which are ugly and not at all self explanatory. I am also less than happy that a married couple should be referred to as 'the Purchaser' – it would only take a little extra effort to refer to them as 'the Purchasers', and to make the required grammatical amendments.

(5) Please note that obligation contained at 12(a) which is in the style recommended by the Deputy Keeper in an article – 'Land Registration Update' January 1995 JLSS 15 and the Registration of Title Practice Book (2nd edn, 2000).

Notes: (1) This offer is made in the firm's standard style, which to my mind is far too long, but see chapter 3 on this point.

(2) It is signed by a partner of the firm and the signature is witnessed. This makes the offer self proving (see Requirements of Writing (Scotland) Act 1995).

12.   E.mail Henry Pink to Wendy Robertson 6 March 2002

I have sent you a long offer for 3 Miller Drive, Inveraray. I am getting too old for this game. What happened to the old five clause offer? What does it all mean? Please draft an acceptance for my approval, and then I'll get Mr. James in and try and explain it to him. HP

Note: Particularly note how law reform and systematic legal education have changed things. Old Pink has been a conveyancer for thirty years, and Wendy Robertson is only just out of University. Yet Henry Pink relies on her. But Pink protests too much. He is no fool. He has been regularly to courses and he reads textbooks. He will keep a pretty close eye on Wendy Robertson's actions, bearing in mind the Law Society's recommendations in Appendix VI, and his responsibilities as a trainer.

13.   Letter received from Black Country PLC enclosing title deeds and a note of deduction of title for the discharge. See 18(c) in this appendix. 7 March 2002. Short acknowledgement sent.

14.   File Note by Henry Pink 7 March 2002

Meeting between Henry Pink and Wendy Robertson and Mr. and Mrs. James 7 March 2002. Going through the clauses and taking instructions for acceptance. They seemed perfectly happy with the offer, and basically left "all the technical bits" to us. Mrs. James mentioned that a friend of hers had sold her house but she had to wait for six weeks before the missives were concluded, and had been quite ill with worry. Agreeing that this appalling, and stating that it would not happen here. Engaged 30 minutes. HP

Notes: (1) This note is very important, and it is good practice to make a note when instructions are given. Not only does it give some evidence that the points were agreed, but it also provides a note of how much time was spent on the transaction in case detailed charges have to be made. It is amazing what disappears from the human memory, even after a short time

(2) The point about an early conclusion of missives is a good one and is dealt with in clause G of the qualified acceptance below.

15.   Acceptance from Brown Jarvie & Walker to Mair & Kildare 9 March 2002

Brown, Jarvie & Walker,
Solicitors,
42 Registration Row,
Glasgow G1 3XX.

Messrs Mair & Kildare,
Solicitors,
35 Magister Street,
Paisley PA1 4ZZ.

DX PA5000

URGENT COURIER DELIVERY

9th March 2002

DEAR SIRS,

On behalf of our client Mr John James of 3 Miller Drive, Inveraray, (hereinafter called 'the seller') we hereby accept the offer dated 5th March 2002 made on behalf of Mr and Mrs MacLachlan (hereinafter called 'the Purchasers') to purchase the detached dwellinghouse at 3 Miller Drive, Inveraray, as described in your offer, and that at the price of ONE HUNDRED THOUSAND POUNDS (£100,000) and that on the terms and conditions contained in your said offer to purchase, but subject to the following qualifications:-

A. Payment of the purchase price in full on the date of entry is of the essence of the contract. In the event of the purchase price or any part thereof remaining outstanding as at the date of entry, then notwithstanding consignation or the fact that entry has not been taken by your clients, your clients shall be deemed to be in material breach of contract and further, interest will accrue at the base lending rate of 4 per centum per annum above The Royal Bank of Scotland plc base lending rate from time to time until full payment of the price is made or in the event of our clients exercising their option to rescind the contract until such time as our clients shall have completed a resale of the subjects and received the resale price and further interest shall run on any shortfall between the purchase price hereunder and the resale price until such time as the shortfall shall have been paid to our clients. In the event that the said purchase price is not paid in full within fourteen days of the date of entry, our clients shall be entitled to treat your clients as being in material breach of contract and to rescind the missives on giving prior written notice to that effect to your clients without prejudice to any rights or any claims competent to our clients arising from the breach of contract by your clients including our clients' rights to claim all losses, damages and expenses sustained as a result of your clients' breach of contract including interest on the price calculated as set out in this clause. For the purposes of computation of our clients' loss, the interest element of that loss shall be deemed to be a liquidate penalty provision exigible notwithstanding the exercise by our clients of their option to rescind the contract for non-payment of the price or any repudiation of the contract by your clients. This clause shall have effect always provided that any unreasonable delay in settlement is not attributable to us or our clients.

This clause, where inconsistent with clauses 1 and 2 of your offer, shall be the ruling clause of the two.

B. The time limit in your Offer (if any) shall be withdrawn.

C. In Condition 11 of your Offer, the word 'the Purchaser' where it occurs in the last line shall be deleted and 'both parties to this contract' shall be substituted.

D. With reference to clause 6 of your Offer, the title deeds shall be dispatched to you at the earliest opportunity, and your clients shall have seven days to intimate any objection to their terms, failing which they will be deemed to have satisfied themselves.

E. Clauses 12 (b) and (c), 13 and 16 will be deleted as inappropriate.

F. Double glazing was fitted to the windows throughout four years ago, but the Company has gone out of business, and the Guarantee is thought to be worthless.

G. An acceptance of the terms of this letter, which will conclude missives, shall be received in this office by 12.00 pm on Tuesday 12th March 2002 failing which this letter, if not sooner withdrawn, shall be treated pro non scripto.

We shall be pleased to receive your acceptance of these qualifications and conclusion of the agreement.

Yours faithfully,

BROWN, JARVIE & WALKER   Witnessed

cc Mr James

Note: This qualified acceptance deals with the following points arising from the terms of the offer:

A. Late settlement
B. Deletion of all earlier time limits
C. Spreading the concept of mutuality of conditions
D. Sending the title deeds to allow the purchasers to satisfy themselves
E. Deleting inappropriate clauses, relating to Companies selling, and to tenement flats and to survival of missives
F. Correcting factual information.
G. Time limit for acceptance which shall conclude the deed and avoid missives remaining unconcluded.

1. A long offer indicates a long acceptance. This is not too bad an example.

2. Letters of the alphabet are used for acceptance conditions to differentiate them from offer conditions. This is good practice, but is a matter of choice.

3. The main part of the acceptance is the delay in settlement clause, which is discussed at Chapter 4. This is crucial. It may appear harsh, but is only harsh to a purchaser who has not made his or her arrangements properly, and who causes a lot of distress to the seller. Sellers have been known to have nervous breakdowns where there has been a delay in settlement, and this clause provides a mechanism to rectify the position with only minimum distress. Damages for general inconvenience have been awarded (*Mills v Findlay* 1994 SCLR 397) but solatium is not a competent head of damages.

4. Note the time limit for acceptance. This should always be realistic – not too long and not too short.

16.   Letter concluding missives 11 March 2002.

Dear Sirs

On behalf of our clients Lachlan and Jean MacLachlan, we hereby accept the qualifications contained in your letter of 9 March 2002, being a qualified acceptance of our offer, dated 5 March 2002 for the purchase of 3 Miller Drive, Inveraray.

We are accordingly holding the bargain between our respective clients as concluded on the basis of (1) our offer of 5 March (2) your qualified acceptance of 9 March and (3) this letter.

Please let us have the title deeds and other papers to enable us to complete the conveyancing.

Yours faithfully

Mair & Kildare   Sandy Sneddon (Witness)

The firm's signature is adhibited by Kenneth Kildare, a partner of the firm. and witnessed by Sandy Sneddon , Law Accountant, 35 Magister Street, Paisley

Note: 1. This letter concludes the missives, or what is known technically as "the bargain". This terms does not mean that either party has got a bargain. Both parties are completely in agreement *in idem* (in the same thing) as they must be.

3. The conclusion of missives initiates a sequence of events as follows:-

(a) Inform client that missives are concluded. That should put Mrs. James' mind at rest!

(b) Inform Black Country PLC of sale and ask for the amount required to redeem the loan around the date of entry, and for a daily figure for interest in case there is a delay in repayment;

(c) Send title deeds to the purchaser's agent;

(d) Make future diary entries to make sure the transaction does not fall asleep.

Letters (a) and (b) are routine in their terms and are not reproduced here.

17. File Note of meeting with Mrs. James 11 March 2002

Wendy Robertson meeting with Mrs. James (engaged ½ hour). I explained to her the importance of her consent to the deed of sale as a non entitled spouse having an occupancy right under the Matrimonial Homes Act. I explained to her that she was entitled to seek independent advice before signing the Disposition, but she said she was quite happy to be advised by me. She had worked in a law office, anyway, and knew exactly what her signature meant, and she was perfectly happy about the whole thing. She was also extremely happy that missives were concluded, and that they knew where they stood. WR.

Note: "All this palaver", as Mr. Pink describes it, is better left to a younger person. Briefly it covers the requirement for the less dominant party in a transaction to be given independent advice, and not being told to "sign there" without further attention. This is covered in the cases of *Smith v Bank of Scotland* 1997 SLT 1061 and *Clydesdale Bank plc v Black* 2002 SLT 704 which lay down the standards of advice which should be given to what are, unflatteringly, referred to as "cautionary wives".

18. (a) Letter from Brown Jarvie & Walker to Mair & Kildare 12 March 2002

Dear Sirs,

Mr. John James
Mr. and Mrs. MacLachlan
3 Miller Drive, Inveraray

We refer to the conclusion of the agreement for sale and now enclose the following:-

(a) the title deeds of the property, as stated on the enclosed form 4;
(b) draft Discharge of our client's Standard Security;
(c) Form 10A Report and draft Form 11;
(d) Draft Letter of Obligation;
(e) Feuduty Redemption Receipt.

There is a non-entitled spouse Mrs. Agnes Miller. Can you please include a consent in the draft Disposition?

Yours faithfully

BJW

18   (b) Form 4 with details of deeds being sent.

REGISTERS OF SCOTLAND EXECUTIVE AGENCY
(Land Registration (Scotland) Rules 1980 Rule 9(2))

	FORM 4

INVENTORY OF WRITS RELEVANT TO APPLICATION FOR REGISTRATION *(see Note 1)*
(to be completed in duplicate)

Mair & Kildare
35 Magister Street
Paisley
PA1 4ZZ

(see Note 2)

Title Number(s)
(to be completed for a dealing with registered interests in land.)

Subjects *(see Note 3)*   **3 Miller Drive
Inveraray
PA32 5XX**

Registration County   **Argyll**

Applicant's Reference

Please complete Inventory overleaf as in this specimen

Item No.	Please mark "S" against writs submitted	Particulars of Writs *(see Note 4)*		
		Writ	Grantee	Date of Recording
		Land Certificate*		
		Charge Certificate*		
1	-	Feu Charter*	Upright Builders Ltd	2 May 1938

*Delete if inapplicable

Notes 1-4 referred to are contained in Notes and Directions for Completion of Inventory of Writs Relevant to Application for Registration.

FOR OFFICIAL USE ONLY

APPLICATION NUMBER	DATE OF RECEIPT	TITLE NUMBER

The writs marked "S" on this inventory were received on the Date of Receipt stamped on this page.

Published by **everyform**   User Identifier

INVENTORY

Particulars of Writs *(see Note 4)*

Please mark "S"
against writs
Item No.   submitted

		Writ	Grantee	Date of Recording
		xxbankCertificatex		
		xChargeCertificatex		
1	S	Feu Disposition	Jeremiah James	2 June 1974
2	S	Confirmation	Executor of J James	
3	S	Disposition	John James	5 April 1997
4	S	Standard Security	Black Country Building Society	5 April 1997
5	S	Feuduty Redemption Receipt	John James	

*delete if inapplicable

User Identifier

Published by *everyform*

Note: You can of course send the deeds with a traditional Inventory of Writs, but why not take advantage of the Form 4 made possible by Land Registration, which greatly simplifies matters?

18 **(c) Draft letter of Obligation in a First Registration transaction.**

Messrs. Mair & Kildare
Solicitors
35 Magister Street
Paisley

Dear Sirs

John James
Mr. and Mrs. MacLachlan
3 Miller Drive, Inveraray

With reference to the settlement of this transaction today, we herby:

1. Undertake to clear the records of any deed, decree or diligence (other than such as may be created by or against your clients) which may be recorded in the Personal register or to which effect may be given in the Land Register in the period from ....(date of Form 10A or 11A report) to 14 days from the date hereof inclusive (or the earlier date of registration of your clients' interest in the above subjects) which would cause the Keeper to make an entry on, or qualify his indemnity in the Land Certificate to be issued in respect of that interest; and

2. Confirm that to the best of knowledge and belief, the answers to the questions numbered 1 to 14 in this draft form 1 adjusted with you (in so far as these answers relate to our client or to our client's interest in the above subjects) are still correct.

3. We also undertake to deliver to you within 14 days of this date the duly executed Discharge of the existing Standard Security granted by our client, with our Forms 2 and 4 thereanent and our cheque made payable to the Keeper for registration thereof.

Yours faithfully

Notes: 1. The Letter of Obligation, which is recognised as the lubricant which enables transactions to be settled, even though a clear search can never be presented up to the date of settlement. The letter provides that a clear search will be presented to the purchaser within 14 days of settlement. Failing that the seller and his agent are responsible, jointly and severally, for any consequences that result.

2. Further the letter certifies that the various questions asked by the Keeper in the Form 1 are still answered correctly by the purchaser's agent, even although the seller last saw the answers some time before.

3. The third paragraph, which will not be required if the seller has the Discharge signed and returned before settlement, states that if this is not the case, the Discharge will be delivered with 14 days with the forms 2 and 4 and cheque that will enable it to be registered in the Land Register. The registration is made by the purchasers' agents, along with the Disposition giving their client a title, and any Standard Security the purchaser may have granted.

4. For the law of Letters of Obligation, see 8.11. As the obligation is given by the lawyer and the client, jointly and severally, the lawyer is usually chosen to be the principal obligant. This is because lawyers are covered by Indemnity Insurance. For cases involving lawyers, see Chapter 8.11.

5. The final letter of Obligation is written on the firm's notepaper, signed by a partner of the firm, and often witnessed, so as to be self proving.

6. In terms of the missives, which remain alive after settlement, the seller is bound to ensure that the purchaser gets a Land Certificate without restriction of indemnity.

REGISTERS OF SCOTLAND EXECUTIVE AGENCY (Land Registration (Scotland) Rules 1980 Rule 9(1)(a))	**FORM 1**	*Please complete in BLACK TYPE* No covering Letter is required

APPLICATION FOR FIRST REGISTRATION

1 Presenting Agent Name and Address (see Note 1)

Mair & Kildare

35 Magister Street
Paisley
PA1 4ZZ

Keeper of the Registers of Scotland
Meadowbank House
153 London Road
EDINBURGH EH8 7AU
Telephone: 0131 659 6111

Part A

2 FAS No. (see Note 2) 4444	3 Agent s Tel No. (include STD Code) **0141 887 654X**	4 Agents Reference **MacL2002/34**

5 Name of Deed in respect of which registration is required **Disposition**	6 County (see Note 3) **Argyll**	Mark X in box if more than one county

7 Subjects (see Note 4)

Street No.	3	Street Name	**Miller Drive**		
Town	**Inveraray**			Post code	**PA32 5XX**
Other					

8 Name and Address of Applicant (see Note 5)

1. Surname **MacLachlan**   Forename(s) **Lachlan**

Address **3 Glenlivet Road, Glasgow**

2. Surname **MacLachlan**   Forename(s) **Jean**

Address **3 Glenlivet Road, Glasgow**

and or company/ firm or council, etc   Mark X in box if more than 2 applicants

Address

9 Granter/Party Last Infeft (see Note 6)

1. Surname **James**   Forename(s) **John**

2. Surname   Forename(s)

and or company firm or council etc.   Mark X in box if more than 2 granters

10 Consideration (see Note 7) **£100,000**	Value (see Note 8)	Fee (see Note 9) **£220.00**	Date of Entry **18 April 2002**

11 If a Form 10 Report has been issued in connection with this Application please quote Report No.

12 I/We apply for registration in respect of Deed(s) No. **3** in the Inventory of Writs (Form 4) I/We certify that the information supplied in this application is correct to the best of my/our knowledge and belief.

FOR OFFICIAL USE

Signature   Date

Notes 1-9 referred to are contained in Notes and Directions for completion of Applications for First Registration

Published by *everyform*   Users Identifier

PART B

Delete **YES** or **NO** as appropriate
N.B. If more space is required for any section of this form, a separate sheet, or separate sheets, may be added.

1. Do the deeds submitted in support of this application include a plan illustrating the extent of the subjects to be registered?   **YES**/NO
    If **YES**, please specify the deed and its Form 4 Inventory number:

    If **NO**, have you submitted a deed containing a full bounding description with measurements?   **YES**/**NO**

    If **YES**, please specify the deed and its Form 4 Inventory number:

    N.B. If the answer to both the above questions is **NO** then, unless the property is part of a tenement or flatted building you must submit a plan of the subjects properly drawn to a stated scale and showing sufficient surrounding features to enable it to be located on the Ordnance Map. The plan should bear a docquet, signed by the person signing the Application Form, to the effect that it is a plan of the subjects sought to be registered under the attached application.

2. Is a Form P16 Report issued by the Keeper confirming that the boundaries of the subjects coincide with the Ordnance Map being submitted in support of this Application?   YES/**NO**

    If **NO**, does the legal extent depicted in the plans or descriptions in the deeds submitted in support of the Application cohere with the occupational extent?   **YES**/**NO**

    If **NO**, please advise:-

    (a) the approximate age and nature of the occupational boundaries, or

    (b) whether, if the extent of the subjects as defined in the deeds is larger than the occupational extent, the applicant is prepared to accept the occupational extent as viewed, or   **YES**/**NO**

    (c) whether, if the extent of the subjects as defined in the deeds is smaller than the occupational extent, any remedial action has been taken   **YES**/**NO**

3. Is there any person in possession or occupation of the subjects or any part of them adversely to the interest of the applicant?   **YES**/NO
    If **YES**, please give details:

4. If the subjects were acquired by the applicant under any statutory provision, does the statutory provision restrict the applicant's power of disposal of the subjects?   **YES**/NO
    If **YES**, please indicate the statute:

5. (a) Are there any charges affecting the subjects or any part of them except as stated in the Schedule of Heritable Securities etc. on page 4 of this application?   **YES**/NO
        If **YES**, please give details:

    (b) Apart from overriding interests are there any burdens affecting the subjects or any part of them, except as stated in the Schedule of Burdens on page 4 of this application?   **YES**/NO
        If **YES**, please give details:

Users Identifier

(c) Are there any overriding interests affecting the subjects or any part of them which you wish noted on the Title Sheet?
If **YES**, please give details:

YES/NO

(d) Are there any recurrent monetary payments (eg feuduty, leasehold casualties) exigible from the subjects or any part of them?
If **YES**, please give details:

YES/NO

6. Where any party to the deed inducing registration is a Company registered under the Companies Acts

Has a receiver or liquidator been appointed?
If **YES**, please give details:

YES/NO

If **NO**, has any resolution been passed or court order made for the winding up of the Company or petition presented for its liquidation?
If **YES**, please give details:

YES/NO

7. Where any party to the deed inducing registration is a Company registered under the Companies Acts can you confirm

(a) that it is not a charity as defined in section 112 of the Companies Act 1989 and

YES/NO

(b) that the transaction to which the deed gives effect is not one to which section 322A of the Companies Act 1985 (as inserted by section-109 of the Companies Act 1989) applies?

YES/NO

Where the answer to either branch of the question is **NO**, please give details:

8. Where any party to the deed inducing registration is a corporate body other than a Company registered under the Companies Acts

(a) Is it acting *intra vires*?
If **NO**, please give details:

YES/NO

(b) Has any arrangement been put in hand for the dissolution of any such corporate body?
If **YES**, please give details:

YES/NO

9 Are *all* the necessary consents, renunciations or affidavits in terms of section 6 of the Matrimonial Homes (Family Protection)(Scotland) Act 1981 being submitted in connection with this application?

YES/NO

N.B. If sufficient evidence to satisfy the Keeper that there are no subsisting occupancy rights in the subjects of this application is not submitted with the application then the statement by the Keeper in terms of rule 5(j) of the Land Registration (Scotland) Rules 1980 will not be inserted in the Title Sheet or will be qualified as appropriate without further enquiry by the Keeper.

Users Identifier

10. Where the deed inducing registration is in implement of the exercise of a power of sale under a heritable security

    Have the statutory procedures necessary for the proper exercise of such power been complied with?   YES/NO

11. Where the deed inducing registration is a General Vesting Declaration or a Notice of Title pursuant on a Compulsory Purchase Order

    Have the necessary statutory procedures been complied with?   YES/NO

12. Is any party to the deed inducing registration subject to any legal incapacity or disability?   YES/NO
If **YES,** please give details:

13. Are the deeds and documents detailed in the Inventory (Form 4) all the deeds and documents relevant to the title?   YES/NO
If **NO,** please give details:

14. Are there any facts and circumstances material to the right or title of the applicant which have not already been disclosed in this application or its accompanying documents?   YES/NO
If **YES,** please give details:

SCHEDULE OF HERITABLE SECURITIES ETC.
N.B. New Charges granted by the applicant should not be included

Standard security in favour of Black Country Building Society registered 5 April 1997.

SCHEDULE OF BURDENS
Writ No. 1 of Form 4

18 (d) Draft Discharge of Standard Security

WE BLACK COUNTRY PLC incorporated under the Companies Acts having our registered office at Arnold Street, Stoke –on- Trent, in the County of Derby in consideration of the sum of SIXTY FIVE THOUSAND POUNDS (£65,000) being the whole amount secured by the Standard Security aftermentioned paid by JOHN JAMES residing at Three Miller Drive, Inveraray, PA 32 5XX HEREBY DISCHARGE a Standard Security by the said John James in favour of Black Country Building Society registered in the County of Argyll on Fifth April Nineteen Hundred and Ninety Seven; WHICH STANDARD SECURITY was last vested in Black Country Building Society as aforesaid and from whom Black Country PLC acquired right on Fourth December Two Thousand by (one) a Transfer Agreement pursuant to Section 97 of the Building Societies Act 1986 between Black Country Building Society and the said Black Country PLC dated Ninth May Two Thousand and (two) Confirmation of the transfer by the Building Societies Commission pursuant to Section 98 of the Building Societies Act 1986 dated twenty eighth September Two Thousand: IN WITNESS WHEREOF

Notes: 1. Please see the deduction of title linking up the the new PLC with the old Society, to whom the security was granted.

2. There is no warrant of registration. This deed is to be registered in the Land Register, where warrants of registration are not required.

18 (e) Feuduty Redemption Receipt

WE, HIGHLAND ESTATES, Having our registered office at Jail Square, Inveraray Argyll PA 32 6QQ acknowledge to have received from JOHN JAMES the sum of ONE HUNDRED AND TWENTY FIVE POUNDS in redemption in terms of Section 4 of the Land Tenure Reform (Scotland) Act 1974 of the feuduty of SEVEN POUNDS FIFTY per annum exigible as at Martinmas Two Thousand and One in respect of Three Miller Drive, Inveraray.

Dated this Fifteenth day of November 2001

Note: Such receipts (Under the 1974 Act Schedule 1 Form 2) are relatively uncommon these days, because most feuduties have been redeemed, either under the terms of the 1974 Act sections 1 to 6 on a sale of the property, or voluntarily, to be rid of them. The reason why this has not been done here is that the house was bought in 1973 by John James' uncle, who lived there for many years, and who never felt the need to redeem the feuduty. When he died in 1996, he left the house to John, who borrowed money from the Building Society to bring it up to date and build on an extension. He did not redeem the feuduty until 2001. This receipt will now be registered with the title to the house, and need never be exhibited again, as a record of the redemption will be made in the Land Certificate.

18   (d) Draft Form 11.

REGISTERS OF SCOTLAND
Executive Agency

· p r o p e r t y REPORTS s e r v i c e ·
FORM 11

(Land Registration (Scotland) Rules 1980 Rule 24(2))

APPLICATION FOR CONTINUATION OF REPORT PRIOR TO REGISTRATION OF THE SUBJECTS DESCRIBED BELOW

Note: No covering letter is required and an existing Search should not be submitted.
VAT Reg No. GD 410 GB 888 8410 64

Please complete in DUPLICATE and in BLACK TYPE

From **Brown, Jarvie & Walker** **42 Registration Road** **Glasgow** **G1 3XX**	FOR OFFICIAL USE
	Report Number
	Date of Receipt
	Fee

County	**Argyll**		Previous Report	

Search Sheet No. [1]			FAS No.	**7777**

Applicant's Reference	**HP/WR/Jame.123**		FAX No.	**0141 204 432X**

Telephone No.	**0141 204 123X**		FAX response required (X here)	

POSTAL ADDRESS OF SUBJECTS

Street No.	**3**	House Name			Street Name	**Miller Drive**

Town	**Inveraray**		Postcode	**PA32 5XX**

OTHER:

Description of Subjects	**Detached house at above address**

I/We apply for the Report to .... [2]   against the above subjects to be brought down to date.

1. *Number obtainable from previous Report.*
2. *Date obtainable from previous Report.*

Faxed applications should not be followed up by a written request and may not be accepted if a plan is included.

DIARY SERVICE:

Please state date and time you require report

Date _____ Time _____
NOTE: If you do not state we will assume a 48 hour turnaround

User Identifier _____

Meadowbank House, 153 London Road, Edinburgh EH8 7AU
www.ros.gov.uk DX 555338 EDINBURGH 15 reports@ros.gov.uk
Tel: 0845 6070162   Fax: 0131 479 3651/3683/3667

Published by everyform

· p r o p e r t y **REPORTS** s e r v i c e ·
FORM 11

The following parties (in addition to those notes on the previous report) should be searched against in the Register of Inhibitions and Adjudications, viz.

1. Surname(s)		Forename(s)	

Address(es)	

2. Surname(s)		Forename(s)	

Address(es)	

3. Surname(s)		Forename(s)	

Address(es)	

4. Surname(s)		Forename(s)	

Address(es)	

5. Company/ Firm/ Corporate body	

Address(es)	

6. Company/ Firm/ Corporate body	

Address(es)	

NOTE: Insert full names and addresses of the persons on whom a Report is required.

Signature: _____ Date: _____

Published by *everyform*

User Identifier

19.   E.mail from Wendy Robertson, trainee, to Veronica Vanbrugh, administrator, 11 March 2002

Dear Veronica. Please make the following double diary entries for the sale of 3 Miller Drive, Inveraray.

11 March	Titles sent out.
28 March	Disposition to be received by now.
4 April	Check that everything is in order for settlement.
11 April	Send Form 11 away. Make arrangements for settlement.

Note: This is a very important procedure for a busy law office. Wendy will make her own diary entries, but is also asking the administrator to make a double entry. Veronica will remind Wendy of these dates when they come. At all costs, a last minute rush should be avoided, but there is still a nasty surprise to come!

20.   Letter from Mair & Kildare to Brown Jarvie & Walker 23 March 2002

Dear Sirs,

John James
Mr. and Mrs. MacLachlan
3 Miller Drive, Inveraray

We refer to our previous correspondence and return the title deeds and your various drafts, all duly approved. We also enclose our draft Disposition and Forms 1 and 4 for your approval and return.

Kindly attend to the following observations:-

1.   Please let us have the Form 11A report before settlement.
2.   Please confirm that there are no outstanding liabilities for any moveable items included in the sale.
3.   Please let us have your State for Settlement.
4.   Please let us have the usual letter confirming that there are no outstanding Notices.
5.   Please confirm that you will inform the Council of the change of ownership for Council Tax purposes.
6.   Please let us see a Building Warrant, Completion Certificate, and superior's consent for the new window that your client put in looking over the loch, approximately seven years ago.

Yours faithfully

M& K

Note: The enquiries on title are few. The title basically consists of a Feu Disposition in favour of the seller's uncle, Confirmation in favour of his Executors, a Disposition to the seller, and the Standard Security. If there is no difficulty, why make one? The query regarding the window is quite in order, and no doubt will cause enough of a flap at Brown Jarvie & Walker.

21 (b) Note of telephone call Wendy Robertson to Agnes James 24 March 2002

Telephoning Mrs. James and asking her if she had the necessary consents for the making of the window. Noting that she was not married to Mr. James at the time, and did not live in the house. She did not therefore know if he had got consents or not. The work was part of the reconstruction of the house, but she thought had not been done by the main contractor, but by a firm who specialised in replacement windows. Mr. James was abroad on business for the next 10 days, but he might phone in, and she would ask him. (10 minutes).

21 (c) E.mail Wendy Robertson to Henry Pink 24 March 2002

Sorry to say that everything's gone pear shaped in John James' sale. Please see file for details. What do you suggest?

21 (d) Reply from Henry Pink

Try Argyll County Council for a Letter of Comfort, and Highland Estates for a retrospective permission. Better be nice to the superiors. You might get your head chopped off. Can you deal with this when I'm away playing golf at Valderama! HP.

Note: Senior partners are generally a nuisance, but they do have their moments of being an oasis of calm in the tempest . . . Note that Mr Pink has not quite caught up with local government changes.

21 (e) Telephoning Argyll & Bute Council and explaining what had happened here. Noting that the Council took a very serious view of such breaches, but that we should write in and request a letter of comfort. (10 minutes)

21 (f) Telephoning Highland Estates and explaining position to them. Noting that they took a very serious view of such breaches of the feuing conditions, but that we should write in, and explain the position, and they could see what might be done (10 minutes).

21 (g) Telephoning Mair & Kildare and explaining what had been done. Noting that they were concerned about the matter, and might have to advise the purchasers to withdraw.

Note: Potentially this is a very serious situation. Argyll & Bute Council have the power to order that the owner apply retrospectively for Building Warrant and Completion Certificate, and if this is not obtained to order that the property to be restored to its original condition. Meanwhile if the purchasers are not kept happy, they may withdraw from the transaction (see offer clause 7(111)). The Superiors, since the passing of the Abolition of Feudal Tenure Etc. (Scotland) Act 2000 thankfully now have no power of irritancy of the feu, for a breach of feuing conditions. They would however have, until the whole feudal edifice is brought down, a right to claim specific implement of the conditions, and damages. Mr. James is out of the country, Mrs.James doesn't know much about it, Mr. Pink is probably playing golf in Spain, Mair & Kildare are threatening, and the whole mess falls upon Wendy Robertson to sort out.

21.   Letter from Brown Jarvie & Walker to Argyll & Bute Council 25 March 2002

Dear Sirs

John James
3 Miller Drive, Inveraray

I refer to my conversation yesterday, and regret to confirm that it would appear that a window has been formed at the above address, looking southward over Loch Fyne. This window was formed in 1995 by a firm which specialised in such matters, and who assured the owner that "everything was in order". It now turns out that this was not the case, and there was no Building Warrant or Completion Certificate obtained.

The owner very much regrets that this alteration was made without permission, and requests that the Council can see their way to grant a letter of comfort.

As there is some urgency in this matter, we shall be obliged if you can deal with the matter as urgently as possible. Please let us know your charges in the matter.

Yours faithfully

BJW

Note: A handsome apology and an offer of money may help to appease.

22. Letter from Brown Jarvie & Walker to Highland Estates Limited
25 March 2002

Dear Sirs

John James
3 Miller Drive, Inveraray

I refer to my conversation with you yesterday, and would confirm that it unfortunately appears that a window was formed in the gable wall at the above address, overlooking Loch Fyne to the South, and that permission of the Superiors was not requested or received.

The owner greatly regrets that this has happened. The window was formed by a specialist firm from Glasgow, who assured the owner that everything was perfectly in order.

The owner apologises for this breach of the feuing conditions, and requests that a retrospective permission be now given.

Yours faithfully

BJW

Note: A suitably contrite letter. Mr. Pink, had he been in the country, would have probably suggested that it be finished off with the valediction – "We have the Honour to Remain, Sirs, Your Humble and Obedient Servants" – which, honestly, was the way people used to end these letters. Wendy Robertson, having been President of the Students' Union, wouldn't even think of it!

23. Telephone call from Argyll Council 27 March 2002

Attendance on the telephone with Argyll & Bute Council. Noting that they had inspected the property, and would grant a letter of comfort. The cost of the inspection would be Fifty Pounds. If we sent the cheque they would let us have the Letter of Comfort by return. Drawing cheque and sending it. (10 minutes) WR

Note: It should be clearly stated that the Argyll & Bute Council in this example is a purely fictitious body, and bears no connection to the real Argyll & Bute Council in Inverary. The real Council could, therefore, possibly act differently from the fictional one. It is the same with Highland Estates Ltd.

24.   Telephone call from Highland Estates Limited 28 March 2002

Attendance on the telephone with Argyll Estates Limited. Noting that they took an extremely serious view of this breach of feuing conditions, but in all the circumstances would issue a retrospective permission. Could we please send our cheque for £50. Drawing cheque and sending it. (10 minutes) WR

Note: Wendy took the bull by the horns and must be mightily relieved that she did so. The seller is out of a tight corner. Will he be grateful? We'll see.

25.   (a) Letter from Brown Jarvie & Walker to Mair & Kildare 1 April 2002

Dear Sirs

John James
Mr. and Mrs. MacLachlan
3 Miller Drive, Inverary

Thank you for your letter of 23 March. We have revised your draft Disposition, draft Forms 1 and 4, and return these. We are obliged to you for including the matrimonial consent in the Disposition.

We would deal with your enquires *seriatim*:

1.   We shall obtain a Form 11A report and fax it to you before settlement.
2.   We enclose letter from the Council re Notices etc. and the Coal Authority regarding mining. We also our draft State for Settlement.
3.   We are obtaining Letter of Comfort and retrospective Superior's permission for the offending window.
4.   We confirm paragraphs 4 and 5 of your letter.

Yours faithfully

BJW

Notes: (1) The Council and Mining Certificates are not printed here, as they are lengthy and quite routine. For examples see Chapter 18.

(2) The word 'seriatim' is a piece of legal jargon, used mainly in Court pleadings and means 'following your numbering'.

25   (b) Draft State for Settlement prepared by seller's agent.

STATE FOR SETTLEMENT
In connection with sale of
3 Miller Drive, Inveraray

Price: 100,000 including £1,500 of moveables.
Entry: 18 April 2002
Seller: John James (Messrs. Brown Jarvie & Walker)
Purchasers: Mr and Mrs Lachlan MacLachlan (Messrs. Mair & Kildare).

2002
18 April Price per Missives   £100,000

Note: Council Tax is being apportioned by the Council.

26   Letter from Brown Jarvie & Walker to Argyll & Bute Council
5 April 2002

Dear Sirs,

John James
3 Miller Drive, Inveraray, Argyll
Roll No. 1234/5678

Please note that Mr. James has sold the above house to Mr. and Mrs. MacLachlan, per Mair & Kildare, 35 Magister Street, Paisley with effect from 18 April 2002.

As Mr. James is moving to a temporary address in London, please send any communications to him at this address.

Please apportion the Council tax around the date of entry.

Yours faithfully

BJW

26.   Letter from Brown Jarvie & Walker to Black Country PLC 5 April 2002

Dear Sirs

Mr. John James
3 Miller Drive, Inveraray, Argyll
Roll No. 9876/6789Z

We enclose Discharge of Standard Security which please have executed by the Company. The date of entry is 17 April 2002.

Please let us have a note of the sum to repay the loan on the date of entry, and send the Discharge to be held undelivered pending repayment in full.

Please cancel the Fire Insurance at the 17 April 2002, and refund any excess premium paid.

Yours faithfully

BJW

Notes: (1) It is as well to send this early. Since many Societies demutualised it is a common complaint that standards of service have slipped, and that matters are dealt with very slowly, because staff have been cut in the interests of shareholders' dividends and directors' bonuses. The obligation in paragraph 3 of the Letter of Obligation (see 18(c)) may be needed.

(2) Most lenders prefer to arrange the Fire Insurance, but the Borrower is entitled to look elsewhere, and may save substantially by doing so. Obviously Mr James has just taken the package offered by the lenders.

27.   Letter from Mair & Kildare to Brown Jarvie & Walker 6 April 2002

Dear Sirs

Mr. & Mrs. MacLachlan
John James
3 Miller Drive, Inveraray

We now enclose Disposition for signature by your clients, together with schedule of witnessing. We also enclose the draft Disposition for comparison and return.

Yours faithfully

M&K

28 (a) Letter from Brown Jarvie & Walker to Mair & Kildare 7 April 2002

Dear Sirs

John James
Mr. & Mrs. L. MacLachlan
3 Miller Drive, Inveraray

We now enclose the letter of comfort from Argyll & Bute Council, and a letter from the superiors, both concerning the unauthorised windows.

We trust that these will prove suitable for your purposes.

We return your draft Disposition.

Yours faithfully

BJW

28 (b) Letter from Argyll & Bute Council 5 April 2002

Dear Sirs,

Building (Scotland) Acts 1959/70
Building Standards (Scotland) Regulations 1990
3 Miller Drive, Inveraray,

I write to confirm that, following your application for confirmation of completion received on 30 March 2002, a survey of the above property has now been carried out. The purpose of the survey was to inspect the building operations carried out, in the opening of a window on the south facing gable of the house at the above address, which did not receive permission, and comment is therefore restricted to this. No responsibility for the condition of any concealed elements of the structure can be accepted.

Following inspection of the property, it has been ascertained, as far as practical, that the operations have been completed. I can therefore confirm that this Authority shall take no action with regard to the absence of a Building warrant and a Certificate of Completion relative to this operation.

Yours faithfully

Principal Building Control Officer

Notes: (1) This is a fictional case, and nothing should be taken as an indication that the real Council would take this course in a similar application, although it isd not unreasonable to suppose that they might.

(2) Please note the letter is guarded in its terms and, in particular, does not bind future authorities, and that the purchaser does not have to accept it in fulfilment of the terms of the Missives, see *Hawke v Mathers* 1995 SCLR 1004. However, the purchasers want the house, the alteration is not structurally dangerous, and it would be unreasonable not to accept the Letter of Comfort. The best course would have been for Mr. James to "confess" to his lawyers at the outset, and for a Letter of Comfort to have been obtained prior to completion of Missives. Then it could have been made a condition of missives that the purchaser accepted the Letter of Comfort. There is much to be said for planning to meet such eventualities.

28   (c) Letter from Highland Estates to Brown Jarvie & Walker
5 April 2002

Dear Sirs

3 Miller Drive, Inveraray

We refer to your recent request for retrospective permission to open a window on the south facing gable at the above address.

While the superiors take a serious view of the breach of feuing conditions, they are nevertheless willing to grant the request retrospectively, on the condition that all statutory consents that are required, shall be obtained.

We acknowledge receipt of your cheque for the fee of £50.00 plus VAT of £8.75.

Yours faithfully

Highland Estates Limited

Note: Superiors make a reasonably healthy income from requests like this. They should enjoy it while they may. The Abolition of Feudal Tenure Etc. (Scotland) Act 2000, when it becomes operational, will see an end to it.

29   Fax from Black Country PLC 8 April 2002

Amount required to redeem loan on 17 April 2002 is £59,876.00. Daily interest thereafter is £10.35. Signed Discharge follows by post.

30   E.mail Veronica Vanbrugh, administrator, to Wendy Robertson, trainee, and replies 8 April 2002

Wendy. Please note that there is a diary entry today to send Form 11 and make arrangements for settlement. Veronica.

Thanks Veronica. Please check that we have the following on file:

(1)   draft state for settlement (approved by other side).
(2)   Draft Letter of Obligation (also approved)
(3)   Discharge by Black Country signed and forms 2 and 4
(4)   Disposition signed by Mr. and Mrs. James.

Wendy

Wendy. All present and correct. Veronica.

VV Thanks WR.

Note: Its all going like clockwork now.

31   Postcard from Gibraltar airport. Received 10 April 2002

Weather here wonderful. Golf not quite so good. See you all soon. Hope Wendy managed to straighten out things with John James' house. Henry Pink.

Note: Good to know he's keeping his finger on the pulse!

32   Note of telephone call Mr. James to Wendy Robertson 11 April 2002

Attendance on telephone with Mr. James. Noting that they were moving out on 14 April, and would drop keys in at office the following day. Informing Mr. James that he should take meter readings for gas and electricity, inform the suppliers and British Telecom, and that he should cancel all standing orders relating to the house eg Council tax, Black Country PLC, home and contents insurance etc. (10 Minutes)

33   Note of telephone call from Mair & Kildare 16 April 2002

Wendy. Someone called from Mair & Kildare and said that they knew you from University. They were looking forward to seeing you at settlement, but unfortunately they are busy that day. They will send the cheque by courier firm, Hot Wheels. VV

Note: The rule for settlement is that the cheque goes to the Disposition. Settlements used to be social occasions, but, with pressures of business, they are commonly done by couriers or by post.

34   Letter from Brown Jarvie & Walker to Mair & Kildare 18 April 2002

Dear Sirs

John James
Mr. and Mrs. MacLachlan
3 Miller Drive, Inveraray

We received your cheque for £100,000 this morning, and therefore now enclose:-

1.   The keys (two sets).
2.   The signed Disposition and particulars of signing (you already have the draft).
3.   The deliverable writs.
4.   Form 11 A Report as at 14 April 2002.
5.   Our letter of obligation and draft, dated to run from 14 April, the date of the Form 11A report.
6.   Feuduty Redemption Receipt.
7.   Receipted State for Settlement and draft. .
8.   Discharge of the Standard security, the draft, Forms 2 and 4, and cheque made payable to the Registers of Scotland for registration dues.

Please confirm that these papers are all in order, and return our drafts.

Yours faithfully

BJW

Note: The Letter of Obligation is that given in draft form at 18 (c) supra. The dates to be inserted are 14 April 2002 (date of 11A Report) and 2 May 2002 (14 days after settlement).

35.   Letter from Mair & Kildare to Brown Jarvie & Walker 19 April 2002

Dear Sirs

Mr. and Mrs. L.MacLachlan
Mr. John James
3 Miller Drive, Inveraray

Thank you for your letter of 17 April, with its enclosures, which were all in order.

We return you draft letter of obligation, state for settlement and discharge.

Yours faithfully

M&K

36. Letter from Brown Jarvie & Walker to John James 19 April 2002

Dear Mr. James

Sale of 3 Miller Drive, Inveraray

We have now completed the sale of your house and have pleasure in enclosing cheque for £ 39,678.50 being the free proceeds of sale as undernoted.

We trust that your move to London was trouble free, and that you will have a successful stay there.

We would take this opportunity of thanking you for your instructions in this matter.

Yours faithfully

BJW

Note Referred To:

Amount received at settlement		£100,000
Repayment of the loan £59,876 plus 2 days at £10.35		59,670.50
		£40,329.50
Less: Fees and Outlays per our estimate and receipted account	£533.50	
Fees payable to Argyll & Bute Council and Highland Estates Limited in connection with window not allowed for in quotation	117.50	651 .00
Sum due to you		£39,678.50

37. Letter to Black Country PLC 18 April 2002

Dear Sirs

John James
Sale of 3 Miller Drive, Inveraray
Roll No. 9876/6789Z

We now enclose cheque for £59,670.50 being the redemption figure with two days interest added. Please acknowledge receipt.

Yours faithfully

BJW

37.   Letter from John James to Henry Pink 20 April 2002

Dear Mr. Pink

Thank you for your letter and cheque which I got today, and for your very efficient handling of my sale, particularly the unfortunate matter of the window.

We are settling down in London, but hope that we will be posted North again, when I shall contact you.

In the meantime I have recommended your services to Jim Parsley, who is moving North to take my place.

Yours sincerely

John

Notes and Reflections: 1. Not a word about Wendy and Veronica's sterling work! Never mind, Wendy will be a partner soon, and will be able to bathe in reflected glory, like Henry Pink! Veronica is doing a part-time LLB.

2. You will note that the opportunity was not taken to charge extra for the work done with the window, although the estimate would have allowed this. It is therefore doubtful if the transaction was economically viable. On the other hand, the firm has kept their client happy, there is talk of repeat business, and new business from Mr. James' friends. All of these things have to be balanced out.

It should be noted that, under the old scale Fees, the fee would have been nearer £1000, which should be approximately the same as the fee charged by a stockbroker today for investing £100,000 in, say, 20 shares. The difference is that the stockbroker deducts a relatively small fee on each transaction.

38.   Letter from Mair & Kildare to Brown Jarvie & Walker 31 July 2002

Dear Sirs

Mr. and Mrs. L. MacLachlan
Mr. John James
3 Miller Drive, Inveraray

We have today received the Land Certificate, without restriction of indemnity, and accordingly return the Letter of Obligation marked as implemented.

Yours faithfully

M& K

Note: This was acknowledged with a note on a Compliments slip. A full letter is not required. Unnecessary letters should be avoided, as they just cost money, which at this level of fee is simply not justifiable.

39. E.mail exchange – Wendy Robertson to Veronica Vanbrugh
3 August 2002

Veronica. When you return from holiday, please let me have Mr. James' file for the sale of 3 Miller Drive. I will check the odds and ends, and we can then put it into storage. Hope you had a great holiday! Wendy.

Wendy. I'm back, worst luck. Here's the file. V.

Veronica. Returned with thanks. Please put away. I have checked the file. Roll on Christmas! W.

Appendix II

SOME FORMS UNDER THE MATRIMONIAL HOMES (FAMILY PROTECTION) (SCOTLAND) ACT 1981

1 **For use in both sale and security transactions where the subjects are not a matrimonial home within the meaning of the Matrimonial Homes (Family Protection) (Scotland) Act 1981 as amended by the Law Reform (Miscellaneous Provisions) (Scotland) Act 1985, s 13 (See 1986 JLSS 214).**

I, AB (design), proprietor of the subjects known as *(the subjects of sale/the security subjects), do solemnly and sincerely swear/affirm as follows:

With reference to *the sale of the subjects of sale to
/*the grant by me of the standard security over the security subjects in
favour of   the *subjects of sale/security are not a
matrimonial home in relation to which a spouse of mine has occupancy
rights, the expressions 'matrimonial home' and 'occupancy rights' having
the meanings respectively ascribed to them by the Matrimonial Homes
(Family Protection) (Scotland) Act 1981 as amended. Sworn/affirmed by
the above-named at

on the   day of   in the presence
of XY (design)
Notary Public
(*Delete where inapplicable)   (*Witnesses – see note 4*)

Notes: 1.   The 'dealing' referred to in the forms of consent in respect of a loan should, for consents signed after 30th December 1985, be 'the granting of the security' as opposed to 'the taking of the loan'.

2.   In cases where Registration of Title is applicable, the Keeper formerly required a statement from the applicant's solicitor to the effect that the relative consent, renunciation or affidavit as delivered at or before delivery of the disposition as standard security. Since the passing of the Law Reform (Miscellaneous Provisions) (Scotland) Act 1985 it has been competent to deliver consents retrospectively, and this question has been dropped from the new Forms 1, 2 and 3.

3.   The term 'Notary Public' includes any person duly authorised in the law of the country (other than Scotland) in which the swearing or affirmation takes place to administer oaths or receive affirmation in that other country.

4. Witnesses are also required if the Affidavit is to be registered in the Books of Council and Session.

5. It is not competent for an Attorney to grant the consent et cetera on behalf of the constituent.

6. Since the LR(MP)(S) Act 1985 it has been competent to grant the affidavits and renunciations retrospectively.

Exempt from Stamp Duty by virtue of Finance Act 1949, Part IV, Section 35, Schedule 8, Part (1)(2).

2   For use where the title to the matrimonial home stands in the name of one spouse only.

FORM OF RENUNCIATION OF OCCUPANCY RIGHTS

I, A (design) spouse of B (design) hereby renounce the occupancy rights to which I am or may become entitled in terms of the Matrimonial Homes (Family Protection) (Scotland) Act 1981 as amended in the property known as   being intended to become a matrimonial home as defined in the said Act: And I hereby swear/affirm that this renunciation is made by me freely and without coercion of any kind: And I declare these presents to be irrevocable.

Given under my hand at   this
day of   19   in the presence of (design)
Notary Public, and in the presence of these witnesses:–

. . . . .Witness

. . . . .Full name

. . . . .Address   . . . . .A

. . . . .Occupation

. . . . .Witness

. . . . .Full name

. . . . .Address   . . . . NP

. . . . .Occupation

Note: Liable for fixed Stamp Duty of 50p under the Head of Charge 'Release or Renunciation' as set out in the First Schedule to the Stamp Act 1891.

3   Consent by a non-entitled spouse to a sale of the matrimonial home by the entitled spouse (as provided in The Matrimonial Homes (Forms of Consent) (Scotland) Regulations 1982).

SCHEDULE 1

CONSENT TO BE INSERTED IN THE DEED EFFECTING THE DEALING

(The following words should be inserted where appropriate in the deed. The consenter should sign as a party to the deed.)

. . . with the consent of A.B. (*designation*), the spouse of the said C.D., for the purposes of the Matrimonial Homes (Family Protection) (Scotland) Act 1981 as amended . . .
[To be attested].

SCHEDULE 2

CONSENT IN A SEPARATE DOCUMENT

I, A.B. (*designation*), spouse of C.D. (*designation*), hereby consent, for the purposes of the Matrimonial Homes (Family Protection) (Scotland) Act 1981 as amended, to the undernoted dealing with the said C.D. relating to (*here describe the matrimonial home or the part of it to which the dealing relates: see Note 1*).
Dealing referred to:–
(*Here describe the dealing: see Note 2.*)
[To be attested].

Note 1
The expression 'matrimonial home' is defined in section 22 of the Matrimonial Homes (Family Protection) (Scotland) Act 1981 as follows:–

'"matrimonial home" means any house, caravan, houseboat or other structure which has been provided or has been made available by one or both of the spouses as, or has become, a family residence and includes any garden or other ground or building attached to, and usually occupied with, or otherwise required for the amenity or convenience of the house, caravan, houseboat, or other structure.'

Note 2
The expression 'dealing' is defined in section 6(2) of the Matrimonial Homes (Family Protection) (Scotland) Act 1981 as follows:–

'"dealing" includes the grant of a heritable security and the creation of a trust but does not include a conveyance under section 80 of the Lands Clauses Consolidation (Scotland) Act 1845.'

Note 3
The consent is not liable to Stamp Duty.

Appendix III

ORGANISATION OF THE REGISTERS OF SCOTLAND

With the introduction of Registration of Title into:
(1) the County of Renfrew on 6 April 1981
(2) the County of Dumbarton on 4 October 1982
(3) the County of Lanark on 3 January 1984
(4) the County of the Barony and Regality of Glasgow on 30 September 1985
(5) the County of Clackmannan from 1 October 1992
(6) the County of Stirling from 1 April 1993
(7) the County of West Lothian from 1 October 1993 and
(8) the County of Fife from 1 April 1995
(9) Aberdeen and Kincardine from 1 April 1996
(10) Ayr, Dumfries, Kirkcudbright and Wigtown from 1 April 1997
(11) Angus, Perth and Kinross from 1 April 1999
(12) Berwick, East Lothian, Peebles, Roxburgh and Selkirk from 1 October 1999
(13) Argyll and Bute from 1 April 2000
(14) Inverness and Nairn from 1 April 2002
(15) Banff, Caithness, Moray, Orkney and Zetland, Ross and Cromarty, and Sutherland planned for 1 April 2003

The Department now comprises the Land Register of Scotland and the 14 other Registers which already existed and which are grouped under four offices with which they are historically and administratively connected, namely the Sasine Office, the Deeds Office, the Chancery Office and the Horning Office.

Office	Registers
Sasine Office	Register of Sasines
Deeds Office	Register of Deeds
	Register of Protests
	Register of English and Irish Judgments
Chancery Office	Register of Service of Heirs
	Register of the Great Seal
	Register of the Quarter Seal
	Register of the Prince's Seal
	Register of Crown Grants
	Register of Sheriffs' Commissions
	Register of the Cachet Seal

Horning Office

Register of Inhibitions and Adjudications
Register of Entails
Register of Hornings (abolished by the Debtors (Scotland) Act 1987, s 89)

Appendix IV

MAPS OF SCOTTISH LOCAL GOVERNMENT AREAS

(a)   Scottish Counties before 1975

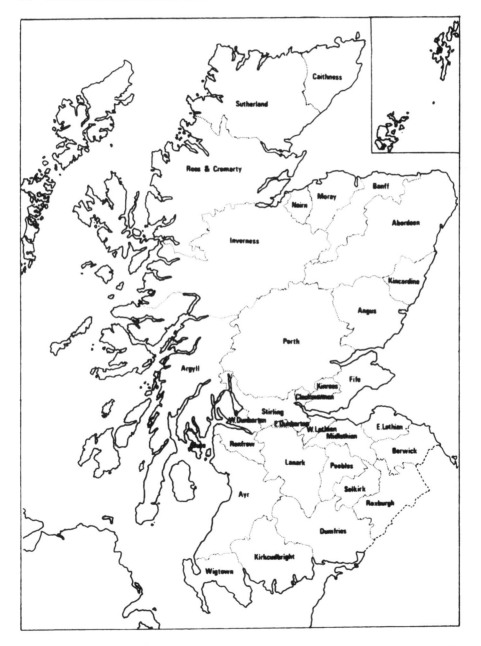

(b)   New Scottish administrative areas

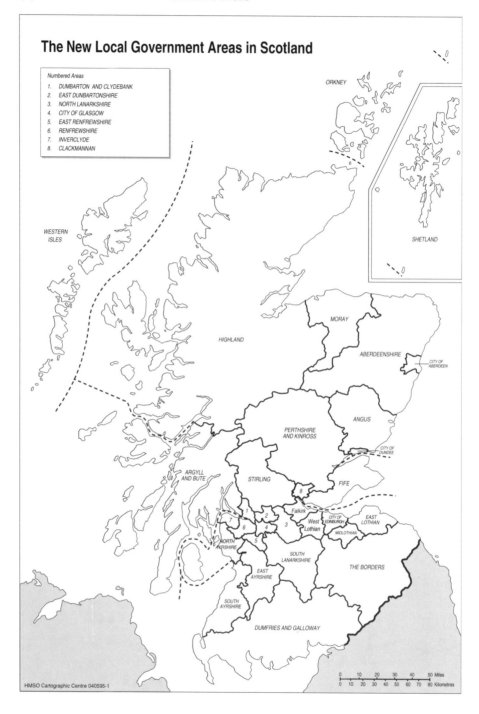

The New Local Government Areas in Scotland

Numbered Areas

1.   DUMBARTON AND CLYDEBANK
2.   EAST DUNBARTONSHIRE
3.   NORTH LANARKSHIRE
4.   CITY OF GLASGOW
5.   EAST RENFREWSHIRE
6.   RENFREWSHIRE
7.   INVERCLYDE
8.   CLACKMANNAN

ORKNEY

SHETLAND

WESTERN
ISLES

MORAY

HIGHLAND

ABERDEENSHIRE

CITY OF
ABERDEEN

ANGUS

PERTHSHIRE
AND KINROSS

CITY OF
DUNDEE

ARGYLL
AND BUTE

STIRLING

FIFE

8

Falkirk

West
Lothian

CITY OF
EDINBURGH

EAST
LOTHIAN

MIDLOTHIAN

NORTH
AYRSHIRE

SOUTH
LANARKSHIRE

THE BORDERS

EAST
AYRSHIRE

SOUTH
AYRSHIRE

DUMFRIES AND GALLOWAY

HMSO Cartographic Centre 040595-1

0   10   20   30   40   50 Miles
0   10 20 30 40 50 60 70 80 Kilometres

Appendix V

ENFORCEMENT OF STANDARD SECURITIES

References are to the Conveyancing and Feudal Reform (Scotland) Act 1970.
SC – Standard condition of loan under Sch 3 to Act.

1. Calling-up notice	2. Notice of default	3. Insolvency of proprietor	4. Petition to sheriff to exercise remedies
ss 19, 20; Sch 6, Form A SC 9(1)(a)	ss 21–23; Sch 6, Form B SC 9(1)(b)	SC 9(1)(c)	ss 24, 29(2)
Debtor does not comply Debtor redeems loan and creditor grants discharge; s 17; Sch 4, Form F	Debtor appeals notice to sheriff and is upheld Debtor does not comply Debtor remedies default	Apparent insolvency; Trust deed; Arrangement with creditors; Judicial factor appointed; Company wound up or liquidator, receiver or administrator appointed; Possession taken of assets under floating charge	Application specifies nature of default. Additional or alternative to notice of default if granted.

At this stage the borrower, or certain other people, may petition the Court to suspend procedures under the Mortgage Rights (Scotland) Act 2001. Please note that this applies only to residential properties, and it does not apply in cases of apparent insolvency. See chapter 12.

DEBTOR IN DEFAULT – CREDITOR'S REMEDIES

Traditional remedies: 1. Personal action 2. Adjudication 3. Poinding of the ground	Any remedy outwith Act given by standard security: SC 10(1)	Sale of security subjects: SC 10(2). If sale is not possible then the remedy is **foreclosure:** SC 10(7) (sheriff court action)	Entering into possession and letting: SC 10(3)–(5) **Note:** this remedy may be accompanied by a court warrant for ejection in terms of the Act of Sederunt 1990 SC 1990(6) It is not strictly necessary on the expiry of a calling-up notice but may in practise be desirable. In most cases possession is sought first before exercising any other remedy.	Repair reconstruction and improvement: SC 10(6).

Appendix VI

PROFESSIONAL INDEMNITY INSURANCE

'Welcome to the world of professional claims – a world where your worst nightmares come true – a world full of snakes and very few ladders – a friendless world of reporters, notoriety – and financial ruin – and it could all be so different – friends, riches, acclaim.'

(Neil Douglas, indemnity solicitor, talk to diploma students)

Archie McPherson on Radio Clyde: 'Well, I don't know why the ref ruled out that goal. He didn't look offside to me. Possibly handball? What did you think, Davie Provan?'

Provan: 'Archie, the ball hit the side-netting. It's a bye kick to Hibs.'
(*The Herald*)

To err is human and most solicitors will have had at some time – whatever they may say – the horrible feeling that they may have done something, or not done something else, that may give rise to a claim in professional negligence.

At such times it is reassuring to know that you have your indemnity policy standing between you and a financial chasm. The minimum cover per solicitor is currently £1.25 million but this may not be enough. I believe that some larger firms insure for much larger sums per partner, but of course the bigger the firm, the bigger the business and volume of business, and thus the possibility of a bigger mistake. In any event it is really not a good idea to try to save expense by cutting down this cover. The premiums are obviously expensive, but thanks to careful management, have not reached the levels ruling in England, which in 1995 were 4% of the firm's turnover. In many cases this is a huge sum.

Examples of conveyancing mistakes that have occurred in the past and should not therefore recur, but probably will, are as follows.

1. The very worst mistake a solicitor can make is to forget the strict provisions of the Companies Act 1985, s 410 relating to the registration of charges created by a limited company. This covers not only floating charges, but also fixed charges, such as standard securities. Thus if a limited company grants a standard security over its land, the lender's agent must first record this document and obtain a date of recording from the Keeper. The recording date, in either the Register of Sasines or the Land Register, is the date of creation of the security, and within 21 days of that date the lender's agent must register particulars of the charge with the Register of Charges, kept at Companies House, 37 Castle Terrace, Edinburgh EH1 2EB. Failure to do this

will mean that the charge is void against a liquidator or creditor of the company, and the lender will rank only as an ordinary creditor instead of being secured. The loss due to the solicitor's error is potentially huge. Another danger is revealed in a letter from the Registrar of Companies in 1985 JLSS 11. The Registrar points out that details of such a charge should be intimated to him in Forms 410 (Scot), 413 and 413(a) (Scot) and 416 (Scot) in terms of the Companies (Forms) Regulations 1985. If one of these forms has to be returned to the solicitor for correction, it must be returned to the Registrar in correct form within 21 days, or again the registration is not complete as required.

2. Another point to watch is when you send your standard security to be recorded in the General Register of Sasines and you receive a recording date, and you then duly lodge your particulars of charge. Then disaster strikes, and the Keeper returns your standard security for correction. When you have made your corrections, you must then re-record the security, and *again* register details of the charge. The first notification is invalid. Fortunately this cannot happen in the Land Register.

3. You sell land for a client and allow the client to grant absolute warrandice, even though you know that ownership of part of the land is doubtful. The new owner is then interdicted from building on the area of doubtful ownership, and claims against your client under absolute warrandice. As a result your client has to buy the land in question at an extortionate price and looks to you for recompense.

4. Check all boundaries and areas carefully, and particularly, access to the property.

5. Ensure that building warrants and completion certificates are to hand at an early date, also agreement for replacement windows.

6. Don't undertake to deliver anything in a letter of obligation that you may not be able to deliver (eg a property inquiry report disclosing old adverse notices). See article by Professor Robert Rennie in November 1993 JLSS 431. See also *McGillivray v Davidson* 1993 SLT 693.

7. When acting for a lender, read the lender's instructions carefully and follow them. See Rennie 'Negligence, Securities and the Expanding Duty of Care' February 1995 JLSS 58.

For your own sake and for the sake of the profession, who have to pay sharply increased premiums each year, please try and avoid mistakes like these.

In a publication (September 1989) prepared by the Law Society and the Indemnity Insurance Brokers, entitled *Better Practice in Practice*, certain guidelines are laid down for solicitors. While, hopefully, all of these have been stressed throughout this book, these guidelines present a useful summary:

- Take clear instructions from all your clients direct – that is to say, not solely through intermediaries.
- Record properly all communications, all meetings, all telephone calls, in writing.
- Enforce a good diary system – a double diary system, if necessary.
- Read and check the file, and think before taking a decisive step.

- Review all files regularly.
- Always know what your assistants are doing.
- Copy all important correspondence to clients immediately.
- Only provide Letters of Obligation that you can personally meet. (**8.11**)
- When going on holiday, leave adequate file notes.
- Where reliance is placed on words, express them clearly, fully, and accurately and, wherever possible, in plain English.
- Take expert advice in areas of uncertainty – legal or otherwise.
- If you are using a lawyer in another town as a correspondent, bear in mind that your responsibility to your client is nevertheless not reduced.
- Similarly, if you are acting as correspondent to another lawyer, keep the instructing solicitor constantly advised.

Every practising solicitor should be thoroughly familiar with the contents of this booklet.

To these guidelines, I would add another:

- Never forget that you are responsible for all documents that you prepared. You should, therefore, check every document that you have prepared, *before* it leaves the office and is signed. It is not enough to leave the checking to staff, especially junior staff who may have just left school and who are set to comparing documents between making tea and doing the deliveries, and who cannot be expected to have any idea of legal terminology.

As an example of this, I saw a deed from a respected firm which stated 'I grant drainage rise' instead of 'I grant warrandice'. Such intelligent, but totally wrong, guesses of bad writing are always the hardest to spot, simply because they are so plausible to the untrained eye. (See also *Hunter v Fox* 1964 SC (HL) 95).

Written amendments on typed or word processed documents should also be carefully checked. One such mistake through a misreading of poor writing – I'm sorry to say it was my own – was to transform the term 'three miles' into 'three metres'. Had it not been caught in time, the result could have been hideous, as this was the area in which the seller of a business was not allowed to trade for a certain number of years!

When drafting deeds, approved styles should be used wherever possible. Conveyancing styles may be found in the excellent style book issued to diploma students, or in most conveyancing texts. Much useful information may also be gained from consulting English style (or 'precedent') books, most particularly Butterworth's *Encyclopaedia of Precedents*. *Care must however be used when following a style, and this must never be done uncritically, particularly in the case of English styles.* A cautionary tale unfolds in *Tarditi v Drummond* 1989 SLT 554 – a style from Halliday *Conveyancing Law and Practice* (II, 15–138) was followed, but the Court ruled that it was 'difficult to understand, and should not be followed slavishly in future.' This excellent advice applies to all style books.

In a speech reported briefly in the *Glasgow Herald* of 9 November 1985, Judge David Edward QC is reported as saying to newly admitted solicitors that they should not imagine that they could get through their professional lives without making mistakes, and it was important to admit when they had been made. He continued to say that 'clients and insurers are surprisingly sympathetic to the lawyer who admits to his mistakes.'

This is sound advice, for if an attempt is made to hide a mistake, it only gets worse. One would, I think however, have to be very careful about the exact admission made in case this prejudiced a valid insurance claim.

Please note carefully that any circumstances which might lead to a claim should be reported immediately to the indemnity insurers. Early notification can greatly ease matters.

Lastly, please use language carefully, and use language that can be understood by the average intelligence. Avoid horrors like the following definition of a bed:

> 'A device or arrangement that may be used to permit a patient to lie down when the need to do so is a consequence of the patient's condition rather than a need for active intervention such as examination, diagnostic intervention, manipulative treatment, obstetric delivery or transport.'
>
> (NHS staff circular)

INDEX